D0898204

£28

OXFORD HISTORICAL MONOGRAPHS

Editors

BARBARA HARVEY   A. D. MACINTYRE

R. W. SOUTHERN   A. F. THOMPSON

H. R. TREVOR-ROPER

TUDOR YORK

BY

D. M. PALLISER

Lecturer in Economic and Social History
University of Birmingham

OXFORD UNIVERSITY PRESS
1979

DA
690
.Y6
P3
1979

Oxford University Press, Walton Street, Oxford OX2 6DP

OXFORD LONDON GLASGOW
NEW YORK TORONTO MELBOURNE WELLINGTON
KUALA LUMPUR SINGAPORE HONG KONG TOKYO
DELHI BOMBAY CALCUTTA MADRAS KARACHI
NAIROBI DAR ES SALAAM CAPE TOWN

© *D. M. Palliser 1979*

Published in the United States by
Oxford University Press, New York

All rights reserved. No part of this publication may be reproduced, stored in a retrieval system, or transmitted, in any form or by any means, electronic, mechanical, photocopying, recording, or otherwise, without the prior permission of Oxford University Press

British Library Cataloguing in Publication Data

Palliser, David Michael
Tudor York. — (Oxford historical monographs).
1. York, Eng. — History
I. Title   II. Series
942.8'43'05   DA690.Y6   79-40611
ISBN 0-19-821878-8

Typeset by Hope Services, Abingdon

Printed in Great Britain
at the University Press, Oxford
by Eric Buckley
Printer to the University

FOR
F. H. LEGG
AND
IN MEMORY OF
MY PARENTS

PREFACE

English urban history has become a flourishing subject in the past decade, with its own *Yearbook* which contains an impressive annual bibliography of publications. The focus of interest remains, however, the period of large-scale urbanization of the last two centuries, despite the appearance of several recent books on the early modern period. Historic cities like York have, of course, a plethora of publications to their credit, but many are antiquarian in approach; and there are still almost no monographs of individual provincial cities in the sixteenth century, taking account of recent approaches to local history, other than Professor MacCaffrey's on Exeter and Dr Dyer's on Worcester. It has therefore seemed worthwhile to study another Tudor city at length, combining political and ecclesiastical with economic and social history in an attempt to view an urban community in its totality, or as much as the records permit. There is no easy answer to the choice of chronological and geographical limits or to the arbitrary organisation of what is part of a seamless web. The dates 1485 and 1603 have been taken as terminal points, but have not been adhered to pedantically where important evidence is found earlier or later.

The chief manuscript sources on which the book is based are listed in the bibliography. In general, the Public Record Office provides the same riches for York as for other towns, notably taxation returns and judicial records. The one disappointing exception concerns the equity courts of Requests, Chancery and Star Chamber. These provide numerous invaluable York pleas of the early Tudor period, but very little after about 1560. The probable reason is that suitors after that date turned increasingly to the King's Council in the North, the records of which are, alas, lost. Much of this study is based on the ecclesiastical archives at the Borthwick Institute of Historical Research, which include most of the surviving city parish registers, several churchwardens' accounts, a huge collection of copies of wills, numerous 'cause papers'

from the church courts, and the recently rediscovered records
of the Northern Ecclesiastical Commission. The only dis-
appointment of the collection is the almost total absence of
the probate inventories which originally accompanied each
will, and of which Professor MacCaffrey and Dr Dyer were
able to make such effective use in their own studies.

The corporation archives, now housed in the City Library,
include the 'House Books' or corporation minutes for almost
the entire period, the complete register of freemen's admissions, many though not all of the city's financial accounts,
and some of the surviving records of the trade guilds; the
records of the merchants' and tailors' guilds are still separately
preserved by the surviving companies. The only major dis-
appointments among the civic archives are the disappearance
of the records of the court of orphans and of the market
tolls, both of which would have added greatly to our understanding of the economic and social structure. An extensive
selection of corporation minutes has been edited by Canon
Raine under the title *York Civic Records*, and as his edition is
widely available and frequently quoted, it is perhaps worth
pointing out that it is in many respects defective: major omissions and errors are where possible indicated here in the foot-
notes.

This book grew out of a thesis submitted for the degree of
Doctor of Philosophy at Oxford, begun in 1964 and completed in 1968. It has been completely rewritten to make it
more suitable for publication, new sections being added,
recent publications taken into account, and lengthy arguments
more suitable for a thesis than a book being compressed or
simply omitted, with an appropriate reference to the original
argument. Latin quotations are translated, but extracts from
contemporary English have been left in their original spelling,
though with punctuation and use of capitals modernized, and
contractions expanded without indication. Christian names
have been modernized, but not surnames, and I have adopted
consistently that version of a man's surname which was most
often used. 'Herbert' and 'Peacock', for example, are here
rendered 'Harbert' and 'Paycok', since they were the usual
spellings and probably reflected local pronunciation. To
avoid frequent repetition of 'townsmen' and 'citizens' the

contemporary term 'Yorkers' has been revived here and used occasionally. Most officials and places have been given their modern names for ease of identification. The exceptions include the contemporary 'common clerk' for town clerk and 'Common Hall' for town hall, i.e. the present-day 'Guildhall', which I have preferred as expressing a sixteenth-century concept of what was 'common' or public.

I have accumulated many obligations in the course of writing the thesis and the subsequent book. In particular, I would like to thank Professor W. G. Hoskins, who supervised the original thesis, and whose kindly encouragement and help have been invaluable, and Professor A. G. Dickens for his encouragement and for the benefit of his many publications on York and the North. Much of this study would have been far more difficult without the existence of his general survey of Tudor York in the *Victoria County History*. I am also grateful to many colleagues and friends for helpful advice, information and criticism, especially to Professor G. E. Aylmer, Dr M. H. R. Bonwick, Dr C. E. Challis, Dr C. L. Cross, Professor A. M. Everitt, Mr G. C. F. Forster, Dr E. A. Gee, Dr J. H. Harvey, Mr C. Phythian-Adams, Dr P. A. Slack, Dr H. M. Spufford, Dr J. Thirsk, Professor R. B. Wernham, Dr P. H. Williams, and the staff of the York branch of the Royal Commission on Historical Monuments. My debt to Dr Cross includes her lending me an advance copy of her chapter in the recent *History of York Minster* edited by G. E. Aylmer and R. Cant (Oxford, 1977), an important volume which appeared too recently to be consulted in print. I am greatly indebted to Professor R. B. Dobson and the late Mr J. P. Cooper, who, in addition to much other help, read the book in draft, and to Dr J. N. Bartlett, Dr E. W. Ives, Dr C. J. Kitching, Dr R. B. Smith, Dr P. Tyler, and Miss B. M. Wilson, who allowed me to read and to make use of their unpublished theses. The History of Parliament Trust kindly allowed me to consult and cite their files on MPs between 1558 and 1603; I was in turn invited to write their biographies of York MPs for the period 1509–58, which I have occasionally cited here. I would also like to thank Mrs C. S. Busfield and Miss S. P. Swann for typing successive drafts, and the staff of the record offices and libraries in which I have worked for their helpfulness and courtesy, especially those of the Borthwick Institute of Historical Research, York, York City Archives and York City Library, York Minster Library, the Public Record Office, the British Museum, the Bodleian Library, and the University Libraries of Keele and Birmingham. I am much indebted to Worcester College and New College, the University of Oxford and Stone-Platt Industries Ltd., for making full-time research on the original thesis possible. Finally, I am more grateful than I can express to my wife for her help and support.

CONTENTS

	List of maps and tables	xiii
	List of abbreviations	xiv
I	York and its setting	1
II	The City and the State	40
III	City Government	60
IV	The Office-Holders	92
V	Population, Poverty, and Wealth	111
VI	The Occupational Structure	146
VII	Commerce and Trade	179
VIII	Poverty and Decay, 1460–1560	201
IX	Religion and the Reformation	226
X	Stability and Recovery, 1560–1600	260
	Conclusion	288
	Bibliography	299
	Index	311

LIST OF MAPS AND TABLES

Map 1   Areas of secular and ecclesiastical
        jurisdiction governed from York   xv

Map 2   Early Tudor Yorkshire   xvi

Map 3   York c.1500   xvii

Table 1 Baptism and burial rates, 1541–1610   126

Table 2 Distribution of taxable wealth, 1524
        and 1546   136

Table 3 York trades, 1500–1600   156–7

Table 4 The leading occupations, 1500–1600   159

Table 5 Bequests of testators' souls in York wills,
        1501–1600   250–1

LIST OF ABBREVIATIONS

A.P.C.	*Acts of the Privy Council*
B.I.H.R.	Borthwick Institute of Historical Research, York
B.L.	British Library
Borth. P.	Borthwick Papers (York, 1951 to date; described as St. Anthony's Hall Publications to no. xxvi inclusive)
C.C.R.	*Calendar of Close Rolls*
C.P.R.	*Calendar of Patent Rolls*
D.N.B.	*Dictionary of National Biography*
Econ. H.R.	*Economic History Review*
H.M.C.	Historical Manuscripts Commission
L.P. Hen. VIII	*Letters and Papers, Foreign and Domestic, of the Reign of Henry VIII*
Palliser, 'York'	D. M. Palliser, 'Some aspects of the social and economic history of York in the sixteenth century', Oxford University D.Phil. thesis, 1968
P.R.O.	Public Record Office
R.C.H.M. *York*	Royal Commission on Historical Monuments, *An Inventory of the Historical Monuments in the City of York*
Test. Ebor.	*Testamenta Eboracensia*
V.C.H. East Riding	*The Victoria County History of Yorkshire: East Riding*
V.C.H. North Riding	*The Victoria County History of Yorkshire: North Riding*
V.C.H. York	*The Victoria County History of Yorkshire: the City of York*
V.C.H. Yorkshire	*The Victoria County History of Yorkshire*, general volumes
Y.A.J.	*The Yorkshire Archaeological Journal*
Y.A.S.R.S.	The Yorkshire Archaeological Society Record Series
Y.C.A.	York City Archives
Y.C.R.	*York Civic Records*, ed. A. Raine
Y.M.L.	York Minster Library (including Dean & Chapter Archives)
Y.P.R.S.	Yorkshire Parish Register Society

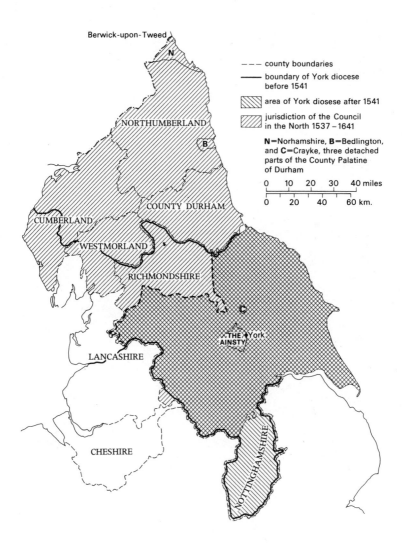

Berwick-upon-Tweed

N

NORTHUMBERLAND

B

COUNTY DURHAM

CUMBERLAND

WESTMORLAND

RICHMONDSHIRE

C

THE AINSTY

York

LANCASHIRE

CHESHIRE

NOTTINGHAMSHIRE

--- county boundaries

— boundary of York diocese before 1541

area of York diocese after 1541

jurisdiction of the Council in the North 1537–1641

N=Norhamshire, **B**=Bedlington, and **C**=Crayke, three detached parts of the County Palatine of Durham

0   10   20   30   40 miles

0   20   40   60 km.

Map 1   Areas of secular and ecclesiastical jurisdiction governed from York

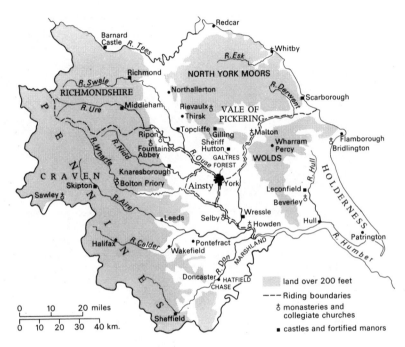

Map 2   Early Tudor Yorkshire

Redcar

Barnard
Castle *R. Tees*

R. Esk

Whitby

Richmond

NORTH YORK MOORS

RICHMONDSHIRE

Northallerton

R. Swale

R. Derwent

Scarborough

R. Ure Middleham

Rievaulx

VALE OF
PICKERING

Thirsk

Ripon Topcliffe

Gilling

Malton

Flamborough

Sheriff
Hutton

Wharram
Percy

Bridlington

Fountains
Abbey

GALTRES
FOREST

WOLDS

R. Wharfe

R. Nidd

R. Ouse

Knaresborough

HOLDERNESS

R. Hull

CRAVEN

Bolton Priory

Ainsty

York

Skipton

Leconfield

Sawley

Beverley

R. Aire

Leeds

Selby

Wressle

Hull

Howden

Patrington

Halifax *R. Calder*

Pontefract

R. Humber

Wakefield

R. Don

MARSHLAND

Doncaster HATFIELD
CHASE

P E N N I N E S

land over 200 feet

Sheffield

– – – Riding boundaries

☩ monasteries and
collegiate churches

■ castles and fortified manors

0   10   20 miles

0   10   20   30   40 km.

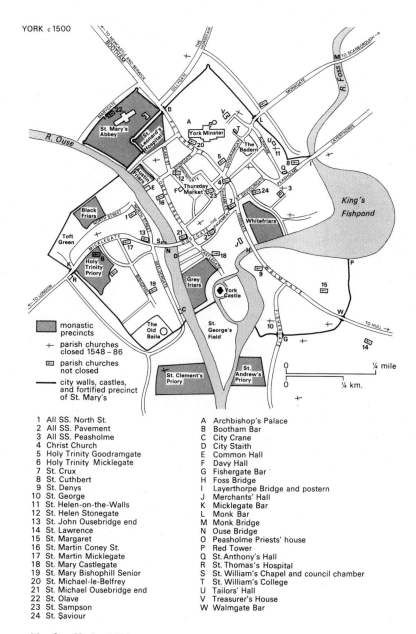

YORK c 1500

monastic precincts
+ parish churches closed 1548 – 86
⊟ parish churches not closed
— city walls, castles, and fortified precinct of St. Mary's

1 All SS. North St.
2 All SS. Pavement
3 All SS. Peasholme
4 Christ Church
5 Holy Trinity Goodramgate
6 Holy Trinity Micklegate
7 St. Crux
8 St. Cuthbert
9 St. Denys
10 St. George
11 St. Helen-on-the-Walls
12 St. Helen Stonegate
13 St. John Ousebridge end
14 St. Lawrence
15 St. Margaret
16 St. Martin Coney St.
17 St. Martin Micklegate
18 St. Mary Castlegate
19 St. Mary Bishophill Senior
20 St. Michael-le-Belfrey
21 St. Michael Ousebridge end
22 St. Olave
23 St. Sampson
24 St. Saviour

A Archbishop's Palace
B Bootham Bar
C City Crane
D City Staith
E Common Hall
F Davy Hall
G Fishergate Bar
H Foss Bridge
I Layerthorpe Bridge and postern
J Merchants' Hall
K Micklegate Bar
L Monk Bar
M Monk Bridge
N Ouse Bridge
O Peasholme Priests' house
P Red Tower
Q St. Anthony's Hall
R St. Thomas's Hospital
S St. William's Chapel and council chamber
T St. William's College
U Tailors' Hall
V Treasurer's House
W Walmgate Bar

Map 3   York c.1500

I

YORK AND ITS SETTING

This is the second city of England, the finest of this
region [Yorkshire] and indeed of the whole North, as
well as its principal fortress. It is pleasant, large, and
strongly fortified, adorned with private as well as
public buildings, crammed with riches and with
people, and famous as the seat of an archbishop.
William Camden, 1586[1]

York, still the ecclesiastical capital of northern England, at
least for Anglicans, was also its chief administrative centre
until the seventeenth century and its social and intellectual
capital until the early nineteenth century. It is worth emphasizing its role as a regional capital at the outset because,
despite its rich historical fabric, it no longer has the atmosphere of an Edinburgh or even of a Bristol or a Newcastle.
Yet that is precisely what it was until relatively recently, one
of that select band which 'in each province of England, above
all in the peripheral regions . . . played the part of capital
cities'.[2] It is therefore necessary, if York is to be rightly
understood, to consider its regional context. Even a small
county town like Dorchester 'was the complement of the
rural life around; not its urban opposite',[3] but the links
between town and hinterland were even more important in
the case of a provincial capital. It is not possible in brief com-
pass to do justice to the diversity of York's region, or to the
royal and ecclesiastical institutions which made it their capital, but to ignore them and to consider only the city and the
citizens would be to paint a very distorted picture.

The Vale of York is an extension of the midland plain,
thrust north into an upland zone. Hills encircle the Vale on

---

[1] W. Camden, *Britannia* (London, 1586), p. 407 (translated).
[2] W. G. Hoskins, *Provincial England: Essays in Social and Economic History*
(London, 1963), p. 86.
[3] Thomas Hardy, *The Life and Death of the Mayor of Casterbridge* (Wessex
edn., London, 1912), p. 68.

all sides except the south, where it widens out to merge imperceptibly into the level Humber basin and the Vale of Trent. Consequently, almost the entire Yorkshire river-system drains into the Vale, which forms a convenient area from which to dominate or to govern the uplands. Furthermore, the main lines of communication between London and the Scottish border, whether by road or rail, have always followed the corridor east of the Pennines rather than the Lancashire route. This combination of advantages as a centre of communications, both long-distance and local, by water and by land, meant that until the Industrial Revolution the only feasible location for a northern capital lay within the Vale.

A neighbouring gentleman described York in 1589 as lying 'in the centre of this goodly plain . . . upon a confluence of the waters of Ouse and Foss . . . situate in a choice part of this island to command both the kingdoms of England and Scotland', having 'besides the fertile soil . . . good passages as well to bring in by water as to utter by land any such commodities as England usually interchangeth'.[1] The Ouse was still navigable above York, so that the city was in direct communication with the midlands (via the Trent), the east coast, London and the Continent, in an age when bulky cargoes were much cheaper to transport by water than overland. Between 1524 and 1529 goods were shipped upstream through York to Boroughbridge, Ripon, Northallerton, Topcliffe, Knaresborough, Bedale and Whalley, and even to Penrith and Cockermouth.[2] Downstream, York was linked with all the main ports along the eastern coast. Early in the sixteenth century, for instance, Yorkshire lead was bought in the city by merchants from London, King's Lynn, Boston, Hull, and Newcastle.[3]

Yet if the Ouse and its tributaries made York a convenient political and commercial centre, they also made life there uncomfortable; it has always been, as an Icelandic Viking tersely described it, 'York town, the dank demesne'.[4] Much of the alluvial Vale was marshy and liable to flood until very

[1] B.L., Lansdowne 119, fo. 110^V; D. M. Palliser, 'A hostile view of Elizabethan York', *York Historian*, i. 20.
[2] Y.C.A., C 2, fo. 191^r; C 3, pt. 1, pp. 42-3, 141, 237-8.
[3] *Y.C.R.* iii. 17.
[4] A. G. Dickens, 'York before the Norman Conquest', *V.C.H. York*, p. 13.

recent times, and only at two points, where glacial moraines crossed the Vale, was a large settlement feasible. By choosing York the Romans settled for a well-drained and easily defensible site with a good harbour, and one which was in easy communication north and south by river and east and west along the moraine. The existence of this ridge thus made possible the very existence of York, but it has also paradoxically made flooding a perennial danger. When heavy rain falls, or snow melts, in the Pennines, the Ouse can rise very rapidly. The York moraine creates a bottleneck for the waters, and the extent of 'washland' or floodable land just above the city is very limited. Heavy floods therefore invade the city instead of passing harmlessly through between the river banks. The Tudor corporation, like their successors, were familiar with the problem,[1] and they suffered a major disaster when ice piled up against Ouse Bridge during the hard winter of 1564–5. A sudden thaw on 6 January caused 'such a water that it overthrew two bowes within one arch and twelve houses standing upon the same bridge, and by the fall thereof was drowned 12 persons'.[2]

From its strategic road and river junction, York controlled or served a wide area. Economically, its sphere of influence stretched from the Humber to the Cumbrian coast, though it had been losing ground to other towns since the fifteenth century, and only in the Vale itself was its supremacy unchallenged. Politically, however, there was no such decline; York remained the secular and ecclesiastical capital of a very large part of England (see map 1). In the first place, it was the county town of the largest English shire, covering some 6,000 square miles, almost equivalent to Cornwall, Devon, Dorset, and Wiltshire combined. The high sheriff (not to be confused with the two city sheriffs) ruled from York Castle, which was physically within the city though outside its jurisdiction. There the county courts and the twice-yearly assizes were held; there MPs were elected for the county; and there prisoners were held in the county gaol. One gauge of the

[1] *Y.C.R.* iv. 118; viii. 118.
[2] Bodley, Gough *Yorks.* 8, p. 116, confirmed by B.L. Add. 33,595, fo. 42. A. Raine, *Mediaeval York: A Topographical Survey based on Original Sources* (London, 1955), p. 219, is in error in saying that the exact date of the collapse is not known.

effect of all this on York's shops and inns is that a crowd of
close on 6,000 Yorkshiremen assembled at the Castle for the
parliamentary election of 1597.[1] In short, courts and assem-
blies for the county as a whole were invariably held in the
county town; and, what is less well known, so were many of
the local wapentake (hundred) courts. Villagers at odds over
transactions in corn and wool travelled nearly twenty miles
to sue one another at the castle.[2]

When the crown wished to make use of institutions with a
wider jurisdiction than the county, whether military, fiscal or
judicial, York was usually chosen as the northern centre. In
the early Tudor period York Castle housed the only royal
mint in England apart from the Tower of London. The city
also possessed an admiralty court, apparently with delegated
power from the lord high admiral over the whole north.[3] Most
important of all, the city housed the King's Council in the
Northern Parts, a powerful administrative and judicial agency
which controlled the north on behalf of the Privy Council
and acted as a regional equivalent to the Courts of Requests
and Star Chamber. It brought a great deal of business to
York, and by the end of the sixteenth century it was hearing
between one and two thousand cases a year.[4] It must have
been a boon to the citizens, but it was also of great use to
many other northerners, who no longer needed to make the
lengthy and occasionally dangerous journey to the capital to
settle a lawsuit over property.[5]

The church, like the state, possessed a judicial and administrative apparatus of some complexity. The ecclesiastical
equivalent to the county was the diocese of York, which until
1541 comprised all Yorkshire and Nottinghamshire together
with much of Cumbria and North Lancashire. Even after the
transfer of its north-western outliers to the new diocese of
Chester in 1541, York was still a vast diocese, and with

---

[1] J. E. Neale, *The Elizabethan House of Commons* (London, 1949), p. 83.
[2] *V.C.H. East Riding*, iii. 4; *Select XVI Century Causes in Tithe*, ed. J. S.
Purvis (Y.A.S.R.S. cxiv, 1949), p. 36.
[3] J. S. Purvis, *The Records of the Admiralty Court of York* (Borth. P. xxii,
1962).
[4] R. R. Reid, *The King's Council in the North* (London, 1921), pp. 344, 359.
[5] e.g. S. J. Watts, *From Border to Middle Shire: Northumberland 1586–1625*
(Leicester, 1975), p. 35.

215,000 communicants in 1603 it included almost 10 per cent of the recorded English population.[1] Furthermore, the bishops of Durham, Carlisle, and (after 1542) Chester were subject to the archbishop of York as metropolitan, who thus ruled a Northern Province of eight counties. The archbishops were frequently absent from the city after 1373, and almost always between 1501 and 1530, but in one sense it did not matter, for they left an efficient body of administrators to govern in their absence.[2] There were four main courts for the province and diocese sitting at York, as well as numerous lesser courts; and from 1561 to 1641 the city was also the seat of an Ecclesiastical Commission for the Northern Province. A single ecclesiastical court, the archbishop's chancery, heard on average something like 400 cases a year.[3] Furthermore, synods of the diocesan clergy were held there twice a year; and before the Reformation the city benefited substantially as a centre for pilgrims and for the business activities of the northern monasteries, many of which retained a town house there, or at least owned property which they leased out to citizens. On the eve of the Reformation at least thirty-seven Yorkshire religious houses, as well as Durham, Furness, and Cockersand, owned dwellings or rents in the city.[4]

This brief summary has inevitably oversimplified the picture; in practice, the intricate interrelationship of jurisdiction, lordship and land-ownership, and the existence of numerous liberties exempt from sheriffs and bishops, greatly complicated northern government. It remains true, nevertheless, that for many purposes the inhabitants of six or eight counties looked to York for government, justice and pastoral care, rather than to Westminster or Lambeth. Clearly it was a regional capital

---

[1] T. H. Hollingsworth, *Historical Demography* (Sources of History series, London, 1969), p. 83.

[2] M. D. Knowles, *The Medieval Archbishops of York* (Oliver Sheldon Memorial Lecture, 1961), pp. 5, 11-15.

[3] R. A. Marchant, *The Puritans and the Church Courts in the Diocese of York 1560-1642* (London, 1960), p. 8.

[4] Beverley (St. Giles), Bolton, Bridlington, Byland, Coverham, Drax, Easby, Ellerton, Fountains, Grosmont, Guisborough, Healaugh, Kirkham, Kirkstall, Knaresborough, Malton, Marton, Meaux, Molsby, Mountgrace, Newburgh, Nostell, Nun Appleton, Nun Monkton, Pontefract, Rievaulx, Roche, Salley, Selby, Swine, Synningthwaite, Thicket, Warter, Watton, Whitby, Wilberfoss, Yedingham. Most relevant references are in *L.P. Hen. VIII* or in the *Valor Ecclesiasticus*.

in the loose sense of providing government and services for a wide area; could it also be described as the capital of a coherent region, a province with a true sense of identity? Many earlier historians have accepted that a northern region did exist, manifesting itself in grievances against sovereigns who visited the north more and more rarely; and the events of 1536 have often been interpreted in terms of a northern provincial rebellion. Such views have received the qualified support of Professor Hexter, but not of Professor Dickens and Mr Beckingsale, who deny the existence of a homogeneous north with its own regional identity.[1] The conflict of opinion is perhaps more apparent than real. Recent researches have certainly rendered untenable the old simplifications which made England north of the Humber a homogeneous region with an economy, society and religion different from those of the midlands and south. Local regional diversity in Tudor England was much more complex than that.

Yet it can be argued that northerners as a whole viewed themselves as different from other Englishmen. The strong support for Richard III north of the Humber, and much of the dislike of him south of it, can be partly explained by a long residence in the north which had strongly coloured his loyalties and affinities. The experiments of Richard and of Henry VII with a Northern Council recognized that the region needed separate government, if only by reason of its distance from Westminster. The Pilgrimage of Grace in 1536–7 expressed in part a widespread sense of neglect by northerners, especially as the Tudors had ceased to visit the north in person after 1487, while their Northern Council had ceased to be very effective. The Pilgrims' demands at Pontefract included four of a regional nature, and some of the rebel poems could almost be described as appeals to a northern nationalism. Certainly by their thorough reorganization of the Northern Council in 1537 Henry VIII's ministers recognized that northerners had legitimate grievances over government if not over religion. The success of the reorganized Council was one

---

[1] J. H. Hexter, *Reappraisals in History* (London, 1961), p. 36; A. G. Dickens, *Lollards and Protestants in the Diocese of York 1509–1558* (Oxford, 1959), p. 4; B. W. Beckingsale, 'The characteristics of the Tudor North', *Northern History* iv (1969), 67.

reason for a gradual decline of this embittered northern senti-
ment, and the gradual binding together of the English regions
by growing trading links, and the union of the crowns in
1603, contributed their part. Undoubtedly the sense of a
northern identity weakened as the sixteenth century ran its
course; but it would be wrong to underestimate its importance or to antedate its decline.

2

Ideally a study of York would be prefaced by a detailed
description of the whole Tudor north. Space does not permit
such a survey, but some brief consideration of Yorkshire, at
least, will allow the city to be better understood (map 2).
Administratively, it consisted of a large number of townships,
which were grouped into wapentakes and they in turn into
the three Ridings, North, East, and West. Only York and Hull,
as counties corporate, stood outside this administrative structure. There was a parallel structure of ecclesiastical government in the diocese of York, the basic units equivalent to the
townships being the parishes, which were grouped into
deaneries and archdeaconries. The only peculiarity to which
attention need be drawn was the anomalous position of
the Ainsty, one of the twelve wapentakes of the West Riding,
which lay just west of York and was nearly surrounded by
the rivers Nidd, Ouse, and Wharfe. Under the name of 'the
county of the city of York' it had been granted by the crown
to the city's jurisdiction, and as fiscal and military assessments
were always levied jointly on York and the Ainsty it will
occur frequently in the following pages.
    More important than these man-made divisions were the
physical and geological differences which gave Yorkshire a
greater variety of landscape and agriculture than any other
English county.[1] William Camden, who visited the shire in
the 1570s or 1580s, said that

if in one place the soil be of a stony, sandy, barren nature, yet in
another it is pregnant and fruitful; and so if it be naked and exposed in

[1] J. Thirsk, 'The farming regions of England', in *The Agrarian History of
England and Wales: Volume IV: 1500-1640*, ed. J. Thirsk (Cambridge, 1967),
pp. 28-40.

one part, we find it clothed and sheltered with great store of wood in another; Nature using an allay and mixture, that the entire county, by this variety of parts, might seem more pleasing and beautiful.[1]

The western third of Yorkshire, forming part of the Pennine chain, was Camden's 'naked and exposed' area. Much of it consists of bleak uplands, moors and mountains, though the tributaries of the Ouse, flowing east and south-east, form fertile valleys or dales between the hills. The agrarian economy was mainly pastoral, with a predominance of cattle- and sheep-farming. It is sheep and wool which are associated with the popular image of the Yorkshire dales, so it is worth stressing that cattle probably played a larger part in the region's economy. The Fountains Abbey estate in the time of Henry VIII had two cows to every sheep,[2] and the importance of the leather industries in Tudor York would suggest that the proportion was not exceptional. Even the abundant but often rough grazing could not, however, provide a living for all the uplanders. Many dalesmen emigrated in search of work, and will be found playing a large part in the life of York, but the local custom of partible inheritance encouraged others to remain at home on smallholdings and to look for supplementary means of livelihood. This social and demographic pressure helps to explain the rise of important industries in the dales, notably weaving, hand-knitting, and coal- and lead-mining. There were four important Pennine leadfields, three of them wholly or partly within the county, and they helped to create wealth not only for the dalesmen but also for York, as most of the lead passed through the city on its way downstream to the east coast ports or the Continent.[3] Nevertheless, one should not exaggerate the poverty of the Pennines; R. B. Smith's study of the West Riding has established a definite geographical shift in wealth from Vale to Pennines, measured by tax assessments, between 1334 and 1543-7.[4]

East of the Pennines, the river valleys broaden and unite to

[1] W. Camden, *Britannia*, ed. E. Gibson (London, 1695), col. 705.

[2] R. B. Smith, *Land and Politics in the England of Henry VIII: the West Riding of Yorkshire: 1530–46* (Oxford, 1970), pp. 19 f.

[3] A. Raistrick and B. Jennings, *A History of Lead Mining in the Pennines* (London, 1965), *passim*; map of leadfields on p. xvi.

[4] Smith, *Land and Politics*, pp. 28-33.

form the fertile Vale of Ouse, where mixed husbandry has always been practised. The northern part, the Vale of Mowbray, is merely a narrow corridor between Pennines and moors, but south of Northallerton it broadens into the Vale of York proper, while to the north-east of York the River Derwent flows into the widening plain from the Vale of Pickering. The Vales were more fertile than the hills, and there was much less reliance on secondary occupations to supplement agriculture except in the towns—York, Ripon, Leeds, Wakefield, Pontefract, and a few others. Yet even in the Vale of York not all the land had the prosperous face it has today, for woodland, scrub, and marsh were all extensive. In the vicinity of York itself, the contrasts were sharp. To the north, the wapentake of Bulmer was largely covered by Galtres Forest, a poor, scrubland district despite its extensive grazing. To the south-east, Ouse and Derwent wapentake suffered from poor drainage and the flooding of the two rivers that bordered it and gave it its name, but between the washlands it was very fertile. West of York, the Ainsty was a rich and well-drained wapentake of mixed arable and pasture.

South of York, where the Ouse is joined by the Derwent, Aire, and Don, and then unites with the Trent to form the Humber, the Vale merges imperceptibly into the midland plain. Until the seventeenth and eighteenth centuries much of the lower Vale was marshland, often under flood, but noted for rich arable and pasture when the waters subsided or were permanently channelled away in drains. Further south again, the huge fenland of Hatfield Chase straddled the Lincolnshire border. It still supported its own fenland way of life, though in 1626 Vermuyden began the long process of draining it against the wishes of many of the inhabitants.

The Vale had been traditionally a well-wooded area, supplying timber for the citizens' buildings and fuel for their fires. However, these activities, together with charcoal-burning, gradually eroded the woodland. Sir John Uvedale, visiting York in 1540, sent Cromwell a suggested draft for a parliamentary bill against excessive malt-making there which, he alleged, had consumed all the woods within twenty miles of the city.[1] He may have exaggerated, but one parish eight

[1] *L.P. Hen. VIII* xv, no. 515; Addenda, i. no. 1453.

miles from York had by 1542 lost its extensive medieval tree-cover so completely that there was not enough timber to repair existing buildings.[1] In 1549 the city's MPs were instructed to seek a remedy against the destruction of wood within eight miles of York, and in 1553 to urge a statute 'agaynst the great destructyon of wood within xvj myles of this Citie'.[2]

The Yorkshire vales are flanked on the east by hilly regions very different in character from the Pennines. East of the Vale of Mowbray lie the North Yorkshire Moors, or the Cleveland and Blackamore hills as they were known in the sixteenth century, a mainly sandstone plateau stretching to the coast, and specializing in sheep-farming, though with some arable land in the valleys. Further south, the gentle chalk wolds—Yorkswold was the Tudor name, a coinage similar to Cotswold—had also a sheep–corn husbandry. Finally, beyond the Wolds lies Holderness, another lowland region which ends in a long peninsula between Humber and North Sea, and which formed, together with north Lincolnshire, a major granary for Tudor Yorkshire.

Such, in brief outline, were the varied natural divisions of the county. The vales were naturally more densely peopled than the dales and uplands, but even they had few large settlements. York itself, with a sixteenth-century population varying between about 8,000 and 12,000, was the only large town by contemporary England standards, and was indeed the largest town north of Humber with the possible exception of Newcastle. Ripon, with about 2,000 people in 1532, was probably the largest town in the West Riding. By the early seventeenth century it had been overtaken by Leeds, with an estimated population of 5–6,000. More reliable is an exact count of the population of Sheffield in 1616, which totalled only 2,207.[3] Most Yorkshiremen lived in villages, hamlets or scattered farmsteads. It is possible to glimpse the nature of one such settlement at the beginning of the Tudor period from the recent excavations at Wharram Percy, a wolds

[1] *V.C.H. East Riding*, iii. 117.   [2] *Y.C.R.* v. 24, 87.
[3] Smith, *Land and Politics*, p. 8 and n.; *The Early Modern Town: A Reader*, ed. P. Clark (London, 1976), p. 282; J. Hunter, *Hallamshire*, revised edn. by A. Gatty (London, n.d.), p. 148.

village seventeen miles east of York. A substantial community until the mid-fifteenth century, it then decayed, until the last sixteen residents were evicted some time before 1517. Apart from the manor house, the villagers' houses, even in the last generations of the settlement, were all 'long-houses' of timber, wattle and daub, with living rooms at one end and a byre for animals at the other. They were insubstantial structures which had to be rebuilt from the ground, on average, once every generation.[1]

Wharram Percy is an important site because it has been deserted and can therefore be excavated to reveal a complete village of about 1500 uncomplicated by later phases or by surviving buildings. Nevertheless, it would be unwise to assume that it was typical of the settlement context of York in the period with which this study is concerned, partly because of improved housing standards during the sixteenth century (at another village near Wharram, deserted about 1600, the long-house had become obsolete), and partly because housing types could vary greatly over quite short distances. Mrs Hutton has studied thirty-four timber-framed houses of a type she identifies for convenience as 'Vale of York houses'; they probably range in date from the fifteenth to the seventeenth century, and are superior to those excavated at Wharram Percy. The characteristic type is a timber-framed house of one or two storeys, with no wings or jetties: the majority possess or possessed a continuous outshot which is a relic of an aisled hall open to the roof. They are common enough to have been characteristic of the more prosperous houses in the Vale in the sixteenth century, but differ radically from surviving timbered buildings in York itself, which all have jetties or upper-floor halls.[2]

3

Wharram Percy, as its name suggests, was originally a manor of the great Percy family, and is a reminder that one should

---

[1] M. Beresford and J. G. Hurst, eds., *Deserted Medieval Villages: Studies* (London, 1971), pp. 76–144, 167; J. G. Hurst in *The Times*, 12 Sept. 1975.

[2] B. Hutton, 'Timber-framed houses in the Vale of York', *Medieval Archaeology*, xvii (1973), 87–99.

not neglect that territorial geography of lordship and land-holding which was at least as important to the citizens as the physical or economic context of their city. In legal theory they held their liberties directly of the king, with no mesne lord interposed between them and him. However, the wishes of the county magnates could not lightly be denied, and the corporation were careful to keep on friendly relations with them. Thomas Lord Roos (d. 1543), for example, was not only lord of Helmsley and other estates but the heir to a troublesome claim on part of York's fee-farm.[1] One June morning in 1522, the city councillors learned that he was to enter York at 2.00 p.m. that day, it being 'the first tyme of his cumyng to the said City sens he came to his lands'. They hastily decided to welcome him 'after the lovyngest manner', and spent £3. 13s. 7d. on entertaining him to a dinner of fresh pike.[2] York was not only a city and county corporate held of the king but the capital of a county controlled by its leading nobles, gentry, and churchmen, whose interests it had always to take into account.

The greatest territorial lord in Yorkshire, even before his seizure of the monastic estates, was the king. In the West Riding alone, in 1535, he held the lordships of Conisbrough, Doncaster, Hatfield, Sowerby, and Wakefield, while as duke of Lancaster he also possessed the honours of Pontefract, Tickhill, and Knaresborough. Besides all this, he enjoyed the honours of Holderness in the East Riding, and of Richmond and Pickering in the North Riding, making him lord of more than half of Yorkshire.[3] When to the crown lands are added the great ecclesiastical estates, the traditional view that the Percys and other nobles controlled the north before the Pilgrimage of Grace in 1536 can be seen to be fallacious. Nevertheless, the northern lords did have enormous power, not only because of their own estates and revenues, but also because of the crown lands which they administered in the name of their distant sovereign. The Pilgrims' easy successes north of the Don were facilitated by the neutrality, if not

[1] See below, pp. 48, 215 f.
[2] *Y.C.R.* iii. 83; Y.C.A., C 2, fo. 119[r].
[3] Smith, *Land and Politics*, pp. 51-61, 282-7; Reid, *King's Council in the North*, map at end.

open support, of the local lords, and by Lord Darcy's surrender of the king's castle of Pontefract.[1] The problem was not a lack of royal lands in the north but the entrusting of those lands to the right hands, as Sir Thomas Gargrave told Lord Burghley in 1572.[2]

There is a danger in assuming the inevitability of the Reformation and anticipating the decline of ecclesiastical wealth and power that it involved. It is salutary to remember that throughout Henry VII's reign and the first half of his son's reign the archbishop was the most powerful and wealthy man in Yorkshire next to the king and the earl of Northumberland, with an income in good years of perhaps £2,000 from temporalities alone.[3] Other great ecclesiastical individuals and corporations, such as the Dean and Chapter of York, the abbot of St. Mary's and the abbot of Selby, while not as wealthy as the archbishop, certainly ranked in influence with the nobles rather than the gentry. No anachronism was perpetrated when Henry VII entrusted the leadership of the Council in the North successively to William Sever, abbot of St. Mary's and bishop of Carlisle, and to Thomas Savage, archbishop of York. The Reformation did, of course, mark a revolution in landownership, with not only the redistribution of the extensive monastic estates but also with serious inroads into the landed possessions of the archbishops. Forced exchanges between Henry VIII and Archbishops Lee and Holgate were so unequal that the archbishop's *nominal* temporal income of 1597 was almost exactly what it had been in 1536, despite an enormous inflation in the sixty years between and a considerable increase in most lay lords' incomes which kept pace with the inflation or even moved ahead of it.[4] The archbishops remained very influential figures, but they never regained their pre-Reformation position.

Until 1527 the greatest territorial lords in Yorkshire next

---

[1] Smith, *Land and Politics*, pp. 165-212.

[2] *Chapters in the History of Yorkshire*, ed. J. J. Cartwright (Wakefield, 1872), p. 64.

[3] C. Cross, 'The economic problems of the see of York: decline and recovery in the sixteenth century', in J. Thirsk, ed., *Land, Church and People: Essays presented to Professor H. P. R. Finberg* (*Agricultural History Review*, xviii (1970), Supplement), p. 68.

[4] Cross, op. cit., p. 83.

to the king were the earls of Northumberland. The fifth earl, Henry the Magnificent (1478-1527), enjoyed over £3,000 a year from his estates, which included at least thirty-three Yorkshire manors.[1] He lived chiefly at three manors, Wressle, Leconfield, and Topcliffe, within a day's journey of York, and made bulk purchases for his household in the city.[2] His grandfather the third earl (1421-61) had actually died at his York house and been buried in St. Denys's church nearby; the fifth earl was content with lodgings in York or with a chamber in the Austin Priory, but his relations with the city council remained close.[3] The strength of Percy support can be glimpsed during the Pilgrimage in 1536, when Sir Thomas Percy—the fifth earl's younger son—rode through the city, and the commons 'showed such affection towards him as they showed towards none other'.[4] In 1537 the king seized the Percy estates as heir to the feckless sixth earl, but the majority were eventually restored to the family, and by 1581 the eighth earl was owner of most of the Yorkshire manors once more, and still a power to be reckoned with in the Vale.[5]

In some counties a single noble family was supreme, like the Percys themselves in Northumberland. Yorkshire was, however, too large to be dominated by any one family. The Talbots, earls of Shrewsbury, controlled Hallamshire from Sheffield castle, and the Cliffords, created earls of Cumberland in 1525, ruled Craven from their castle at Skipton: in 1537 the landed income of the two earls was returned as £1,533 and £1,333 respectively. On a more modest scale, Thomas Lord Darcy, with a landed income of £333, was the leading figure in the Pontefract area until his attainder for complicity in the Pilgrimage of Grace.[6] In the North and East Ridings the declining power of the Percys was matched by the rise of the Manners family, Lords Roos and from 1525 earls of Rutland. To an inheritance of Helmsley lordship, the

---

[1] J. M. W. Bean, *The Estates of the Percy Family 1416-1537* (Oxford, 1958), pp. 3, 36–41, 127, 140, 159.

[2] *The Regulations and Establishment of the Household of . . . the Fifth Earl of Northumberland*, ed. T. Percy (London, 1827), *passim*.

[3] *Y.C.R.* iii, 8, 30, 84; *L.P. Hen. VIII*, iv (2), no. 3380 (9).

[4] *L. P. Hen. VIII*, xii (1), no. 369.

[5] E. B. de Fonblanque, *Annals of the House of Percy* (London, 1887), ii. 582.

[6] Smith, *Land and Politics*, pp. 134 f.

first earl (d. 1543) made advantageous purchases and exchanges, including Rievaulx Abbey and the estates of Warter
Priory. In particular, he took over and expanded the monks'
ironworks at Rievaulx, which his successors worked so profitably that it constituted a major share of their revenue. Their
average net profit from the works rose from £530 per year in
the mid-1590s to over £1,000 in the early seventeenth century; and as early as 1582 chapmen flocked to the earl's
storehouse in York to buy his iron.[1] Also to be reckoned
with were the families of the gentry, of whom Dr Cliffe has
counted no fewer than 557 in Yorkshire at the start of Elizabeth's reign.[2] They varied greatly in wealth and importance,
as his thorough study shows, but the greater gentle families—
such as the Constables, Saviles, Fairfaxes, Gascoignes, and
Tempests—had an influence in their own districts equal to
that of the noblemen.

The influence of noblemen and gentlemen permeated early
Tudor York in many ways. They came to town regularly for
the assizes, for elections of knights of the shire, or simply to
meet socially and to buy in the shops. In 1530 Oswald Wilstrop, a gentleman of the Ainsty, inaugurated regular horse
races between local gentry, making York, like Chester and
Carlisle, one of the earliest centres of the sport.[3] Town houses
were owned by nobles and gentry, and many citizens wore
their liveries or badges, despite royal orders and acts of parliament. In 1547 a York tailor confessed that 'he was servaunt
and reteynyd with Sir John Ellerker, knyght', who 'dydd
gyve hym mete and drynk and xls. fee by yere', and as late
as 1577-8 there were nine presentments in one ward alone
'for wearyng of lords and gentlemans lyveray', the offenders
being threatened with disfranchisement.[4]

The situation can be paralleled elsewhere; at Worcester, for
example, orders against citizens wearing liveries were repeated

---

[1] L. Stone, *Family and Fortune: Studies in Aristocratic Finance in the Sixteenth and Seventeenth Centuries* (Oxford, 1973), pp. 165-208; H.M.C., *MSS.
of the Duke of Rutland*, i. 138.

[2] J. T. Cliffe, *The Yorkshire Gentry from the Reformation to the Civil War*
(London, 1969), p. 16.

[3] *Y.C.R.* iii. 131-2; G. H. Martin, *The Town* (London, 1961), p. 26.

[4] *Y.C.R.* ii. 14; iii. 1; iv. 157; Y.C.A., E 31, fos. 55ᵛ, 56ʳ. Raine does not print
the latter entry (14 Oct. 1577), but only the sequel in Feb. 1578: *Y.C.R.* vii. 168.

until at least 1555. Dr Dyer points out that 'the survival of livery and maintenance long after the familiar campaigns of the early Tudors against these dangerous habits is probably a more general phenomenon than is often realized', and that the practice was especially dangerous in county towns: 'the most likely place for a clash between rival bands of retainers was in the county capital where their masters normally settled their affairs'.[1] The records of Star Chamber fully bear him out. Assizes were held at York twice annually, during the Lent and Trinity law vacations, leading to such incidents as a clash in Aldwark between the retainers of two feuding esquires up for the assizes, where one, if not two, servants were killed.[2] The holding of the Lent assizes in 1534 provoked a clash between more powerful gentry—the irascible Sir Robert Constable of Flamborough and his brother-in-law Sir William Percy, brother of the fifth earl. It began with a trivial incident worthy of the Montagues and Capulets: one of Percy's servants acquired and flaunted a Constable buckler, provoked the Constable servants in a tavern, and was killed in a street fight in Fossgate. The Constable servants were gaoled by the assize judges, but no jury of citizens would convict them—because of Constable bribery, according to Percy, who retailed his version to the Court of Star Chamber. The verdict is unfortunately not known, but the whole case throws a vivid light on the difficulties of enforcing law and order even in assize week in the county town.[3] Constable himself, at the time of the riot, was an East Riding justice of the peace. It seems to have been an exceptionally violent case, but there are numerous other examples of justices allegedly conniving at or even involved in breaches of the law.[4]

It would, however, be unfair to think of the gentry's involvement in the law only in terms of corruption. Some of the gentry of the Vale made the law their profession, and had

[1] A. D. Dyer, *The City of Worcester in the Sixteenth Century* (Leicester, 1973), pp. 212 f.

[2] *Yorkshire Star Chamber Proceedings*, ii, ed. H. B. McCall (Y.A.S.R.S. xlv, 1911), 67–73. De la River was lord of the manors of Brafferton and Brandsby, and Barton of Whenby.

[3] *Yorkshire Star Chamber Proceedings*, iii, ed. W. Brown (Y.A.S.R.S. li, 1914), 18–28; M. H. and R. Dodds, *The Pilgrimage of Grace 1536–1537 and the Exeter Conspiracy 1538* (Cambridge, 1915), i. 47–8.

[4] e.g. *Yorks. Star Chamber Proceedings*, ii. 54–6, 94–6.

distinguished careers in the royal courts. Of 170 sergeants and barristers of the period 1461-1518, the majority were drawn from southern and eastern England, and only twenty-four from the six northern counties. However, of those twenty-four, eleven were born within twenty miles of York and five in the area south of Doncaster near the Great North Road, a concentration perhaps owing to the regional influence of York and its close contacts with the capital. Three were born in the Ainsty, including Sir Guy Fairfax of Walton and Steeton (d. 1495), successively Justice of the King's Bench and Chief Justice of Lancaster. His eldest son William was Justice of the Common Pleas, and a younger son Thomas was a sergeant. A similar family tradition in the law was maintained by the Palmes of Naburn, one of York's suburban villages.[1]

Gradually, from the mid-sixteenth century, the city and county moved into a different relationship with their leading lords. The permanent presence of the Council in the North in the York area from 1537 changed the balance of power, and the lords president, by virtue of their royal commission, gradually replaced the local nobles as the most powerful men in the north. Admittedly all the early presidents, from 1537 to 1568, were leading northerners in their own right, but Elizabeth's next two choices were noblemen conspicuously loyal to herself and with no northern power base. Thomas Radcliffe, earl of Sussex, suppressed the Rising of the Northern Earls despite his sympathies with their party; Henry Hastings, earl of Huntingdon, consolidated royal power in the north and ruled firmly, justly and impartially for almost a generation (1572-95). The failure of Northumberland and Westmorland in 1569 to raise much support except in the areas through which their army passed indicates how much Yorkshire had changed since 1536.

By then, livery and maintenance was virtually a dead issue, and the gentry were no longer closely associated with rival noble leaders. An early example of one such gentleman,

<hr />

[1] E. W. Ives, 'Some Aspects of the Legal Profession in the late fifteenth and early sixteenth centuries', unpublished University of London Ph.D. thesis, 1955, pp. 63 f., 95, 120-1, 124-38, 185 and Table I; T. Widdrington, *Analecta Eboracensia*, ed. C. Caine (London, 1897), pp. 87 f., 149 f.

exceptional only in the degree of his success, was Sir Thomas
Wharton (d. 1568), who began his career as an officer of the
sixth Percy earl but ended as a crown official, a major land-
owner in his own right, and first Lord Wharton; in 1544 he
became one of the first two Marcher wardens not drawn from
the traditional northern noble families. He acquired a bloc of
fertile estates near York, the former Percy manors of Healaugh
and Catterton, together with the dissolved monasteries of
Healaugh and Synningthwaite. Though he rose so high, he
was of minor gentry stock; and one of his Westmorland
cousins did not disdain to marry the daughter and heiress of
John Beane, innholder and alderman of York.[1]

The dissolution of the monasteries, from which Wharton
profited, had of course enormous consequences for the distribution of land among the gentry, even though it is now
known that most purchasers were already of landowning
stock and were not the 'new men' of popular belief. For
some established lords, it provided an opportunity to acquire
an estate conveniently near the city. Sir Thomas Tempest, a
lawyer with the Northern Council, found regular attendance
at York expensive, so he acquired Synningthwaite Priory, a
property which was later exchanged with Wharton.[2] Leonard
Beckwith was nearer the popular idea of a monastic purchaser: the son of a minor gentleman of Stillingfleet in the
Vale, he became a leading crown agent in the suppression of
the Yorkshire monasteries. He used his position ruthlessly to
acquire Selby Abbey and Holy Trinity Priory at York, as well
as interests in the estates of Byland and Fountains; and he
turned Holy Trinity into a town-house for his family.[3] The
careers of Beckwith and Wharton, however exceptional, are a
salutary reminder of the mobility and fluidity of the Yorkshire gentry. J. T. Cliffe calculates that the 557 gentry families of 1558 increased to 679 by 1642, but points out that
the net increase is misleading, for 181 families died out in

[1] M. E. James, *Change and Continuity in the Tudor North: the Rise of Thomas First Lord Wharton* (Borth. P. xxvii, 1965), *passim*; R. Davies, *Walks through the City of York* (London, 1880), p. 184.
[2] Smith, *Land and Politics*, p. 246.
[3] Smith, op. cit., pp. 224-5; B. A. English and C. B. L. Barr, 'The records formerly in St. Mary's Tower, York', *Y.A.J.* xlii (1967-70), 366-7, 517.

the male line, 30 disappeared without trace, and 64 left the county.[1]

One cannot safely generalize about so large and diverse a group, but many of the Elizabethan gentry appear to have poured their energies into litigation and building. There is little evidence of the bloody feuding of early Tudor times, though the disappearance of the records of the Council in the North may distort the picture. G. C. F. Forster is inclined to accept that the Council did curb feuds between the gentry, but draws attention to a resurgence of rioting, as well as quarrelling and litigation, in the early seventeenth century when the Council was weakened.[2] Even so, litigation rather than physical violence was becoming the normal expression of quarrelling. As to building, their other costly indulgence, at least 280 Yorkshire manor houses were rebuilt or enlarged between 1558 and 1642, often on a lavish scale. In Elizabeth's reign, Sir Robert Stapleton rebuilt his ancestral mansion at Wighill in the Ainsty, 'a palace the model whereof he had brought out of Italy . . . fitter for a lord treasurer of England than a knight of Yorkshire'.[3] Building was usually a mark of growing prosperity, but for some gentry it was one of the forms of extravagance which led to financial difficulties. Nearly one half of the Yorkshire gentle families were in financial difficulties at one time or another, and many had to resort to borrowing from merchants in York, Hull, and other towns.[4] Even noblemen had on occasion to resort to the York money-lenders.[5] To some indebted gentry York was, not a place to negotiate loans, but a haven where one could live privately and cheaply without the expense of hospitality on one's estate.[6]

A perhaps more typical relationship between a gentle family and their county town is glimpsed in the notes of the first English woman diarist, Margaret Lady Hoby (1571-1633). Her surviving journal covers the period between 1599 and 1605, when she was living at Hackness near Scarborough,

[1] Cliffe, *Yorkshire Gentry*, p. 16.
[2] G. C. F. Forster, 'Faction and county government in early Stuart Yorkshire', *Northern History*, xi (1976), 70-86.
[3] Cliffe, *Yorkshire Gentry*, pp. 102-4. [4] ibid., p. 145.
[5] Fonblanque, *Annals of the House of Percy*, i. 574-5; P.R.O., C1/1426/51, 52.
[6] Cliffe, *Yorkshire Gentry*, pp. 20, 151, 165.

and had married the Puritan gentleman Sir Thomas Hoby. During that time she stayed in York at least seven times, for periods varying from a night to two weeks. They were partly social visits, including dinners with her cousin (the wife of Lord President Burghley), the archbishop and the dean; but she also took the opportunity for medical treatment and legal consultations. In 1600 the Hobys bought a house in the city, for Sir Thomas, as a member of numerous government commissions, was often there on business; and Lady Margaret, knowing the York shops, was able to use his visits to obtain groceries not available locally.[1]

The Hobys were typical of many Yorkshire gentry who, by the time of Elizabeth, were visiting York frequently to shop, to consult doctors and lawyers, to give evidence in lawsuits, to vote in parliamentary elections, or simply to be entertained. The horse-racing between local gentry from 1530 was followed by similar diversions such as archery contests in 1555 and 1582, and by regular cock-fighting from 1568.[2] Understandably, the corporation appreciated the patronage of the gentry. They were prompt in agreeing to the gentlemen's request for a cockpit, as it would 'cause muche money to be spent bothe emongs vytelers and other craftsmen', and equally prompt to compel repaving in Stonegate when the drainage became defective, as 'gentlemen and straingers passing that way did much compleyn thereof'.[3]

By this time it was becoming commoner for noble and gentle families to acquire, as the Hobys did, town houses in York. Well-known Yorkshire families like the Fairfaxes, Eures, Constables, Salveyns, Saviles, and Scropes all possessed messuages in York in the later years of Elizabeth. George, earl of Cumberland, acquired two tenements in Lendal in 1580, and even the queen's chief minister, Lord Burghley, acquired property in 1592, though it is not clear why he

[1] *Diary of Lady Margaret Hoby 1599–1605*, ed. D. M. Meads (London, 1930), pp. 72–4, 112–15, 146–7, 149, 188–9, 195, 202–3, 268, 279.

[2] *Y.C.R.* v. 127; vi. 135; W. Elderton, *Yorke, Yorke for my Monie* (1584); B.L. Add. 33595, fo. 43; D. M. Palliser, 'York under the Tudors: the trading life of the Northern capital', *Perspectives in English Urban History*, ed. A. Everitt (London, 1973), pp. 57 f.

[3] *Y.C.R.* vi. 135; B. M. Wilson, 'The Corporation of York, 1580–1660' (Univ. of York, M.Phil. thesis, 1967), p. 168.

should have felt the need to establish a base at York in his old age unless it were as a staging-post *en route* to Scotland and to the queen's heir presumptive James VI.[1] The acquisition of town houses increased still further under the early Stuarts, and by the time of the civil war at least two dozen nobles and gentry owned dwellings in the city.[2]

There were therefore many ties connecting the gentry with the citizens; and indeed it would be wrong to think of them as two separate groups, for many citizens were themselves either drawn from the ranks of the gentry or connected with them by marriage. The recordership of York was held almost always by local gentry with a legal training, some of whom married citizens' daughters. The recorders were professional and non-resident members of the corporation, but many other city councillors were also of gentry stock. Of fourteen Tudor councillors born outside the city whose fathers' rank is known, ten were of gentle families, including the Halls of Leventhorpe who provided younger sons to the city council in three successive generations.[3] Numerous other examples could be collected of citizens, chiefly merchants, who came from a similar background. Edward Exelby, who became free as a merchant in 1568–9 and died in the great plague of 1604, was of a junior branch of the Exelbys of Dishforth. Marmaduke Sothabie, made free as a merchant in 1576–7, was the third son of a gentleman of Pocklington. Thomas Marshall, a mercer who took up the franchise in 1586–7, was the third son of a gentleman of Middleton near Pickering.[4] Such examples could be multiplied, as could cases of York natives who married the daughters of gentlemen or whose daughters were married by them. There was no social gulf between the 'mere' gentry of the county and the more prosperous citizens.

[1] *Feet of Fines of the Tudor Period*, ed. F. Collins (4 vols., Y.A.S.R.S. 1887–90), ii. 36, 107, 149; iii. 24, 146, 178, *et passim*; F. Peck, *Desiderata Curiosa*, i (London, 1732), lib. v, p. 41.

[2] Cliffe, *Yorkshire Gentry*, pp. 20 f.; 'Proceedings of the Commonwealth Committee for York and the Ainsty', *Miscellanea Vol. VI* (Y.A.S.R.S. cxviii, 1953), pp. 12 f.

[3] See below, p. 95.

[4] *Register of the Freemen of the City of York from the City Records*, ed. F. Collins (2 vols., Surtees Soc., 1897, 1900), ii. 9, 17, 27; *Y.A.J.* x (1889), 496–7, 500; xiv (1896–8), 106; vii (1882), 101–2.

4

York was, therefore, a capital to the 'county community' of England's largest shire, an administrative and judicial centre for eight northern counties, and an active centre of trade and commerce in its own right. Contemporaries saw it as one of the very few provincial cities worthy of mention. Indeed, the Venetian ambassador's secretary, visiting England in 1496-7, said that apart from London there were scarcely any towns of importance in the kingdom except Bristol to the west and 'Boraco alias Orchi, which is on the borders of Scotland'.[1] The last phrase betrays the ignorance of the Italian diplomat based in London, and indeed there were other cities as wealthy or as populous as York, if not both. Nevertheless, seasoned travellers more familiar with English towns than the Venetian all considered York to be one of the finest. The Scot John Major placed it second only to London: 'in circuit it is great, though not', he added significantly, 'in population or in wealth'. John Speed, like Camden, thought it 'a pleasant place, large, and full of magnificence, rich, populous, and not onely strengthened with fortifications, but adorned with beautifull buildings, as well privat as publike'.[2] It must have been at the height of its glory before the dissolutions of religious institutions and the consequent destruction. Patrick Nuttgens goes so far as to say that 'York probably looked its best at the time of the accession of Henry VIII; it probably looked its worst by the end of the century'.[3]

The early Tudor city, like any other large town, reflected in its street-pattern and buildings its complex past (map 3). It had begun as a Roman legionary fortress and civilian town, which had later been absorbed into the Anglian state of Deira and thence into the kingdom of Northumbria. This period left a permanent legacy in the form of the cathedral, for the first king converted to Christianity, Edwin, had in 627 founded an episcopal church of St. Peter which was the seat

[1] *A Relation, or rather a True Account, of the Island of England*, ed. C. A. Sneyd (Camden Soc. xxxvii, 1847), p. 41.
[2] *A History of Greater Britain . . . by John Major*, ed. A. Constable (Scottish Hist. Soc., x, 1892), p. 15; J. Speed, *The Theatre of the Empire of Great Britaine* (London, 1611), p. 78.
[3] P. Nuttgens, *York: the Continuing City* (London, 1976), p. 59.

of an archbishop from 735. The Danes captured the city in 866, and from then until 954 it was intermittently the capital of independent Danish and Norwegian kingdoms, while the Scandinavian influence remained paramount even after the north was conquered by the kings of Wessex. It was the Anglo-Scandinavians who turned York into an international mercantile city trading overseas by way of the Ouse, and they who extended the old walled area south to protect the angle of the Ouse and Foss, laying out a large new market area in the Pavement, Shambles and Ousegate district. It was they who created new thoroughfares and renamed the old ones, for to this day the central streets are almost all called 'gate', from the Old Scandinavian *gata*.

The Norman Conquest also left its mark on the physical development of the city. The burning of York in the revolt of 1069, like the accidental fire of 1137, was a great catastrophe which was obliterated by later recovery and rebuilding; but more permanent was the action of William I in clearing one-seventh of the built-up area to make way for two motte-and-bailey castles, dominating the river approach to York from the south. The castle on the right bank was soon abandoned, and by the Tudor period its earthworks were used only for musters and military drill, but the other, rebuilt in stone in the thirteenth century, was kept defensible as the sheriff's headquarters and county gaol. It was also the Normans who founded St. Mary's Abbey and several other religious houses, and who completed the city's earth-and-timber defences. By about 1200 the shape of York as it remained until the sixteenth—and indeed the nineteenth—century was complete, and the intervening period witnessed elaboration and rebuilding rather than dramatic change. In the thirteenth century six friaries were added to the stock of religious houses of which four survived until the Reformation. Between about 1250 and 1380 the city's stone walls were erected on the existing ramparts, and the Minster was rebuilt in its present form between about 1230 and 1472. In the fourteenth and fifteenth centuries many parish churches were rebuilt and enlarged, while corporation and social and mercantile guilds built the four great guildhalls which still survive today.

The city walls in their final form made a circuit of over

two miles in length, continuous except where they met the two rivers and the marsh by the Foss.[1] They enclosed an extensive area between the Ouse and Foss, together with the Micklegate and Bishophill district west of the Ouse and the Walmgate area east of the Foss, totalling 263 acres. The earthen banks with their stone walls were set between inner and outer moats, probably dry for most of their length. Five well-defended 'bars' or gates guarded the entrances from the main roads into the city, while seven smaller gates or posterns were placed where the walls met the rivers. The walls were by no means an anachronism, and throughout the Tudor period a very clear distinction was maintained between the city and the suburbs, the walls dividing the two. The walled city was large by contemporary English standards, though much less than the square mile of London or Norwich. It can now be crossed in fifteen minutes' brisk walking, but distances must have seemed much greater on foot with the narrow, crowded, badly surfaced streets, almost unlit at night. Bootham and St. Sampson's parish were considered 'remote' from Petergate in the fifteenth century, though both are within five minutes' walk of it today.[2] Not until late in the sixteenth century did the city council order all householders to hang out street lights, though they imposed this requirement on themselves in 1527.[3]

The churches and religious houses were almost the only stone buildings except the city walls. Before the Reformation they included the cathedral and its numerous ancillary buildings; the Benedictine monasteries of St. Mary's, Holy Trinity, and St. Clement's; St. Andrew's Priory; St. Leonard's Hospital; four friaries; the priests' college at Peasholme; forty parish churches; two civic bridge chapels, and numerous other chapels, hospitals and *maisons dieu*. St. Mary's Abbey, standing outside the city walls by the main road to the Scottish border, had long had its own defences, but even the intramural religious houses had gatehouses and precinct walls, as did the Minster.

[1] For a detailed description of the walls see R.C.H.M. *York: Volume II: the Defences* (London, 1972).
[2] J. S. Purvis, *A Mediaeval Act Book* (York, n.d.), p. 27.
[3] *Y.C.R.* iii. 110; Y.C.A., B 28, fo. 159ᵛ (1584).

Secular public buildings were very few. Only four of the city craft guilds are known to have had their own guildhalls, though after the Reformation the other guilds were allowed the use of St. Anthony's Hall. The corporation had two alternative meeting places, a council chamber on Ouse Bridge and the larger Common Hall of 1446–59 off Coney Street, where meetings attended by the commons were held. There was no official mayoral residence until the eighteenth century, and Tudor mayors used their own homes for official business and for civic hospitality.[1] Other officers must have carried out many of their official duties from their homes: a description of the house of Thomas Rogerson (common clerk 1590–1602) in Castlegate, with the benches and royal arms in the hall, and tables, shelves, rails, and benches in the 'office', suggests that most of his business was carried out there.[2] Where private houses proved too small, meetings and courts would be held in the most convenient large building, which was usually a church.

Public buildings did, however, include a number of corporation structures for specialized purposes. The city walls have already been mentioned: intended originally for defence, they had become equally useful as barriers for the efficient collection of tolls, or for excluding undesirables like beggars or plague suspects. The highest compliment paid to a deceased alderman in 1483 was that 'he was like another town wall to the citizens'.[3] There was also a tendency to use the gates for non-military purposes after about 1570, when the military threat from Scotland diminished. Monk Bar and Fishergate Bar were turned into prisons, while Bootham, Micklegate, and Walmgate Bars were extended at the rear to form dwellings; the timber-framed house built on to Walmgate Bar still survives.[4] The city also maintained several bridges, notably Ouse Bridge and Foss Bridge, which were both lined by corporation-owned houses, shops and public buildings. The former was the only bridge over the Ouse, and crossings at other points had to be made by boat. One corporation ferry

[1] e.g. Davies, *Walks*, p. 265; F. Drake, *Eboracum: or the History and Antiquities of the City of York* (London, 1736), p. 132.
[2] Y.C.A., B 32, fo. 245^r and 245^v.   [3] Drake, *Eboracum*, p. 295.
[4] R.C.H.M. *York*, ii. 95, 116, 125, 129, 142–3, 152.

operated where Lendal Bridge stands today, and a second
civic ferry came into use by 1541 near the site of Skeldergate
Bridge. The smaller river Foss was easier to bridge; it was
crossed, apart from Foss Bridge, by smaller bridges at the
ends of Monkgate and Layerthorpe, while in 1583 a fourth
was added at Castle Mills.[1] South of Ouse Bridge the corporation kept up a large 'staith' or quay on the east bank and a
common crane on the opposite shore; and finally they maintained a number of prisons, stocks, pillories and gallows, as
did the owners of the various private jurisdictions in the city.

York was full of visual contrasts, and has been pictured,
with perhaps only slight exaggeration, as 'a city of exquisite
architecture rising out of a midden'.[2] Cheek-by-jowl with the
castle, cathedral, churches, and city walls were narrow, filthy
streets of huddled houses and cottages. The Shambles seems
very narrow today, especially where the upper stories of
timber-framed houses nearly meet, yet it was a main street;
many houses must have pressed still closer together along the
narrow, sunless lanes, as they still do in Lady Peckitt's Yard.
Congestion was severe in the heart of the city, for the walled
area housed four times the population that it does today. Nor
was the housing evenly distributed, for large spaces—the
Minster close, the castle and the religious liberties—were un-
available for building. Housing was most densely packed into
the central district between Minster, Ouse and Foss; the
Micklegate and Walmgate areas had much more open space,
and after the late medieval population decline each consisted
essentially of one long main street. Camden, entering the city
at Micklegate Bar by the London road, admired the 'long and
broad street' of Micklegate running downhill to Ouse Bridge,
'flanked on both sides by handsome buildings which back on
to fine gardens', while 'behind the gardens fields for musters
stretch to the city walls'. Once across the bridge, however, he
found the centre 'all crowded with buildings and narrow
streets'.[3] Indeed, the congestion caused by shopkeepers'
stalls in Low Ousegate, just over the bridge, was a constant
concern of the corporation.[4]

[1] K. J. Allison, 'Bridges', *V.C.H. York*, pp. 515–20.
[2] Viscount Esher, *York: a Study in Conservation* (London, 1968), p. 2.
[3] Camden, *Britannia*, pp. 407 f. (translated).   [4] *Y.C.R.* ii. 119, 185.

The lesser streets and lanes were even narrower, and probably lined with one- or two-roomed hovels very different from those prosperous timbered houses which survive today. Both streets and lanes were also much more squalid than can easily be pictured. Repeated corporation orders to cleanse the streets, remove garbage heaps, and drive out scavenging pigs are eloquent enough of normal conditions, and passers-by risked being spattered as chamber-pots were emptied.[1] The main intramural streets were paved by the fifteenth century, and the four main roads out of the bars in 1541,[2] but the paving was apparently only a rough kind of cobbling, and some streets did not even have that. Micklegate, the main street which Camden admired and which brought London visitors into the heart of the city, must still have been unpaved in the winter of 1571, when it was too 'myery' for the corporation to be willing to walk up it.[3] Even where paving was laid down it was easily broken up by cartwheels, so much so that in 1493 4d. a year was levied on all ironbound carts passing over the bridges or through the bars, towards maintenance of the street surfaces; while in 1523-4, after the main streets had been 'newe pavyd' at great expense, dung carts with ironbound wheels were forbidden altogether.[4]

One of the most remarkable features of Tudor York is how relatively little change there seems to have been to its physical fabric over such a long period. Throughout England, the Reformation virtually brought church-building to an end, but at York poverty had already put a stop to it a full generation earlier, apart from the total rebuilding of St. Michael-le-Belfrey between 1525 and 1536, and the partial reconstruction of St. Helen, Stonegate, in the 1550s.[5] Extensive rebuilding of the city walls in the Walmgate sector was undertaken between about 1490 and 1510, but after that the corporation committed themselves to no major works except for the unavoidable rebuilding of Ouse Bridge in 1565-6. The only large new buildings were town houses put up by gentry and northern

[1] e.g. Y.C.A., B 33, fo. 82ᵛ.   [2] Y.C.R. iv. 57; Y.C.A., B 15, fo. 30ᵛ.

[3] Register of the Guild of Corpus Christi in the City of York, ed. R. H. Skaife (Surtees Soc. lvii, 1872), p. 308.

[4] Y.C.A., B 7, fo. 94ʳ; Y.C.R. iii. 89-91.

[5] N. Pevsner, Yorkshire: York and the East Riding (Harmondsworth, 1972), pp. 117, 119, 124; J. Harvey, York (London, 1975), p. 56.

officials: Thomas, first Lord Fairfax, erected a mansion on
Bishophill early in Elizabeth's reign, another was built simul-
taneously at Heslington by Sir Thomas Eynns, secretary to
the Council in the North, and a third was added to Treasurer's
House, just by the Minster, by George Young about 1600.
The King's Manor was also enlarged for the Council in the
North at various times under Elizabeth I and the early
Stuarts.[1] The one major change at York was negative: the
suppression of the religious houses during the Reformation.
Most of their buildings seem to have been demolished fairly
quickly, but the surprising thing is that their sites long remained open spaces. After all, the century after the Reformation saw York's population increase by a half, restoring it
almost to its medieval peak, yet there is very little evidence
indeed for new domestic building during the century. The
vacated monastic sites remained unbuilt on, and were still
mostly indicated as open spaces as late as 1750.[2] The extra
population was apparently crammed into the existing stock
of buildings, or into courtyard developments in their back-
yards.[3]

The lack of new building on the monastic sites can be explained by the reluctance of the new owners to lose the
extensive gardens and orchards that they had acquired, but
equally striking is that the suburbs did not greatly expand
during the Elizabethan population rise. An apparently precise
and hitherto neglected census of 1639 records 1,786 houses
within the walls and 370 without, a proportion confirmed by
Widdrington, according to whom the suburbs before their
destruction in 1644 'amounted to a sixth part of the city'.[4]
As there was little new building in the sixteenth century, the
proportions of city to suburbs are not likely to have been
very different a century earlier. It can thus be suggested that

[1] *The Life of Marmaduke Rawdon, written by Himself*, ed. R. Davies (Camden
Soc., lxxxv, 1863), pp. 124 n., 125 n.; *V.C.H. East Riding*, iii. 70; R.C.H.M. *York*,
iv. 30-43.

[2] Peter Chassereau, *A Plan of the City of York* (London, 1750). A. L. Rowse,
The England of Elizabeth: the Structure of Society (London, 1950), p. 162, errs
in stating that York's 'monastic sites and gardens' were built over in Elizabeth's
reign.

[3] See Palliser, 'York', pp. 345-56.

[4] Bodley, Rawl. C886, pp. 51 f.; Widdrington, *Analecta Eboracensia*, p. 120.

in Tudor York only one person in six lived outside the walls: a very different state of affairs from, for instance, Exeter, where in the 1520s the proportion was one in four, or Leicester or Winchester, where it approached one in two.[1] Admittedly York's walled area was larger than theirs, but the fact remains that its suburbs were smaller under the Tudors and Stuarts than they had been in the thirteenth century.

There were extensive areas of open, mainly agricultural, land between the walls and the city boundaries. Part of it was occupied by the city's common lands, which included 'strays' or permanent pastures like Hob Moor and Knavesmire, and arable fields over which the freemen enjoyed 'average' or grazing rights after harvest. There are even traces of ridge-and-furrow ploughing surviving in places, as at Yearsley Bridge Hospital, for most of the city's arable was originally open-field, though mainly enclosed by the mid-sixteenth century.[2] The arable around the city was considerable enough to support numerous windmills, and one can list at least twenty in the suburbs and satellite villages in the sixteenth and early seventeenth centuries.[3] The pasture rights of the freemen were perhaps even more important to them than the arable fields, for many citizens owned cattle, sheep, and horses, and it is clear from the violence with which enclosures of the common lands were met that many poorer citizens relied on their 'stint' of one or two cows in the fields to supplement their earnings from their craft.

Indeed, the common lands of the city extended beyond the boundaries of its liberty into the three ridings. A careful analysis of the various city bounds has shown that the walled city was at the centre of two concentric but very irregular areas. The smaller was the liberty of the city, not mapped until 1850 but apparently virtually the same as it had been in the sixteenth century, taking in the walled city, Knavesmire, Hob Moor, Bishop's Fields and very little else. The citizens

[1] W. T. McCaffrey, *Exeter 1540–1640: the Growth of an English County Town* (Harvard, 1958), p. 13; Hoskins, *Provincial England*, p. 89; D. J. Keene, 'Suburban growth', in M. W. Barley, ed., *The Plans and Topography of Medieval Towns in England and Wales* (London, 1976), p. 78.

[2] R.C.H.M. *York*, iii. 1 f.; iv. 1 f.

[3] Raine, *Mediaeval York*, pp. 257, 280, 284–5, 301, 309–10, 319; R.C.H.M. *York*, iii. 57; iv. 1; *V.C.H. East Riding*, iii, 33, 72.

had full jurisdiction within this territory, except for the smaller liberties within it like the cathedral and castle; but their chartered rights did not run beyond it, except on the western side where the Ainsty wapentake formed a huge jurisdiction of a special kind. Rather larger than the city's liberty was the tract perambulated by the corporation almost annually in the Tudor period; it has often been identified with the city's liberty, but was in fact the land over which the citizens enjoyed rights of pasturage. It is noteworthy that even this larger area excluded the neighbouring townships and villages: York had no direct jurisdiction even over villages like Heworth and Clifton, within a mile of the walls. On the other hand, the ecclesiastical position was more complicated. The parochial system was so ancient and irregular that the city's parishes included all or part of several nearby villages: Clifton, Copmanthorpe, Dringhouses, Fulford, Heworth, Heslington (half), Holgate, Knapton, Middlethorpe, Naburn, Rawcliffe, and Upper Poppleton.[1]

It is not possible in a study of the city of this length to consider these villages in detail, nor would it be appropriate, for they were self-contained rural communities outside the city's jurisdiction. Nevertheless, the villages of York's hinterland had inevitably a close relationship with the large city in their midst. This was especially true of the dozen communities which were within York's parish system, for even if they had chapels of their own they were under the authority and jurisdiction of urban priests. An extreme case was Naburn, a village of perhaps thirty households four miles south of York. Most of the village and manor lay within the parish of St. George's, York, and all those dwelling in that part had to be brought to be buried in the churchyard of St. George's.[2] Even if they were not actually baptized or buried in the city, most rural parishioners had their vital events recorded in the register of their mother church, which means that calculations of the city's population based on parish figures—almost the only possible basis—involve a blurring of the line between town and country. In the case of the extramural parish of St.

[1] For this paragraph see P. M. Tillott and K. J. Allison, 'The boundaries of the city', V.C.H. York, pp. 311–21.
[2] Raine, Mediaeval York, p. 109; V.C.H. East Riding, iii. 81.

Olave's, it is possible to state that exactly two-thirds of those baptized had homes in the suburbs and one-third in the villages; but most registers are not so helpful.[1] The rural parishioners were also, of course, subject to tithe to the city priests. Indeed, as tithe could be levied easily only on crops and livestock, very few cases of tithe disputes appear between priests and citizens, and the enforcement of tithe is normally mentioned only in connection with the rural hinterland. The only tithe case in Dr Purvis's selection involving city parishes concerns a long-lasting dispute over sheep at Heworth, a township divided between three York parishes. The grazing on Heworth Moor was held to belong to the whole village and thus to all three parishes, and the only means of deciding which of the three priests received the tithe of a particular flock was the location of the owner's house within the village.[2]

5

Enough evidence remains, both archivally and in surviving buildings, to provide considerable information about the housing standards of at least the rich and middling citizens, more indeed than can be surveyed here.[3] Almost all the houses known to have been either built or lived in during the Tudor period were oak-framed, and York certainly conformed to William Harrison's generalization that 'the greatest part of our building in the cities and good townes of England, consisteth only of timber'.[4] They ranged in height, even in the city centre, from one storey to four; the multi-storey houses were made more stable by the use of a jetty or overhang. The roof members and tie-beams of most surviving houses were numbered for ease of assembly, and from the late sixteenth century the studs or timber uprights were also numbered. The Plumbers' Arms of about 1575 even preserves some

---

[1] *The Parish Register of St. Olave, York*, i, ed. F. Harrison and W. J. Kaye (Yorks. Par. Reg. Soc. lxxiii, 1923), 24-6, 36-62.
[2] *Causes in Tithe*, ed. Purvis, pp. 9-16.
[3] For documentary references see Palliser, 'York', pp. 345-56, 394 A-C; for surviving buildings, R.C.H.M. *York, passim*.
[4] W. Harrison, *Description of England in Shakespere's Youth*, ed. F. J. Furnivall (New Shakespere Soc., 2 vols., 1908), i. 233.

original window frames which were 'shop-made units ready to be jammed into position between the pegged framing'.[1] With such methods of construction, there was no great difficulty in dismantling a house either to renew it or even to rebuild it on a different site entirely.[2] Any unevenness in appearance would probably have been masked by plastering the façade. Almost all Tudor building accounts include payments for plaster, and when a royal visit was expected in 1575, householders were ordered to 'repare, plaistir, trym and well decke decently their houses of the foresydes'.[3] The plasterwork would also be made gayer by colour-washing. In preparing for James I's entry of 1603, the corporation ordered all inhabitants to 'painte the owteside of ther howses with some collors to the strete forwardes'.[4]

The complete absence of thatchers from the freemen's register, and the fact that building disputes were reserved to the carpenters' and tilers' guilds, suggest that thatched roofs were rare, and they were forbidden altogether from the 1580s, presumably because of the fire risk.[5] The tilers' guild provided not only roof-tiles, but also the 'wall-tiles' or thin bricks which were commonly used as infilling between timbers, in preference to wattle-and-daub. Conservative York remained, however, slow and grudging in its acceptance of brick as a building material. The abbots of St. Mary were rebuilding their house by the abbey in brick by 1483 or earlier, and they were imitated by Archbishop Rotherham (1480–1500) at Bishopthorpe Palace, but the citizens were slow to copy their example except for the new tower on the city walls added in 1490.[6] Eynns's Heslington Hall of 1565–8 was built entirely of brick, but no completely brick house is recorded in York itself until 1610, when one such was standing in Micklegate, its rarity indicated by its name of 'le read brick howse'.[7] Brick was certainly in domestic use well before this date, but was apparently reserved for ovens,

[1] R.C.H.M. *York*, iii, pp. lxv, lxxiv, lxxviii.
[2] e.g. *Y.C.R.* iii. 119; iv. 138; vi. 8.
[3] ibid., vii. 105.   [4] Y.C.A., B 32, fo. 249[V].
[5] Y.C.A., E 31, pt. 1, pp. 53, 55 etc.; B 29, fo. 15[r].
[6] R.C.H.M. *York*, ii. 139; iv. 13, 21, 30, *et passim*; N. Pevsner, *Yorkshire: the West Riding* (Harmondsworth, 2nd edn., 1967), p. 108.
[7] Y.C.A., E 27, fo. 123[r].

hearths, floors, chimneys, and internal walls.[1] There was apparently an aesthetic prejudice against its display on façades.

The houses of the very poor have left no trace either in surviving fabrics or in inventories, but it would not be surprising if many were still one-roomed hovels; after all, as late as 1901 there were 284 one-roomed houses in York.[2] Even among those rich enough to merit an inventory, the carpenter Thomas Cok (1520) was little above this level, for his house consisted simply of a hall and a 'bowtyng hows'; in the latter room he slept and stored 'his stuff that pertenyth to his occupacion as axys and other thyngs'.[3] The smallest houses described in inventories were generally those of priests. The vicar of St. Lawrence (1523-4) had only a hall, a parlour in which he slept, and a kitchen, while a cantarist of St. Saviour's (1547) and the rector of St. Helen-on-the-Walls (1551) had even smaller houses, with only a hall and parlour. In both, the parlour served as a bedroom, while in the former house at least, the hall was used for cooking.[4] At the other end of the ecclesiastical social scale, the pre-Reformation dignitaries of the cathedral had huge and impressive residences. An imperfect inventory of the treasurer's house lists fifteen rooms, including a library and three different larders, while the chancellor's house also contained at least fifteen rooms.[5]

Laymen's houses were similarly of very varying size, as four inventories of similar date show. Isabel Fisher, widow, had a sparsely furnished house of only three rooms, a hall and two parlours. The tailor Henry Bowrow of Petergate apparently had a five-roomed house, with hall, kitchen, shop, and two chambers, and a buttery which perhaps formed only a partitioned corner of the hall. A larger house was that of John Litster of Belfrey parish, draper and member of the

[1] Palliser, 'York', pp. 363-5.
[2] B. S. Rowntree, *Poverty: a Study of Town Life* (London, 3rd edn., 1902), p. 160.
[3] B.I.H.R., original probate records, inventory of T. Cok 1519 (O.S.). Almost all surviving York inventories occur in this collection; later references will give only the name and date of each. See D. M. Smith, *A Guide to the Archive collections in the Borthwick Institute of Historical Research* (York, 1973), pp. 155 ff.
[4] B.I.H.R., inventories of T. Barton 1523; J. Watson 1547; R. Agrig 1551.
[5] *Testamenta Eboracensia*, ed. J. Raine *et al.*, 6 vols. (Surtees Soc., 1836-1902; hereafter *Test. Ebor.*), iv. 279-307; v. 253-5.

Twenty Four—his inventory indicates a three-storeyed house of eight or nine rooms—while his neighbour Neville Mores, stationer, possessed a house in Stonegate with a hall, two parlours, kitchen, five chambers, and shop.[1] Almost all laymen's inventories, in fact, listed a hall and a kitchen, and one or more parlours or chambers, usually used as bedrooms. Several inventories listed a brewhouse, and some a 'bolting house' where flour was sifted before bread was made.

Despite the city's poverty, and the limited extent of rebuilding, York shared in a modest way in the gradual improvement of housing standards and domestic comfort. The medieval hall, for instance, rising two storeys in height and open to the rafters, was gradually abandoned in favour of smaller rooms divided by walls and ceilings. Several late fifteenth-century houses were still built with open halls; the scarcity of buildings in the first half of the sixteenth century makes it impossible to date the change, but Elizabethan houses were never built with an open hall, and by about 1600 those of late medieval date were being converted by the insertion of an intermediate floor. The late sixteenth century also saw the introduction of attics; previously the roof had been open to whatever rooms lay below, but the insertion of an extra floor created more living-space and also made heating the rooms below easier.[2] Ladders were in common use for access to upper floors, and the 'payre of stayres' down which an old man fell to his death in 1599 was probably such a ladder.[3] Some houses already had structural staircases by the late fifteenth century, sometimes inconveniently provided in a rear annexe so as to rise in one uninterrupted flight to the second floor; by the early seventeenth century, at latest, the internal stairwell had replaced them.[4]

The open hall had been heated by a central fire under a louvre, and even multi-storeyed houses could be heated, if at all, by braziers. The humble Church Cottages of the late fifteenth century, of 'one up and one down' type, have no

[1] B.I.H.R., inventories of I. Fisher 1548; H. Bowrow 1538; J. Litster 1541; N. Mores 1538.

[2] R.C.H.M. *York*, iii, pp. lxii–lxvi, 72, 88, 96, 104-6, 109.

[3] Yorkshire Archaeological Society Library, transcript of par. reg. St. John's, Ousebridge, York, p. 32.

[4] R.C.H.M. *York*, iii, pp. lxiii, lxxvii.

structural evidence of any fireplaces before the eighteenth century. A revealing incident during the enclosure riots of 1536 involved a shoemaker sending a servant 'for fyer' to a neighbour at 11.00 p.m., to use in burning the offending gates.[1] Nevertheless, there are several references to chimneys in the houses of the more prosperous early Tudor citizens, and even to a specialist craft of 'chymmaker'.[2] Some Elizabethan houses were constructed from the beginning with brick fireplaces and chimneys, allowing safe heating on each floor; this was indeed one of the chief early uses for brick, like the 200 'breke teill' which the church wardens of St. Martin's, Coney Street, bought 'for maikynge uppe chimies . . . whiche blewe downe with the wynde'.[3] Domestic fires were apparently in more common use, and neighbours and landlords were concerned to ensure that fireproof chimneys were inserted.[4]

Two other improvements made by the more prosperous during the sixteenth century were the insertion of glass into windows and the covering of walls with wainscot panelling. In 1575 the tenement at the Common Hall gates, for example, contained 72½ yards of 'sealing of waynescot' and 104 feet of glass in the windows, all of which had been placed there by the outgoing tenant. One of the conditions of the new lease was that the next tenant should buy them for the use of the corporation, to prevent their being removed; York men were, in fact, like townsmen elsewhere, slow to regard glass windows as fixtures.[5] Even so, York must have struck country visitors by 1600 by the amount of domestic glass in use; Yorkshire inventories in general suggest that its use was very rare before about 1620. Probably, as in Oxfordshire, such improvements were introduced into the county town well before they spread into the countryside.[6] Gradually the civic

---

[1] op. cit., p. 99; *Y.C.R.* iv. 3.

[2] York Merchants' MS, D 62; B.I.H.R., prob. reg. vi, fo. 31; Y.C.A., B 9, fos. 30ᵛ, 74ʳ.

[3] R.C.H.M. *York*, iii, p. lxxvi; B.I.H.R., Y/MCS 16, p. 75 (1568).

[4] York Merchants' MS, D 82; Y.C.A., E 31, pt. 1, fo. 85ʳ.

[5] Y.C.A., B 26, fo. 28ʳ. For other York examples, see Palliser, 'York', pp. 374-5.

[6] D. W. Crossley, 'The performance of the glass industry in sixteenth-century England', *Econ. H.R.* 2nd ser. xxv (1972), 424; M. A. Havinden, ed., *Household and Farm Inventories in Oxfordshire, 1550–1590* (H.M.C. J.P. 10, 1965), p. 26.

élite, anxious to preserve their improvements for the benefit of their families, directed that wainscot and windows were not to be removed after their deaths. The first to do so was Alderman John Lewes, who in 1552 bequeathed 'the waynskott and seallinge aboute the hall' to remain as heirlooms in his High Ousegate house, copied in 1558 by his colleague William Holme. Alderman Hall, in 1564, was more comprehensive, ordering that 'all maner of sealinges of waynescott, all bynks, portalls, dores, lockes and glasse in the wyndowes . . . shall remayne and contynewe in my now dwelling howsse as hairelomes for ever'. Gradually such injunctions became almost standard, and by 1600 ten aldermen had made such provisions for their panelling, six of them also safeguarding their glazing.[1]

Furniture in the home, like fittings, reflected a gradual increase in domestic comfort, at least among the will-making class. For example, frame tables began to supplement the normal trestle tables, just as chairs were supplementing the less comfortable stools and benches. Both novelties were possessed by William Craven, who in 1581 bequeathed 'a longe table and a rounde table standinge upon frames' and 'iij greate turned chaires and one lesser' in the hall, and 'a square table and frame' in the hall chamber, to remain in his Micklegate house as heirlooms; by doing so he drew attention to their rarity.[2] Carpets, of course, where they were used, covered tables and not floors, but table cloths were sometimes used instead. The efficient household of the Minster Treasurer in 1508–9 included eleven table cloths marked with different letters of the alphabet, as well as thirteen pairs of lettered sheets and fourteen lettered towels.[3]

The room where cooking was carried on, often but not always the kitchen, included equipment varying with the wealth of the household, but nearly always contained pots and pans, a kettle and a spit. Brewing, and the sifting of flour, were usually carried on in separate outbuildings. Another task that must have been necessary in all well-to-do households

[1] B.I.H.R., prob. reg. xiii, fo. 1005 (Lewes); xv, pt. 3, fo. 229 (Holme); xvii, fo. 477 (Hall); xviii, fo. 122 (Coupland); xxi, fo. 441 (Appleyarde); xxiii, fo. 326 (Beckwith); xxiv, fos. 158, 365 (Robinson, Harbert); xxvi, fo. 382 (May); xxvii, fo. 596 (Brooke).

[2] B.I.H.R., prob. reg. xxii, fo. 196.   [3] *Test. Ebor.* iv. 284–7.

was the salting down of meat, but the only trace of it in the inventories is John Litster's 'kennelle for saltynge of flesshe'. Food was usually eaten off wooden trenchers or pewter plates, but the richer citizens owned silver or silver-gilt plate. Litster left plate worth nearly £12 in 1541, amounting to about a quarter of the value of his personal possessions if his very large trading stocks are excluded. In the same year a mayor's widow referred in her will to silver spoons 'that is served at my table daylie'.[1] The plate was collected for ostentation, but also because it could be readily converted or melted down and was a flexible investment. A quite normal transaction was that by which a waxchandler delivered a piece of silver, six silver spoons and £3 in money to a goldsmith for him to 'make a staydyng cupp of the said pece sponez and money'.[2]

A rich citizen usually slept in a feather bed with expensive linen, and a bedcover which might be decorated with a merchant's mark or shield, the image of a saint, or a flower pattern.[3] Chamber pots were in widespread use, while a few rich citizens owned a 'chair of ease', a more elaborate arrangement with a pot incorporated into a seat. Beds were often shared, and servants might have to sleep wherever there was room. One chamber in a tapiter's house in St. Denys's parish contained 'the chyldren-bede with the clothes' and 'a nother bed for the norse and other chyldren', while 'the maydyng bedd' stood in the 'boultyng hows'.[4]

The inventories did not, of course, include any of the very poor, but some of the houses described were very modest indeed. The rector of St. Helen-on-the-Walls, who died in 1551, perhaps of the plague then raging, lived in a house of two rooms, and his goods were worth little more than £5. In the hall he had a counter, an aumbry, five cushions, a folding board, two forms, and a 'haulyng', and in his parlour a purse, a board, a feather bed (with two blankets, two coverlets, and two pairs of sheets), and his limited wardrobe: three gowns, a tippet, a jacket, two doublets, a pair of hose, two bonnets,

[1] B.I.H.R., original probate records, J. Litster 1541; prob. reg. xi, fo. 574.
[2] P.R.O., C1/555/13, dated 1528.
[3] e.g. B.I.H.R., prob. reg. x, fo. 20; xi. fos. 85, 249; Y.M.L., prob. reg. iii, fos. 6, 36.
[4] B.I.H.R., original probate records, R. Hewton 1553.

and a cap.[1] At the opposite end of the social scale was the wealthy lawyer and alderman James Birkeby, who left a great house of thirty rooms or so at his death in 1610. He and his wife had separate bedchambers, while the maids shared another. The alderman had a study with desks, stool, coffers, and books, and his lady her own closet at the end of the gallery. The rooms were well furnished: Birkeby's own bedchamber, for instance, contained a bed, apparently a four-poster, with a buckram tester and curtains of red and white say; a chair and cushion; a desk; a livery cupboard (in which food and drink could be kept); a curtain before the window; and a fireplace with tongs, shovel and bellows. Altogether three chambers had fireplaces, as did the kitchen, and there was another in the dining parlour, used for eating in preference to the hall. The house contained many luxuries, such as looking glasses, framed pictures and maps, a 'warminge handball', a horn lantern, 'a chesboard and men belongeinge the same', and twenty-two table cloths. His total goods and ready money were worth £508, of which no less than £210 was in the form of silver and silver-gilt plate, kept in 'the chist in the dyninge parlor'.[2]

6

Such, then, was York under the Tudors: a city with about the population of present-day Selby, though by contemporary standards one of the largest English towns; a city of large and imposing churches rubbing shoulders with small and unimposing timbered houses, the whole still encircled by defensive walls which nearly, but not quite, marked the line between town and country. Much of it would seem squalid and shabby by today's standards, but what struck well-travelled contemporaries most about York was the beauty and not the squalor, which they doubtless took for granted. Even at so early a period York was a magnet for visitors who can only be described as tourists, such as the Hanseatic merchant who rode over from Hull simply to view the town.[3] The

[1] B.I.H.R., original probate records, R. Agrig 1551.
[2] B.I.H.R., D/C. C.P., R. VII H. 767.
[3] *Yorks. Star Chamber Proc.* iii. 83–5.

city merchants themselves, however hardheaded they appear in their business dealings, were by no means insensitive to the beauty of their city. The act of parliament of 1553 permitting the rebuilding of St. Helen's church, Stonegate, asserted that its demolition had 'muche defaced and deformed' York, as it had stood 'in a principall place of the said Citie'—a wording probably taken from the local petition that secured the act.[1] More explicit were petitions sent by the corporation to Lord Burghley and Sir John Fortescue in 1596, protesting at the partial destruction of Clifford's Tower, the castle keep; they could almost be called the earliest requests for a preservation order in York. The tower was described as 'one of the fairest and hiest buildings for showe and buetifyinge of this Cittye . . . and doth most grace buetefye and set forth the showe thereof (Yorke Mynster onelye excepted)'.[2] The following pages will necessarily concentrate on those issues on which contemporaries have left most record, but even the worst phase of York's sixteenth-century economic depression needs to be pictured against an urban environment which could evoke praise from discriminating visitors, and which the citizens referred to so little only because they accepted it without question.

[1] *Statutes of the Realm*, iv. 216.
[2] Y.C.A., B 31, fo. 190^V; Davies, *Walks*, pp. 83-7.

II

THE CITY AND THE STATE

> Trusty and welbeloved we grete you well; and havyng
> by the assistance of Allmighty God and the helpe
> from good and lovinge subjects discomfited Wyet and
> thother rebells of our County of Kent . . . we cannot
> but give you our hartie thanks for the redynes that
> youe have beyn withe the force of our said Citie to
> have servyd us if neyd shuld have beyn . . .
>
> Mary I to the Corporation, 11 February 1554[1]

English towns never acquired the political independence of
the Italian communes or the Imperial cities of Germany; but
the larger ones did obtain, by royal permission, considerable
autonomy within their own bounds. York's enfranchisement
was very gradual, beginning in 1212-13 when it was freed
from the financial control of the county sheriff and began to
elect its own leader or mayor. During the thirteenth and fourteenth centuries it acquired further privileges, and the business
of royal government and peacekeeping passed more and more
into the hands of a powerful group of citizens assisting the
mayor, men who came to form a senior bench of aldermen
and a junior body called the common council. Their privileges
were acquired and maintained not by right but by royal grace
and favour, as indeed remained the position until 1688, and
Edward I did not hesitate to remove the city's rights of self-
government in 1280-2 and again in 1292-7. To view English
urban history in terms of a natural opposition between royal
and municipal power would, however, be fallacious. Town
councillors wished for autonomy in day-to-day affairs, but
they needed the protection, patronage and justice of the
crown even more. If Edward I overrode the city's liberties, he
also, like his son and grandson, brought much business to
York by making it a centre of operations for war with the
Scots. For several short periods between 1296 and 1336 York

[1] *Y.C.R.* v. 100 f.

was the capital of England and the seat of Exchequer, Chancery, King's Bench and Common Pleas. Again, Richard II transferred the departments of state to York from Westminster for a few months in 1392. The unlucky king had a special liking for York, and in 1393 and 1396 he granted it by charters the widest possible measure of local self-government, making it a corporate borough and a county of itself, of which the mayor and aldermen were *ex officio* justices of the peace.[1] It was now entirely detached from its shire, and answerable directly to the crown in all matters, financial, judicial, and administrative. The only exception to the new powers of the 'county of the city of York' was the castle, which was excluded from its jurisdiction so that the county sheriff would not in any way be subject to the citizens. The charter of 1396 was the final coping-stone to an elaborate structure of royal privileges, and the city government remained essentially unchanged thereafter until 1835.

The golden age of York's medieval prosperity lasted until the mid-fifteenth century, after which decline set in, a decline which is more properly analysed in the context of the urban economy.[2] Many of the actions of the Yorkist and Tudor sovereigns are explicable only in terms of this catastrophic depression, which they had no reason to doubt. Yet even in the midst of its decline, York remained a regional capital, with sufficient wealth, independence and civic pride to continue electing (and paying) its own citizens as parliamentary burgesses at a time when lawyers and gentry were invading the smaller northern boroughs.[3] Furthermore, it retained importance as a strategic centre, essential to hold if the north was to be controlled. When Edward IV invaded Yorkshire in 1471 in an attempt to regain the throne, his peaceful capture of the city was rightly seen as a turning-point. And Edward's brother, Richard duke of Gloucester

---

[1] *York Memorandum Book*, i, ed. M. Sellers (Surtees Society cxx, 1912), 143-6, 157-63. On relations between King and city see J. H. Harvey, 'Richard II and York', in *The Reign of Richard II: Essays in Honour of May McKisack*, ed. F.R.H. du Boulay and C. M. Barron (London, 1971), pp. 202-17.

[2] See below, ch. VIII.

[3] P. Jalland, 'The "revolution" in Northern borough representation in mid-fifteenth-century England', *Northern History*, xi (1976), 33-6, 47-51, corrected in *Northern History*, xiii (1977), 265 f.

(1452-85), was responsible for a development which in the long run helped to offset York's decline. When in 1471 he was granted the broad estates of the Nevilles in Yorkshire and Cumberland he put a council in charge of them, a council which was later incorporated into a royal household at Sheriff Hutton castle near the city. Such was the modest beginning of what finally became the King's Council in the Northern Parts.

Gloucester was, in P. M. Kendall's words, 'the Lord of the North' for fourteen years before he became King as Richard III. His role in northern history has still not received the attention it deserves, and an adequate consideration of it would go beyond the scope of the present work. It is, however, not possible to understand the citizens of Henry VII's reign without taking account of the potent memory of his predecessor. The corporation minutes record many instances of Richard's favours to the city and friendships with its leading citizens. His patronage and generosity earned him a fierce loyalty from the corporation and from many of the more substantial citizens, though the reasons for and extent of that loyalty are still debated.[1]

The corporation always responded promptly to Richard's appeals for military support, whether against domestic rebels or Scots, and when they heard on 16 August 1485 that the Earl of Richmond had invaded the realm they did not even wait to be asked. Straight away they sent John Sponer, one of the mayor's sergeants of the mace, and a messenger, to find the King at Beskwood Lodge near Nottingham, and to offer him aid. Within three days the messenger was back in the council chamber bearing the King's reply, and the council decided to muster a contingent of eighty armed men the same afternoon to set off to join the royal army, under the captaincy of the city macebearer. In other words, no time was lost, though the men arrived too late to fight for Richard at Bosworth. The most astonishing evidence of the corporation's loyalty, however, was their minute of 23 August, the

[1] *Y.C.R.* i, pp. vii f., 76–121; *Extracts from the Municipal Records of the City of York*, ed. R. Davies (London, 1843), *passim*; E. Miller, 'Medieval York', *V.C.H. York*, pp. 61–3; P. M. Kendall, *Richard the Third* (London, 1955), *passim*; A. Hanham, *Richard III and his Early Historians 1483–1535* (Oxford, 1975), pp. 60–4.

day after the battle, when John Sponer, who must have gal-
loped home without stopping, brought news of it. They were
angry enough to record that

King Richard, late mercifullye reigning upon us, was, thrugh grete trea-
son of the Duc of Northfolk and many othre that turned ayenst hyme,
with many othre lordes and nobilles of this North parties, was pitiously
slane and murdred, to the grete hevynesse of this Citie.[1]

Such a show of defiance was unprecedented, for in 1461,
1470, and 1471 the city fathers had accepted dynastic
changes equally enough. Nor can it be easily argued, as Dr
Hanham tries to do, that the commons were less favourable
to Richard. On 24 August Sir Roger Cotam arrived to pro-
claim the new King; the councillors went to meet him at an
inn within the protection of the castle, for Cotam 'durst not
for fere of deth come thrugh the Citie' to speak with them, a
clear enough hint of the feeling in the streets. Their minutes
relate how Cotam greeted them from 'the King named and
proclamed Henry VII', as they meaningfully described him,
and promised that Henry would be their good and gracious
lord.[2] Nevertheless, the city began the Tudor period emo-
tionally committed to a fallen regime, for the first time since
dynastic war had begun thirty years before.

2

Neither King nor corporation could afford mutual hostility.
In 1486 the city spent £66 on Henry's first visit to York;
along his route was presented a series of pageants and
speeches, all stressing his virtues and his hereditary right, and
culminating in a representation of Our Lady, promising her
son's aid for the King.[3] The flattery can scarcely have been
sincere, for throughout the first year of Henry's reign he
was being politely but firmly thwarted by the city council
over his wish to nominate to the offices of recorder and

---

[1] Y.C.A., B 2-4, fo. 169ᵛ, pr. in Drake, *Eboracum*, p. 121; Davies, *Extracts*,
p. 218; *Y.C.R.* i. 119. Raine, curiously, thought the original was lost, and printed
Drake's transcript, which misreads 'mercifullye' as 'lawfully'. The reference to
Norfolk, who died fighting for Richard, is a mistake.

[2] Drake, *Eboracum*, p. 121; *Y.C.R.* i. 119 f.

[3] *Y.C.R.* i. 155-9; Y.C.A., C4/1; S. Anglo, *Spectacle, Pageantry, and Early
Tudor Policy* (Oxford, 1969), pp. 23-8.

swordbearer.[1] Yet in 1487, when invasion by Lincoln and Simnel was expected, the corporation were prompt in guarding the city against attack. Alderman Wells, personally taking charge of the guard at Bootham Bar, was murdered by a citizen in an incident that may reflect political discontent. Certainly, the King heard 'senistre reportes' of the murder which the corporation were anxious to deny, and they were ostentatiously loyal when the expected rebellion materialized.[2] Henry, on a second visit, expressed his thanks by knighting Mayor William Todd and Alderman Richard York, within the next three years granting them annuities of £20 and £40 for life.[3] The city fathers may well have come to accept the new regime, either out of a sense of political realism or from a weariness of political disorder; but Henry's troubles with York were not yet over, perhaps because many lesser citizens still grudged his success. In 1488 he found it necessary to order the mayor and sheriffs to see good rule kept, or he would 'sharpelie lay it to your blame and charge' with severe punishment of the offenders. The council recorded nothing of the reason for his displeasure, but they immediately summoned the guild searchers and lectured them on the need for law and order.[4] In the following year the fourth earl of Northumberland, trying to levy an unpopular tax in Yorkshire, was murdered by the commons at Cocklodge near Thirsk, a victim to 'the continual grudge that the Northern men bore against him sith the death of King Richard'. In the ensuing rebellion, York corporation failed to hold the city because the 'commonalty' sided with the rebels, who were able to 'burn' Walmgate and Fishergate Bars, or at least their wooden gates, enter the walls, and compel the aldermen to grant them military help. When it was all over, the corporation had to appease the King's anger, and they shut the stable door by blocking up Fishergate Bar instead of rebuilding it. The rebellion was suppressed, and Henry met no further serious opposition in Yorkshire, but Bacon commented on the rising that Richard's memory 'laid like lees at the bottom

[1] *Y.C.R.* i. 124–60; Kendall, *Richard the Third*, pp. 385–8.
[2] *Y.C.R.* ii. 10–19.
[3] *Y.C.R.* ii. 20–8; *C.P.R. 1485–94*, pp. 256–7, 303.
[4] Y.C.A., B 6, fos. 121–2; *Y.C.R.* ii. 34.

of men's hearts, and if the vessels were once stirred, it would rise'.[1]

Yet if Henry faced no more serious sedition than this after 1489, York was by no means peaceful, for internal strife had also to be reckoned with. For the first nine years of his reign, the citizens and the Minster Vicars choral battled over rights of winter common in the Vicars' Leas. Every Michaelmas from 1485 there was an enclosure riot as the citizens enforced these rights, until in 1494 the King summoned the mayor before him and told him that if he could not keep order, 'I most and woll put in other rewlers that woll rewle and govern the Citie accordyng to my lawez'. The earl of Surrey and the abbot of St. Mary's mediated between the parties, and an award was made in 1495 in favour of the Vicars.[2] In 1504 there was violence of a different kind, the 'commons' of the city rioting over grievances against the city oligarchy at the mayor's election and installation, and the King ordering the corporation to take a firm line in restoring order.[3] Henry never visited York after 1487, and instead relied heavily on the northern Council created by Richard to keep the city orderly. He also made use of York as a minting centre in what has recently been identified as a major recoinage of 1495-9. Outside the main London mint he used mints at Canterbury, York, and Durham to issue the cheaper denominations of silver; and the special importance of York in meeting a deficiency of coin in the north was indicated by the fact that royal and ecclesiastical mints were in use simultaneously.[4]

Late in the reign the Council in the North was virtually abolished, leaving a dangerous vacuum in the north until 1537. Its absence may explain why York politics became violent again soon after Henry VIII's accession. On 23 November 1514 the King issued a proclamation announcing measures taken against 'enormities' committed in the city,

[1] Kendall, *Richard the Third*, p. 384; *Y.C.R.* ii. 45-53; John Stow, *Annales* (1631 edn.), p. 474; R.C.H.M. *York*, ii. 142, n. 7.

[2] *Y.C.R.* ii. 105-17, 123; Y.M.L., V, Box XII; F. Harrison, *Life in a Medieval College* (London, 1952), pp. 320-2.

[3] *Y.C.R.* ii. 191-4; iii. 1-7.

[4] D. M. Metcalf, *Sylloge of Coins of the British Isles: 23: Ashmolean Museum, Oxford: Part III: Coins of Henry VII* (London, 1976), pp. ix-xix.

suburbs, and county of York; the corporation took care not to refer to these disorders in their minutes, but they were clearly very serious. A junior councillor was threatened with death at a council meeting in December 1513, and in 1514 a former MP was summoned before the King's council, presumably to explain matters.[1]

The city was not quiet for long. On 1 February 1516 a tie occurred among the aldermen in voting for a new colleague, and many citizens took sides with the two chief candidates, John Norman and William Cure. 'Dyvers grett riotts and affrayez' ensued, until the leaders of the two factions among the aldermen (Thomas Drawswerde and William Neleson) were summoned to appear before Wolsey and the royal council on 6 April. The council gave judgement on 4 June that neither candidate should be elected, and Drawswerde and Neleson promised on behalf of their colleagues that no alderman would be chosen without Wolsey's consent. However, by 12 January 1517 a second alderman had died, and the corporation coolly chose to regard the dispute as terminated by electing both Norman and Cure to the two vacant places. To make matters worse, on 15 January they elected as mayor Neleson, who was then a prisoner in the Fleet, presumably for his part in the troubles. The King sent the corporation a blistering message of his 'gret mervaylle and dyspleasour', ordering them to install his own nominee as mayor, and to depose the two new aldermen. The corporation made no attempt to thwart his wishes as they had his father's, and his orders were promptly obeyed. And on 18 July 1517, to avoid the quarrels of the past few years, the King issued letters patent reorganizing the city's common council on a less popular basis.[2]

3

A quiet period followed the troubles of 1513–17. No doubt the royal anger had a part in it, and also the corporation had

[1] *Tudor Royal Proclamations*, ed. P. L. Hughes and J. F. Larkin, i (New Haven and London, 1964), 125–6; Y.C.A., B 9, fo. 75ʳ; *Y.C.R.* iii. 44 f.

[2] *Y.C.R.* iii. 51–61. The 1516–17 disputes are recounted here at length because the account in *V.C.H. York*, p. 137, is not quite correct.

a friend and protector once more: Thomas, Cardinal Wolsey, archbishop of York from 1514 to 1530, and the most powerful man after the King. He interceded for them with Henry in 1517, when he expressed his 'gret love and good mynd' towards them, 'all beyng our parysshons, and of the chief and princypale place of our provynce and dyoces'. The thankful corporation granted their office of swordbearer to one of his servants, a favour they had denied to Henry VII.[1] The cardinal also did what he could to bolster the city's overseas trade. He was instrumental in persuading the King to grant letters patent in 1523 allowing the citizens the right to ship overseas wool and fells from almost all Yorkshire apart from the West Riding clothing areas—a coveted exemption from the Staplers' monopoly of wool exports. Significantly, this grant was repealed by Parliament in 1529, just after Wolsey's disgrace,[2] and it is probably also Wolsey's fall which explains a sudden change in York's representation in that same Parliament. One of the two burgesses, elected on 27 September 1529, was the city's recorder Richard Page, a protégé of the Cardinal, but he was immediately replaced, without explanation, by one of the aldermen.[3]

The city was thus bereft of a powerful patron, but the corporation were quick to cultivate the next great minister instead. Thomas Cromwell became a leading royal councillor late in 1531, and by February 1532 they had 'grete confydence and truste' in him and were asking him to help their representatives with various matters. He was granted a fee, and, like Wolsey, was honoured by the rare privilege of nominating one of the city's officers.[4] The man apparently responsible for persuading Cromwell to be 'good mayster' to York was Sir George Lawson, alderman from 1527 to 1543, and an MP for the city at the time. Lawson, the wealthiest York layman, combined residence and high civic office in York with a series of important crown offices in the north, notably the treasurership of Berwick-upon-Tweed (1517-43)

[1] *Y.C.R.* iii. 58, 64, 66.   [2] *Statutes of the Realm*, iii. 301-2.
[3] *Y.C.R.* iii. 119, 127; S. E. Lehmberg, *The Reformation Parliament 1529-1536* (Cambridge, 1970), p. 22. Lehmberg has missed the second reference, which proves that Page cannot have taken his seat even for a short period.
[4] *Y.C.R.* iii. 139 f.; iv. 4, 23. For Cromwell and York, see G. R. Elton, *Reform and Renewal: Thomas Cromwell and the Common Weal* (Cambridge, 1973), pp. 77 f.

and membership of the Council in the North (c. 1525-34 and
c. 1540-3). During the early 1530s he was on close terms with
Cromwell, and did much to implement the government's
revolutionary policies in the north.[1]

During this period, government help enabled the corporation to weather another crisis. Since the reign of Richard III
they had had increasing difficulty in meeting all their financial
commitments, as the volume of their trade and the number
of their taxpayers steadily decreased. The most burdensome
was the royal fee-farm of £160 a year; the Roos family of
Helmsley had been receiving £100 of it since 1322, and St.
Stephen's Chapel, Westminster, another £35. 14s. 7d. since
1351.[2] For a long time the corporation were allowed to compound for the £100 by a payment of £13. 6s. 8d., but from
1526 Lord Roos (now earl of Rutland) tried to enforce payment of the full sum.[3] At the same period he was pursuing a
suit against the city of Lincoln, whose fee-farm he had also
inherited.[4] Both corporations struggled desperately to avoid
full payment, York threatening more than once to surrender
its liberties to the King rather than meet the claim.[5] Eventually, Cromwell found time to study York's economic problems, and it was partly owing to him that the city was able to
solve the crisis in 1536. Rutland agreed to accept £40 a year
in all, and an Act of Parliament was passed ratifying the
agreement and freeing the city of several other financial
burdens.[6]

Meanwhile York was suffering again from internal strife.
In 1529 five junior councillors plotted to deprive the mayor
of his fees, no doubt because local as well as national taxes
were becoming insupportable; they stirred up 400 of the
commons to revolt, and the Council in the North had to intervene to support the mayor.[7] In 1533-4, by contrast, the ruling
oligarchy was itself divided. Corruption and mismanagement

---

[1] For Lawson (not in *D.N.B.*), see my biog. of him in *History of Parliament
1509-1558*, ed. S. T. Bindoff (not yet published).

[2] *V.C.H. York*, pp. 33, 65.

[3] *Y.C.R.* iii. 106, 113, 116-17, 137, 139, 146, 150-2, 165, 169, 174.

[4] J. W. F. Hill, *Tudor and Stuart Lincoln* (Cambridge, 1956), pp. 26-9.

[5] *Y.C.R.* iii. 113, 137.

[6] *L.P. Hen. VIII*, vi, Nos. 904-5; viii, No. 804; ix, No. 705; *Statutes of the
Realm*, iii. 582-4.

[7] *Y.C.R.* iii. 120-8.

were alleged against the Guild of SS. Christopher and George, which was closely linked with the corporation and helped to maintain the fabric of the Common Hall. Three aldermen who were former masters of the guild clashed with the rest of their colleagues, the case being taken before Chancery, Star Chamber and the Council in the North, and involving a confusing mass of allegations about corrupt politics and finance. On 12 December 1533 Star Chamber confirmed the depositions of two of the aldermen, but for some unspecified reason the King ordered them to be restored the following May.[1] And only two years later there was further trouble from below. The corporation enclosed Knavesmire, the largest of the common pastures, only to find a serious riot on their hands, with the new gates burned down at night. The ringleaders were caught and punished, but the lesson was learned, and half the pasture was left open.[2]

The enclosure riots of 1536 were, however, quickly eclipsed by greater events. The riots had been fanned by rumours of what Lawson had said about the actions of Parliament. He and his colleague George Gayle had been attending what has come to be known as the Reformation Parliament, which from 1532 onwards had been revolutionizing the relationship of church and state. York had seemed to the nervous government a possible springboard for a *coup d'état* by Wolsey in 1530, and his arrest just as he was to be at last enthroned in the city may have been precipitated by fear that he would publish a papal bull and rally resistance in the Northern Convocation.[3] In the event the citizens were apparently unaffected by the break with Rome in 1534, but the fate of institutions long established in their midst was a different matter.[4] In 1536 Parliament allowed the King to suppress religious houses worth under £200 a year, including two York priories, St. Clement's and Holy Trinity. Hard on the heels of these and other suppressions in the north, there broke out a widespread revolt in Yorkshire against recent government policies, the Pilgrimage of Grace, a revolt which

[1] *Yorks. Star Chamber Proceedings*, ii. 13-36; *Y.C.R.* iii. 154-68; P.R.O., C1/872/69.
[2] *Y.C.R.* iv. 1-3.   [3] Lehmberg, *Reformation Parliament*, pp. 108-9.
[4] For religious attitudes at the time see D. M. Palliser, *The Reformation in York 1534-1553* (Borth. P. xl, 1971), *passim*.

was supported by the York 'commons'. The corporation admitted the rebels within the walls after only half-hearted resistance, and the city became the rebel headquarters, a grand council being held there in November.[1] The revolt, despite the doubts of some modern historians, should probably be interpreted chiefly as a protest against recent government policies, especially the monastic suppressions. Certainly, sixteen of the fifty-three suppressed northern houses were restored by the rebels, including both York priories and Healaugh Priory in the Ainsty.[2] After the rebellion was over, the King exacted no vengeance on the city, but he did order the duke of Norfolk to execute several leading rebels there, culminating in the hanging in chains of Robert Aske, the 'Grand Captain', on 12 July 1537.[3] Henry thought of visiting the north in the summer of 1537, to demonstrate his power and his mercy, but the progress was postponed for four years. In September 1541, in company with his fifth queen, he entered York, having sent artillery by sea from London to overawe the citizens. Mayor Robert Hall and the corporation made a humble submission to the King for their share in the rebellion, and presented the royal couple with £140 in silver-gilt cups.[4]

4

The revolts of 1536 had shown Henry the need for a stronger Council in the North, and in 1537 it was placed on a more permanent and satisfactory basis. Over the next century, the existence of this powerful commission often led to clashes of jurisdiction with the city corporation; but York gained far more than it lost, both in terms of peace and justice, and also of business brought to the city. The architect of the revitalized Northern Council was Robert Holgate (c. 1481-1555), a Yorkshire gentleman and cleric who was its mainstay from

---

[1] Dodds, *Pilgrimage of Grace*, i. 174-84, 311-18.
[2] Palliser, *Reformation in York*, pp. 9-11; P.R.O., C1/881/31; Smith, *Land and Politics*, p. 187.
[3] *L.P. Hen. VIII*, xii (2), Nos. 205, 229.
[4] *Y.C.R.* iv. 68-70; N. Williams, *Henry VIII and his Court* (London, 1973), pp. 206-7. For the similar submission of Lincoln, which York used as a precedent, see Hill, *Tudor and Stuart Lincoln*, p. 51.

1537 and Lord President from 1538 to 1549. His biographer has depicted him as a firm and successful administrator who did much to integrate the north with the rest of England, and who did not hesitate to override York's municipal privileges if they stood in the way. As a close associate of the duke of Somerset he lost the presidency in the purge of 1549, but by then he was also archbishop of York (1545-54), so that for nearly twenty years he governed the north as its secular or ecclesiastical head. He deserves, perhaps, more credit than any other single man for keeping the north peaceful after 1536.[1]

In Holgate's time the central government itself came to the aid of York, which was now at the lowest point of its economic fortunes. The 1536 Act, besides reducing York's fee-farm payments, relieved civic finances further by suppressing seven chantries and three obits, granting their endowments to the corporation. An Act of 1540 allowed York (together with thirty-five other corporations) to compel the rebuilding of decayed houses under threat of confiscating the sites. In 1543 the city obtained a statutory monopoly of coverlet-making in Yorkshire, and the right of search for faulty coverlets in all fairs and markets north of Trent. Finally, an Act of Edward VI's first Parliament (1547) allowed the suppression of the poorer parish churches in York. As a result, about fifteen of the forty churches were closed by 1553, and most were demolished at once.[2]

Meanwhile the city also enjoyed a limited revival of its ancient importance as a military and administrative centre for border war and defence, especially during the Scottish war of 1542-50. Mercenaries from Cleves were billeted there in 1545, followed by a thousand Germans in 1549.[3] Even in time of peace, York had a part to play as a military treasury. The government deposited large sums at St. Mary's Abbey during the 1520s and 1530s, and Sir George Lawson, treasurer for the Berwick garrison, regularly came to York to collect it.[4]

---

[1] A. G. Dickens, *Robert Holgate* (Borth. P. viii, 1955), *passim.*

[2] *Statutes of the Realm*, iii. 582-4, 768-9, 908-9; iv. 14 f.; D. M. Palliser, 'The unions of parishes at York, 1547-86', *Y.A.J.* xlvi (1974), 87-102.

[3] *Y.C.R.* iv. 133; v. 24.

[4] *L.P. Hen. VIII*, iii. No. 3528 (2); iv. Nos. 1821-2, 1843, 2069-70, 2977, App. 96; v. Nos. 1285, 1590, 1630, 1671; etc.

As late as 1552 Lawson's successor on occasion collected his garrison's wages at York, though more usually he went only to Newcastle.[1] Perhaps it was to avoid the inconvenience of transmitting such sums from London that the Royal Mint at York was reopened in 1545, bringing further prosperity to the city; Alderman George Gayle was put in charge of it.[2] Indeed, the post was so important that Protector Somerset tried in vain to prevent Gayle's election as mayor, in case it should interfere with his duties at the Mint. However, the revival of the institution proved short-lived, and it was closed again by February 1554 at latest.[3]

Edward VI died on 6 July 1553, but his death was not officially announced in York until the 13th, when Jane Grey is said to have been proclaimed queen. If this were so, the cautious corporation nevertheless did not copy the proclamation into their minutes, or use any regnal year at all. When, by contrast, Mary was proclaimed queen at York on 21 July there was said to be great public rejoicing, and the proclamation was properly recorded.[4] Her reign was certainly popular at York, and the corporation were resolute in holding the city for her when rebellions broke out in 1554 and 1557. In the latter year rebels seized Scarborough Castle, and the council under Mayor Robert Hall sent a spy to gather news of the 'traytors'. Hall was the mayor who, in his previous term of office, had led the city's submission to Henry VIII in 1541, and now demonstrated to Mary the loyalty so effusively promised to her father.[5] The corporation's loyalty to Mary was reciprocated. Just after the defeat of Wyatt's rebellion she intended, according to the Imperial ambassador, 'to go to York and live there, so as to be [among] Catholic people and to have a sea-port [Hull] near by'.[6] It is scarcely

---

[1] *The Report of the Royal Commission of 1552*, ed. W. C. Richardson (Archives of British History and Culture, iii & iv, Morgantown, 1974), p. 189.

[2] G. C. Brooke, *English Coins* (London, 1942), pp. 179, 189 f.; *L.P. Hen. VIII*, xx (1), No. 620 (42).

[3] *Y.C.R.* v. 8–10; P.R.O., E351/2080.

[4] Bodley, Lat. Th.d. 15, fos. 138–9, pr. in 'Robert Parkyn's narrative of the Reformation', ed. A. G. Dickens, *Eng. Hist. Rev.* lxii (1947), 77 f.; *Y.C.R.* v. 89–91.

[5] *Y.C.R.* v. 100–1, 158–60. Twenty-seven rebels from Scarborough were imprisoned at York: J. Strype, *Ecclesiastical Memorials*, iii (London, 1721), Appendix, p. 263.

[6] *la dite dame delibere aller en York, et resider celle part, pour estre le peuple*

possible that such a desperate measure can have been seriously entertained, but it is significant that rumour could speak in such terms. Certainly Mary, like Richard III before her, responded generously to the city's pleas of poverty. She remitted £50 of their tax in 1553, £50 more in 1555, and £40 in 1558. The last two rebates were apparently granted at the suit of the Catholic alderman William Holme, MP for York in her last three parliaments, who pleaded eloquently the 'great ruyne and povertie' of his city.[1]

5

The death of Mary I in 1558 is the traditional dividing line in Tudor historiography, marking off the 'earlier Tudors' from the Elizabethan age. For York it is a meaningful division, since civic life took new directions after about 1560, some of them the direct result of state policies and others merely coincidental in time. Firstly, the religious settlement of 1559 finally established a Protestant state religion, an event unpopular in conservative York. Secondly, the Queen took steps to enforce obedience to church and state by establishing two powerful royal commissions at York. Thirdly, the city saw much less of those royal visits and military campaigns dear to the older civic historians: the north was quieter, peace with the Scots became the norm, and the new royal agencies at York were remarkably successful in imposing the royal will by delegation. Hence there were no royal visits to the city (other than breaks on the journey between London and Edinburgh) between 1541 and 1639. Finally, the mid-century saw the end of the late medieval decline in prosperity, and the last serious epidemics for fifty years. From about 1560 there was a slow but perceptible revival in York's prosperity, as well as a considerable increase in its population.

The new age of modest prosperity and peace coincides roughly with the establishment at York of the Ecclesiastical Commission for the Northern Province and the Queen's

catholique, et avoir port de mer prochain: P. F. Tytler, *England under the Reigns of Edward VI and Mary* (London, 1839), ii. 308 f., from the original in Brussels.

[1] *Y.C.R.* v. 92, 97 f., 133, 135; Y.C.A., B 22, fos. 121-2.

Council in the North, between 1561 and 1641. The former
was a new creation intended to enforce the new religious
settlement, and it awaited only the right leadership to become a very powerful body. The latter was, of course, old-
established, and its permanent staff had been based in York
since 1539, but their work had been seriously impaired under
Lord President Shrewsbury (1549-60), who had lived away
from the city.[1] Indeed, the effective survival of a Council at
York was ensured only by the devotion of Sir Thomas Gargrave, one of Holgate's former lieutenants, who was vice-
president almost continuously from 1555 to 1579 and did
much to hand on a working machinery from Holgate to the
later President Huntingdon. In 1560 Gargrave told Cecil that
to make York the sole meeting-place would work for the convenience of suitors and also for the prosperity of York.[2] His
plea was answered in 1561, when the Government fixed on
York as the President's official residence, and for the next
eighty years both the Council and Commission attracted
much business to the city.

The presence of such powerful and reliable bodies may
have persuaded Elizabeth that her presence in person was
unnecessary, and projected royal progresses to York in 1562
and 1575 came to nothing. The nearest that Elizabethan
York came to a royal visit was the curious and inconclusive
first 'trial' of Mary, Queen of Scots, the first session of which
was held in the city in October 1568. The extensive correspondence of the commissioners does not locate their
sessions, and all that is clear is that their large retinues
strained the resources of local victuallers.[3] It was a portent
of further visits by Scots as the borders became more peaceful. In 1583 a party of Scots gentlemen could turn aside from
the Great North Road purely as tourists, to see 'the toun
and minster'.[4]

Perhaps the new Government's cautious religious policy
allayed discontent, or perhaps the York corporation had

---

[1] Reid, *King's Council in the North*, pp. 178-9, 186-7.
[2] Cartwright, *Chapters in the History of Yorkshire*, p. 10.
[3] *Cal. State Papers relating to Scotland and Mary, Queen of Scots*, ed. J. Bain,
ii. (1900), 514-43; G. Donaldson, *The First Trial of Mary, Queen of Scots* (London, 1969), pp. 106-21.
[4] *Y.C.R.* viii. 69.

become convinced, during thirty years of religious change, that loyalty to the Crown, and the avoidance of civil war, had priority over religious sympathies. Whatever the reason, their behaviour during the Catholic rebellion of 1569—the Rising of the Northern Earls—was in sharp contrast to their equivocal behaviour in 1536. In 1564 the archbishop reported to the Government that eleven aldermen out of thirteen were 'no favores of religion', but when it came to rebellion, with a Catholic alternative queen almost on their doorstep, those sympathies did not dictate their actions.[1] Vigorous preparations were made to withstand a siege, and the city was made a base for 3,000 Yorkshire levies.[2] The rebels said 'yf they atteyne York, all ys theirs, and yf they mysse yt, yt were better for them to dye lyke men, then to be hanged'.[3] They did indeed miss it; its fortifications deterred them from besieging it, and their failure was a turning-point in the revolt. When all was over, trials were held in York of some of the chief rebels, of whom four were executed; and in 1572 another of the rebel leaders, the seventh earl of Northumberland, was beheaded on the pavement after being handed over by the Scots.[4]

There is no evidence that the Queen or Burghley can be credited with any personal interest in the city's prosperity, such as Wolsey and Cromwell had shown. Nevertheless, Elizabeth's establishment of the Northern Council and Commission at York was of major importance in its economic revival. Even in the old days of Shrewsbury, the absentee President, the Council had been important. In 1552 Shrewsbury had demanded that the corporation should take certain measures against plague on pain of losing the holding of the next Council sitting at York, 'whiche as you well knowe will be no smale hinderaunce to the seide Cytye'.[5] Vice-President Gargrave and Lord President Huntingdon both took a keen interest in York's prosperity, and Huntingdon earned the corporation's gratitude by ending a bitter shipping dispute

---

[1] 'A collection of original letters from the Bishops to the Privy Council', ed. M. Bateson, in *Camden Miscellany*, ix (Camden Soc. N.S. liii, 1893), p. 72.
[2] Cartwright, *Chapters Hist. Yorks.* pp. 34 f.; *Y.C.R.* vi. 161–82.
[3] J. Raine, *Historic Towns: York* (London, 1893), p. 109.
[4] op. cit., pp. 109 f.; *Y.C.R.* vii. 56.   [5] Y.C.A., E 40, No. 77.

between York and Hull.[1] It is no wonder that the loss of the
Council in 1641 was bitterly regretted by the citizens, who
petitioned Charles II several times for its restoration.[2]

The latter half of Elizabeth's reign was overshadowed by
Catholic plots and war with Spain, and the leading citizens,
by now firmly Protestant, reacted to these events in common
with other Englishmen. In 1581 Huntingdon could assure
Walsingham that York was staunchly loyal, and in 1584 some
1,300 citizens, headed by the corporation, subscribed to the
Association for the Preservation of the Queen, in striking
contrast to Coventry, where only 201 subscribed out of a
population nearly as large.[3] There were great rejoicings in the
streets after the exposure of the Babington Plot, and a state
of war hysteria soon developed. A sailor's drunken outburst—
'I wold to God that ther weare as many Spanyards in this
towne as ther are Englishe men in yt'—was treated as a serious
case of sedition.[4] Patriotic feelings, however, were one thing,
and hard cash another. The war with Spain was signalled in
Yorkshire by a series of unedifying 'ship money' squabbles,
as each town attempted to pay as little as possible towards
warships, and an exasperated Privy Council had to mediate.
York struggled repeatedly to avoid bearing a large share of
Hull's assessment, but both towns were able to co-operate
happily when it was a matter of passing on part of their joint
charges to the towns of the West Riding.[5]

The end of the Queen's long reign was brought home vividly
to the citizens in April 1603 when James VI and I broke his
journey there on his way to London and the Crown. He made
a solemn entry accompanied by regalia, coaches, heralds, and
trumpeters summoned from London. The Privy Council had
thought that these trappings need be sent no further than
Burghley House near Stamford, but James insisted that York

---

[1] *Y.C.R.* v–vii, *passim*; C. Cross, *The Puritan Earl* (London, 1966), pp. 172–8,
189–90; Widdrington, *Analecta Eboracensia*, pp. 280–1; *V.C.H. York*, pp. 129 f.

[2] Drake, *Eboracum*, p. 238 and App. xxxvi–xxxviii.

[3] H.M.C., *MSS. of R. R. Hastings*, ii. 27; *Y.C.R.* viii. 81–4; J. C. Jeaffreson,
Coventry Charters and Manuscripts (Coventry, 1896), p. 85.

[4] *Y.C.R.* viii. 123–4; Y.C.A., B 31, fo. 170[r].

[5] *Acts of the Privy Council 1588*, pp. 46, 282, 316, 394–5; *1588–9*, pp. 45 f.;
1595–6, pp. 210 f., 325; *1596–7*, pp. 150–1, 325–7; *1597*, pp. 44 f.; *1597–8*,
p. 66; Y.C.A., B 30, 31, *passim*; Reid, *King's Council*, pp. 217 f., 222–3; Cross,
Puritan Earl, pp. 190–1; *V.C.H. East Riding*, i. 99.

was 'our second city', and that the county contained peers and gentry of the best sort.[1] He was entertained at York with elaborate ceremony, so that he might 'take that state on him which was not known in Scotland'. Pleased with his reception, he promised the citizens that the Ouse navigation would be improved, and that 'he himself would come and be a burgess among them': was this meaningless flattery or a fleeting idea of a new central capital for the joint realms? On leaving the city, James knighted the lord mayor, Robert Watter, the first knight to hold the mayoral office for exactly a century.[2] The York he left behind had come a long way, both in prosperity and in loyalty, since the last visit of a reigning sovereign in 1541.

6

This outline of relations between Crown and corporation has concentrated on the relationship from the Crown's viewpoint. The sovereign's main interest lay in seeing that towns paid their taxes and were 'quietly governed'. Corporations were expected to suppress rioting and disorder, to enforce political and religious conformity, and to supply the Crown with military forces on occasion. From the corporation's point of view, however, the relationship might seem very different. Local issues and local prosperity were of paramount importance, and national political issues were viewed from a local angle. The Reformation was seen at York—after the vain resistance in 1536—largely in terms of ownership of the confiscated religious houses and hospitals. The Scots, French, and Irish wars were seen chiefly as distractions which drew away from the city manpower and taxes.

The difference of viewpoints is made clear in considering the Tudor Parliaments, in which burgesses greatly outnumbered knights of the shire. It was an established part of medieval thinking that the local communities should be represented in Parliament to give their assent to royal policies (especially to taxation), and in return to demand redress of grievances. York nearly always elected citizens as its two

[1] D. H. Willson, *King James VI and I* (London, 1956), p. 162.
[2] Drake, *Eboracum*, pp. 131-2.

members, unlike many other boroughs which from the fifteenth century, and increasingly during the sixteenth, allowed
outside gentlemen and lawyers to represent them at Westminster. It thought so highly of their service that it was prepared to pay for aldermen and recorders as its representatives,
rather than allow local gentry to serve in return for waiving
their fees. The corporation's lists of instructions to their
members, however, and the letters from the members themselves, show that their importance was conceived purely as
fostering local interests. The MPs were never instructed to
take a stand on the national issues which dominate Sir John
Neale's *Elizabeth and her Parliaments*, but rather to fight for
local statutes, for reductions in the city's tax, or for sympathetic government action over local problems. Obviously the
corporation was affected by national legislation, and by
Elizabeth's reign the MPs were bringing back the printed
statutes for the Clerk's use;[1] but there is no evidence that
they ever took an active part in supporting or opposing
public statutes. Where evidence survives of lobbying by the
city's burgesses, it concerns local or private legislation such as
the remission of their fee-farm in 1536, or of pressure on
behalf of influential groups of citizens like the guildsmen.[2]
    The only recorded activity of the city's members in Edward
VI's first Parliament, when a new Protestant settlement was
being created, was lobbying for a local act to reduce York's
parishes. William Holme, one of those members, also sat
through three of Mary's five Parliaments, and witnessed an
equally dramatic reversal of the Edwardian settlement. All
his energies, however, seem to have been expended on fighting for the city's interests, and when in 1558 he was publicly
rewarded for his services as MP, it was because he had secured
two substantial tax reductions for York, as well as a large
gift from Sir Martin Bowes, a York native who had become a
London alderman. This may seem a very narrow-minded view
of Parliament, and so perhaps it was, but it is important to
remember that York was in the 1550s at the lowest point
of its economic fortunes after a century of accelerating

---

[1] *Y.C.R.* vii. 33, 115-16.
[2] e.g. J. Hatcher and T. C. Barker, *A History of British Pewter* (London, 1974),
p. 173 n.; *Y.C.R.* iv. 92.

depression, and that persistent attempts to reduce its tax burden were only natural. Furthermore, the city had since 1523 been feeling the effects of the heavier taxation introduced by Henry VIII, with a wider incidence than any taxes for two centuries; the burden was severe enough in the country as a whole, but was particularly heavy on a community the prosperity and population of which were in decline. If the Elizabethan corporation devoted less energy to combating tax demands, it owed less to any increasing sense of public duty than to a growing civic prosperity, combined with a national tax burden which in real terms was declining sharply.

These economic fluctuations of York's Tudor century will be traced in detail later, but it may be asked at this stage how far, if at all, relations between city and State altered under the Tudors. There can be little doubt that the city did, indeed, lose some freedom of manoeuvre: the heady days of 1455-85, when York could open or shut its gates to a claimant to the throne, and when the city's military contingent could be worth wooing, were over for ever. After 1537, and especially after 1561, York was firmly and permanently under the close supervision of the central Government; and though the organ of state which made it possible was dismantled in 1641, the achievement was not undone. On the other hand, York's merchants doubtless regarded the growing trade and internal peace of Elizabethan England well worth buying at the cost of a dubious local independence; and there is a sense in which, after 1547 at least, the power of the Crown could advance only in step with the power of the local county and city communities, for it was a state which depended on the consent of the politically active members of society, urban aldermen as well as county justices. Henry VII and Henry VIII, despite strong warnings, never followed Edward I in confiscating the city's liberties, and Elizabeth I, faced with an increasingly important House of Commons, was even less able to act despotically than her father and grandfather. The York of 1603, or at least the small group who acted in its name, was perhaps more influential than the York of 1485.

III

CITY GOVERNMENT

Sirs, I knowe non havyng governaunce and rewle of
any citie or place within my royalme may more boldly
rewle or governe then ye may do that my Citie of
York, for within your fraunches and libertiez ye may
rewle accordyng to my lawez as and I were ther my
nawn person and so I will ye do.

Henry VII's address to a civic delegation, 1495[1]

Since 1396 York had enjoyed the desirable status of county
corporate, first granted in 1373 (to Bristol), and even by
1603 held by only sixteen provincial towns. Its government
was formally a corporation, able to hold land and to pursue
legal actions just like an individual, a concept familiar for
religious houses but still novel for urban councils.[2] Simultaneously, and unlike many other corporate towns and cities,
it had been completely separated from the county of York
for administrative and judicial purposes. The county sheriff
had been superseded by two city sheriffs, and the county
justices of the peace excluded by the aldermen as *ex officio*
justices. As a token of the new liberties, Richard II had given
the mayor a sword, which was to be borne before him point
upwards except in the king's own presence.

Thenceforth the corporation considered themselves
responsible only to the king, and emphasized their autonomy
by fining or disfranchising any citizen suing another citizen
in any but a civic court. Their touchiness expressed itself at
any threat of interference by local magnates. When Lord Clifford tried to advise them about the royal visit of 1486, the
recorder spelled out to him 'that under the King the Maier
. . . is lieutenant, having full power and auctoritie under the
King and lawes to rul and gyde the Cite'.[3] The one external

---

[1] *Y.C.R.* ii. 115.

[2] M. Weinbaum, *The Incorporation of Boroughs* (Manchester, 1937), *passim*.

[3] *Y.C.R.* i. 154.

authority that could not be excluded, since it was an extension of the king's own power, was the Council in the North, and even the Council usually found it politic to avoid injuring civic pride. In 1504 Archbishop Savage, then head of the Council, offered advice to the mayor over the election riots, but tactfully added that 'ye be corporate and by reason therof no person oweth to entermytte amonggs bot your selves for the redressyng of any your causes'.[1] In the 1540s Archbishop Holgate was more cavalier towards the city's liberties, and provoked a bitter clash.[2] Under Elizabeth and James I it became clear to the reluctant corporation that the overriding power of the Council was not to be resisted, but they still stood on their dignity as far as possible. When Lord President Sheffield tried in 1608 to have the mayoral sword abased in his presence, they obtained a verdict of the earl marshal's court against him.[3]

The city's governmental structure remained substantially unaltered from 1396 to 1835. Throughout that long period, all important decisions were taken by the mayor and his fellow-aldermen, a junior council called the Twenty-Four (corresponding to the common council of many other towns),[4] two sheriffs, a recorder and a common clerk or town clerk. Altogether they numbered usually about thirty-five, though Professors Miller and Dickens, accepting the Twenty-Four as a numerical description, have made the total higher and have calculated attendances accordingly; on two occasions when the Twenty-Four were counted, they actually numbered eighteen.[5] These thirty to forty men, the mayor, aldermen and Twenty-Four, were the real councillors, who met irregularly but frequently to govern the city, and it is they who are hereafter described for convenience as the corporation or city council. To add to the confusion, however, there was also a common council or commonalty, meeting only occasionally, and not here comprehended within the

[1] *Y.C.R.* iii. 3.

[2] *Y.C.R.* iv. 178 f., 182; v. 1 f., 7, 12 f.; Dickens, *Robert Holgate*, pp. 14 f.

[3] Drake, *Eboracum*, App. pp. xxiii f.

[4] The Twenty-Four were often called the common council until 1517, when the term was transferred to the larger body of craft representatives. To avoid confusion, 'common council' is used in this book solely for the latter body.

[5] *V.C.H. York*, pp. 78, 139; *Y.C.R.* v. 172 n.; viii. 85.

term city council. It was known before 1517 as the Forty-Eight from an extension of the symmetry of Twelve and Twenty-Four, but actual numbers again varied, as it was composed of the searchers of all the city's craft guilds.

2

There were always thirteen aldermen, including the mayor, who was invariable elected from their number. They were the city's justices of the peace, and any three of them, including the mayor, formed a quorum for holding the city's petty and quarter sessions. They were also the senior part of the city council, and would on occasion hold a council meeting without apparently summoning the Twenty-Four. The norm was for the retiring sheriffs each year to join the Twenty-Four, and for aldermanic vacancies to be filled from that body. Exceptionally, four Tudor aldermen were elected straight from the office of sheriff, and two, George Gayle and William Harryngton, even before they were sheriffs, while Nicholas Lancaster and George Lawson moved straight to the inner council without ever holding that onerous post. Lancaster, Lawson and Gayle were not only wealthy but were Crown officials, and their privileged rise to power was very much the exception.

Between 1500 and 1600 inclusive, 106 men served as aldermen, their tenure of office increasing as the century wore on. In the first half-century there were 58 aldermen, serving on average 12½ years each, while the 48 aldermen of the second half had a mean tenure of nearly 18 years. This increase must have come about through earlier promotion, or increased longevity, or both. Most aldermen held office for life, but four were discharged by royal command after the disorders of 1516–17, and four others by the corporation after local political squabbles, though two of the latter were reinstated by Henry VIII. In addition, Alderman Hogeson was replaced while a prisoner in Scotland, another resigned because he had left York and was in debt to the corporation, and seven others because of age, sickness or poverty. As in other towns, the corporation felt an obligation to aid former colleagues,[1]

[1] J. H. Thomas, *Town Government in the Sixteenth Century* (London, 1933), p. 37.

and at least five of the last nine were granted pensions for life. These could be used as a lever; in 1556 the chamberlains were ordered to stay the payment of Robert Elwald's annuity because he had wilfully pulled down a house in the city.[1] Pensions were also paid to the widows of aldermen if they had fallen on hard times.

The mayor's responsibilities gave him great power. Not only did he dominate the council and have a casting vote there, but as escheator he answered to the king for the necessary arrangements on the deaths of tenants in chief. He was held personally responsible by the king for good order in the city, and could make arrests on his own authority.[2] As clerk of the markets, he was responsible for fixing market prices, and was expected to go round in person on the three weekly market days to ensure that they were observed. Thus in 1555 William Beckwith 'went through the market to see reasonable priez of vitalls' when, seeing a butcher 'sellyng his fleissh excessyvely', he ordered him to sell certain pieces at prices 'reasonable to the poor'.[3] This function of the mayor probably affected ordinary citizens more than any other.

His power and prestige were such that he could act almost despotically, though he always had to remember that once his mayoralty was over he might face retaliation. In 1503 Alderman Neleson burst out, 'Master Maier, ye do me wrang, and if ye do me wrang this yere I trust to be your felawe the next yere.' Ironically, he was fined for this behaviour in accordance with an Act passed in his own mayoralty.[4] In 1572 Aldermen Beckwith and Harbert were disfranchised and imprisoned for refusing to join Mayor Allyn in watching the Pater Noster play, but next year Harbert succeeded Allyn as mayor, and within a month Allyn was being persecuted over the sale of city cloth and was disfranchised in turn. The two issues were not connected, but it is likely that the cloth accusations were used as a pretext by Harbert to take his revenge on Allyn.[5] It seems to have been common practice for mayors and aldermen not to enforce all of the vast number of bylaws, making it easy for a mayor to take revenge on an

[1] Y.C.A., B 22, fo. 6ᵛ.   [2] e.g. *Y.C.R.* iii. 20.
[3] *Y.C.R.* iv. 129; v. 125; vi. 32; viii. 133.
[4] Y.C.A., B 9, fos. 1, 2ᵛ, 9ʳ.   [5] *Y.C.R.* vii, 49 f., 67–73.

enemy by punishing offences which might otherwise be overlooked. When the mayor in 1504 was levying a royal tax of £160, a merchant hinted darkly that if forfeits were to be levied on all ex-mayors for not enforcing laws, it would bene- fit the king by three or four times that sum.[1]

The mayor was usually chosen from among recently elected aldermen. It may seem strange that such despotic power should have been entrusted to newcomers, but the office was onerous, and the senior aldermen were probably glad to leave it to their younger colleagues; indeed, there are hints that a mayoral election could be a mere formality, ratifying a choice they had already made informally.[2] Among the reasons of Thomas Appleyarde II for wishing to resign his aldermanship in 1596 were that he was old and infirm, and if re-elected mayor, would be unable to fulfil his duties.[3] After 1392 a mayor could not be re-elected until his colleagues had all been mayor, and from 1517 he was to be chosen from among those aldermen who had not been mayor twice already and who had not held office within the past six years. Conse- quently most mayors held office only once, and none more than twice. The 1517 regulation ensured that all aldermen should be mayor if they lived long enough, and this must have been bitterly regretted by some, as it gave the city mayors of such variable quality. Of the 106 aldermen during the sixteenth century, 97 were at some time mayor.

The mayor was elected on 15 January, and held office for a year from 3 February. For secular purposes this was the most important dating-year in York, more important even than the regnal year. The corporation minutes normally referred to previous events by mayoralties, and civic annals were compiled on the same basis.[4] A midwife testified to the date of birth of a girl she had delivered eleven years previously 'by accomptinge of the yeres of theme that were lorde maiors'. At the relevant time John Lewes had been mayor, for she 'many times did se the sword and mace borne before hime that same yere'; and as further evidence she named

---

[1] *Y.C.R.* iii. 9.   [2] e.g. *Y.C.R.* vi. 31; Y.C.A., B 23, fo. 44[r].
[3] Y.C.A., B 31, fo. 190[r].
[4] In 1617 one councillor bequeathed 'my role of the Maiours of this cittie': R. H. Skaife, 'Civic officials of York and parliamentary representatives', 3 MSS volumes, York City Library, *sub* P. Brooke.

correctly the two mayors who had preceded him.[1] A mayor's term would long be remembered, and he would be held to account for its failures. Sixteen years after the Vicars Choral had won their enclosure battle with the corporation, a miller insisted that 'Maister Kyrke shulde never be Maire [again] for he lost the Vycar Lees'.[2]

During the Tudor period the mayor's dignity was increased by elaborating his title, just as at the same time the sovereign came to be addressed as 'your Majesty' instead of 'your Grace'. In the late fifteenth and early sixteenth centuries he gradually came to be called Lord Mayor: 'my lord the mair' and 'my Lord Maier' seem first to occur in the 1480s, and the same process occurred at London, where the title lord mayor was used regularly by the city council from about 1535, and spread into general use some ten years later.[3] A more curious development was that the mayor's wife was entitled Lady, not only during her husband's term of office, but for life, a practice which also seems to date from the 1480s.[4] York was, in fact, the only English town besides London where such titles were used, perhaps in a vain attempt to maintain that it was still the second city of the realm. The Venetian ambassador noticed in 1551 that outside the capital civic office was held with less dignity 'except in the city of York, which is on a par with London'.[5]

The mayor was assisted in governing the city by two sheriffs, elected annually on 21 September to take office for a year beginning at Michaelmas (29 September). Unlike the mayors, they were never called on to take office twice, and 204 different men held the post during the sixteenth century, as four died in office. The sheriffs assisted the mayor in every way; they had, like him, power of arrest; and they had their own prison or prisons. They also held their own court, and they could greatly abuse their powers, if complaints filed in

---

[1] B.I.H.R., C.P. G 1037 [1561]. For another case, ibid. G 32.

[2] *Y.C.R.* iii. 36.

[3] T. P. Cooper, *York: the titles 'Lord Mayor' and 'Right Honourable'* (York, n.d.).

[4] Y.C.A., B 6, fo. 92ᵛ.

[5] *eccetto quello della città d'York, il quale è all'istessa condizione di Londra*: E. Alberi, ed., *Relazioni degli Ambasciatori Veneti* Ser. i, vol. ii (Florence, 1840), 241; *Calendar of State Papers Venetian 1534-54*, p. 345.

Chancery against them may be believed. A sheriff's widow (who ought to have known) said she could have no justice at York because the sheriffs there had 'the rule of all the commen jurours and questmongers of the citie', while a Minster canon complained that as he was being sued by an ex-mayor and an ex-sheriff, he 'coude nat . . . have eny lerned in the lawe to be of councell ayenst theym'.[1] All these powers, however, were subject to the overriding control of the mayor and aldermen, who were quick to intervene if the sheriffs disobeyed them.[2]

The sheriffs were rewarded for their pains by joining the Twenty-Four after their term of office ended. A study of the corporation's attendance lists for the sixteenth century shows that of the 200 sheriffs who survived to the end of their term of office, 182 joined the Twenty-Four. Analysis of the membership of the Twenty-Four in this work is confined to the 182 known members, although this may be erring on the side of caution, since there is some evidence late in the century that sheriffs joined the Twenty-Four before they relinquished office.

The Twenty-Four, or Privy Council as they were often called by Elizabeth's reign, were a part of the regular city council, but without the weight and prestige of the aldermen. A series of corporation resolutions in 1567–8 laid it down that the Twenty-Four were to attend all meetings of the mayor, aldermen and sheriffs, but were to have no share in electing to any of those three categories.[3] Early Tudor corporation meetings were frequently unattended by any of the Twenty-Four, though they participated more during Elizabeth's reign.

Most important decisions were taken by the city council as so far described, whether by aldermen alone or with the Twenty-Four, and in view of the frequent quarrels and divisions among them it is worth noting how their decisions were reached. Maitland pointed out long ago that the unanimity required of gatherings in the early Middle Ages, tested by a shout, gradually gave way before the modern concept of

---

[1] P.R.O., C1/330/22; C1/258/16. The cases are datable 1508X13 and 1500X10.
[2] e.g. YCA., B 31, fos. 194–5.
[3] *Y.C.R.* vi. 123 f., 130 f., 141 f.

decision by a majority vote.[1] At York decisions were still recorded as made by the whole council until the beginning of the sixteenth century, though voting by a show of hands or voices must often have been needed. The lid was lifted once, during the disputed aldermanic elections of 1516–17. The mayor and four aldermen voted for John Norman, the mayor 'clamyng after the custome of the said citie to have two voicez in every election'. Six other aldermen chose William Cure, and one Simon Vycars, so that there was a tie. Such an open division was exceptional, and the council promised Wolsey 'to be alway from hensforth in oon unite and concord withoute any parte takyng in any eleccion'.[2] The precedent had been set, however, and in 1522 occurred the first peaceful election of an alderman openly recorded as made by the 'moste voyces' of the councillors. In 1538 John North was elected mayor on a frank majority basis, the voting figures being given, and his mayoralty saw the first case of routine business settled by 'the moste voycez'.[3] Election by voices meant what it said, and counting was needed only if numbers were nearly equal. At a meeting of the much larger common council in 1564, the members 'so diffusely answered, the part cryeng "All, all" and otherz holdyng their peace, that it could not be well knowne whither the more part assented thereto'. The mayor and recorder thereupon counted their votes individually, and found thirty-three in favour of the motion concerned and twenty-two against.[4]

3

The common council was a separate body from the council so far described, and was supposed to represent the 'commonalty' or whole body of freemen; it met only for elections, or when specially summoned by the city council for its advice. This was the only part of the civic constitution to be altered by the Tudors.[5] From the 1390s there had been a theoretically concentric system, with the regular council of Twelve (aldermen) and Twenty-Four joined for occasional

[1] F. W. Maitland, *Township and Borough* (Cambridge, 1898), p. 34 f.
[2] *Y.C.R.* iii. 52 f.   [3] *Y.C.R.* iii. 84; iv. 28, 30.   [4] Y.C.A., B 23, fo. 159.
[5] For this paragraph see *V.C.H. York*, pp. 71 f., 78, 80, 83 f.

purposes by the Forty-Eight or commonalty. During the fifteenth century this wider body came to consist of the searchers of the city's craft guilds. Aldermen at that period filled their own vacancies, and sheriffs were effectively chosen by the aldermen and Twenty-Four. In the election of mayor, however, the procedure was (in the periods 1464–73 and 1490–1517) for the Forty-Eight to nominate two aldermen, from whom the aldermen and Twenty-Four selected one to be mayor. Even this limited power of the Forty-Eight seemed dangerously democratic to the aldermen, especially as commoners who had no official status also attended the mayoral elections. The aldermen's forebodings must have seemed justified when there were riots at the mayoral election of 1504, and when the Forty-Eight tried to participate in the sheriffs' election as well. Finally, in response to the riots of 1516–17, the King altered the composition of the larger council. The Forty-Eight were replaced by a body of forty-one men called the common council, consisting of two representatives each of thirteen major crafts and one each from fifteen lesser crafts. It was to meet when summoned, and also—assisted by the twenty-eight senior searchers of the crafts—to elect mayors, aldermen and sheriffs.[1] In one way this spread responsibility more widely, for the common council had a share in aldermanic and shrieval elections as well as those for mayor. In each case they were allowed to choose candidates, from among whom the aldermen and sheriffs made a final choice. In reality, however, the new regime was less democratic than the old, for the common council did not directly represent the crafts as the Forty-Eight had done. It was itself an indirectly elected body, the twenty-eight specified crafts putting up candidates from whom councillors were chosen by the aldermen and Twenty-Four. Furthermore, after 1517 commoners not on the common council were strictly barred from mayoral elections.

Henry's intervention in 1517 was very much of a piece with royal policy towards the corporate towns. In 1489 the mayors and ex-mayors of Northampton and Leicester had been empowered by statute to nominate electoral Councils of Forty-Eight, and the reason was frankly acknowledged to

[1] Drake, *Eboracum*, p. 207.

be fear of the multitude, 'beyng of lytill substaunce and haveour and of no sadnes discrecion wisdome ne reason'.[1] In 1497 a royal charter confirmed the recent practice at Exeter by which the Council of Twenty-Four had become self-electing.[2] The Crown was fearful of the risk of popular tumult in the towns, and the York election riots of 1504 and 1516–17 must have confirmed Henry VIII's worst fears. Consequently the city joined the growing band of corporations where the Crown was establishing small, self-perpetuating and, it was hoped, trustworthy oligarchies.[3]

Yet the common council should not be thought of merely as a creature of the corporation after 1517. Given the right leadership, it was capable of putting forward constructive programmes of reform on behalf of the freemen at large, and averting conflicts between the corporation and the lesser freemen. Its reorganization in 1517 'proved a development of major significance in the history of York', A. G. Dickens observes, and 'played its part in procuring stabler relationships'.[4] It is noteworthy, for example, that from 1555 onwards the corporation often consulted the common council about proposed instructions for the city's MPs.

For a short period, one common councillor emerged from obscurity and threatened to give the council an independent policy. Miles Cooke was a merchant who by the early 1560s had become, officially or unofficially, spokesman for the common council, twice putting forward petitions in their name. On the second occasion, at the meeting to elect a mayor in 1563, Cooke 'in name of the rest of the Common Consell requyred' certain articles 'to be forthwith enacted by my Lord Mayour Aldremen and Pryvay Consell'. These demanded easier loans to freemen, lower charges by the millers, and the consent of the commons to all leases of city property. The final point, and perhaps the most important, was that some of the twenty-eight crafts allowed to take part

---

[1] Mrs J. R. Green, *Town Life in the Fifteenth Century* (London, 1894), ii. 287; C. A. Markham, ed., *The Records of the Borough of Northampton*, i (Northampton, 1898), 101.

[2] E. A. Freeman, *Historic Towns: Exeter* (London, 1895), p. 150.

[3] P. Clark and P. Slack, *Crisis and Order in English Towns 1500–1700* (London, 1972), pp. 21 f.

[4] *V.C.H. York*, pp. 138 f.

in electing mayors and sheriffs had died out; Cooke wanted the letters patent amended so that other crafts could take their places. When the mayor said the articles would be considered, Cooke replied that no mayor would be elected until the articles were agreed to. The mayor and his colleagues pretended to give way so as to secure a peaceful election, but this only produced a renewed outburst when the common council were again gathered to elect an alderman. Finally the city council agreed to the articles, having first pointed out that it was not for the common council to dictate them.[1]

The revision of the letters patent of 1517 eventually came to nothing for lack of money to obtain new ones; matters became worse, as more of the twenty-eight crafts declined or vanished, while others without representation flourished. Eventually, in 1632, a new charter was obtained which cut the Gordian knot by abandoning altogether the principle of election on a craft basis, and reconstituting the common council to represent the four wards.[2]

Below the common council ranked the offices of chamberlain, bridgemaster, and muremaster, positions frequently held by future aldermen as their first civic office, though more often by humbler citizens who never rose so far. The chamberlains were the city's treasurers, elected for a year on the same day as the mayor (15 January). Their number varied between three and ten, with the exceptional number of twenty for the year 1537–8 only, and no fewer than 571 men held the office during the sixteenth century. The bridgemasters took charge of the revenues assigned for the upkeep of the two chief city bridges. They kept their own account rolls, but were responsible to the chamberlains, who accounted to the city council for all civic finance. Bridgemasters were elected annually on 15 January, and there were four, two each for Ouse Bridge and Foss Bridge, until 1569, when their numbers were reduced to two, for both bridges jointly. The muremasters were two or more in number and elected yearly for most of the Tudor period. Their job was to see the city walls kept in good repair; from 1585 their posts were

[1] *Y.C.R.* vi. 3 f., 51–3. For Cooke's career and the office of 'chief' of the Common Council see Palliser, 'York', pp. 151–4.
[2] *Y.C.R.* vii. 50 f., 66; *V.C.H. York*, pp. 174, 178 f.

replaced by that of the City Husband. All chamberlains were expected to pay a fine unless they had previously been bridge-master or muremaster, so that in theory the latter posts formed a necessary first step on the ladder of civic promotion, but it must have been common to pay the fine or to ignore the rule altogether. Nearly all sixteenth-century aldermen had previously been chamberlains (99 out of 106), but during the century they ceased to take up the office of bridgemaster beforehand.

The elective offices and councils reviewed so far formed a recognized ladder of promotion for the ambitious citizen. Such a man, soon after becoming free of the city, would first take on the office of bridgemaster or muremaster, if he had not paid a fine instead; then he would be elected chamberlain, after which he would advance into the outermost circle of power, the common council. The decisive step towards the inner circles was election as sheriff, which ensured, at the end of his term, almost automatic membership of the Twenty-Four. The Twenty-Four in turn provided candidates for vacancies among the aldermen, and these in turn could all expect at least one term as mayor if they lived long enough.

This *cursus honorum* can best be illustrated by looking at the careers of those city councillors whose age can be deter-mined. Unfortunately, the exact birth dates of only three Tudor aldermen are known, but various records can be made to yield the approximate year of birth of fifteen other alder-men and of fifteen members of the Twenty-Four.[1] The mean age of the eighteen aldermen was about twenty-four on attain-ing the freedom of the city, thirty-three on election as cham-berlain and forty on election as sheriff, so that they joined the Twenty-Four, on average, at forty-one. Their mean tenure of a place on the bench of aldermen was from forty-six until death at the age of sixty-seven. The fifteen members of the Twenty-Four who did not rise to the bench made rather slower progress. Freemen at a mean age of twenty-six, they were elected chamberlains at thirty-six, sheriffs at forty-six,

[1] Twenty-seven refs. cited in Palliser, 'York', pp. 193–5, plus six further in-stances. P.R.O., C 142/255/180 has the age of Robert Askwith II, while those of W. Coupland, J. Blads, J. Hydwyn, W. Wood, and J. Rasyng are in B.I.H.R. CP. (refs. G 172, G 204, G 205, G 1430, and one ref. lost).

and were members of the Twenty-Four from forty-seven until death at sixty-one. But though these figures illustrate the career profiles of over thirty councillors, they cannot be entirely representative of the whole body. It is sufficient to point to the fact that the eighteen aldermen sat on the bench for an average of twenty-one years each, a longer tenure than was enjoyed by most of their colleagues.

4

Outside the hierarchy so far described, the corporation employed many other officers, of whom the most important were the city's Members of Parliament. Two Members were summoned from York to every Tudor Parliament, and the ancient importance of the city was commemorated on the opening day, when, by custom, the Members for London and York sat on the Speaker's right, next to the privy councillors.[1] Formally, the MPs were elected by the freeholders in the city's county court, but in practice, until 1563, they were chosen by the aldermen and Twenty-Four, the county court apparently accepting their choice without question; indeed, there are signs that the county court was simply the corporation under another name. In Elizabeth's reign, however, responsibility was spread rather more widely, the selection being made jointly by the city council and a special assembly of between thirty and forty commoners.[2] Both practices were widespread among Tudor boroughs, elections being usually made or at least controlled by the corporations.[3]

The electors took care that those chosen should have the city's interests at heart, and York's representation was still confined almost entirely to local men. Forty-six men served as MPs under the Tudors, of whom forty were city aldermen, and three others were, or had been, city recorders. Such overwhelmingly local representation was rare. Only five provincial boroughs always elected residents as MPs during

[1] Neale, *Eliz. House of Commons*, p. 365.

[2] e.g. *Y.C.R.* v. 92, 109; viii. 43 f., 80, 127 f.; Y.C.A., B 31, fos. 297–8. Raine does not print lists of electors, but that of 1584 is in Drake, *Eboracum*, p. 358.

[3] Lehmberg, *Reformation Parliament*, pp. 11 f.; Neale, *Eliz. House of Commons*, pp. 246 ff.

Elizabeth's reign, and York almost qualifies as a sixth.[1] The only Tudor MPs not members of the corporation were Thomas Gargrave (1547–52), Reginald Beysley (1555) and John Bennett (1601). All were York residents, although in service with Church and State: Gargrave was a resident member of the Council in the North for a third of a century, Beysley was clerk of the castle and a notary and advocate in the church courts, and Bennett the archbishop's chancellor. They all appear to have justified the corporation's confidence by working for the city's interests: it was, for example, Bennett's concern for the grievance felt in York at the monopoly on salt that provoked him to a courageous speech on monopolies.[2]

To secure the advantages of colleagues as their MPs, the corporation were prepared to pay. Although boroughs were expected to pay their representatives 2s. a day, many came to choose gentry who, in return, agreed to serve *gratis*. York refused to be tempted by this approach. The city's MPs, until 1558, were each paid 4s. a day during their absence from York, a sum expected to cover the expenses of one member, two servants, and their horses. Four shillings was the customary wage of a knight of the shire, twice that of a burgess, for the MPs of counties corporate like York and Bristol ranked officially as both.[3] The total cost would absorb a considerable share of the civic budget, as in 1542, when the two members received £35. 4s. 0d. for an absence of eighty-eight days. The mid-century inflation, however, made even such sums inadequate. In 1562 the corporation raised the daily rate from 4s. to 6s. 8d.,[4] and later increased the members' payments further by lump sums as 'rewards'.

The MPs were of course only occasional officers of the city. Of the permanent civic officials, the most important was the recorder. He was the corporation's chief legal adviser, and although not expected to attend their every meeting, he was summoned whenever knotty legal points arose. Time after

[1] Neale, *Eliz. House of Commons*, pp. 163 f.
[2] S. D'Ewes, *The Journals of all the Parliaments during the Reign of Queen Elizabeth* (London, 1682), p. 645.
[3] M. McKisack, *The Parliamentary Representation of the English Boroughs during the Middle Ages* (Oxford, 1932), pp. 32, 86.
[4] *Y.C.R.* vi. 49 f.

time the city council agreed that some matter should be deferred until Master Recorder's advice could be had. In fact the office was so important that from the late fifteenth century a second lawyer was sometimes retained as deputy recorder; no other town is known to have employed a deputy so early.[1] Nevertheless, the recorder's fee remained throughout the Tudor period, despite inflation, 20 marks and an official livery. The recorders were usually drawn from an interrelated group of local gentry who gave conscientious legal advice and who were sometimes very eminent lawyers in their own right. Guy Roucliffe, for example, was recorder in the 1450s; his son Brian was a baron of the Exchequer, while his grandchildren Brian and Guy Palmes became sergeants at law, and Brian Palmes also served York as recorder (1496-1509). William Fairfax, another local gentleman, was recorder for a time (1490-6) before becoming Justice of the Common Pleas. Other local gentry who held the office included Sir William Gascoigne of Gawthorpe (1523-7), William Byrnand of Knaresborough (1573-82), and William Hildyard of Winestead in Holderness (1582-1608), a member of the Inner Temple and of the Council in the North. The Tankerds of Boroughbridge, however, came nearest to a family tradition of legal service to the city. Richard Tankerd was recorder from 1509 to 1519 and married an alderman's daughter; and his nephew, William Tankerd, served the city satisfactorily for the record period of thirty-seven years (1537-73), managing to combine the office with the position of a county justice and eventually with membership of the Council in the North. William not only married the daughter of John Pulleyn (common clerk 1507-10 and recorder 1534-7), but was also brother-in-law to Miles Newton, common clerk from 1519 to 1550.[2]

The common clerk was another professional lawyer permanently retained by the corporation. His regular work was to write their records and keep them safely; many of them he apparently stored at his house, since unlike the recorder he was normally resident in the city. Among the lesser legal

[1] Ives, 'Aspects of the legal profession', pp. 368 f.
[2] Skaife, 'Civic officials', *sub* Tankerd; *North Country Wills*, ed. J. W. Clay, 2 vols., Surtees Society (1908-12), i. 207-10.

officers under the corporation were three city coroners, and at least two common clerks added to their other duties by holding one of the coronerships.[1] Furthermore, the clerk was often chosen by the corporation as their emissary to the government and to neighbouring magnates. Miles Newton was sent at least twelve times to London, besides taking part in several deputations to the archbishop and one to the duke of Norfolk.[2] The clerk's traditional fee was £5 plus his liveries, but this was far from representing his real income, since he was entitled to charge fees for his official services, even from freemen. In 1508 he was regularly exacting 2s. for actions involving recognisances, and the commons wanted him to take only 8d.[3]

The corporation also employed gaolers, cooks, chaplains and minstrels, a keeper and clerk of the common crane, a bellman to make public announcements, a mason to keep up the walls, and a pavier to maintain the pavements. The mayor's dignity was enhanced by the provision of eight servants: a swordbearer, a macebearer, and six sergeants at mace, all clothed in the city's livery. He was expected to be preceded through the streets by the sword and mace as symbols of his justice, and during council meetings on Ouse Bridge the two esquires were to guard the door of the council chamber, while the six sergeants kept watch downstairs.[4] Most of these officials received salaries, and some were granted pensions if they had to retire. One of the waits, replaced in 1486 after over forty years' service, was granted a 13s. pension and a rent-free house for life.[5] Furthermore, besides the salaried posts there were others whose holders instead paid the corporation for the privilege, expecting of course to recoup more than they paid. Such were the ferrymen of the two ferries over the Ouse, and the farmers of the tolls of the city markets.

The lesser civic offices were much less permanent than the greater ones, which tended to remain little altered from the fourteenth century to the nineteenth. The chaplains, for instance, ceased to be employed when the two bridge chapels

[1] *Y.C.R.* v. 56.   [2] *Y.C.R.* iii–v, entries indexed under Newton.
[3] *Y.C.R.* iii. 25.   [4] *Y.C.R.* viii. 29, 71.
[5] *Y.C.R.* i. 170–1. The last line on p. 170 misreads 'service' as 'since'.

were closed in Edward VI's reign, and it proved impossible
to retain a city mason later in the century. Instead, an outside
mason was retained to inspect and repair the stone civic
buildings once a year. His first assignment was the rebuilding
of Ouse Bridge in 1566, and he was still retained by the corporation in 1598.[1] *Per contra*, new offices were created to
meet new or growing needs. Oversight of beggars and paupers
led to the appointment of master beggars about 1530 and of
poor law officials in 1588; the condition of the Ouse and of
the city moats to that of a water bailiff in 1541; and street
cleansing prompted the employment of four scavengers in
1580.[2] Also in 1580, growing Puritanism among the corporation led to the appointment of a city preacher, whose salary
was usually a substantial £40 a year.[3] The most influential
new post to be created was that of high steward, an office
granted to a leading politician in return for his good offices.
Although, as the corporation said in 1591, 'there haith bene
for the most parte continuallie untill of late tyme, one of her
Majesties most honourable Privie Counsell which haith bene
towards this Corporacon', it was not until that year that they
created a regular position of steward for a privy councillor,
and appointed Sir John Fortescue at £10 a year. Fortescue
held the office until 1607, and in the following year Sir
Robert Cecil, already high steward of Hull, succeeded him.[4]

5

Despite the elaborate governmental structure already
described, the city was too large to be administered entirely
from Ouse Bridge or the Common Hall. Instead, a three-tier
system of administration, law enforcement, and justice had
evolved, the city being subdivided into wards, and the wards
into parishes. The parishes were primarily units of church
government, the incumbent of each being assisted by a clerk

[1] *Y.C.R.* vi. 113–14, 128, 139, 141; vii. 8, 49; viii. 28; Y.C.A., B 27, fo. 210^r;
B 28, fos. 44^v, 99^v; B 29, fo. 191^r; Y.C.A. CC 9, 1598-9 book, p. 193; R.C.H.M.
York ii. 35, 174.

[2] *Y.C.R.* iii. 133; iv. 54, 57 f.; viii. 31, 38, 158.

[3] *Y.C.R.* viii. 31, 35, 46, 51 f., 56–8, 71, 79, 91 f., 98.

[4] Y.C.A., B 30, fos. 220^r, 234; Wilson, 'Corporation of York', p. 214; H.M.C.,
Hatfield MSS. vi. 436.

and by a number of laymen elected annually as church-wardens. The corporation also found the parishes useful as civil units, and both civic rates and national taxes were assessed parochially, while each parish had two or three constables to keep the peace. Justice at its humblest level was enforced there too, for most churchyards contained a pair of stocks. As the volume of Tudor legislation increased, the parish was used more and more as a convenient civil unit for such matters as poor relief, road making, policing and the storing of armour; and the corporation delegated much administration and law enforcement to the parochial officers, wardens as well as constables, and to the newly-established overseers of the poor. The ordinary householders in each parish, too, were involved, for they still shared in rotation the traditional burden of watch and ward.[1] Ecclesiastical and civil parishes were identical until 1586, when the former were reduced from forty to twenty-three.

For ecclesiastical purposes, a dozen of the forty late medieval parishes formed part of the peculiar jurisdiction of the Minster Dean and Chapter, while the others were included in the rural deanery of York and its suburbs. This was one of five subdivisions of the York archdeaconry, which in turn was one of five archdeaconries in the diocese. For civil purposes the corporation grouped the city parishes into six wards, rearranged during the 1520s as the familiar four-ward system (Micklegate, Monk, Bootham, Walmgate) which remained unaltered for three centuries. The thirteen aldermen all acted as wardens, each group having a general responsibility for one ward and for holding a court twice yearly. The surviving wardmote records reveal that their main business involved public hygiene and street paving, and each ward had its stocks for the punishment of beggars, vagabonds, and other 'mysdoers'.[2] Policing was carried out by the wardens in person: Alderman Moseley himself searched the premises of a man accused of pig-keeping, and found seven swine in his 'backsyde and styes'. Policing his ward must have been one of an alderman's most onerous tasks, and the reason given for

[1] e.g. Y.C.A., B 31, fo. 306^r; F 86, end folio.
[2] Bodley, Rawl. B 451, fos. 2-5 [1517]; Y.C.A., E 31 [1575-86]; *Y.C.R.* ii. 165, 171.

demanding Alderman Appleyarde's residence in the city was that the mayor and his other colleagues were having to shoulder his share of ward business.[1]

Naturally the initiation of policy was confined to the city councils, but even at parish level an officer was not without power and influence. It is worth reflecting that a large minority of freemen must at any one time have been holding office; in Elizabeth's reign councillors and civic officials will have numbered over 120, with at least as many more in ward and parish offices, even allowing for some duplication of personnel. This would suggest that one freeman in five may have held public office at any time, and the proportion holding office at some time in their careers will have been considerably greater. In some parishes almost every eligible male must have had the opportunity to serve. That of St. Martin's, Coney Street, with under a hundred adult males, had four wardens, and there were fifteen candidates for the posts in 1576 and twenty in 1578.[2] One noteworthy feature of office-holding is that not one woman appears to have held even the humblest office, although in other areas women are known to have served at least as churchwardens. This may merely reflect the fact that office in York was confined almost exclusively to the franchised class, of which women formed less than one per cent.

The ward and the parish may well have been the units most immediately affecting the lives of ordinary citizens; but their powers were of course subject to the overriding civic and ecclesiastical courts. The city sheriffs held three distinct courts: a twice-yearly tourn for the Ainsty only, a monthly county court, which they held jointly with the coroners, and a court of common pleas, normally held thrice weekly. The last, the most important, specialized in pleas of debt, but had jurisdiction also over affrays, trespass, and the assize of bread.[3] The lord mayor presided over another group of courts: the weekly court of husting or common pleas, for miscellaneous pleas and the enrolling of deeds and wills; a court of mayor and aldermen, difficult to distinguish from the ordinary meetings of the corporation, which judged a

[1] Y.C.A., B 30, fo. 341ʳ; B 32, fo. 4ʳ.   [2] B.I.H.R., Y/MCS 16, p. 126.
[3] Drake, *Eboracum*, pp. 189–95; *V.C.H. York*, p. 75.

wide variety of offences; and a group of lesser courts under
the latter, including a court of orphans, a court of chamberlains (with jurisdiction over apprenticeship), a coroner's
court and an escheator's court.[1] Unfortunately almost nothing survives of the records of most of the mayor's and sheriffs'
courts, but the minutes do survive (notably for 1560-99) of
the court of quarter sessions of the city and Ainsty, held by
the mayor and aldermen in their capacity as Justices of the
Peace, and dealing with a great variety of business.

York was thus, for its size, equipped with a judicial and administrative system of some complexity. Backed by the
authority of the king and his courts, it presented to the
potential lawbreaker a wide array of powers, impressive on
paper at least. The chief purpose of the whole system was the
preservation of law and order: externally, by levying troops
or taxes to defend the realm or to attack others, and inter-
nally, by averting or punishing breaches of the peace. How
strictly law and order were in fact enforced in York is not
easy to assess. Certainly the fear of punishment was enough
before the Reformation to make many law-breakers flee to
sanctuaries, not only those in the city, but also others far
away. Between 1501 and 1539 two York murderers and fourteen debtors took refuge at Beverley, while during the same
period three York men, a murderer and two debtors, sought
sanctuary at Durham.[2]

The city aldermen, like many of their contemporaries,
found rights of sanctuary a serious obstacle to law enforcement, and tried with varying degrees of success to whittle
them away. In 1487 the sheriffs seized various persons who
had sought sanctuary in St. Andrew's Priory, and were called
to account by the archbishop.[3] There were other powerful
defenders of the system. The Minster Dean and Chapter seem
to have successfully enforced a claim that it covered all city
churchyards subject to their Liberty, and as late as 1534 the

[1] Drake, *Eboracum*, pp. 197-9; *V.C.H. York*, pp. 75 f. It is incorrect to say
that 'there is no trace of an orphans' court at York' (C. Carlton, *The Court of
Orphans*, Leicester 1974, p. 109).

[2] *Sanctuarium Dunelmense et Sanctuarium Beverlacense*, ed. J. Raine (Surtees
Soc. v, 1837), pp. 49, 56, 69, 112, 118, 126, 130, 142, 167, 172, 177, 187, 191,
193-5, 209.

[3] *V.C.H. Yorkshire*, iii. 256.

city had to release, at the behest of the Lord Chancellor, prisoners whom they had seized from sanctuary in the White-friars.[1] The problem was largely solved when the religious houses were suppressed in 1536-9, though an Act of 1540-1 fixed on York as the location for one of eight English sanctuaries, and an unnamed site in the city was designated for it by the corporation.[2]

What must have been galling to the corporation's critics was the councillors' natural but reprehensible habit of imposing double standards in their own favour. When the Midsummer Play was performed in 1585, charges were levied on those before whose doors it was played. Distresses were levied on two householders who refused to pay, yet two aldermen in the same position were spared.[3] Humble folk guilty of adultery and even fornication were publicly humiliated, at least under the stricter mayors, yet no action was taken against Francis Bayne of the Twenty-Four, who confessed 'that he committed adultery with the said Anne now his wief in the lief time of his former wief'. Mayor Henry May, according to hostile report, escaped unpunished for similar behaviour.[4]

The basic test of the corporation's competence, as Henry VII and his son made very clear, was their ability to prevent serious breaches of the peace; and their record in those reigns was not a happy one. Attention has already been drawn to the serious election and enclosure riots of 1485-94, 1504, 1514, 1516-17, 1529, and 1536, and to the corporation's surrender to rebels in 1489 and 1536. Nor were those all, for enclosure riots also occurred in 1524, 1534, and 1546, a religious riot in 1536, and a riot over the city bounds in 1539.[5] The last serious Tudor riots were raised in 1550 by local rural labourers, perhaps in protest against the city's policy of requisitioning corn supplies,[6] and the reigns of Mary and Elizabeth were apparently free of major disorder. But the corporation were not allowed to become complacent,

---

[1] *Y.C.R.* iii. 35, 168.
[2] *L.P. Hen. VIII* xv, No. 498 (12); Y.C.A., B 15, fo. 10^V; *Y.C.R.* iv. 63.
[3] Y.C.A., B 29, fo. 53^r.
[4] *Y.C.R.* vii. 52; Y.C.A., B 25, fos. 23^V, 36^V, 45^V; B.I.H.R. H.C./A.B. 11, fo. 44^r; *Ampleforth Journal* lxxvi. 29.
[5] Palliser, 'York', p. 161.   [6] *Y.C.R.* v. 42-9.

for the sovereign was now able, through her local representatives, to pay closer attention to the enforcement of statutes. The House Books between 1561 and 1578, for instance, record no fewer than twenty-one letters to the city from the Council in the North, urging stricter enforcement of statutes, and usually complaining of the city's negligence. The commonest complaint was of neglect of the anti-recusancy laws, with which the city council were plainly out of sympathy until the late 1570s. It was the same problem which Tudor governments met in dealing with any body of JPs, whether rural gentry or urban aldermen: unpaid and unsupervised officials would enforce only those laws with which they were in sympathy.

The evidence of their minute-books, however, does reveal the corporation making a valiant effort to enforce many statutes, if not always successfully. And perhaps more interesting is the way in which this period saw them begin to enlarge their sphere of activities, often anticipating what was later to be enacted by Parliament. There had always been issues beyond law and order on which the corporation had felt it necessary to legislate through by-laws: issues such as public health and food manufacture. Many social problems, however, the late medieval aldermen had tended to ignore as irremediable, or to leave their solution to private charity or to the church; and one of the most interesting aspects of Tudor urban government is the way in which corporate control was exercised over many of these problems for the first time, to be followed tardily by Parliament as the initiative justified itself. One such was the massive problem of poverty. York, by a system of licensing beggars, made the important distinction between those who would not and those who could not work as early as 1515,[1] a distinction not made by statute until 1531. The essential support for any system of poor relief, a system of compulsory contributions, was introduced temporarily in 1538 and permanently in 1550,[2] whereas Parliament did not follow suit until 1572. Similarly, the same period saw towns begin to tackle epidemics by other means than prayer alone. London and Oxford

[1] *Y.C.R.* iii. 46.
[2] Y.C.A., B 13, fo. 127^r; *Y.C.R.* v. 33–5.

made the first recorded anti-plague measures in 1517, and York followed in 1538.[1]

But if York's record as a pioneer in legislation was a good one, it had less to be proud of in terms of major public works. Some cities, such as Bristol and Exeter, were very active during this century,[2] but York, like Lincoln, Winchester and other decayed cities, was unable to afford the necessary expense. It lived on the fat of its earlier prosperity with its stock of public buildings as in other ways, and so the city council were taken aback when Ouse Bridge collapsed in 1565. It was rebuilt only after a delay of nearly two years, and the city's poverty can be judged from the proposal, seriously entertained, to rebuild the bridge in wood.[3] The corporation's policy towards the Ouse navigation also showed up their inertia or want of means. Several times during the century or so after 1550 there were proposals to make the Ouse deep enough for larger ships, or to improve the flow of the river by a cut, but all these schemes came to nothing.[4]

6

This poor record of the corporation raises again the problem of their solvency. Three series of financial accounts were maintained. The muremasters and bridgemasters each compiled their own, and handed over any surplus to the chamberlains, who kept the main accounts. The muremasters' records are altogether lacking, as are many of the bridgemasters' rolls. The most important records, the audited rolls of the chamberlains, are also too few to provide a full picture. They survive intact only for 1486-7, 1501-2, 1506-7, 1508-9, 1561-2, 1576-9, 1580-3, 1597-9, and 1602-3: fourteen years in all, and none from the vital half-century after 1510 which saw the corporation's financial plight at its worst.

[1] D. M. Palliser, 'Epidemics in Tudor York', *Northern History*, viii (1973), 58.

[2] MacCaffrey, *Exeter 1540-1640*, pp. 67-9, 76, 114, 126-36, 157; Rowse, *England of Elizabeth*, p. 178.

[3] *Y.C.R.* vi. 97.

[4] *V.C.H. York*, pp. 128, 169; Wilson, 'Corporation of York', pp. 137-43; B. F. Duckham, *The Yorkshire Ouse* (Newton Abbot, 1967), pp. 38-50. Duckham, pp. 44 f., speculates that the grandiose scheme for a tidal canal may go back before 1616; and this is confirmed by Y.C.A., B 32, fos. 279-80 [1603].

Fortunately, they can be supplemented by other rolls, incomplete or damaged, and by the surviving chamberlains' books. The books were the day-to-day accounts from which the chamberlains later extracted summaries in roll form to present for audit. The greatest value of the books is that they expand the bare summaries in the rolls, and for one period, 1597-1600, three consecutive years can be studied from both sources.[1]

Taking income first, the total under Henry VII was of the order of £200, whereas under Elizabeth I it rose from about £350 to between £500 and £600. These absolute figures mean little, of course, since there was inflation for most of the sixteenth century, and of more interest is the annual balance. The year 1486-7 saw a heavy deficit, caused mainly by an expensive royal visit, and added to an even larger one carried over from the previous year, it produced a total deficit nearly as large as the year's income. In 1490 the corporation was still in 'greit det', and pleading for gifts of money to reduce it.[2] The position gradually eased, and in the last year of Henry VII there was even a small surplus. The real financial crisis, of course, occurred during a period not covered by any complete surviving rolls, but one fragment indicates the gravity of the situation. It is a stark summary of the year 1536-7, as audited on 9 February: 'Summa totalis of all the said allowances £680. 5s. 6d. wherof deduct the aboue wryttyn som of recept of £197. 7s. 8d. And so the said accomptantes are in surplusage [i.e. deficit] this yere— £482. 17s. 10d.' This disclosure was swiftly followed by emergency measures, including the gift of over £200 by chamberlains, ex-chamberlains and others.[3]

When the surviving rolls begin again, the crisis had been weathered. 1561-2 saw a net surplus of £50 or £200 (there is a puzzling discrepancy in the roll) and the position was further improved when much unprofitable urban property was sold in 1563 and rural leases purchased instead. This laid the foundation for a strong recovery. The total surplus handed over by the retiring chamberlains—their own balance, together with the reserves they had inherited—rose to £160 in 1578

[1] The following section is based on Y.C.A., C 4-C 10 (rolls) and CC 2-10 (books).
[2] Y.C.A., B 7, fo. 15ᵛ. [3] Y.C.A., C 6:8; *Y.C.R.* iv. 17-20.

and to £265 in the following year. In 1580-2 it dropped to a
£40 level, but by the end of Elizabeth's reign it was back to
between £145 and £170 each year.

The largest source of income was real estate. The traditional medieval source was the 'bridge rents', a stock of urban
houses, gardens and closes administered by the bridgemasters.
They accounted for £55 in 1486-7, and their yield remained
fairly level throughout the first half of the period, rising substantially under Elizabeth to reach a level of £120 to £130.
In real terms, however, inflation meant that these rents fell
in value, especially during the mid-sixteenth century. By
1562 the city fathers had to recognize that 'the most part'
of their urban properties cost more in repairs than they
yielded in rent. After various discussions, large numbers of
houses were sold in the winter of 1562-3. Records survive of
the sales carried out on a single day, when sixty-seven separate
parcels were disposed of; twenty-seven of the parcels are
known to have raised £243. 12s. 0d.[1] Pruned of these un-
economic properties, the bridge rents moved into a healthier
period; and furthermore, the 'bridge rents' income recorded
in the chamberlains' rolls no longer represented total receipts.
The rents tended to remain at traditional levels, and the corporation, like other landlords, solved the problem of erosion
by inflation by imposing large 'gressums' or entry fines rather
than by raising the rents. By the end of the century much
city income was in the form of 'casual receipts', and the £98
of such receipts in 1597-8 consisted mainly of gressums and
rents.

Furthermore, the corporation tried several times to increase
their rent-roll by enclosing and leasing parts of the common
lands, but sturdy opposition from the freemen always de-
feated them.[2] They were more successful with Tang Hall
Fields, which they leased from the prebendary of Friday-
thorpe in 1525, with the aim of sub-letting for profit. During
Elizabeth's reign they were paying the canon about £25 a
year for the lease, while from the sub-tenants they recouped
income rising gradually from £42 to £67. For a short period
they became more ambitious, and practised the same policy

[1] *Y.C.R.* vi. 43, 46 f.; Y.C.A., E 22, fos. 1-26.
[2] *V.C.H. York*, pp. 500 f.

with lands and even whole manors well away from the city, acquiring them for a term of years and then sub-letting. The account rolls for 1576–83 show a temporary increase in income from rural rents to between £72 and £88 a year, but for some reason the policy was abandoned by 1597. By that time another urban source was being exploited instead: the Castle Mills brought in £20 a year in 1597–9 and the Abbey Mills £6. 6s. 8d. in 1597–1600. Furthermore, the market tolls, which had been insignificant under Henry VII, were farmed out for £16. 13s. 4d. during most of Elizabeth's reign.

Next to property, the largest regular source of income was payments for the admission of new freemen. Total annual receipts from this source increased gradually from £34 in 1486–7 to a peak of £78 in 1599–1600. The other substantial income from freemen consisted of fines levied for exemption from civic office. Such fines regularly produced between £30 and £40, and therefore diminished in real value during the century. The reason was a change in the system. Under Henry VII a few rich men paid very large sums to avoid the expensive offices of chamberlain and sheriff, but by the end of the century, civic office was no longer desperately avoided by the wealthy, and instead standard fines were levied on those chamberlains who had not been bridgemasters or muremasters.

Under Henry VII there were two other substantial sources of income for the chamber. The King regularly remitted £40, and later £60, of the city's fee-farm, and this sum, though collected by the sheriffs, was transferred to the chamberlains. They also received the sums collected by the searchers of the craft guilds from their members as fines for trading and manufacturing offences. Such fines amounted to nearly 10 per cent of civic income in 1486–7 and 1501–2, but for some reason dwindled in real terms during the sixteenth century.

The income side of the Elizabethan rolls is complicated by the presence, at their head, of a large and increasing item, 'Treasure in store'. It covers not only the balance handed over by the outgoing chamberlains, but also a series of special items which were carried through the year and handed on at its end. With one exception they consisted of the city plate, which was beginning to increase through bequests, and of cash bequests made for the benefit of the corporation or of freemen. Considerable sums were involved: two bequests totalling £100 were handed over in 1561, but by 1602 they had increased to twelve bequests totalling £605.

Most of the twelve bequests were of a kind new to the city, the revolving loan fund. The aim of the testator was to help citizens short of capital, especially young tradesmen wishing to set up their own shop or business. A lump sum would be bequeathed to the corporation or other trustees, who were to lend it out in parcels, at low interest or none at all. W. K. Jordan has discovered no such endowments in Yorkshire prior to 1577, but the earliest at York occurred in or by 1560, when Nicholas Girdlyngton, gentleman, left £40 to the corporation 'to be lent gratis to poor citizens'.[1] Then in 1566 Sir Thomas White created a fund to pay nearly £100, to go in turn to twenty-three specified corporations. The money was to provide ten-year loans of £25, free of interest, to poor clothiers or other tradesmen.[2] The York chamberlains received £100 under this scheme in 1577 and another £100 in 1600. The citizens and their neighbours were slow to emulate White and Girdlyngton. In 1585 William Drewe, butcher and city councillor, gave £40 to be lent to butchers, but otherwise bequests of this kind became common only at the end of the century:

James Cottrell	1595	£100
Alderman Robert Askwith I	1597	£20
Alderman Robert Brooke	1598–9	£10
Christopher Turner	1600	£20
John Burley	1601	£100[3]

Such were the corporation's major assets and sources of revenue. On the debit side, their greatest expenditure was on the fees, wages, and liveries paid to the mayor and to the permanent officials. The mayor's annual fee remained at £50

---

[1] W. K. Jordan, *The Charities of Rural England 1480–1660* (London, 1961), p. 292; Widdrington, *Analecta Eboracensia*, p. 296; Y.C.A., B 23, fo. 4ᵛ.

[2] *V.C.H. York*, p. 438; Jordan, *Charities of Rural England*, p. 292; Drake, *Eboracum*, p. 221.

[3] Listed, but without dates, in Widdrington, *Analecta Eboracensia*, p. 296. Further, William Woller set up a £100 loan fund in 1597, but under the merchants' company: *The York Mercers and Merchant Adventurers 1356–1917*, ed. M. Sellers (Surtees Soc. cxxix, 1918), p. 288.

throughout the Tudor age, but other components of the wages bill were more variable. Before the Reformation over £40 was paid annually to a large staff of civic chaplains. This expenditure dwindled almost to nothing by 1561-2, but from 1581 it was replaced by a preacher's fee of £40. Consequently the total regular wages bill, about £150 under Henry VII, fell to £115 in 1561-2 and then climbed to over £180 at the end of the century. In real terms, therefore, the declared stipends of the mayor and the secular officers fell considerably; but with payment of wages, as with income from property, the later rolls are misleading. The draft account books for 1597-9 allow a breakdown of the large 'foreign payments' item in the rolls, and reveal that by then the fixed stipends, especially of the mayor and recorder, were being supplemented by substantial entertainment allowances in the form of hogsheads of wine. In addition, the chamberlains had to meet wages and expenses of a less predictable kind. Besides claims from the MPs after every session of Parliament, there were often bills of expenses from aldermen and recorders visiting London on corporation business. The most costly years were 1581-2 and 1598-9, when parliamentary expenses exceeded £70. In comparison, other variable fees and wages were small, a few pounds being spent yearly on the reception of noblemen and justices, on travelling minstrels, players and bear-wards, and on pensions for retired councillors or their widows.

Poor relief payments by the corporation were always modest, whereas expenditure on civic privilege and prestige was sometimes considerable. Nearly £27 was spent in 1580-1 on making a great mace and a case for it. Royal favours could also be costly. £13 was spent to obtain letters patent in 1486, though it was money well spent, since the letters granted an annual fee-farm remission of £60. Another £14. 7s. 4d. was spent in 1523 on securing a local monopoly of the export of wools and fells, and £44 on a new charter in 1563. The citizens were probably relieved that royal visits were rare, for Henry VII's first visit in 1486 cost them £35. 18s. 6d. in preparations and £30. 3s. 8d. on presents to the King and his retinue. A more frequent expense was the equipping of soldiers conscripted by the government; normally, however,

such military expenses were recouped by levying assessments
on the parishes. The only other substantial expenditure was
on maintaining civic property, notably the walls, bridges,
pavements and causeways. The cost of repairs varied greatly,
depending on their urgency and on the state of the chamber's
finances: £168 was spent in 1580-1, but only £12 in 1602-3.

7

The system of government outlined in this chapter did not
apply within the liberties or exempt areas within the city.
Of the two secular liberties, much the more important was
the castle, which had lost most of its military functions, but
remained a useful headquarters for the high sheriff of the
county and his officials, conveniently located within the
county town but outside its jurisdiction. Its seven acres contained the county gaol and law courts, though not the county
gallows: most condemned criminals were executed at
'Tyburn', on Knavesmire. The other secular liberty, the
quarter acre Davy Hall in Davygate, had originally been the
residence and gaol of the larderer of Galtres Forest. It passed
into the hands of the Thwaites family, and then by marriage
to the Fairfaxes in the early sixteenth century. The corporation tried to override the Fairfaxes' jurisdiction in 1533, but
presumably without success, and by the late seventeenth
century its exempt status had made it a popular residence of
poor and unfree shoemakers.[1]

Before the Reformation, York was also honeycombed with
religious liberties. The Minster, St. Mary's Abbey, St. Leonard's Hospital, and the seven priories were apparently completely independent of the corporation, and the many meetings
and arbitrations held in the friaries by citizens often represented a deliberate choice of 'neutral' ground. Craftsmen
living in those areas had no need to take up the freedom of
the city or to join a craft guild; two of the guilds, at least,
met this threat by ordering their members to give no work to
inhabitants of the liberties.[2] No more is heard of these

---

[1] Widdrington, *Analecta Eboracensia*, pp. 249-60; P.R.O., C1/790/29; Davies,
Walks through York, pp. 27 f.
[2] *York Memorandum Book*, ii. 285; *Y.C.R.* iii. 91, 183.

privileges of the seven priories after their dissolution in 1536–8, but the three greater liberties retained theirs until the nineteenth century. The reason was probably that it suited the interest of the Crown to maintain islands of exemption in the city, for St. Mary's became the home of the Council in the North as soon as the community surrendered, while the revived Royal Mint of 1545–54 was located in the former buildings of St. Leonard's, the site of which became known in consequence as Mint Yard. As late as 1820 a resident of the Yard testified 'that it was a privileged place', and 'that any unfreeman carrying on business there never was disturbed'.[1]

The most important, and best recorded, of the liberties was that of the Dean and Chapter. They enjoyed 'sole and absolute jurisdiction' in two areas within the city, as well as in other extramural areas: the Minster Garth, or cathedral close proper, and the Bedern, or College of Vicars Choral.[2] The inhabitants of the liberty had their own judicial system: separate sessions of the peace were held every quarter, a court leet and view of frankpledge every six months, and a court for debts, trespasses, and small offences every three weeks.[3] The city coroners were excluded from the Minster Garth, and the corporation petitioned Parliament in vain to allow the craft guilds' searchers to enter the close.[4]

The 'sole and absolute jurisdiction' of the Dean and Chapter within the close is not in doubt; what is uncertain is how far it extended to other parts of the city. A charter of Richard II had excluded from the corporation's power not only the close and Bedern, but also all houses without the close which belonged to the prebendaries or their tenants. The Minster about 1533 claimed jurisdiction over its appropriated parish churches in the city, over the whole parish of St. Michael-le-Belfrey, and over all or part of several streets, notably Petergate and Stonegate.[5] It was obviously of vital importance to the citizens whether or no the Minster liberties extended to

---

[1] Y.M.L., F1/1/4s, fo. 6ʳ.　　　　[2] Y.M.L., L1(7), p. 526.
[3] *A List of the Noblemen and Gentlemen in the Commission of the Peace for the Liberty of St. Peter* (York, 1789), p. 15. The evidence is late, but Y.M.L., F1/3/1, shows the three-weekly courts in action in 1445–6.
[4] *Y.C.R.* viii. 23 f., 82.
[5] J. S. Purvis, *A Mediaeval Act Book* (York, n.d.), p. 44.

these churches and houses; but unfortunately the evidence is conflicting. Some of the wealthier craftsmen of Petergate and Stonegate in the early Tudor period do not figure in the freemen's register, and a claim in 1511 that St. Lawrence's church was within the Minster Liberty was at least partially conceded by the corporation.[1] In 1599, on the other hand, the corporation laid claim to forfeited goods in Stonegate, which the Dean and Chapter also claimed as owners of the house in question.[2] By the early nineteenth century the Minster liberty was clearly confined to the Yard and Bedern, but there were hints that it had not always been so.[3] Probably the position in Tudor times was that a wide medieval interpretation of the liberty was being gradually challenged more frequently, and that eventually it was eroded away until only the close remained.

York was typical of corporate towns in the friction displayed between the jurisdiction of the corporation and that of the exempt areas. It was also typical in its success in gradually reducing the scope of the cathedral liberty, for the sixteenth century was a propitious time for corporate towns to seek Crown support against the pretensions of bishops and cathedral chapters. The changes in the nature of the city's government, however, were more important than those in its precise geographical extent. The apparent continuity of that government from 1396 to 1835 masked a gradual tightening of control by the mayor and aldermen, seen especially in the ending of tumultuous popular elections, in the reorganization of the common council in 1517, and in the ending of all pretence that parliamentary elections involved the burgesses at large. The narrowness of that oligarchy was demonstrated in 1597, when in a disputed election for knights of the shire, a crowd of some 6,000 voters assembled at the castle, while less than a mile away the election of burgesses to represent the city and Ainsty was decided by an assembly of sixty-one.[4] It has been said that 'the continuous growth of

---

[1] D. M. Palliser and D. G. Selwyn, 'The stock of a York stationer, 1538', *The Library*, 5th ser. xxvii (1972), 208; *Y.C.R.* iii. 35.
[2] Y.C.A., B 32, fo. 48ᵛ.
[3] Y.M.L., D 2; F1/1/4s.
[4] Neale, *Eliz. House of Commons*, p. 83; Y.C.A., B 31, fos. 297–8.

oligarchic magistracy is the most obvious theme in English urban history from 1500 to 1700', and certainly the example of York does nothing to undermine that assertion.[1]

[1] Clark and Slack, *Crisis and Order in English Towns*, p. 25.

IV

THE OFFICE-HOLDERS

> Understandyng that ye mynd tellecte George Gaill to
> the rome of maryaltie, the same beyng under tresourer
> of the mynt shall not be hable to supple bothe chargs
> . . . therefore we requyre you that at the contemplacon
> hereof . . . ye will forbere telecte hym yeur Maier.
>
> *Protector Somerset* to York Corporation, 1549[1]

The councillors were the most powerful, wealthy and influential group of citizens, and for that reason more is known of their careers and their personalities than of any others. The leading inhabitants of the liberties are of more importance for a study of the county or the diocese,[2] but within the jurisdiction of the city the corporation were easily the most influential, in spite of occasional interference by the archbishop or the lord president. The present chapter attempts a brief analysis of the 225 men who were aldermen, members of the Twenty-Four, or both, at any time between 1500 and 1600.

The city council included, unsurprisingly, nearly all the richest citizens, for only such men could afford to hold office when councillors were expected to meet large deficits temporarily out of their own purses, and probably only the rich and powerful would have been sufficiently respected in the thankless task of keeping law and order. A man's 'worship' or respect was equated with his wealth, and casual references suggest well-understood rules about the level of wealth necessary for particular offices. In the early Tudor period, for instance, several men were spared election as sheriffs simply

---

[1] *Y.C.R.* v. 8 f.

[2] Reid, *King's Council in the North*, has much useful information on councillors, and Cross, *Puritan Earl*, is an excellent biography of one President. Short biographies of some other Crown officials resident in York are in English and Barr, 'Records formerly in St. Mary's Tower', parts II and III. A monograph on one resident archbishop is Dickens, *Robert Holgate*, and one on a leading lawyer is J. D. M. Derrett, *Henry Swinburne* (Borth. P. xlvi, 1973).

for being worth less than £100 in goods, a floor which could be raised as high as £200.[1] Nevertheless, wealth was never an automatic passport to civic office. Alan Staveley, elected a chamberlain in 1494, was only a fortnight later blackballed by the corporation from being sheriff until he should be 'able and sufficient as well in reson and discrecion and as in havour of his guds'. Yet five years later they endorsed his election as sheriff, while on his election as alderman in 1502 he was 'right discret and honest'. Presumably time and experience had tempered youthful indiscretion.[2] Although criticisms and insults were often directed at the council from below, they almost always reflected grievances against specific measures or particular aldermen, like Nicholas Roger's outburst in an alehouse that 'he wolde not awayl his bonet to non aldermen except iij for he sayd they gafe hym nether mete ne drinke'.[3] Never does the dominance of the city by an élite seem to have been challenged in favour of a more democratic system. It was generally accepted that political power should be distributed according to wealth, and there were no fundamental attacks on this even by the unprivileged.

This attitude can be partly explained by the prevailing emphasis on obedience and subordination in the Tudor period, but in part it may have stemmed from the oligarchy's ability to recruit new families. The 225 councillors during the century had 168 different surnames, and thus represented at least 168 families. Power was shared by more families than in other large provincial cities. Taking as a criterion the number of families sharing the mayoralty in Elizabeth's reign, York's total (thirty-three families among thirty-nine mayors) was substantially higher than those of Exeter and Norwich and marginally higher than Bristol's. Only the smaller cities of Chester and Winchester had mayoralties as open as York's. The corollary of this openness was an absence of dynasties on the York council. Only in twenty-six cases were a father and son both councillors, and there was probably no case of a family represented on the council for three successive generations.[4]

[1] Y.C.A., B 7, fo. 142^r; B 8, fos. 96^r, 117^r; B 9, fo. 60^v.
[2] Y.C.A., B 7, fo. 108^r; *Y.C.R.* ii. 179.
[3] *Y.C.R.* iii. 36. [4] Palliser, 'York', pp. 167–9.

Since a place on the council was not hereditary, the way was open to lesser freemen to push their way into the ranks of the oligarchy if they could acquire the necessary wealth. One such may have been Alderman Metcalf, whose origins are obscure; for in 1500 a Yorkshire knight told the mayor, 'I wald ye take no sample by a carle, your neghbour, John Metcalf, which ye knawe is comen lightly up and of smale substance and wilbe maid glade shortly to knawe his negh-bours for his better.'[1] And the career of another alderman, John Beane, certainly suggests a rise from obscurity to the top of the civic ladder. The son of a capper, he became free as an innholder in 1523-4, and just afterwards was taxed on wages of £1 a year. From these humble beginnings he rose to be twice mayor, an alderman for the record period of forty years (1540-80), and the lord of a rural manor.[2]

How far were vacancies on the council filled by lesser free-men who prospered, like Beane, and how far by men from outside the city? The birth places are known of seventy-seven of the city councillors, of whom thirty-nine were natives of the city, and twenty-eight others were Yorkshire men, mostly from rural areas of the county. A handful originated further afield, including Christopher Harbert, the son of a Monmouth-shire man who had settled in Yorkshire.[3] The most distant arrival was Martin Soza, goldsmith, who was 'born in Sapher in Spayne', probably Zafra, became free of York in 1530-1, and was naturalized in 1535.[4] Soza may have been held back by his foreign birth, for while he was sheriff in 1545-6 and then joined the Twenty-Four, he did not progress any further. He was certainly an exotic exception on the council, though it would be wrong to treat the sample of seventy-seven as typical of the whole council in their origins. No less than half of the sample were born within the city, but this result is distorted by including all the councillors who were made free by patrimony. There is reason to believe that almost all citi-zens who did not take up their freedom by patrimony were

---

[1] *Y.C.R.* ii. 156.   [2] Palliser, 'York', pp. 170, 192.
[3] R. Davies, 'A memoir of Sir Thomas Herbert', *Y.A.J.* i (1870), 183.
[4] Bodley, Dodsworth 161, fo. 17ʳ; *Register of Freemen*, i. 250; Y.C.A., E 23, fo. 103ᵛ. The last has a copy of the letters patent of denization, which are not in *L.P. Hen. VIII.*

born outside York,[1] in which case the proportion of natives on the city council can be inferred as not more than a fifth, rather than a half.

Information about councillors' fathers is even scantier, and the York archives naturally provide more information about the fathers who were York natives than about those who were not, thus ensuring another biased sample. A search has revealed the trade or status of the fathers of only sixty-one councillors. Forty-seven were York men, twenty-three of them city councillors like their sons, and the rest lesser citizens. The other fathers included ten gentlemen, one yeoman, one husbandman, a mayor of Doncaster, and an alderman of Hull. It thus seems probable that a majority of York city councillors originated in other parts of the shire, and the small sample suggests that their fathers were often gentry. The evidence is too scanty, however, to show whether it was chiefly the traditional younger sons who came to York to make a business career. Alderman Robert Askwith I, from Potgrange in Masham parish, was an eldest son, although a younger brother, Thomas, followed him to York and rose to be one of the Twenty-Four. A family which did conform to the practice of putting only younger sons into trade was that of Hall, of Leventhorpe near Leeds. Robert, the head of this family of minor gentry, was succeeded at Leventhorpe by his eldest son William, while his third son, another Robert, became a York merchant, and rose to be mayor in 1541-2 and 1557-8. William, in turn, left the family home to his eldest son Michael, while Ralph, his second son, became a York merchant, and was mayor in 1558-9 (succeeding his uncle) and 1576-7. George, another son, also became a merchant of York and rose to the Twenty-Four. Finally, while Michael was followed at Leventhorpe by his eldest son William, his fifth son Henry also became a York merchant, and was mayor in 1600-1 and 1610-11.[2] Thus in three successive generations the family sent at least one younger son to York to make good in trade.

[1] See below, p. 128.
[2] York historians have differed about the Halls' relationships. This account is based on J. Hunter, *Familiae Minorum Gentium*, ed. J. W. Clay, iii (Harleian Soc., xxxix, 1895), 941-2.

2

Although the oligarchy was open, perpetually recruited from new families, this provides only half the picture. When new councillors entered the governing circle, they frequently became bound to the others by marriage, providing a social cement among the governing class where blood relationships were often so lacking. Numerous aldermen's wills in which the testator left large legacies, or an executorship or supervisorship, to his 'brother', another alderman, show how these relationships could indeed bind the council together. The number of intermarriages among the members of the corporation was quite astonishing. It has been possible to construct two interlocking genealogical trees linking nearly half the sixteenth-century aldermen and a fifth of the Twenty-Four.[1] Many other councillors were united into smaller kinship groups; for instance, thirty-two other aldermen were related to at least one other city councillor, so that only a quarter of the aldermen had no known relationship to other members of the governing body. The city council took official cognisance of the importance of marital, as well as of blood, relationships. In assessing a pension for Robert Paycoke II they bore in mind not only that he and his father had been mayor, but also that he had married the daughter of another mayor.[2]

It is difficult to say how many councillors and their children intermarried respectively with the gentry and with fellow citizens, partly because information about wives' parentage is often lacking, and partly because the borderline between gentry and citizens was blurred by the gentle origin of some aldermen. There are, however, instances where a marriage must clearly have represented a social rise for a family hitherto entirely urban. Alderman Beane, the capper's son, lived to see his daughter, Mary, wed Anthony Wharton, a Westmorland esquire distantly related to the Lords Wharton, and it was from their marriage that the modern dukes of Northumberland were descended on the female side.[3] Alderman Birkeby, another York native, married into the gentry

---

[1] Palliser, 'York', Table 6.   [2] Y.C.A., B 33, fos. 276-7.
[3] *Reg. Corpus Christi Guild*, ed. Skaife, p. 66 n.; Davies, *Walks through York*, pp. 184-7.

himself, his first wife being the granddaughter of Sir Brian Stapleton of Wighill, while his second wife was the widow of a Yorkshire esquire.[1]

The marriages of councillors, whatever their success in binding families together in alliance, were not always a success in producing sufficient heirs. The openness of the council chamber to new families suggests either that councillors had too few sons to create urban dynasties, or that their sons did not follow them into civic careers in sufficient numbers. There is no completely satisfactory source for answering the question, and the best available is the mentions of sons in wills. The seventy-seven surviving wills of aldermen during the sixteenth century suggest an average 1.35 male heirs before 1550 and 1.75 in the second half-century. As the wills of York's fifteenth-century mayors reveal an average of only 1.09 sons, the number of surviving heirs was rising during the fifteenth and sixteenth centuries, but was still not very high.[2] However, statistics from wills are minimal figures, generally understating the number of sons.[3] The most important reason is that an eldest son and heir may not be mentioned because he is already provided for, and at least one of the wills analysed above is known to suffer from this omission. It has also been suggested that in pre-industrial societies generally, only some 60 per cent of families would have male heirs, in which case York's Tudor aldermen, 65 per cent of whom before 1550 had male heirs, and 74 per cent after 1550, were relatively fortunate.[4]

A number of aldermen left provision in their wills for the 'governing' by friends or relatives of sons who were still under age. This establishes that at least 14 of the 52 male heirs in the first half of the century (27%) and 12 out of 60 in the second (20%) were orphaned under age. These proportions are much lower than those discovered for London by

[1] Skaife, 'Civic Officials'; J. E. Neale, ed., *History of Parliament, 1558–1603* (forthcoming).

[2] J. N. Bartlett, 'Some Aspects of the Economy of York in the Later Middle Ages, 1300–1500', University of London Ph.D. thesis, 1958, p. 259.

[3] G. Williams, *Medieval London: from Commune to Capital* (London, 1963), pp. 316–7. He is criticizing S. L. Thrupp, *The Merchant Class of Medieval London* (Ann Arbor, 1962), from which this method is taken.

[4] J. Goody, 'Strategies of heirship', *Comparative Studies in Society and History*, xv (1973), 16.

Professor Thrupp, but they are again minimum figures only.[1] Some aldermen may have tacitly left to their widows the guardianship of minors. It is not possible to say how many of these orphans died before reaching maturity, so reducing the number of aldermen's heirs who could themselves hope to marry and carry on the line.

Of those who did reach maturity, not all followed their fathers into trade. The professions of eighty-nine sons of sixteenth-century aldermen are definitely known,[2] and of these, seventy (79%) took up a trade in the city, a proportion rather higher than the two-thirds found in late medieval London.[3] Three took up trades (capping and glove-making) which would effectively disbar them from becoming aldermen themselves, but the others all became merchants or other socially acceptable traders; yet those who actually succeeded in emulating their fathers' careers were few. Of the 67 aldermen's sons who grew up and took up one of the major York trades, only 13 became aldermen themselves. There can be little doubt that many were forced to remain excluded from the city's governing circles: that there was, in fact, a situation of 'downward mobility' in which, as abler or more pushing men from outside the city joined the council, or rose into it from among the lesser freemen, many aldermen's sons were unable to maintain the rank of their fathers.

Only nineteen aldermen's sons (21%) did not follow their fathers into trade. Two practised law, one of them the now-forgotten poet Christopher Brooke, and six entered the church, including Christopher's brother Samuel, who was successively chaplain to Prince Henry, James I, and Charles I, and later archdeacon of Coventry. The Brooke brothers have a small place in literary history, for Christopher was a close friend of John Donne, and when Donne secretly married, it was Samuel who officiated and Christopher who gave the bride away. Samuel's career in the church, successful as it was, was outshone by Thomas Morton (1564–1659), whose father Richard was one of the Twenty-Four. Thomas went

---

[1] Thrupp, *Merchant Class of Medieval London*, p. 202.

[2] Here the group differs from that used earlier. It includes sons of aldermen who died intestate and of aldermen who died after 1600.

[3] Thrupp, *Merchant Class*, p. 205.

to Cambridge, and then in 1598 'his provident Father . . . procured a good Parsonage for him, called *Long Marston*'.[1] This was the parish which witnessed the decisive battle of 1644, but long before then Thomas had left his rectory behind, being promoted successively to the deaneries of Gloucester and Winchester and the sees of Chester, Lichfield, and Durham.

Nine others—10 per cent of all identified sons of aldermen —entered the gentry, illustrating the classic use of urban wealth to buy rural land and status. They were taking part in an exodus which had begun at least by the thirteenth century, one of the earliest cases being that of the well-known Fair-faxes.[2] Not surprisingly, the richest and most powerful alder-men had the best chance of setting up their sons in this way. Sir George Lawson's son Thomas, who held at least two manors in the Vale of York, lived away from the city as a country gentleman, even though he became an alderman like his father.[3] Francis, elder son of Alderman Gayle, the city mintmaster, became an esquire and lived at Acomb Grange near York, an estate which remained in the family for at least two more generations.[4] The common clerk Leonard Belt fathered an even more distinguished family. His sons Robert and William, though knighted, remained members of the corporation, but both founded families of gentry in the sur-rounding countryside, the Belts of Bossall and Overton respectively. Not all gentry families built on city money proved so stable, however. Christopher Harbert, the alder-man from Monmouthshire, came to York about 1550, and he and his son Thomas proved successful as merchant-aldermen. Thomas was able to amass considerable Yorkshire estates before his death in 1614, and to hand on to his son Christo-pher a country seat at North Otterington and numerous other properties. Christopher, however, quickly fell into debt, and by the time of his own death at the early age of forty had sold his entire inheritance.[5]

[1] R. Baddily, *The Life of Dr. Thomas Morton* (York, 1669), p. 8.
[2] *V.C.H. York*, p. 45.   [3] Palliser, 'York', pp. 181 f.
[4] Skaife, 'Civic Officials', *sub* Gale.
[5] P.R.O., C142/669/27; Cliffe, *Yorkshire Gentry*, pp. 163 f.

3

Increasingly, however, it became less necessary to leave a town and set up on a country estate before acquiring the coveted title of 'esquire' or 'gentleman'. A growing number of men were recognized as gentlemen, or at least assumed the title, while living in towns; some were gentry of the traditional kind merely choosing not to live on their estates, but a larger number were professional men, or even merchants, striving to join them. The city councillors of York themselves had ambitions in this direction.

At the beginning of the Tudor age the only gentry involved in civic government were the legal officials, especially the recorders. Even with men like these, the strict social classification of the age was not always willing to concede them the title. In 1486 a kinsman of the common clerk John Harington, described him as 'a poore gentilman' from Eastrington near Howden, but admitted that his status was marginal, for Harington's father was 'a poore gentilman borne thof he never werr taken heir but for a yoman'.[1] But from the 1490s, the aldermen and the recorder were commonly referred to in the council minutes as 'master', the designation of a gentleman or an esquire. In the early 1530s it became usual to call the sheriffs 'master' also, and soon the Twenty-Four claimed the privilege. In the 1560s it began to be used for the chamberlains as well, but at this point further extension of the privilege was halted for at least two centuries, as Drake's description of the office of chamberlain reveals:

As a feather to the place, the title *master*, or *Mr.* is always prefixed to their names . . . ever after. In *London*, they are so well bred as to give this appellation of Mr. to a *porter*, or a *cobler*; but in *York*, when any one is called so that has not passed this office, or is of so mean an account as not to be thought worthy of it, *Mr. quoth'a, pray who was lord-mayor when he was chamberlain?* an opprobious question often used in this city by the vulgar.[2]

Once the title of 'master' had percolated down as far as the chamberlains, the senior councillors probably felt the need to go one rank higher to distinguish themselves again. So towards the end of the sixteenth century formal documents

[1] *Y.C.R.* i. 169.   [2] Drake, *Eboracum*, p. 183.

began to style the aldermen and the recorder esquires, while the Twenty-Four remained gentlemen.

A very few aldermen achieved the rank of knighthood. Mayor Todd and Alderman York were knighted when the King came to York in 1487, thus becoming members of a national élite which was then less than 400 strong. Knighthood was, of course, widely regarded as a burden rather than a privilege, and it is significant that within three years the two were granted life annuities of £20 and £40 respectively from the Hull customs.[1] It is not surprising that in 1500 Mayor Neleson and Alderman Gilliot were fined rather than accept the honour, nor that three years later Neleson fined for it again.[2] But in 1501 Gilliot accepted, becoming one of the only two York aldermen knighted during the sixteenth century.[3] The other was George Lawson, knighted about 1531, though presumably for his services to the Crown rather than for his civic position.[4] From his death in 1543 there was no knight on the bench until 1603, when King James knighted Mayor Robert Watter on his way south from Scotland.

Civic knights were thus always exceptional; but their colleagues, with their assumption of the style of gentlemen and esquires, were demonstrating their dominance within the city. The only inhabitants who could rank with them, or even above them, were the leading professional men who lived in the city liberties, and especially the lawyers and surgeons of Minster Yard. These men stood somewhat apart from the civic hierarchy of York since they formed the apex of a separate social pyramid. But as it was impossible for two groups in the same city to take equal place at ceremonies and services, the professional men came just ahead of the city councillors on such occasions. Notaries public, for instance, were 'to give place to the Sheriffes of Yorke . . . but shall goe before all other cittiezens, yea such as have past that office'.[5] Their marriages, however, in an age when 'disparagement' was

[1] *C.P.R. 1485–94*, pp. 256–7, 303.
[2] W. J. Kaye, 'Yorkshiremen who declined to take up their knighthood', *Y.A.J.* xxxi (1932–4), pp. 362, 364.
[3] W. A. Shaw, *The Knights of England* (London, 1906), i. 147.
[4] ibid. ii. 46 dates his dubbing *c.*1527–9, but this is unlikely. He is regularly styled 'Sir' in *L.P. Hen. VIII* only from 1532.
[5] C. I. A. Ritchie, *The Ecclesiastical Courts of York* (Arbroath, 1956), p. 51.

so frowned upon, show that the two groups were much on a level. The daughter of William Harryngton, mayor during the Pilgrimage of Grace, married William Fawkes, the archbishop's registrar, and Alderman Dyneley wedded the daughter of Christopher Beeseley, another York notary.[1]

More unequal were the relations between the city councillors, even those from gentle Yorkshire families, and the great lords of the north with whom they curried favour. *Yorke, Yorke for my Monie* celebrates a series of archery matches held there, probably in 1582, by the Earls of Cumberland and Essex. The writer was cheered to see

> . . . lords and aldermen so agree,
> With such according cummunaltie . . .

but the one-sidedness of the relationship emerges in his praise of 'the good earle of Cumberlande'

> Whose noble minde so courteously
> Acquaintes himself with the communaltie,
> To the glory of his nobilitie . . .[2]

Such relationships cannot, however, have seemed so unequal to a baron like William, Lord Eure, who had to borrow £40 from a York bowyer, the future Alderman Criplyng, and was sued by him for alleged non-payment.[3] And with the lesser country gentry, as has been seen, city councillors often intermarried and were on terms of equality. They might also have an equal friendship with the great ecclesiastics of the city. Before the Reformation it was not unusual for councillors to dine with canons of the Minster,[4] and though the archbishops were then somewhat grand and aloof, their Protestant successors, poorer and more often resident, were less condescending. Archbishop Young asked Mayor Robert Paycok I to act as godfather to his son, and Archbishop Hutton could refer to one alderman as 'myne ould verie good frend'.[5]

---

[1] *Reg. Corpus Christi Guild*, ed. Skaife, pp. 168 n., 236 n.

[2] W. Elderton, *Yorke, Yorke for my Monie* (London, 1584); *The Ballads and Songs of Yorkshire*, ed. C. J. D. Ingledew (London, 1860), pp. 117-18; E. M. Tenison, *Elizabethan England*, v (Leamington, 1936), 113-8.

[3] P.R.O., C1/1426/51-2 [1553-5].   [4] *Y.C.R.* ii. 116.

[5] *Y.C.R.* vi. 131-2; P.R.O., REQ. 2/159/156.

4

There were good reasons why the city councillors should have assumed the style of gentlemen. They were often either of gentry stock themselves, or married into it; some set up their children as country squires to begin new gentle families. Furthermore, councillors came increasingly to own rural property—one of the tests of gentle status—while remaining active traders.

Investment in country property was not new, but it became heavy in the late fifteenth century, perhaps because trading opportunities were narrowing and urban rents falling.[1] It must have become normal by 1544, when the council agreed not to fine 'any of the seyd presens in wantyng of hys servaunt is [in?] ridyng to his fermald ne adjonyng to this City'.[2] It is difficult to say how much rural property was held by councillors at different times, since many references to land owned are given with either no indications, or else unrealistic ones, of area and value. In spite of its drawbacks, the best method is perhaps to consider the number of manors which councillors owned. These must represent substantial investment in rural property, even though they would vary greatly in size and value. Alderman Thomas Neleson (d. c. 1484) acquired the manor of Skelton by marriage, and it remained in the hands of his descendants until 1573, while his son Alderman William Neleson, besides inheriting Skelton, acquired a country estate at Riccall.[3] The Nelesons were exceptional in their property holdings, but soon the acquisition of manors became more common. Between 1525 and 1600 at least fifteen and a half manors were held by aldermen, in some cases being owned in turn by more than one councillor. The largest collector, William Robinson, acquired eight and a half Yorkshire manors between about 1580 and his death in 1614, while his colleague Robert Watter showed equal zeal in amassing ecclesiastical properties and rights, acquiring the rectories or tithes of four country parishes, as well as two manors and other properties, before his death in 1612.[4]

[1] *V.C.H. York*, p. 113. [2] *Y.C.R.* iv. 99.
[3] *V.C.H. North Riding*, ii. 169; *Reg. Corpus Christi Guild*, ed. Skaife, p. 114 n.
[4] Palliser, 'York', pp. 203–5.

Regularly living outside the city was, however, another matter. Alderman Thomas Lawson (1560-8) seems normally to have been non-resident, but his behaviour was very much resented.[1] When Alderman Allyn moved to Gateforth about 1580, he was given the choice between resigning and returning.[2] But gradually residence came to be less strictly enforced. In or before 1596 Thomas Appleyarde II moved back to his ancestral village of Heslington, but remained an alderman, in spite of criticism, until his death.[3] Sir Robert Watter died at his country seat at Cundall in 1612 while still an alderman, and Christopher Concett, alderman from 1597 until his death in 1615, seems to have lived throughout at Riccall, except when mayor.[4]

The mayor was in a special position, because of his need to be constantly accessible as an embodiment of justice and civic dignity. Not only was he to reside throughout his year of office in York, but actually within the 'city', which in Tudor parlance meant the walled city. Robert Criplyng, mayor in 1579-80, lived in the suburb of Layerthorpe, only just outside one of the posterns, but this was not enough. The aldermen complained that when elected he had promised to come to dwell within the city by Easter, 'for otherwise he could not have bene elected to the said office', and yet he continued to live the whole year 'without the precynctes of this Citie; a thyng never hard of before'.[5] Criplyng was under attack chiefly for his recusant sympathies, but his unprecedented choice of a mayoral home may have contributed significantly to his unpopularity. Certainly the commons took prompt action when the situation was likely to be repeated ten years later. Thomas Jackson, of St. Olave's parish, was about to be elected, and the commons made him promise that, if chosen, he would live within the city with the sword and mace during his mayoralty.[6]

Rural and even suburban homes remained the exception; nearly all councillors lived within the walls, and within that area they concentrated in the richer parishes in the centre.[7]

[1] *Y.C.R.* vi. 26, 101.   [2] *Y.C.R.* viii. 39, 48 f.
[3] Y.C.A., B 31, fos. 190^r, 196^v; B 32, fo. 4^r.
[4] Skaife, 'Civic officials', *sub* Watter; *Reg. Corpus Christi Guild*, p. 317 n.
[5] *Y.C.R.* viii. 28.   [6] Y.C.A., B 30, fo. 76^r.
[7] Palliser, 'York', p. 197 and map.

Where the locations of their houses are known, they were nearly always situated in the same few main streets, notably Micklegate, Ousegate, Pavement, Coney Street, Stonegate, and Petergate, and as the annual Corpus Christi plays were performed along just these streets, it was not difficult for the aldermen to hire performances outside their own doors.[1] But their house-ownership was not usually confined to a home for themselves, as urban rents seem to have formed a normal part of their income. John Gilliot II, by his will in 1509, left fourteen houses and an unspecified number of other city 'landes'. John North in 1558 made specific bequests of nineteen houses, nine closes, two gardens, two orchards, a bowling alley, and a dovecote in the city, while Thomas Harper died in 1567 seised of seventeen tenements and cottages and two gardens, besides the reversion of the Greyfriars.[2] Some of these houses were kept as family homes. Thomas Appleyarde I lived in a capital messuage in Coney Street, and also owned a house round the corner in High Ousegate in which his son Thomas II lived. The father's will provided that his widow should take over the Ousegate house, while his son should move into the family home.[3]

5

The city oligarchs were, then, residents in York and urban landlords, though many also owned rural properties. This way of life marked them off from most of the Yorkshire country gentry, but it was not unknown for 'true' gentry to live in cities, particularly if they held office under the Crown, as several did with the Council in the North. Furthermore, the city councillors were often members of the gentry class by birth. What really distinguished them from the gentry, in the eyes of social conservatives, was their source of income. They might own property on a large scale, but their chief financial support came from trade. Merchants, according to

[1] A. J. Mill, 'The stations of the York Corpus Christi play', *Y.A.J.* xxxvii (1948-51), 492-502.

[2] *Test Ebor.* v. 14-17; B.I.H.R., prob. reg. xv (2), fo. 289; P.R.O., C142/150/157.

[3] B.I.H.R., prob. reg. xxi, fo. 441.

this philosophy, ranked above mere craftsmen but below the gentry.

By these standards, York's council was of even lower social status than those of some other towns, for although it was dominated by merchants, they shared power with a considerable number of mere craftsmen. Of the one hundred and six aldermen during the sixteenth century, sixty were merchants proper, ten were drapers and four were haberdashers, mercantile rather than handicraft occupations. Altogether, then, seventy-four (70%) of the aldermen were merchants and wholesale traders, while six more were lawyers and gentlemen, but the other twenty-six were craftsmen and retailers—four goldsmiths, four tailors and hosiers, three pewterers, and so on. The spread of occupations on the bench was still restricted; of over ninety separate trades and crafts practised in York, only eighteen were represented there, and more than half the aldermen were merchants, whereas among the freemen as a whole the proportion was only one in ten. Even so, the corporation was less dominated by merchants than were other towns of the same size. Merchants provided 72 per cent of the Elizabethan mayors of Norwich, 86 per cent in Bristol, and 92 per cent at Exeter,[1] whereas at York they accounted for 19 or 20 out of 39, or exactly one half. In relative terms, the Tudor age was clearly an ebb period for the influence of York's merchants, falling between two more prosperous periods. In the fifteenth century they held the mayoralty for three years out of four, in the sixteenth for one year in two, in the seventeenth for three out of five.[2]

The Twenty-Four, as might be expected, were less merchant-dominated than the bench of aldermen, and more open to craftsmen. Of 115 members during the sixteenth century, only twenty-five were merchants, and several crafts were represented on the junior bench, such as bakers, mariners, and saddlers, which were not to be found among the aldermen. The most striking instance was that of the butchers, who provided twelve members of the Twenty-Four but not a single alderman. In all, of the ninety or so trades

[1] W. G. Hoskins, *Old Devon* (Newton Abbot, 1966), p. 76.
[2] *V.C.H. York*, pp. 71, 179; Palliser, 'York', p. 207.

and crafts in York, about thirty-three secured representation among the Twenty-Four.

By and large crafts were represented on the council in proportion to their wealth, understandably when holding civic office could be expensive. To rely purely on a wealth bar, however, would have left the door open to rich individuals from trades considered socially inferior. Two scraps of evidence suggest that, as in other Tudor towns, well-understood rules limited the trades open to aldermen. In 1504 John Petty was elected alderman, 'and he to leve his kepyng of hostery and take down his signe apon payn of forfettour of the payn provided'. Six years later, when the draper Thomas Bankhows became an alderman, he was allowed to practise as a tailor—through his servants—for the next two years, but not after that on pain of £10 a year fine.[1] Nor did any butcher become an alderman; but the bar on innkeepers gradually broke down, probably because their numbers and importance increased enormously during the century. No restriction appears to have been placed on John Beane (1540), the first of four Tudor innholders to be elected to the bench.

6

If trading and shopkeeping were the normal vocations for city councillors, they were not the only possibilities. The numerous institutions of church and state which were housed in the city provided much employment. Most such posts were filled by outsiders—clerics, civil servants and northern gentry —but participation by members of the corporation was not altogether lacking. The church, for example, employed several councillors before the Reformation. Thomas Gray was master of the archbishop's mint in 1487, just before he became sheriff of the city, and later William Wright was appointed by Wolsey to the same office when already an alderman.[2] Christopher Horner became master mason of the Minster in 1505 and probably retained office until his death in 1523, although in 1513 he had joined the Twenty-Four.[3] William Harryngton

[1] *Y.C.R.* iii. 10; Y.C.A., B 9, fo. 57.
[2] *Reg. Corpus Christi Guild*, pp. 80 n., 159 n.
[3] J. Harvey, *English Mediaeval Architects* (London, 1954), p. 138.

was in 1512 respited of civic office for six years at the request
of the archdeacon of Richmond, and in 1517 he became
bailiff of the Liberty of St. Peter, a post which he held until
his death in 1540, although he was an alderman by 1531.[1]

In Elizabeth's reign, the three notaries on the city council
—Thomas and John Standeven and Edward Fawcett—all acted
as proctors in the church courts,[2] while William Allyn, a
common councillor, was bailiff of St. Peter's Liberty, until in
1579 the corporation peremptorily dismissed him from the
council for bringing in an outside coroner to hold an inquest
on the body of a man slain in the Minster Yard. Two years
later Allyn was in trouble for suing a fellow-freeman before
the Council of the North, an action forbidden to freemen.
He refused to give up the suit, 'saieng further that Mr. Deane
and the Church of York would beare him forth therin, if it
cost one hundreth poundes'.[3] The commonest church office
held by city councillors after the Reformation was membership of the Northern Ecclesiastical Commission. The government clearly intended the city to have a share in controlling
this important new institution, and appointed two aldermen
as members when it was first established in 1561. Between
27 February 1562, when the surviving act books begin, and
4 April 1603, at least fourteen mayors and aldermen, and
two recorders, attended sessions.[4]

A number of city councillors also held secular government
office in the north. George Gayle was master of the Royal
Mint at York about 1528—and possibly of the archbishop's
mint as well—and when the former was re-opened in 1545 he
became its under-treasurer. He was a wealthy goldsmith, and
his access to ready money was of great use to his colleagues.
In 1549 he was able to pay over £200 out of his own pocket
for a city purchase of guild property, although he was quickly
reimbursed by the corporation.[5] Thomas Standeven was

---

[1] Y.C.A., B 9, fos. 65ʳ, 90ᵛ; Y.M.L., MSS F2 a and b.

[2] R. A. Marchant, *The Church under the Law* (Cambridge, 1969), pp. 50, 55 f.,
249.

[3] *Y.C.R.* viii. 23 f., 55 f.

[4] T. Rymer, *Foedera*, xv (1713), 611; xvi (1715), 386 f.; *C.P.R. 1560-3*,
pp. 170 f.; information by Dr P. Tyler from the Commission's act books.

[5] *L.P. Hen. VIII*, v, no. 1695; xx(1), no. 620 (42); *Y.C.R.* iii. 142, v. 17; *C.P.R.
1549-51*, p. 31.

clerk of the court of Admiralty, while Alderman Holme (d. 1558) and Reginald Beysley (d. 1564), were vice-admirals.[1]

In a class of his own stood Sir George Lawson, receiver-general for the garrison of Berwick from 1517 to 1543, a Yorkshire Justice of the Peace in 1532-3 and 1536-42, a *Valor* commissioner in 1535, a commissioner for the surrenders of religious houses in 1537-8, and by 1538 also bailiff of St. Mary's Liberty. Most important of all, he was an official, and later a member, of the Council in the North at Sheriff Hutton and York. By 1525-6 he became cofferer to the duke of Richmond, a post from which he was dismissed in 1534 against the King's wishes, and in spite of his equivocal role in the Pilgrimage of Grace he became a member of the reconstituted council by 1540.[2] Lawson must have found a York residence useful, and he acquired one by 1523; he was elected alderman in 1527, an election which the King ordered to be annulled, as it would interfere with Lawson's other duties.[3] Nevertheless, he remained an alderman until his death in 1543, serving the city once as mayor and twice as MP, including service throughout the lengthy Reformation Parliament. He was to York what David Cecil was to Stamford: the exceptional councillor whose success rested on Crown offices rather than trade.

Lawson was not the only member of the corporation to hold office with the Council in the North. Sir Richard Page (recorder 1527-33/4) was vice-chamberlain to the duke of Richmond in 1525-6, and possibly later,[4] while William Tankerd (recorder 1537-73) was a member of the Council from 1566 to 1572, when he was removed on the ground of age.[5] James Birkeby, an alderman and a member of the Ecclesiastical Commission, was by profession an attorney, who practised before the Council in the North, and sometimes required the city council's permission to travel with the court to other parts of the north on his clients' business.[6]

[1] *Y.C.R.* v. 126, 132, 143 f.; Drake, *Eboracum*, p. 305; Bodley, Dodsworth 161, fo. 34ʳ.

[2] *L.P. Hen. VIII*, i-xviii, entries indexed under 'Lawson'; Palliser, *Reformation in York*, pp. 8 f.

[3] *Y.C.R.* iii. 88, 112.

[4] *L.P. Hen. VIII*, iv, nos. 1512, 1596, 1779, 1793, 2608, 2729.

[5] Reid, *King's Council in the North*, pp. 184 n., 196, 198, 210 f.

[6] Information supplied by the History of Parliament Trust, Elizabethan section.

Lawson and Birkeby, it is true, can be represented as un-typical aldermen; but the trouble with descriptions of the corporation as an oligarchy, gerontocracy, or civic élite is that an image is suggested of a coherent group, elderly and wealthy merchants with shared assumptions and a common way of life. Even of this group not as much can be known as one would like, but it is clear that there was no such thing as a 'typical' alderman, and that they differed in almost every way except in their common prosperity. They were drawn from many areas and even in one case from overseas; they included merchants and craftsmen, gentlemen's sons and arti-sans' sons, and, as will be seen, religious conservatives and radicals. Many were related by blood or marriage, but they could also quarrel bitterly among themselves. It is true that, in the last resort, they tended to close ranks rather than risk disorder in the city, but to think of them as a body of similar men with similar backgrounds would be to ignore the very real diversity of types represented on the council.

V

POPULATION, POVERTY, AND WEALTH

Ther is not half the nombre of good men within your
said citie as ther hath beene in tymes past.
The corporation to Henry VII, 1487[1]

The city fathers inevitably figure largely in any account of
Tudor York, but despite the bias of the documentary sources
it is possible to learn a good deal about the citizens as a
whole. The parish registers, used with caution, can yield evidence of the size and structure of the city's population. Taxation returns and poor relief records allow some analysis of
that population in terms of wealth and social structure, while
the freemen's register and guild records permit an analysis of
their occupations.

Unfortunately, from a twentieth-century viewpoint, the
corporation showed little interest in establishing the total
number of people within their jurisdiction, a lack of curiosity
they shared with most Tudor corporations. No census is
known of the kind compiled by Coventry Corporation on at
least four occasions in the sixteenth century, though in 1587
the corporation ordered lists to be drawn up of all householders and their male servants, and weekly certificates of
every immigrant; the returns, if compiled, are now lost.[2] However, sufficient evidence exists to give a rough indication of the
size of the population. For the mid-Tudor period the most
detailed, though still incomplete, count is that made for the
chantry commissioners in 1548. The surveys noted for each
parish the number of 'houslings' or communicants, and the
surviving returns indicate a total of 4,131 in seventeen
parishes. Figures for the other nineteen parishes are missing,
but if their proportion of the total was about the same as it
was fifty years later, they would have comprised another
2,300, making a total for the city of some 6,500 houslings,

[1] *Y.C.R.* ii. 9.   [2] *Y.C.R.* viii. 150 f.

or perhaps 8,000 people in all. The figure can be only very approximate, and much depends on the age of first communion.[1]

A population of 8,000 would have placed York among the largest half-dozen provincial English towns of the early Tudor period, though all were insignificant in a European context. Perhaps twenty-six European cities, including London, had populations of over 40,000, leaving even the largest English provincial town, Norwich, with about 10,000 or 12,000, a long way behind.[2] Another conclusion from York's 1548 total is that it was considerably below the city's earlier and later population levels. The population may have reached a peak of 12,000 or even 15,000 around the year 1400, and it was back at the same level in the seventeenth and early eighteenth centuries. These fluctuations were of fundamental importance to the economy and prosperity of the city, and will be considered in the context of economic change. The recovery is easier to trace than the decline because of Thomas Cromwell's introduction of compulsory parish registration in 1538. The earliest surviving York register, St. Olave's, begins on 7 December 1538, and altogether eighteen parishes out of twenty-three have surviving registers or transcripts begun by 1610.

The registers can, in the absence of better statistics, be utilized to estimate the city's population at the beginning of the seventeenth century, accepting J. C. Cox's assumption that total population may have been some thirty times the number of annual baptisms.[3] The assumption of course entails a considerable margin of error, but the method provides totals reasonably consistent with calculations from other sources where they can be made. For the decade 1601–10, making additions for parishes without registers in proportion to their known later size, the total population indicated is

---

[1] Palliser, 'York', pp. 30–4, 77 f.; W. Page, ed., *The Certificates of the Commissioners appointed to Survey the Chantries . . . in the County of York*, Surtees Soc., 2 vols. (1894–5), 450–71; J. D. C. Fisher, *Christian Initiation: the Reformation Period*, Alcuin Club Collections li (1970), pp. 232 f. An independent calculation reaches 8,300: Bartlett, 'Economy of York', pp. 200 f.

[2] R. Mols, 'Population in Europe 1500–1700', *The Fontana Economic History of Europe*, ed. C. M. Cipolla, ii (1974), 41–3; Hoskins, *Provincial England*, p. 72.

[3] W. E. Tate, *The Parish Chest* (Cambridge, 1951), p. 81.

almost exactly 11,000.[1] Apart from the crude nature of the calculation, one has to bear in mind that the baptismal totals of the decade may have been affected by the epidemic of 1604, and that parish registers probably understated the population by omitting some vagrants and mobile poor. If the total around 1600 was indeed in the range 11,000 to 12,000, then it was almost at the 12,000 level at which it stabilized from about 1630 to 1760.[2] A huge increase in Elizabeth's reign was therefore followed by a century and a half of almost total stagnation, not broken until the last third of the eighteenth century.

From the early seventeenth century it is also possible to assess the stock of housing for the available population. The earliest precise count of houses in the city and suburbs, in 1639, totalled 2,156, indicating about six persons per house.[3] At the first census in 1801, the number of houses had increased to 2,407, and the population to 16,846, so that the ratio changed very little over the two centuries. Recent studies of over 400 English settlements, urban and rural, have shown that the mean and median household size was in the range 4.5 to 5.00 throughout the early modern period, but this does not imply that York had an unusually high average, because a 'household' was defined by the researchers as a separate tenement, and a city might include buildings subdivided into more than one tenement. If one takes instead their 'houseful', the number of people dwelling in a physically separate house, then the English averages were in the range 5.3 to 6.3, putting York within the normal range.[4] In any case, the average of six per house will have masked considerable differences in the degree of crowding in different areas, just as the density of the built-up area varied considerably from one parish to another. The population estimates for 1601–10 indicate a density of twenty persons per acre or even fewer in the Walmgate area, rising to 100 per acre in the small but wealthy central parishes like St. Crux or St. Michael, Ouse Bridge end.

[1] Palliser, 'York', pp. 26–30.   [2] V.C.H. York, pp. 162, 212.
[3] Bodley, Rawl. C 886, pp. 51 f.
[4] P. Laslett and R. Wall, eds., Household and Family in Past Time (Cambridge, 1972), pp. 125–203; houseful averages on p. 197.

2

The calculation of totals of population and houses is, however, of limited value and reliability. Recent research in demographic history has moved away from estimates of total populations, and the most promising line of enquiry is the 'family reconstitution' method originated in France, which has been applied to several English parishes with important results.[1] The method involves analysing in great detail a sample group of families from a parish register, considering only those families with a 'complete' record, in other words those which remained in the parish for a whole generation. It is therefore appropriate only in parishes with a relatively low proportion of migrants, preferably large rural communities. In a city like York with many parishes, where few registers survive without gaps for much of the sixteenth century, the method is inapplicable. Sampling the better registers soon confirmed that very few families could be traced within one parish for a whole generation, and it is unlikely that the method will be successful in any large Tudor city, despite a recent attempt to apply it to Worcester.[2] Quite apart from migration into and out of the city, there was a good deal of mobility between city parishes. Of four parishioners of St. Mary's, Castlegate, testifying in a lawsuit in 1525, not one had been born in the parish.[3] York's close mesh of parish boundaries was similar to that of London, where one parson testified that 'the most part of the parish changeth' every twelve years or so.[4]

The urban historian must therefore fall back on the less

[1] L. Henry and E. Gautier, *La Population de Crulai, paroisse normande* (Paris, 1958), and for the published English example E. A. Wrigley, 'Family limitation in pre-industrial England', *Econ. H.R.* 2nd ser. xix (1966-7), 82-109, and 'Mortality in pre-industrial England: the example of Colyton, Devon, over three centuries', in *Population and Social Change*, ed. D. V. Glass and R. Revelle (London, 1972), pp. 243-73. The techniques of family reconstitution and aggregative analysis are explained in E. A. Wrigley, *An Introduction to English Historical Demography* (London, 1966), pp. 44-159.

[2] Dyer, *Worcester in the Sixteenth Century*, ch. 3, uses a 'simplified version' of the method based on two parishes out of ten, but without explaining his version or citing the number of cases analysed.

[3] B.I.H.R., C.P. G178.

[4] L. Stone, 'Social mobility in England, 1500-1700', *Past & Present*, xxxiii (1966), 31.

satisfactory method of 'aggregative analysis', involving the simple addition of baptismal, nuptial, and burial entries and calculations derived from them. For the purpose of this study all the surviving parish registers have been consulted and sample calculations performed. Ideally such work calls for a full analysis of all surviving records by computer, and a partial study of this type has already been carried out and published by Ursula M. Cowgill. Unfortunately it is marred by some fallacious deductions, and misleadingly described as an analysis of all the registers while in fact being based solely on eight of the published ones, drawn almost entirely from the richer parishes and not socially representative.[1] They reveal more favourable infant mortality rates, for instance, than some of the unpublished registers. Nevertheless some of her conclusions relate to population characteristics which almost certainly did not vary with social class, such as the seasonal pattern of births, and they are drawn on here where appropriate.

It is easy to forget that the registers list baptisms and burials, not births and deaths. There could be a variable interval between these pairs of events, and furthermore the total for a given urban parish need not accurately reflect its fertility or mortality if certain churches were fashionable. However, the most important problems concern the time-span between birth and baptism, and the numbers of children dying unbaptized and perhaps unrecorded. The few dates of birth recorded were almost all three days or less before baptism,[2] and in calculating seasonal fluctuations in conceptions and births, the short interval between baptism and birth can therefore be ignored. It is otherwise with the number of live births omitted because upbaptized, or rather, those who did not survive to be baptized publicly in church. The registers are erratic in including or excluding them, and the statistics of baptisms

---

[1] U. M. Cowgill, 'Historical study of the season of birth in the city of York, England', *Nature*, ccix (1966), 1068; 'Life and death in the sixteenth century in the city of York', *Population Studies*, xxi (1967), 53-62; 'The people of York: 1538-1812', *Scientific American*, ccxxii (1970), 104-12; L. Henry, 'Some comments on Ursula M. Cowgill's article', *Population Studies*, xxii (1968), 165-9; Wrigley, 'Mortality in pre-industrial England', p. 245.

[2] e.g. B.I.H.R., C.P. G272; reg. All SS. North St. *s.aa.* 1602, 1605, 1608, 1610.

cited below should be increased by perhaps 5 to 10 per cent to allow for children dying before baptism or otherwise un-recorded.[1] It would be all too easy to add to the catalogue of qualifications necessary to interpret parish registers, but it is proposed instead to proceed to consider the York findings, while bearing in mind that modern statistical accuracy is not to be expected.

In general, the York registers bear out the pattern estab-lished for many other towns and villages, of a series of long-term and short-term fluctuations in vital rates interacting with each other—the normal pre-industrial pattern in Europe. There were, first of all, the long-term movements of a late medieval decline and stagnation, followed by a recovery of numbers in the early modern period; York's population reflected both of these movements. Superimposed on these long-term trends were short-term oscillations of fertility and mortality every few years, with frequent but irregular demo-graphic crises brought about by disease, harvest failure or a combination of the two. Lastly there were the shorter-term seasonal fluctuations with a fairly regular annual rhythm.

The seasonal fluctuations were more pronounced than they are today. U. M. Cowgill has analysed 1,643 weddings between 1538 and 1601 and shown that there was a peak of double the usual numbers in November, and a trough in March and April when very few couples married. The spring minimum is accounted for by ecclesiastical law, which before and after the Reformation forbade marriages in Lent, though curiously the number of weddings remained normal in December, although Advent marriages were also supposed to be forbidden. Dr Cowgill's guess that the November maximum in weddings represented a rush to marry before Advent is therefore unlikely. Perhaps November was simply a conve-nient month for servants, whose terms of service normally ended at Michaelmas (29 September) or Martinmas (11 November). An analysis of weddings at St. Martin's, Coney Street, lends some support to this suggestion; November was easily the most popular month with all couples, but especially so with servant girls. Baptisms fluctuated more than weddings,

[1] Wrigley, 'Family limitation', pp. 99 f.; Hollingsworth, *Historical Demography*, pp. 182-5.

with the largest numbers recorded in the spring and early autumn, and the smallest at midsummer and midwinter. Assuming an average conception date nine months before baptism, the peaks in conceptions occurred in the months of July, November, and December. The early summer maximum seems to be a constant in England and is probably climatically controlled, being exactly six months displaced in the southern hemisphere. The winter peak, however, which disappeared in the seventeenth century, is more surprising. Dr Cowgill suggests as a partial explanation celebrations around Christmas, but such a charming and bucolic idea seems unlikely, especially as the main peak was *before* Christmas. More convincing is the correlation of the winter conceptions peak with that of marriages, for in an age of high death rates the first births to couples would have had a disproportionate effect on the averages.[1]

The seasonal incidence of mortality was more irregular. In years free of severe epidemics, maximum mortality occurred in the late winter and early spring, probably through a combination of winter illness and diminishing food supplies. However, the city was never entirely free of contagious disease, and as diseases have differing seasonal patterns, the unhealthiest months varied considerably. Two examples of registers during periods free of major epidemics will indicate how irregular was the seasonal death-rate.

	J	F	M	A	M	J	J	A	S	O	N	D	Total
St. Denys, 1581–1600	24	31	24	34	28	21	28	30	32	32	26	36	346
Holy Trinity, Micklegate, 1587–1600	32	31	44	39	33	17	32	20	31	22	28	29	358

There was, however, no such thing as a 'normal' year for mortality; many years saw sudden fluctuations in the total, either upwards under the pressures of malnutrition or disease, or downwards after the crisis was over and the weaker citizens had been carried off; and the seasonal incidence was affected by this, as it depended heavily on the proportion of

[1] Cowgill, 'Season of birth', pp. 1069 f.

different age-groups dying and the prevalence or absence of disease. The mark of bubonic plague, for instance, is not only a sudden increase in mortality but a concentration of that increase in the summer months, and such was the pattern in 1550 and 1604. In the latter year 2,138 burials are recorded in eighteen parishes, of which 1,789 (84%) were concentrated between July and October.[1] On the other hand, disastrous harvests like those of 1587 and 1597 were followed by heavy mortality in the spring, as the effects of malnutrition took hold.

3

The impossibility of family reconstitution makes it difficult to analyse fertility and family size. In default, they have to be estimated from very limited samples, or from the very crude method of dividing total baptisms in a parish by the number of weddings. The admittedly incomplete evidence of aldermen's families reveals only small numbers of children even at this prosperous level, only 2.6 per alderman for the first half of the sixteenth century and 4.0 for the second. A census of city labourers in 1574 gives an even lower figure of 1.1 children per couple. The figure relates to uncompleted families, unlike those for the aldermen, but it does suggest that at York, as elsewhere, the richer families tended to be the largest. In part this was caused by the children of the poor acting as servants in the houses of the wealthy, and the numbers of labourers' children may have been reduced in that way. A more evenly representative group of families is obtained by taking all children born in the last twenty years of the century in a group of seven parishes. A total of 2,357 recorded baptisms was produced by 874 recorded marriages, suggesting an average of 2.7 children per couple and therefore an average household size of less than 4.7, since child and adult mortality ensured that not all parents and children were alive by the time the family was completed.[2] The figure is in the same range as the mean household size of the earliest urban censuses, and it emphasises how vulnerable were these

[1] Palliser, 'Epidemics in Tudor York', pp. 49, 53-5.
[2] Palliser, 'York', pp. 53 f.

pre-industrial towns, with a replacement rate of only a little over unity and the ever-present danger of severe mortality, preventing the population from replacing itself.

Fertility figures for York, as for pre-industrial England generally, reflect almost entirely legitimate fertility, for illegitimacy was infrequent despite folk-beliefs to the contrary. It is true that births outside marriage were not always recorded except by the uncharitable: several parish registers mention none at all, but one cannot believe that this reflects the true position. The largest number of illegitimate births recorded in one decade is in the register of St. Michael-le-Belfrey for 1581–90, totalling eight, or 2 per cent of all recorded baptisms—a figure rather lower than the average calculated for twenty-four Elizabethan parishes.[1] Bridal pregnancy, on the other hand, was rather more common. In two parishes examined for the second half of the century, one couple in five produced a first child within seven months of their wedding. The proportion is very close to the rates calculated by Dr Hair for northern England as a whole, rates which are more than double those for the midlands and south. The contrast may, however, mean only that in some areas espousals, rather than the church ceremony, signalled the start of cohabitation.[2]

Whatever the level of live births per family, it was heavily reduced by infant mortality. Minimum rates can be calculated by taking all baptismal entries in a series of registers, and calculating the proportion per thousand buried within twelve months of baptism. Nine parishes yield reasonably complete statistics for the decade 1591–1600, indicating infant mortality rates ranging from 159 at St. Crux to between 264 and 280 at St. Denys; the rates are in roughly inverse proportion to the taxable wealth of the parishes.[3] Even the horrifying figure for St. Denys's is not likely to have been the worst, for the 1598 subsidy assessed six parishes for lower sums, and none of their registers has survived. Such a level of mortality is quite sufficient to account for the haste in baptizing the

[1] P. Laslett, *The World we have lost*, 2nd edn. (London, 1971), p. 142.
[2] Palliser, 'York', pp. 44 f.; P. E. H. Hair, 'Bridal pregnancy in rural England in earlier centuries', *Population Studies*, xx (1966–7), 237.
[3] Palliser, 'York', pp. 41–3.

newly-born. The sickness of many such children, and the belief in the necessity of baptism for salvation, led the church to permit the practice of lay baptism in cases of urgency.[1] Between 1571 and 1587 twenty-five children in Belfrey parish were baptised 'at home' or 'in the house', usually 'becawse of weakness', and in at least sixteen cases the child was baptized by the 'grace woman' or midwife. Several of these unfortunates died the same day, and the parish clerk found it necessary to make special provision for infant deaths in the table of church fees: 'Ther is due at churching of every woman a crysome and a peny, yf the childe be then lyvinge, and if the childe be then deade, then but a peny.'[2]

Mortality remained severe throughout childhood. Age at death was recorded for 466 people buried in Belfrey parish between 1571 and 1586, and of them 136 died within their first year, another sixty-six before the age of ten, and twenty-three more before the age of twenty, so that only half of those buried were adults.[3] A larger sample has been extracted from the printed parish registers by U. M. Cowgill, based on the life spans of 1,625 people born between 1538 and 1601. She calculates that only 22 per cent of the boys and 18 per cent of the girls lived to be twenty, and only 4 per cent of either to the age of sixty.[4] Her figures almost certainly exaggerate early mortality: the life spans of only 34 per cent of those baptized were traced, probably because there was a great deal of movement from one city parish to another. Yet expectation of life must have been low, and few citizens can have been as lucky as the group of aldermen who lived to an average age of sixty-seven.

Dr Cowgill has drawn survivorship curves for her sample of the York population. They show that these citizens died younger than their contemporaries among the nobility and gentry. This in itself is not surprising, but the gap between the survivorship curves of nobles and citizens is remarkably wide, especially considering that the York sample is drawn

---

[1] e.g. Lee's York injunctions, 1538: *Visitation Articles and Injunctions of the Period of the Reformation*, ed. W. H. Frere and W. P. M. Kennedy, Alcuin Club Collections xiv–xvi (1910), ii. 49 f.

[2] *The Registers of St. Michael le Belfrey*, ed. F. Collins, i (Y.P.R.S. i, 1899), 11–57, 99 f.

[3] ibid., pp. 11–56.   [4] Cowgill, 'Life and death', p. 56.

from the wealthier parishes. Another remarkable finding is that the female death rate in Tudor York was at all ages very slightly higher than that of the males, whereas among the Tudor nobility, as in modern western societies, females had a distinctly greater expectation of life. The ratio of males to females in York, probably 104.6 at birth, rose to 128.5 by the age of twenty. The explanation is perhaps that the citizens, as in other poor societies, nurtured their daughters less well than their sons. However, as with all Dr Cowgill's findings on life expectancy, the distortion of her sampling procedures needs to be remembered.[1]

Those who survived childhood probably married at about the same age as today. There are, it is true, occasional records of those notorious child-marriages which have acquired, perhaps, too large a place in social histories. Such was the marriage of Katherine Neleson, whose alderman father, despite refusing a knighthood, obviously aspired to the status of a gentleman. In 1497 he married her to William Gascoigne, son of a local gentleman, when William was nine (Katherine's age is not recorded), and they cohabited for six years 'in mensa et thoro' in her father's house before setting up their own home. The details are recorded in Katherine's suit for the restitution of conjugal rights, since like many such marriages it turned out badly. The notary George Evers (d. 1520) married one daughter before she was thirteen and betrothed another at the age of six, to another son of the Gascoigne family.[2] The most notorious case, however, was that of Anthony, the son of Alderman John Norman. After his father's death, young Anthony was somehow abducted from his guardians and married, at about the age of eight, to a gentleman's daughter, Barbara Wentworth, aged five or six. The marriage was unhappy and never consummated, but nearly twenty years later it became a cause of scandal when Barbara married Archbishop Holgate.[3] These were probably exceptional cases of marriages arranged early for purposes of property settlement; the few cases where a bride's birth and marriage dates are recorded in the same register suggest an

[1] Cowgill, 'Life and death', pp. 60–2; Henry, 'Some comments', *passim.*
[2] B.I.H.R., C.P. G32, G110: Y.M.L. prob. reg. ii, fo. 124.
[3] P.R.O., C1/659/40; *Test. Ebor.* v. 215; Dickens, *Robert Holgate*, pp. 24–6.

average age at marriage of over twenty. Marriages were often shortlived, however, one partner or other dying before the wife was past child-bearing; it was one reason for the small size of the average family. Remarriages were therefore common. Of the 48 aldermen of the second half of the century, 27 married at least once, 19 twice and 1 three times.

High death-rates were maintained by malnutrition and disease, either of which could flare up into a demographic crisis given unfavourable conditions. A run of bad harvests could produce a subsistence crisis or 'dearth', while a sudden increase in lethal disease produced a 'plague' or 'pestilence'. The two were not entirely distinct, for a combination of the two could occur either coincidentally or because famine drove the sufferers to eat unfit food and so to succumb to dietary diseases, and such crises were naturally much the most lethal. Unfortunately it is easier to list York's crises of mortality than to account for them, because diseases were recorded in forms difficult to identify medically. It is also difficult to establish which coincided with bad harvests, for the series of harvest-prices so far published relate to the midlands, south, and west country, and in an age of regional economies a bad harvest in the south did not necessarily coincide with a northern famine.

Before 1538, indeed, it is difficult even to establish which were the years of high mortality. Early Tudor crises can be identified only from chance literary references, or from noting in which years record numbers of probates were granted. The latter is a device to monitor high mortality in the absence of parish registers, and is a crude method for counting the death-rate among the more prosperous citizens. Epidemics described as a 'plage of pestilence' or 'sekenez of pestilence' struck the city in 1485, 1493, and 1501; they cannot be identified with certainty, though as all three were summer outbreaks they may have been bubonic plague, a disease spread by rat-fleas.[1] The sweating sickness, a lethal but obscure disease probably of virus type, was also present in 1493.[2] No other epidemic before 1538 was recorded at the time, apart from a widespread but mysterious 'sickness' in or about

[1] *Y.C.R.* i. 116–8; ii. 102, 104; Y.C.A., B 7, fo. 106ᵛ; B 8 fo. 115ᵛ.
[2] Drake, *Eboracum*, App. p. lxxvi.

1521,[1] but these four were not the only crisis years between 1485 and 1538. Numbers of wills proved were exceptionally high in 1505-7 and 1520-2; malnutrition may well have been an underlying cause, for in both periods mortality was especially heavy if measured by 'harvest years' (beginning on 1 August), and the harvests of 1519-21 were, according to available grain price-series, generally bad.[2] The former mortality receives casual confirmation in a 'proof of age' taken in 1528. John Appleyarde of Heslington gave evidence that Thomas Kente, his godson, had been born at Midsummer 1507, when his father, a York merchant, 'did sugeorn in Heslington for feyre of the dethe thatt then was in Yorke'.[3] Yet no contemporary record of the 1507 outbreak is known, suggesting that epidemics were still accepted with resignation and were not the subject of special comment.

The first well-recorded epidemic in the city was a 'decese of playg called pestyllence' in the summer of 1538, perhaps bubonic plague again, followed by above-average mortality lingering until 1541.[4] Another cycle of 'plage of pestylence' followed between 1549 and 1552, probably induced by malnutrition, for the late 1540s witnessed a series of bad harvests for which, for the first time, there is corroboration from the York area. The nature of the 1549-52 epidemics must have been complex, for it flourished throughout the winters as well as the summers. Bubonic plague may have been alternating with another disease with a winter incidence; and in 1551 the 'swyttyng' sickness was again recorded.[5] After only a few years' respite, the city was struck again: a 'farvent sekenes' or 'newe agewe' raged in the summer and autumn of 1558, again following a series of disastrous harvests. The outbreak left little trace in the parish registers, but that was simply because they ceased to be kept at the height of the epidemic; the number of citizens' wills proved was higher than for any other year in the century, and in one city parish three successive vicars died within the year 1557-8. The 'agewe' was

---

[1] *L.P. Hen. VIII*, iii, no. 2531; xii (2), no. 186 (21); cf. M. James, *Family, Lineage and Civil Society* (Oxford, 1974), p. 8.
[2] Palliser, 'Epidemics in Tudor York', pp. 47 f.   [3] P.R.O., C1/531/3.
[4] Palliser, 'Epidemics in Tudor York', pp. 48 f.
[5] *Y.C.R.* v, 24, 29, 50 f., 56 f., 68; Palliser, 'Epidemics in Tudor York', pp. 49-51.

apparently the mysterious disease, probably of influenza type, which is now thought to have reduced the total population by almost one quarter.[1]

The evidence suggests that the combined effects of the 1549-52 and 1558 outbreaks were catastrophic, coming as they did at a period of severe economic depression. The city's population, reduced to perhaps 8,000 by 1548, may have been cut by a third or more in the 1550s.[2] However, Elizabeth's reign was almost entirely free of mortality crises at York, giving the city a breathing-space of nearly half a century. Its good fortune was due in part to an absence of 'plague' epidemics, which struck other Yorkshire towns but failed to reach York, either through chance or through the success of the corporation's policy of *cordons sanitaires*.[3] There was also an absence of severe famines, presumably because food production in the Vale of York was sufficient. Even in 1587, when much of England suffered from famine and West Riding men were dying of hunger, there is no sign of abnormal burial rates in York, and corn apparently remained cheap in the district.[4] The next nationwide famine in 1596-8 did, however, involve the city. Exports of corn and beans were forbidden, and York bought grain from the midlands and even from overseas. Yet even at its height, in 1597-8, the dearth produced only a moderate rise in mortality except in four parishes, three of them among the poorer districts.[5] Of course misery and hunger cannot be assessed merely by numbers, and the parish clerks recorded occasional deaths from starvation even in years of average mortality.[6] Nevertheless in York, like the rest of lowland England, major subsistence crises were coming to be a thing of the past by

---

[1] *Y.C.R.* v. 189; Y.C.A., B 22, fo. 131^r; Palliser, 'Epidemics in Tudor York', pp. 51 f.; F. J. Fisher, 'Influenza and inflation in Tudor England', *Ec.H.R.* 2nd ser. xviii (1965), 120-9; D. M. Palliser, 'Dearth and disease in Staffordshire, 1540-1670', in C. W. Chalklin and M. A. Havinden, *Rural Change and Urban Growth 1500-1800: Essays in English Regional History in Honour of W. G. Hoskins* (London, 1974), pp. 57 f.; Hollingsworth, *Historical Demography*, pp. 236 f.

[2] See p. 223-4.

[3] Palliser, 'Epidemics in Tudor York', pp. 52 f., 60-2.

[4] B.L., Lansdowne 54, fo. 141^r; Palliser, 'York under the Tudors', p. 50.

[5] Palliser, 'York under the Tudors', pp. 49 f.; Palliser, 'York', p. 92.

[6] *Belfrey Registers*, ed. Collins, i. 56; *The Parish Register of St. Crux, York*, I, ed. R. B. Cook and Mrs F. Harrison (Y.P.R.S. lxx, 1922), 67.

the end of Elizabeth's reign, and hunger a killer of those on the margin of subsistence rather than a major scourge.[1] Plague was also on the wane, and in 1589 a local gentleman said that York rarely suffered 'any pestylence or other infectinge syck-nes'.[2] The terrible epidemic of 1604, which killed 3,512 people or about 30 per cent of the population, proved to be the last major outbreak of bubonic plague, which recurred on a very small scale in 1631 and possibly in 1637 before vanishing from the city for ever.[3]

The lack of severe demographic crises between 1559 and 1603 must have been an important contributory cause to the growth of York's population under Elizabeth. Helleiner's explanation of the eighteenth-century population upswing was an abatement of demographic crises rather than a reduction of normal mortality, and a similar explanation would fit the case of Elizabethan York.[4] The growth of population can be traced in the surviving parish registers by the simple, if crude, method of counting all baptisms and burials to establish the net surplus or deficit of births over deaths, a procedure which despite the imperfections of the registers yields clear and unambiguous results. Table 1, giving decadal totals for all registers commencing before 1590 (except for the imperfect St. Cuthbert's register), indicates two periods with a net deficit of baptisms over burials separated by a healthier period of about thirty years. Furthermore, such crude totals are likely to understate any natural surplus of births for reasons already stated, whereas the burials figures, except in times of severe epidemics, are more likely to be complete.

The three registers beginning sufficiently early indicate a general surplus of burials in the 1540s and 1550s, which of

[1] Most recorded English subsistence crises after 1600 were in the Highland Zone: Laslett, *World we have lost*, pp. 113-134; W. G. Howson, 'Plague, Poverty and Population in Parts of North-West England, 1580-1720', *Trans. Hist. Soc. Lancs and Cheshire*, cxii (1961), 29-55; A. B. Appleby, 'Disease or Famine? Mortality in Cumberland and Westmorland, 1580-1640', *Econ. H.R.* 2nd ser. xxvi (1973), 403-32.

[2] B.L., Lansdowne 119, fo. 112ʳ.

[3] Palliser, 'Epidemics in Tudor York', pp. 53-6; Y.C.A., B 35, fos. 335, 348; R. Davies, 'The Plague at York in the seventeenth century', *Yorks. Philos. Soc. Annual Report* (1873), pp. 4-34.

[4] K. F. Helleiner, 'The vital revolution reconsidered', in *Population in History*, ed. D. V. Glass and D. E. C. Eversley (London, 1965), p. 85.

TABLE 1
Baptism and Burial Rates, 1541–1610

	St. Crux			St. Martin-cum-Gregory			St. Olave		
	Bap.	Bur.	Surplus	Bap.	Bur.	Surplus	Bap.	Bur.	Surplus
1541–50	(119)	(106)	13	(59)	(104)	−45	107	150	−43
1551–60	(94)	(114)	−20	70	99	−29	(46)	(199)	−153
1561–70	(120)	97	23	(46)	(30)	16	105	93	12
1571–80	157	109	48	70	59	11	167*	143	24
1581–90	200	176	24	(41)	(35)	6	173	162	11
1591–1600	201	146	55	82	116	−34	(177)	(141)	36
1601–10	199	291	−92	80	(147)	−67	(175)	(164)	11

	All Saints Pavement			St. Denys			St. Martin Coney Street		
	Bap.	Bur.	Surplus	Bap.	Bur.	Surplus	Bap.	Bur.	Surplus
1561–70	114	89	25	100	85	15	101	89	12
1571–80	106	58	48	—	—	—	109	99	10
1581–90	78	47	31	(114)	(152)	−38	141	101	40
1591–1600	153*	56	97	178*	194	−16	114	90	24
1601–10	157	225	−68	134	254	−120	108	174	−66

	St. Helen Stonegate			St. John Ousebridge End			St. Michael-le-Belfrey		
	Bap.	Bur.	Surplus	Bap.	Bur.	Surplus	Bap.	Bur.	Surplus
1571–80	—	93	—	93	83	10	331	293	38
1581–90	(117)	93	24	89	59	30	400	367	33
1591–1600	138	102	36	129	93	36	355	364	−9
1601–10	141	209	−68	109	213	−104	(370)	(390)	−20

	All Saints North Street			Holy Trinity Goodramgate			Holy Trinity Micklegate		
	Bap.	Bur.	Surplus	Bap.	Bur.	Surplus	Bap.	Bur.	Surplus
1581–90	78	63	15	(109)	(89)	20			
1591–1600	95	71	24	137	139	−2	195	243	−48
1601–10	98	171	−73	158	250	−92	242	461	−219

Note: Figures in brackets are certainly incomplete—i.e. their registers show manifest gaps.

*These three sudden large increases in baptismal rates may be caused by the unions of parishes, which were ratified in 1586 but effectively occurred earlier.

course covered two series of lethal epidemics. Between 1560 and 1590, by contrast, all the parishes experienced a net surplus of baptisms in every decade, with the single dubious exception of St. Denys's parish in the 1580s. Then followed a less healthy period: five parishes out of twelve had a surplus of burials in the 1590s, though overall there was a considerable surplus of baptisms, and all the parishes (with one doubtful exception) had a burial surplus in the first decade of the seventeenth century. The unhealthiness of the two last decades can be attributed partly to the dearth of 1596–8 and the plague of 1604, but A. G. Dickens has followed the fortunes of five of the parishes throughout the seventeenth century, and found that all suffered a net surplus of burials throughout the century.[1]

It would appear, therefore, that the twelve parishes enjoyed a healthy surplus of baptisms over burials for most of Elizabeth's reign, though not before or after. But the surpluses are not large enough to account by themselves for the doubling of the city's population under Elizabeth, especially as the twelve represent roughly the richer half of the city's parishes. The conclusion seems inescapable that York, like London, was experiencing massive immigration, since a modest number of immigrants was needed even to keep the total population steady, and considerable numbers would be required to double it. Not until the later eighteenth century did the larger English towns begin to generate their own natural growth and cease to depend on large-scale immigration.[2]

4

How can the extent of immigration be measured? There is no systematic source, naturally, comparable to the parish registers, but the chamberlains' account books, not previously exploited for this purpose, provide a useful substitute. Those which survive for the middle third of the century name all those made free of the city and also state their places of

[1] *V.C.H. York*, p. 121.
[2] E. A. Wrigley, 'A simple model of London's importance . . .', *Past & Present*, xxxvii (1967), 44–70; J. D. Chambers, *Population, Economy and Society in Pre-Industrial England* (London, 1972), p. 103.

origin. This information survives for six years between 1535 and 1566, and covers altogether 358 freemen, a large enough sample for worthwhile study.[1] Of these, 102, or 28.5 per cent, were born in York. Nearly all the natives who were freemen became free by patrimony; of the 268 who gained their freedom by apprenticeship or purchase, only twelve were York natives. In other words, sons of non-freemen resident in York had very little chance of becoming freemen themselves, the freedom being reserved almost entirely for freemen's sons and for men from outside the city. The few other studies of Tudor urban immigration suggest that York was not exceptional: only 28 per cent of those apprenticed in Bristol in one sample decade were natives of the town, while a Canterbury sample included only 30.5 per cent natives.[2]

About 108 of the immigrants (42.2%) came from within a twenty-mile radius of the city, 75 (29.3%) from between twenty and fifty miles away, and 73 (28.5%) from more than fifty miles away. The largest proportion of immigrants came from the city's immediate hinterland. Nevertheless, long-distance immigrants formed a greater proportion of the total at York than in smaller towns where statistics are available. At Canterbury four-fifths of the immigrants originated within a twenty-mile radius, and at Sheffield in a rather later period the proportion was two-thirds. The lower proportion at York probably reflects its greater size and importance, and therefore its greater power to attract long-distance immigrants; the extent and geographical range of its pull are broadly similar to those of Norwich and Bristol, its fellow provincial capitals.[3]

However, there was no simple pattern of an even distribution in all directions, diminishing with distance. The district within a ten-mile radius, including most of York's own

[1] Y.C.A., C 3–C 5. For the following analysis see Palliser, 'York', pp. 66–72 and map. Since this section was written, the immigrant sample has been analysed in more detail, and with minor amendments, in D. M. Palliser, 'A regional capital as magnet: immigrants to York, 1477–1566', in M. J. Kitch, ed., *Migration in Pre-Industrial England* (London, forthcoming).

[2] J. Patten, *Rural–Urban Migration in Pre-Industrial England* (Oxford, School of Geography Research Paper vi, 1973), p. 34; Clark and Slack, *Crisis and Order in English Towns*, p. 122.

[3] Patten, *Rural–Urban Migration*, pp. 33–9; Clark and Slack, *Crisis and Order in English Towns*, p. 125; E. J. Buckatzsch, 'Places of origin of a group of immigrants . . .', *Econ. H.R.* 2nd ser. ii (1949–50), 303–6.

wapentake, the Ainsty, did provide York immigrants fairly evenly, but the pattern was quite different for areas more than ten miles away. Almost no immigrants came from the rest of the East Riding, and relatively few from the West, whereas a considerable number came from parts of the North Riding forming a clear belt from York almost all the way to the border of Westmorland, nearly sixty miles away.

There are two probable reasons for this pattern. One is that men would be likely to go as apprentices to those towns with which their fellow countrymen traded. East Riding men, except those of the Vale of York, may have had most contact with Hull, while the West Riding had thriving textile centres of its own, to which surplus population would be drawn. On the other hand the closest connections of Richmondshire were with York, and the normal outlet for the Richmond-shire lead exports was by river to York, where they were weighed and struck at the city crane before being sent on their way. This water route through the city would also be the natural one for stockings and mittens, the knitting of which formed Richmondshire's other industry, for these were exported to Holland as well as to London. The other reason for the influx of Richmondshire men into York was probably the same as that which caused those left behind to take up stocking-knitting—the poverty and overpopulation of the dales.[1]

No fewer than seventy-two out of the sample of 358 (20%) came from outside Yorkshire, and again many more came from the poorer lands to the north-west than from other directions. Thirty-three came from Cumbria, where the soil was poor and the population large. Kendal cloth found its way down to York,[2] and it would not be surprising if Cumbrians wishing to be apprenticed should take the same route. Sufficient references survive to show that Cumbrian migration to York was closely connected with the cloth trade, and that it was no short-term phenomenon of the mid-sixteenth century.[3] Of the other freeman immigrants in the six-year sample, there were eight from Lancashire, all of them from

[1] Thirsk, *Agrarian History*, iv. 12, 31 f.
[2] e.g. *Test. Ebor.* iii. 301; *Y.C.R.* ii. 91, 175.
[3] e.g. *Register of Freemen*, i. 216–22; *Y.C.R.* iii. 130.

the poorer land north of the Ribble. If 'the standard stable partnership is between a poor region with regular emigration and an active town',[1] then York's reservoir region, apart from its immediate hinterland, was clearly the northern Pennines and Cumbria.

The freeman's birthplace lists for the mid-sixteenth century can be supplemented by two series of a rather later date. Both are registers of apprentices, and therefore cover a rather wider social group than the freemen, but unfortunately neither is nearly so comprehensive in its coverage of occupations. The earlier of the two is a book of city apprenticeship indentures starting in 1568, which has been partially analysed by Mildred Campbell.[2] It is not, however, as she believed, a comprehensive calendar. For the period before 1600, at least, it comprises mainly the indentures of those apprenticed to a limited group of trades, especially woodworkers and barber surgeons. Nevertheless, the geographical origins of those listed were broadly similar to those of the freemen's sample. Taking the decade 1591–1600, the earliest satisfactory period for analysis, 107 apprentices' birthplaces are listed. Thirty-nine (36%) were York boys, fifty-eight (54%) came from the rest of Yorkshire, and ten (9%) from further afield. A broadly similar picture emerges from the earliest apprenticeship register of the merchant tailors, which was begun in 1606. Of the 165 boys apprenticed before the end of 1610, thirty-five (21.2%) were city born, 113 (68.5%) were from other places in Yorkshire, and seventeen (10.3%) from other counties.[3]

The alien-born community in York seems to have remained small throughout the Tudor period, and accounted for only 1.5 per cent of the mid-century sample of freemen. The only aliens charged to the lay subsidies were a Dutchman and two Frenchmen in 1524, and three Frenchmen in 1546, though in 1549 nine aliens contributed. They represented only those rich enough to pay, but the 1572 subsidy delved deeper, for it recorded eighteen aliens, of whom fifteen were assessed as worth nothing: most of them do not appear in the freemen's

[1] F. Braudel, *Capitalism and Material Life 1400–1800* (London, 1974), p. 380.
[2] Y.C.A., D 12; M. Campbell, *The English Yeoman under Elizabeth and the Early Stuarts* (New Haven, 1942), pp. 277, 395–7.
[3] Merchant Taylors' archives, York: register of apprentices 1606–1751.

register. Those with nil assessments had mainly Netherlandish names, though a few were Scots. The largest concentration of Dutchmen was five or six in Belfrey parish, while four Scots lived in the parish of St. Helen, Stonegate.[1] The 'Dutch' were probably refugee weavers fleeing from the Spaniards. Two of them were made free as 'arresworkers', and carpet weaving may have been the speciality of the whole group; in 1596 a York widow bequeathed two bedcovers 'comonly called by the name of carpet worke which was wrought of the Douchmen'.[2] One of them, Anthony Ruyskaert, rose to the office of master of the weavers' guild at least four times in the 1590s, providing an instance of the way in which alien-born craftsmen were becoming more accepted in the city.[3]

5

The samples of immigrant freemen and apprentices should be fairly representative of that half of the adult male population who were freemen, but it would be wrong to ignore the humbler immigrants or passage migrants who must have formed a large part of York's population. In a detailed study of urban migration in this period, P. A. Clark draws a distinction between 'betterment' and 'subsistence' migration. Betterment migrants tended to move to a town from a rural birthplace not far away; to move seldom, often only once in their lifetime; and to move in order to rise socially, often by becoming apprenticed to urban masters, who were frequently related to them. They usually retained links with their birthplaces, and the most successful retired back to the countryside after amassing wealth in the town.[4]

This profile fits well many of the York immigrants already investigated. Nearly half came from villages within twenty miles of York, and many were certainly moving to better themselves in a city of greater social mobility than their home villages, often by making use of kin already established

---

[1] *Y.A.J.* iv. (1875-6), 170-1, 176; P.R.O., E 179/217/110, 119; E 179/218/133.

[2] *Register of Freemen*, ii. 12; B.I.H.R., prob. reg. xxvi, fo. 310.

[3] D. M. Palliser, 'The trade gilds of Tudor York', in Clark and Slack, *Crisis and Order in English Towns*, p. 100.

[4] Clark and Slack, op. cit., pp. 134-8.

in York. Thomas Moseley, for instance, a younger son from
North Castle Grange near Cawthorne, first joined the household of Alderman John Beane, a kinsman, and was then
apprenticed to an uncle in York, Ralph Micklethwaite; two
steps on the way to a successful career as a merchant, mayor,
and MP.[1] The York immigrants also, like their Kentish contemporaries, retained links with their native parishes. John
Besby, son of a gentleman of Barrow-on-Humber, moved to
York by 1485 at latest, but when he died fifty years later he
still owned land at Barrow, and made bequests to the poor of
the parish and to the church fabric.[2]

Even servants could hope to rise in York's atmosphere of
social mobility. In 1597 two sisters from Ripon bound themselves servants for four- and five-year terms to Robert Salmon
of York, jerseyman, who in return was to teach them his
trade and to feed them; their widowed mother paid him £3
for his consent to the bargain. This was really a form of
apprenticeship, and the girls presumably hoped to acquire a
craft to support themselves.[3] But there were also the true
domestic servants, driven to York by poverty and much more
mobile. One of the recusants presented in 1576 was Anne
Godfray, servant to a tiler and his wife. She told the wardens
that she had no money to pay recusancy fines:

> We enquyere of hir dame whether she had any goodes or no? and what
> aparell she had? and she answered that she had none, but onely that
> whiche she had apon hir back. And the said dame dothe say that 'She
> is but my servant for a whyle, and I cannot tell when she will go away,
> for she will be here to nyght and away tomorowe'.[4]

Anne Godfray perhaps represents the rootlessness of the 'subsistence migrant'. All over England, and increasing in numbers
during the Tudor age, were the mobile poor, often covering
long distances in search of work. Among them, living-in servants, however often they moved, were relatively privileged;
many others could find no regular work at all, and had to
squat or to crowd into cheap lodging-houses. In the mid-
sixteenth century there was plenty of room for migrant
workers with a little money, for the economic depression

---

[1] Biog. of Moseley in files of History of Parliament Trust.
[2] *Reg. Corpus Christi Guild*, p. 126 n.; B.I.H.R., prob. reg. xi, fo. 147.
[3] Y.C.A., CC 9, 1597–8 book, fo. 77^r.   [4] Y.C.A., E 40, no. 61.

and the population decline had left many cottages available at low rents.[1]

Under Elizabeth the problem worsened, the population of the city doubled, and yet there is little evidence for a housing boom to match the growth in numbers. It is apparent that many poor were crammed into the existing houses, thus accentuating the problems of overcrowding and disease; the devastating nature of the plague of 1604 may well have owed its virulence to such conditions. A little light is shed on the subdivision of tenements by an inquiry into liability for pavement repairs in 1578. The general rule was that householders repaired the street pavements in front of their own houses, but 'dyverse poore persons ar setled in the fyerhouses of certeyn tenements . . . against which tenements the cawsies are in dyverse placis decayed, and . . . unrepaired, by reason of the povertie of the same poore tenauntes'. It was therefore agreed to charge repairs also on the occupiers of the 'garthes and backsides' of the tenements, who were 'the landlords or . . . better tenants'.[2] A firehouse was a dwellinghouse with fireplace, as opposed to an outhouse; the implication is that the owners of the long central house-plots were living back from the streets and letting out the frontages as cheap cottages.

It was understandable, if selfish, that the corporations should seek to keep away poor immigrants in an age of population growth. The York aldermen, like the MPs of the time, took the view that the immigrant poor and beggars should be sent back to their previous domiciles. Statutes from 1531 onwards enacted that vagrants should be whipped and then sent back to their birthplaces, or where they last dwelt 'by the space of three years'. York first adopted the policy in earnest in 1574, when the labourers were 'viewed' by the councillors in the Common Hall. Seventy-seven men and their families were 'appoynted to work trewly for there lyving', but those who had come to York less than three years before were to be returned to their birthplaces or previous domiciles. Fourteen men or families were expelled under the order; half were sent to nearby villages where they had last dwelt, but one man had come from as far away as Sawley on the Lancashire

[1] See pp. 214-15.   [2] Y.C.R. vii. 169.

border.[1] From then onwards the city fathers fought a constant battle against poor immigrants: in 1577, for instance, a Lancashire couple and a family from Barnard Castle were ordered to leave their lodgings in York and return home, and in 1601 a poor man was given a passport from York to Rothwell in Northamptonshire, 'wher he saith he is to be placed in an hospitall for his life'.[2] The later Elizabethan minute-books are crammed with such orders, so many that Canon Raine ceased to include them in his printed editions. There could be no clearer demonstration of the change that had come over the city since it bemoaned its huge population losses of the 1550s.

6

The population of York was divided very unequally, in a variety of ways which tended to come to much the same thing, the powerful on one side and the powerless on the other. Councillors ranked before other freemen and all freemen before non-freemen; masters had power over servants, apprentices, and journeymen; and men over women. A complex series of unwritten rules must have decided, for example, who doffed his cap to whom, and who addressed whom by his Christian name rather than by surname or by a title like 'master'. At bottom, however, a great many of the distinctions were based simply on wealth, which brought power and social respectability in its train. Much more than the countryside, the city was a place of considerable social mobility, where increasing wealth could bring promotion to civic office and poverty could cause enforced resignation.

It is possible to measure levels of wealth among the richer citizens from taxation returns, but most covered only a small minority of the population and assessed taxpayers at unrealistic levels. The most comprehensive and reliable appear to be the lay subsidies of the period 1523 to 1546, and fortunately complete assessments survive for York for the subsidies of 1524 and 1546 as well as incomplete returns for intermediate years. Even the most comprehensive, however,

[1] Y.C.R. vii. 91; Y.C.A., B 25, fos. 125–7.
[2] Y.C.R. vii. 146; Y.C.A., B 32, fo. 134r.

may not have given an altogether accurate picture, since the corporation, who were responsible for the assessment, appear to have taken the opportunity to favour themselves. In 1524 six men were given reductions on their assessments in 1523 (the year of the best and most comprehensive subsidy, the returns of which do not survive for York), and four of the six were councillors. Eleven years later Sir George Lawson complained to Cromwell of three present or future aldermen who had bought up much Lincolnshire and Holderness corn; they had each assessed themselves to the subsidy at less than £20 in goods, but one of them alone was said to have bought corn worth £100.[1] This kind of complaint was not new. In 1498 the bishop of Carlisle and the earl of Surrey had accused the city council of taxing themselves lightly and the poor heavily, and it seems the council tacitly admitted the charge.[2] And there is an even clearer demonstration of underassessment: at the turn of the century £80 or £100 was the minimum property level for a sheriff, yet in 1524 only four York men (none of them ex-sheriffs) were assessed at over £80 in goods, and of the twelve aldermen assessed on goods, none was assessed on over £40.

The subsidy assessment of 9 April 1524 lists 876 taxpayers, who paid a total of £192. 8s. 2½d.[3] Among them were the Corpus Christi Guild and the Guild of SS. Christopher and George. These guilds are omitted from the following analysis, which is confined to the assessments on individuals. The assessment of 14 February 1546 lists 361 taxpayers, charged altogether with £393. 2s. 3d.[4] They included the Corpus Christi Guild (worth £20), the Guild of SS. Christopher and George (£6), the tanners' guild (£7), and the city council (for lands worth £50 a year). These four are also omitted from the following results, and so is the very large valuation of the archbishop's lands (£540 a year), which preceded the parish-by-parish lists and was considered apart from the citizens' assessments. The 1524 assessment was more comprehensive than any other Tudor tax taking in all wage-earners who

---

[1] *L.P. Hen. VIII* ix, no. 456.   [2] *Y.C.R.* ii. 137.

[3] P.R.O., E 179/217/92; a copy was printed by E. Peacock as 'Subsidy roll for York and Ainsty', *Y.A.J.* iv. 170–201.

[4] P.R.O., E179/217/110.

earned 20s. or more a year, as well as those owning goods worth £1 or more. The 1546 subsidy cast its net less widely, omitting the wage-earners and those with goods worth less than £5. These levels of wealth are put into perspective by the fact that in 1536 the Pilgrims allowed into the city were asked to pay twopence a meal.[1]

Table 2 shows how many taxpayers in both years belonged to different levels of wealth, and, in the case of those taxed on goods, what proportion of the total taxable goods in the city was owned by each group. The extreme inequality of

TABLE 2
Distribution of Taxable Wealth by Classes

(a) 1524

Status of Group	No. in Group	% of Tax-payers	Goods owned by Group (to nearest £)	% of Total Goods
Wage earners	330	37.8	—	—
£1 in goods	1	0.1	£ 1	0.0
£2 in goods	176	20.1	£ 352	7.9
Over £2 and under £10 in goods	176	20.1	£ 836	18.6
£10–£19 in goods	83	9.5	£1032	23.0
£20–£100 in goods	59	6.7	£1699	38.0
Over £100 in goods	3	0.3	£ 560	12.5
Income from land	20	2.3	—	—
Unstated (portions for others)	26	3.1	—	—
Totals:	874	100.0	£4480	100.0

(b) 1546

Status of Group	No. in Group	% of Tax-payers	Goods owned by Group (to nearest £)	% of Total Goods
£5–£9 in goods	128	36.1	£ 822	17.1
£10–£19 in goods	109	30.7	£1356	28.1
£20–£100 in goods	80	22.5	£2508	52.0
Over £100 in goods	1	0.3	£ 133	2.8
Income from land, fees and annuities	30	8.4	—	—
Unstated (portions for others)	7	2.0	—	—
Totals:	355	100.0	£4819	100.0

[1] *L.P. Hen. VIII* xii (1), no. 306.

wealth is brought out very clearly, especially in 1524. Over a
third of the taxpayers were wage-earners, owning few or no
possessions. Only a little better off were those worth £2 in
goods; they accounted for 20 per cent of all taxpayers but
owned only 8 per cent of the taxable wealth. At the other
extreme were three men assessed at over £100 each in goods,
who owned between them an eighth of the city's taxed goods,
while those worth £20 or more in goods, forming only 7 per
cent of the taxpaying population, owned more than half of
all the taxable capacity. Even these contrasts will not show
the full extent of inequality, because many, even in 1524,
were too poor to be taxed at all. In that year half the population of Coventry, and a third of those of Exeter and Leicester,
escaped the net, and York's proportion may have been similar.[1] Ten of the forty parishes in 1524 were not credited with
a single taxpayer.

The proportion of taxpayers assessed on wages was very
similar in the major cities. York's 38 per cent may be compared with 40 per cent at Norwich and 46 per cent at Exeter.
The proportions in the smaller towns of Leicester and Nottingham were ostensibly much smaller, but the differences
may be illusory, because both included a large class taxed on
20s. in goods, which accounted for only a single taxpayer at
York. It may well be that they were all wage-earners who
would have been taxed on wages in other towns, and if they
are grouped with the wage-earners the differences become
much smaller. Wage-earners plus those worth £1 in goods
formed 38 per cent of the taxpayers of York, 44 per cent at
Leicester, 47 at Nottingham, and 50 at Southampton. This
might suggest that York's wage-earners formed a smaller
proportion of the population than in other towns, but if, as
there is reason to think, general levels of prices and wages
were rather lower in the north than in the midlands and
south, it may simply mean that a higher proportion of York's
wage-earners escaped the net by earning less than 20s. a year.[2]

[1] Hoskins, *Provincial England*, p. 83.
[2] J. F. Pound, 'The social and trade structure of Norwich 1525-75', *Past &
Present*, xxxiv (1966), 51; MacCaffrey, *Exeter 1540-1640*, p. 250; D. Charman,
'Wealth and trade in Leicester in the early sixteenth century', *Trans. Leics. Arch.
Soc.* xxv (1949), 69-97; C. Platt, *Medieval Southampton* (London and Boston,
1973), pp. 264 f.

At the opposite end of the scale, 7 per cent of York's taxable population owned exactly half of the taxable goods. Leicester's 6 per cent owning 46 per cent is very close, but only if one leaves out of account William Wigston the younger, who alone owned nearly a quarter of the town's wealth. The other large cities for which figures have been published had even more pronounced inequality. Some 6 per cent owned 60 per cent of the lands and goods at Norwich, and at both Coventry and Exeter 7 per cent owned nearly two-thirds.

The figures for 1546 are not as startling as those for 1524, because of the narrower basis of taxation, but they reveal the same broad picture of inequality. In one respect they are more useful, because they allow for comparison with figures for the Ainsty and for the West Riding as a whole in 1546. Dr Smith's analysis of the subsidy for those areas yields the following results:[1]

	Total Number Assessed	% Assessed on Lands			% Assessed on Goods		
		Over £20	£5–£19	£1–£4	Over £20	£10–£19	£5–£9
Ainsty	144	6.3	2.8	9.7	7.1	20.9	48.7
West Riding	4,631	3.0	5.8	29.4	4.4	10.1	46.3

The West Riding had too high a proportion assessed on lands to be easily compared, but the Ainsty can be readily contrasted with York, as the proportion taxed on goods in each was not very different. The city was plainly wealthier than its rural wapentake, having a much higher proportion of taxpayers who were really rich (over £20) than did the Ainsty, even though that area had more than did the West Riding as a whole.

Wealth was unequally distributed geographically as well as socially. Down to the eighteenth century, the very wealthy tended to live in the city centre, and the poor just within the walls or outside in the suburbs. It was a natural pattern when most journeys were made on foot, and even the leading merchants kept shops and lived over the shop. In 1622 the city council defined 'the fairest and cheifest streetes in this Citty'

---

[1] R. B. Smith, 'A study of landed income and social structure in the West Riding . . . 1535–46', Univ. of Leeds Ph.D. thesis 1962, p. 235.

as Spurriergate, Coney Street, Stonegate, Blake Street, Petergate, Ousegate, Pavement, and the lower part of Micklegate,
streets 'wherein men of the best sorte and ranck do frequent
and dwell'.[1] The 1524 subsidy has been analysed to yield the
approximate distribution of taxable wealth, and it reveals a
very clear pattern. A solid bloc of central parishes, stretching
from the Minster down to the Ouse and Foss, and taking in
the two parishes immediately beyond Ouse Bridge and Foss
Bridge, paid over 10s. per acre in tax. All the other parishes
paid 10s. an acre or less: the greater part of the Micklegate
and Walmgate areas, a belt of five poor parishes between
Monk Bar and the Foss, and the extramural suburbs. An
analysis of other tax assessments from 1497 to 1598 has
shown that the ratios between parishes remained fairly constant, except for a very few occasions where a very wealthy
taxpayer distorted the pattern, and that the situation in 1524
was normal.[2]

7

After 1546 the collection of subsidies became less and less
realistic in terms of taxable wealth, and failed completely to
keep pace with inflation. Huntingdon warned the corporation
in 1586 not to charge for armour and weapons only those
who paid subsidies, 'for I doubt not but that maney that are
not in the subsidye booke, are of habylitie to beare parte of
this chardge'. The following year the Council in the North
passed on to the corporation a letter from the Privy Council
complaining of the declining yield of subsidies.[3] Out of
2,000 or more householders in Elizabethan and early Stuart
York, fewer than 400 contributed to subsidies, and only 500
or 600 to the poor rates.[4] Nevertheless the Elizabethan subsidies still provide a guide to the relative ranking of the
wealthy, even if the absolute levels of assessment were quite

---

[1] Y.C.A., B 34, fo. 251[r].
[2] Palliser, 'York', pp. 234–8 and map.
[3] *Y.C.R.* viii. 126, 146–8.
[4] H. Aveling, 'Some aspects of Yorkshire Catholic recusant history', in *Studies
in Church History: Volume IV: the Province of York*, ed. G. J. Cuming (Leiden,
1967), 108 n.

unrealistic. The subsidies for 1524, 1546, 1572, and 1598 have been compared with this in mind.[1]

In this respect 1524 proves to have been an untypical year. The richest taxpayer, assessed on £18 a year in lands, was Alderman Thomas Drawswerde, but of the four richest men assessed on goods not one was a member of the city council. George Lawson, returned as worth £200 in goods, was, as has been seen, a northern civil servant with homes in York, Berwick, and Wakefield, who had obvious reasons for avoiding civic office as long as possible. Equally wealthy was John Roger, a fishmonger who had taken up freedom as early as 1486-7 and had been a city chamberlain in 1508-9, but who avoided the office of sheriff until six months after the subsidy of 1524. He thus came late in life to membership of the Twenty-Four, and may have failed to be elected alderman only because of this victualling business. The richest councillor in 1524 was Robert Petty, tapiter, assessed on £80 in goods, while the mayor was one of a number of citizens—most of whom never joined the council—assessed on £40. Later subsidies did not show this surprising feature. In 1546 all the thirteen citizens assessed on £50 or more in goods were either city councillors or councillors' widows. In 1572 so were all but one of the fifteen citizens assessed on £15 or over, the exception being Archbishop Young's widow. And of the fifteen citizens assessed in 1598 at £14 or more, thirteen were city councillors; the other two were Thomas Scudamore, esquire, and George, the son of Archbishop Young. The senior clergy cannot be directly compared, as they were taxed separately under a different system.

If one takes a wider group of the rich, the wealthiest three dozen on each occasion, the picture is more varied. Most were, or were to be, civic officials of some kind, holding at least the office of chamberlain, but there were some interesting exceptions, apart from the Young family. The grandfather and father of Guy Fawkes were among the number in 1546 and 1572, both of them officials in the church courts: William, the archbishop's registrar, and Edward, the notary public of the Exchequer Court.[2] Another of the number in 1546

---

[1] P.R.O., E179/217/92, 110, 133, 167.
[2] Ritchie, *Ecclesiastical Courts of York*, pp. 48, 52.

was John Skaif, pursuivant to the Council in the North. It was plainly a profitable office, for in 1572 his relative and namesake, who apparently succeeded him as a pursuivant, was also among the richest three dozen. John Fearne, secretary to the Council in the North, was one of the same élite in 1598, while of private citizens two members of small professions were equally wealthy: John Gachet, the French-born publisher, in 1524 and 1546, and Roger Lee, doctor of physic, in 1598.

Clearly the aldermen were collectively the richest citizens, but just how rich were they? In looking for York figures more reliable than subsidy assessments, one is hampered by the great scarcity of surviving inventories. No alderman's inventory has yet been found, apart from that of James Birkeby (1610). Otherwise there are only isolated scraps of information, mostly taken from lawsuits. Fortunately numerous such references survive about early Tudor aldermen. The dyer William White left £433 in goods and chattels in 1505, while Sir John Gilliot in 1509 made charitable bequests assessed by Professor Jordan at over £780. Thomas Bankhows, tailor, who died during his mayoralty in 1521, had movable goods worth £300, and the merchants John Rasyng (1527) and Peter Jakson (1531-2) each left over £600 worth. None of them approached in wealth the non-councillor John Chapman, who was assessed in 1524 on £160 in goods, but who left at his death (1530-1) over £1000 worth.[1]

The inflationary middle third of the century provides sharp contrasts in aldermanic wealth. The goldsmith Ralph Pulleyn, in 1540, doubted whether his goods were worth £138, whereas Sir George Lawson is known to have left £2,630 in money, gold, plate, jewels, 'stuffs', clothes, corn, and cattle at York, besides other goods at Newcastle and Berwick; his total wealth, including recoverable debts, was over £7,500. His fellow civil servant, George Gayle, may have been equally rich, for in 1553 he could spend £615 on a single purchase of ex-monastic property.[2]

[1] P.R.O., C1/371/69; Jordan, *Charities of Rural England*, pp. 230, 372; Bartlett, 'Economy of York', pp. 246 f.

[2] B.I.H.R., prob. reg. xi, fo. 529; xvi, fo. 64; Skaife, 'Civic officials', *sub* Lawson; *C.P.R. 1553*, p. 89.

Elizabeth's reign, with its continued inflation, produced larger estates, though never of the size of Lawson's. From the will of the haberdasher Richard Goldthorpe, in 1560, his estate can be estimated at £2,460, knowing that custom in the York province allowed one third of a testator's goods to his wife and another third to his children, the remainder to be bequeathed at his discretion.[1] Robert Hall, merchant (1565), expected a third of his goods greatly to exceed £227, and William Coupland, tailor (1569), left his wife his house and £333 in full recompense of her third part. In 1610 the hatter and haberdasher Sir Robert Watter made charitable bequests worth £990, and the attorney James Birkeby left goods and money worth £508, £22 in recoverable debts, and over £900 in other debts, mostly 'desperate'; he owed his son Alverey the enormous sum of £2,186.[2]

The leading churchmen and civil servants resident in York were as rich as, and in some cases much richer than, the aldermen. Martin Colyns, the Minster Treasurer, died in 1508 worth £1,437 gross, or £1,141 net. William Maunsell, clerk of York Castle, was a well-to-do government official, worth £813 in goods and £100 in recoverable debts at his death in 1541, though he owed £196 to others. Half a century later the earl of Huntingdon left £633 in goods at York and Sheriff Hutton, a figure that takes no account of his family wealth in the midlands.[3]

Not far below these levels would come the Twenty-Four. John Litster, draper, whose inventory survives, left £178 net at his death in 1541, and Marmaduke Sothabie, who died in 1596, should have left some £1,800 in all, since he bequeathed £200 to each of his three daughters. Even a lesser civic official might have wealth of the same order, like Francis Cook, who died in 1583, only two years after being chamberlain, and who seems to have left about £900 in goods. There were

[1] H. Swinburne, *A Briefe Treatise of Testaments and Last Willes*, 1st edn. (London, 1590), pp. 104 f.

[2] B.I.H.R., prob. reg. xvi, fo. 64; xvii, fo. 477; xviii, fo. 122; xxii, fo. 72; C.P.H. 767; Jordan, *Charities of Rural England*, p. 268 n.

[3] *Test. Ebor.* iv. 279–307; B.I.H.R., prob. reg. xi, fos. 534–5; H.M.C., *MSS. of R. R. Hastings*, i. 355–61. A gross estate is here calculated as goods plus debts owed to the deceased; a net estate is the gross total less debts owed by the deceased and 'desperate' debts owed to him.

wealthy freemen even among those who never reached the rank of chamberlain, like the girdler who left £200 in goods about 1505, or the 'tapiter' whose net estate in 1553 came to £220.[1]

Below this level, there is a gap in the scale of known fortunes until one comes down to the level of about £20 to £30 at 1450–1500 prices. These men included some comfortably-off freemen of various trades, and a few of the lesser clergy. Such, for instance, were two founders whose gross estates were respectively worth £34 (1512) and £29 (1516), two priests worth £29 net (1525) and £34 gross (1547), a draper who left £31 net in 1528, and a tailor who left £25 net in 1538–9. Of the same level, when inflation is allowed for, was a shoemaker who died in 1558 worth £92 net, and a woman of the same trade who left £85 in 1589.[2]

Some freemen, however, were worth far less, possessing under £10 in goods at late-fifteenth-century price levels. A freeman cutler owned goods worth £4. 17s. 7d. when he committed suicide in 1499, and a freeman tailor possessed only 40s. in chattels when he fled after murdering a clerk in 1553. In 1525 four parishioners of St. Mary, Castlegate, gave evidence in a slander suit, of whom two mariners were certainly freemen and the others probably free also. The defence belittled them as men worth little or nothing in goods; and sure enough two were not assessed at all to the 1524 subsidy, and the other two only on 20s. in wages. Many priests were probably equally poor. The rector of St. Helen-on-the-Walls, one of the poor benefices then being united, left only £5. 6s. 9½d. net at his death in 1551.[3]

The very poor do not figure in inventories, and what possessions they had can usually be established only when they had forfeited their goods through committing a crime.

[1] B.I.H.R., original probate records, M. Sothabie 1596, R. Hewton 1553; prob. reg. xxii, fo. 424; xxvi, fo. 413; P.R.O., C1/351/6.
[2] *Test. Ebor.* v. 35 f., 79 f.; B.I.H.R., orig. probate records, J. Tennand 1516, R. Plomer 1525, T. Lytster 1528, N. Mores 1538, J. Watson 1547, J. Tessimonde 1558, anonymous 1589. Estate values have not been converted here into a constant form, but the wheat price table in *Agrarian History*, iv. 863, has been used as a very approximate guide to the extent of inflation.
[3] Y.C.A., C 4/4; P.R.O., K.B.9/585, fo. 216; B.I.H.R., C.P. G178, and original prob. records, R. Agrig 1551.

Inquests held in January 1584 on two suicides show that both were very poor indeed. Nicholas Rabye, of St. Lawrence's churchyard, left goods worth only 19s. 2d. and those of Thomas Moore of Goodramgate were valued at still less. All he owned in the world were a pair of tongs, a 'rekyn', a cupboard, three chairs, a counter, a table with two trestles, three forms, a coverlet, a painted cloth, a coffer, a bedstead, a sheet, a mattress, a coat, a doublet, and a pair of hose. Their total value was 15s. 7d.[1] Even these men, though desperately poor by the standard of an alderman, were probably some way from the bottom level of society. There may have been many labourers and servants, like Anne Godfray, who owned nothing but their tools and clothes. Paupers and beggars were always swarming in the city, as innumerable corporation orders testify; and frequent funeral doles allow the magnitude of the problem to be glimpsed. Three testators between 1493 and 1511 left a farthing or a penny each to a thousand poor, and William Neleson in 1525 left a penny dole 'to every olde man and woman', which implied 1,200 elderly poor alone. Alderman Coupland in 1568 left money for 1,600 poor, all of them children and old people, which would argue a total pauper population of over 2,500.[2]

The extent of poverty was clearly enormous, reflecting a situation of rapid population turnover within a city which did not have the resources, or the flexibility of approach, to tackle so huge a problem. The difficulty in picturing the population of Tudor York lies, perhaps, in the sheer continuity of the physical fabric, with its misleading implications for the nature of the population which thronged its houses and streets. Not only did the total population fluctuate sharply, with devastating short-term epidemics superimposed on the longer term decline and recovery of numbers, but there was also the constant high death-rate which necessitated immigration on a massive scale from the countryside. The long-lasting urban dynasty was, as Caxton pointed out, the exception in England, and the population of a major

---

[1] P.R.O., K.B. 9/661, fos. 72–3.
[2] *Test. Ebor.* iv. 78; v. 5, 199; Y.M.L., MS L2(5)a, fo. 111[r]; B.I.H.R., prob. reg. xviii, fo. 122.

town was constantly renewing itself. A city like York could well be compared, like the contemporary nobility, to 'a bus or a hotel, always full, but always filled with different people'.[1]

[1] L. Stone, *The Crisis of the Aristocracy, 1558-1641* (abridged edn., Oxford, 1967), p. 23.

VI

THE OCCUPATIONAL STRUCTURE

Ye shall . . . no man knowe that usez byying or
sellyng in any crafte or occupacon as maistr and not
franchesst but ye shall make it knowyn to the mayer,
chamberleyns, or the common clerk.
Freemen's oath, late fifteenth century[1]

At the summit of York's society and economy were the professions: the higher clergy, the lawyers, civil servants, doctors,
publishers, and schoolmasters. These groups, with the exception of the last, were wealthy and influential, and tended to
be treated deferentially even by the richest citizens. It is not
necessary, however, to discuss them at length in a study of
the city, as they stood rather apart from it. This was true
even in a physical sense, for most of them lived and worked
in the liberties of the Minster, castle, and King's Manor—the
headquarters respectively of the diocese, shire, and Northern
Council—and were outside civic jurisdiction. Consequently
they had no need to take up the freedom of the city, so that
civic records about them are scanty. Of the five known
printers and publishers active in the early sixteenth century,
for instance, only two became freemen, while very few clergy
and lawyers, and no schoolteachers, figure among those
admitted to the freedom.[2]

There was a strong legal tradition at York, owing to the
presence of the church courts and the Council in the North.
There were six major church courts—three for the province,
two for the diocese, and that of the Dean and Chapter—which
called for a large staff of registrars, proctors, advocates,
notaries, and apparitors.[3] In addition there was much secular

[1] *Register of Freemen*, ed. Collins, i, p. xiv.
[2] Palliser, 'York', pp. 324 f.; Palliser and Selwyn, 'The stock of a York stationer', p. 208.
[3] For the first five, see Ritchie, *Ecclesiastical Courts of York*; for the last,
P. Tyler, 'The administrative character of the Ecclesiastical Commission for the
Province of York, 1561–1585', Univ. Oxford B.Litt. thesis, 1960; 'The Ecclesiastical

employment with the county courts in the castle and the city courts in the Common Hall. What would now be described as civil servants were numerous in York, serving the Council in the North, the Royal Mint, and the admiralty court, while the equivalent of local government officers staffed the various institutions in the castle. Their story, however, belongs primarily to the history of national and county government.

The dominant class in the city proper was that of the citizens or freemen. They were the master craftsmen, traders, and shopkeepers, in other words those who ran businesses or were self-employed. Anyone wishing to enter this class had to do so in one of the three traditional ways: by apprenticeship, by patrimony, or by purchase. The class was further restricted to those of legitimate birth, though in another direction conditions of entry were more liberal, since not only could aliens be admitted, but they could join even without becoming naturalized Englishmen.[1] The freemen were privileged both politically, as the only inhabitants eligible to vote and hold office, and economically. A 'foreigner' or 'stranger' (non-freeman) could buy no goods at York except from a freeman, nor could he sell there except to one.[2] The custom of 'foreign bought and sold', by which the city confiscated all goods exchanged between 'foreigners', was jealously guarded. It might be overborne by the powerful and privileged merchants of London or Newcastle,[3] but it was strictly enforced against lesser men. This position of the freemen as compulsory middlemen is seen to be even more important when it is realized that all non-freemen in York were also foreigners and were thus penalized in their own city. The corporation, in using such phrases as 'all cittizens of the said cittye and all other inhabitantes within the same', were voicing a well-understood division of the population into two basic classes, and in defending their 'foreign bought and sold' custom in 1536, they stated that its abolition would 'be a means to

Commission for the Province of York, 1561-1641', Univ. Oxford D. Phil. thesis, 1965; and 'The significance of the Ecclesiastical Commission at York', *Northern History*, ii (1967), 27-44.

[1] *Register of Freemen*, i. 216; *Y.C.R.* iii. 19, 20.
[2] *Y.C.R.* iv. 186 f.   [3] See p. 187.

make all strangers as free within the said Citie as the Citizens bee'.[1]

Such privileges made the city's freedom desirable for outsiders who wished to trade there regularly, or to make use of York's chartered rights. Thus Thomas Mankyn, a Ripon merchant, took up the freedom of York in 1502, probably to use the 'cover' of its charters, for he then tried to trade toll-free at Hull by showing letters testimonial of his York freedom. However, the corporation never allowed a regular class of non-resident freemen to develop, as Oxford and some other towns did. In 1503 they threatened to disfranchise all freemen who failed to reside in York by Martinmas, though three years later they were still allowing Mankyn and other non-residents a year's grace.[2] Several times later in the century this 'ancient rule' was reiterated, though in terms suggesting that it was often unenforced.[3]

It would be wrong, however, to picture the freemen as an oligarchy dominating a throng of unfree paupers. Far from being a small minority of the working population, they numbered some 1,250 in the 1530s and 1540s, or at least half of all adult males in the city.[4] Furthermore, the correlation between freedom and economic prosperity was only a rough one. Just as some of the wealthier inhabitants, especially the gentry and professional classes, did not trouble to take up freedom, so there were those who were relatively poor yet enfranchised. Michael Dyconson, made free as a tailor in 1538-9, left goods worth only 40 shillings when he fled in 1553 after murdering a clerk.[5]

Detailed examination of the economic structure has to be confined to the freemen, simply because much more is recorded of them than of the foreigners. Every freeman ought to have been recorded, with a note of his trade, under the year of his admission, although a large minority, amounting to perhaps one in five during the fifteenth century, failed

---

[1] Y.C.A., B 32, fo. 285ᵛ; *Y.C.R.* iv. 4.

[2] Y.C.A., B 8, fo. 133ʳ; B 9, fos. 2, 27-8.

[3] *Y.C.R.* iii. 67, iv. 105, vi. 133; Y.C.A., B 24, fo. 91ʳ.

[4] Assuming an average 20.5 years between enfranchisement and death, a figure drawn from a sample of ninety-four freemen dying in the decade 1541-50.

[5] P.R.O., K.B. 9/585, fo. 216.

to be listed.[1] Much can also be learned of the freemen from the archives of the craft guilds, which were managed exclusively by them, as well as from wills and corporation records. By contrast, the many others engaged in economic activity— apprentices, journeymen, and servants—are buried in obscurity. A great deal is known of the free members of the butchers' guild, a prosperous body who lived together in the Shambles, but the very existence of a group of unfree butchers in Micklegate Ward would be unknown but for a single corporation minute.[2] No Tudor will is as informative as that of the mercer Robert Colynson, who in 1450 made bequests 'to the dyers, fullers, cutters, and weavers working with me'.[3]

Apprentices were boys (or occasionally girls) indentured to serve a master craftsman or trader, and to receive board, lodging, and instruction in return for their service. Little is recorded of their lives, their ages, or even their identity. The guilds and the corporation allowed masters a free hand with their apprentices, provided that they imparted genuine instruction and used no excessive brutality, and were concerned chiefly to regulate the numbers of apprentices, and the length of their service. Apprentices' indentures bound them to their masters *in loco parentis*, and ensured a close supervision of their leisure and morals as well as their work. Even in church there was no escape: one church kept four pews reserved for householders and their apprentices, 'to the entent that the sayd masteres myght se the conversacon of the sayd prentises'.[4] Apprenticeship, if not the norm, was a common route to freedom, and it was therefore in the interest of the masters to regulate admission to their own ranks with care. The minimum length of apprenticeship varied from guild to guild, but the seven-year term imposed by Parliament in 1563 was usual at York even in the fifteenth century and universal by 1530, while under Elizabeth some guilds increased the minimum to eight years and even more. Restrictions on the number of apprentices each master might take on were also usual, though

[1] Bartlett, 'Expansion and decline of York', p. 20 n.
[2] *Y.C.R.* viii. 17; cf. *R.C.H.M. York*, iii. 82.
[3] P. J. Shaw, *An Old York Church* (York, 1908), p. 98.
[4] Y.M.L., MS L2(3)d, fo. 22^V (1526).

they were temporarily suspended during the economic depression of the mid-sixteenth century. The ambition of an apprentice was to set up shop as a master himself when his indentures expired, but not all could afford to do so, and without sufficient capital many ex-apprentices remained journeymen, hired assistants to the masters. It was partly to remedy the shortage of capital at the start of a trading career that revolving loan funds were introduced.[1]

A wealthy man might employ several apprentices and servants, but a small master would rely a great deal on his own family, and women especially must have played a large part. A few women even traded on their own account by taking up the freedom of the city. The 6,231 admissions between 1500 and 1603 included forty-four women, though they can have been only a small fraction of those involved in trade. It was common for a widow to maintain the family business without needing to take up freedom herself: thus in 1487 a mayor's widow was carrying on his business as an ironmonger, and was even eligible for office in the ironmongers' guild, and in 1593 a tapiter bequeathed his two looms to his servants 'after such time as my wife shall leave of from workinge upon my occupacion'.[2] Indeed, in 1529 the city council agreed that all freemen's widows, as long as they did not remarry, could continue their family businesses.[3] And in the 1590s at least two guilds, the barber-surgeons and bakers, acknowledged that the employment of women was normal.[4]

2

Economic life in York was controlled by the trade and craft guilds or companies, which were unions of the free masters, although their decisions were binding upon apprentices and journeymen. Though they had social, religious, and charitable sides to them, they were primarily economic organizations, and need to be distinguished clearly from the religious, charitable, and parochial guilds which abounded in the city before

    [1] See p. 85 f.; and on apprentices and guilds generally, Palliser, 'Trade gilds of Tudor York', pp. 86–116.
    [2] Y.C.A., B 6, fo. 92^V; B.I.H.R., prob. reg. xxvi, fo. 65.
    [3] *Y.C.R.* iii. 126 f.   [4] *V.C.H. Yorkshire*, iii. 453 f.

the Reformation. The wealthiest and most powerful was the mercers' or merchants' guild, reconstituted in 1581 by royal charter as the Society of Merchants Adventurers of the City of York.[1] Ruling from its medieval timbered hall by the Foss, it controlled the city's general traders, especially those who dealt wholesale and trafficked overseas, and its 1581 charter granted it a monopoly of all overseas imports except fish and salt. The charter put York on a level with other provincial capitals like Chester (1554) and Exeter (1560), whose merchants had already secured similar monopolies. 'Merchant' was, however, a loose term at that period, and although it indicated a large-scale general trader there were other important traders in York outside the merchants' company. The drapers, or dealers in cloth, formed a powerful group second only to the merchants in importance, especially when they combined with the associated handicraft guilds of tailors and hosiers.[2] A third trading guild was that of the haberdashers, who in 1591 were united with the feltmakers and cappers to form another large company.[3] The numerous other economic guilds in York can be described for convenience as craft guilds, since most were involved in producing and selling goods, though a few were engaged in distribution and service trades. Altogether there were between sixty and seventy organized craft groups in the city—sixty-four were listed in 1579—though not all were formally constituted as guilds or companies with a system of officials and regulations.[4] The pattern is complicated by the frequent creations, unions, separations, and disappearances which make it very difficult to draw up a definite list of the guilds for any given date. Nevertheless, York's complement compared closely to the sixty crafts of London in 1531 and greatly exceeded those of most provincial towns.[5]

Each person admitted to the freedom of the city had, immediately afterwards, to join the appropriate trade or craft

---

[1] *York Mercers*, ed. M. Sellers, pp. 244-54.

[2] B. Johnson, *The Acts and Ordinances of the Company of Merchant Taylors* (York, 1949), pp. 41-3, 128-31.

[3] Y.C.A., B 30, fo. 229^v.   [4] Palliser, 'Trade gilds', p. 89.

[5] G. Unwin, *The Gilds and Companies of London* (London, 1908), p. 169; C. Phythian-Adams, 'The economic and social structure', in *The Fabric of the Traditional Community* (Milton Keynes, 1977), p. 30.

guild if one existed. The freeman's oath bound him to obey the mayor and sheriffs and to observe the city by-laws, including of course the trading regulations, so that each entrant to a guild had already pledged overriding loyalty to the corporation; and to make assurance doubly sure the city councillors insisted on approving the ordinances of all guilds before they could be enforced, while all guild officials had to take their oaths of office before the mayor. Even this degree of control was found insufficient, for the guild searchers, whose task was to inspect the quality of workmanship, had a natural tendency to be lax in punishing fellow craftsmen. In 1519, therefore, power of punishment was taken from the searchers, who were bound on oath to disclose all trading offences to the council for punishment.[1] Only the weavers' and merchants' guilds could claim some exemption from the council's jurisdiction, since their rights stemmed from royal charters and not from the permission of the councillors.

Surviving records suggest that most guilds met quarterly for business, and annually to elect officials and receive accounts. The searchers were empowered to visit members' premises at any time to ensure that regulations were observed, and frequently they would go before the mayor and council to present an offending member, or a non-member poaching on the guild's preserve. The guilds also had a social and charitable side. They were responsible for staging the cycle of miracle plays, performed nearly every year until the 1570s; all held feasts and religious services, and some made provision for financial help to aged and sick members and their dependents. The tailors and drapers, for instance, held an annual feast on their patronal festival of St. John the Baptist, and later a Martinmas dinner as well; they maintained a light of Corpus Christi before the Reformation; and they financed an almshouse for poor brethren. Much of this activity was originally sponsored by the confraternity of St. John, which became in effect the tailors' guild under another name, but the name of the confraternity was discreetly forgotten during the sixteenth century, and hall, almshouse, and feasts carried on unscathed by the Reformation.[2]

[1] *Y.C.R.* iii. 69.
[2] Johnson, *Company of Merchant Taylors*, pp. 18-33, 53.

3

The most satisfactory means of gauging the strength of the crafts is to analyse the register of freemen kept by the corporation. There are several limitations to the conclusions that can be drawn from it: the proportions of trades practised among freemen were not necessarily the same as among the working population as a whole, since some would use more unfree labour than others, and the exemption from freedom of dwellers in the liberties must distort the pattern. Further, the register is manifestly not comprehensive, for some known freemen are not to be found in its folios, while other known masters seem never to have been enfranchised, like most of the master weavers in the period 1461-1502. The case of the weavers also indicates that craftsmen could escape guild membership as well as freedom, for weavers in Minster Yard, Marygate, and St. Lawrence's churchyard made annual payments to the guild in lieu of membership. Yet, with all these limitations, the register provides an invaluable directory of the greater part of the city's master traders and craftsmen.[1]

The register records the admission of 5,997 freemen between 15 January 1500 and 15 January 1600, and it is upon these 6,000 that attention will here be concentrated.[2] A distinction is made throughout between freemen by inheritance and other entrants, and the former grew steadily in numbers during the century. In the quarter-century 1501-26 they accounted for 229 admissions out of 1,348 (17 per cent), whereas by 1576-1601 they numbered 603 out of 1,687 (nearly 36 per cent). Unfortunately the remaining freemen are not subdivided into freemen by apprenticeship and by redemption. It might be assumed that the majority were always ex-apprentices, but for the fact that for the period 1482-8 the register divides the 493 new recruits into three, of which sixty-four were admitted by inheritance and 139 by apprenticeship, but the other 290 belonged to neither class.

---

[1] *Register of Freemen*, ed. Collins, *passim*. Its limitations are discussed by R. B. Dobson, 'Admissions to the freedom of the city of York', *Econ. H.R.* 2nd ser. xxvi (1973), 1-22; Palliser, 'York', 267-72.

[2] The dating of entries by Collins is slightly more than one year out and is silently corrected throughout this book; e.g. his year 1500 is that beginning on 15 Jan. 1501 New Style, and his 1600 begins 15 Jan. 1601.

It would be rash to assume, however, that the proportion of ex-apprentices remained fixed during the Tudor period, since that of freemen by inheritance did not.

The evidence of paternity for freemen by inheritance affords some information on the longevity of family businesses. Throughout the century, fewer than half followed the same trade as their fathers, and a three-generation business was a rarity. An examination of all freemen by inheritance between 1580 and 1603 revealed 241 businesses where father was succeeeded by son, but only fifty-six of them lasted more than two generations. Furthermore, only nine can be clearly traced for more than a century. Of these, the longest-lasting was that of the Wightmans, who were millers for five generations, from 1564 until at least 1711. Such stability was most exceptional, for usually mortality among male heirs, emigration, and upward or downward social mobility, conspired to prevent long-lasting business of any kind.[1]

The freemen admissions can be classified in a variety of ways, any of which involves some arbitrary choices. The method used here, for the sake of comparison, is to adopt the nine groupings used by W. G. Hoskins in his analysis of the freemen of Leicester, adding to them an extra group, 'personal services', consisting chiefly of barbers, surgeons, apothecaries, and scriveners.[2] Of the other groups, 'textiles' accounts for the men who processed wool and other fibres, as well as those who serviced them by making cards, combs, and other tools. 'Clothing' includes all who made, or dealt in, finished garments. 'Leather' comprises tanners, skinners, saddlers, and curriers, but not the important cordwainers, who made shoes to sell retail, and who have therefore been added to 'clothing'. 'Food and drink' is a comprehensive group, taking in fishermen and innholders as well as butchers, bakers, and other victuallers. 'Household' covers those who provided miscellaneous goods for the home, like candles, knives, pewter, and silver. 'Building' includes all trades involved in the construction or repair of houses and churches;

[1] Palliser, 'York', pp. 289–93.
[2] Hoskins, *Provincial England*, pp. 94 f. A different categorization has been employed in an invaluable comparison of nine towns: Phythian-Adams, 'Economic and social structure', pp. 16, 39 f.

'rural' comprises chiefly blacksmiths, spurriers, and yeomen; 'distributive' includes merchants and allied trades as well as porters, sledmen, panniermen, and mariners; and 'miscellaneous' is a residual class, including gentlemen, labourers, armourers, bowyers and fletchers, minstrels, clerks and clergy, parchment makers and stationers.

Table 3 gives the number of freemen admissions to these groups in each decade, both in absolute terms and as percentages of total admissions. It is at once apparent that there were no dramatic changes in the relative sizes of the groups during the century. The clothing trades were the largest, with more than a fifth of all admissions to their credit. The food and drink trades came next, with almost as many admissions, and in the period 1510-40 they temporarily supplanted the clothing trades to become the largest group. The only other group which approached these two in size was the distributive class, inflated by including the largest single trade (the merchants). These three groups between them expanded their share of the total admissions fairly steadily, from 53 per cent in the first decade of the century to 62 per cent in the last, most of the smaller groups shrinking slightly in compensation.

Was this occupational structure typical of a large Tudor town? Similar statistics available for Bristol, Chester, Coventry, Exeter, Hull, Leicester, Lynn, Northampton, Norwich, and Worcester suggest that the major groups of trades were comparable in size.[1] In all eleven towns the basic victualling, clothing, and building trades loomed large: it had to be so, for the townsmen had to feed, clothe, and house themselves and also provide those services for extensive hinterlands. Nevertheless, there were major differences between the towns in their industrial composition. York had relatively small numbers engaged in the leather and textile crafts, while Coventry in 1522 had as many as 33 per cent of its assessed citizens in the textile trades alone, Norwich in 1525 had 30 per cent, and Worcester in the period 1540-90 had over

---

[1] Hoskins, *Provincial England*, pp. 80, 94; Pound, 'Social and trade structure of Norwich', pp. 56, 60; D. M. Woodward, 'The Chester leather industry, 1558-1625', *Trans. Hist. Soc. Lancs. and Cheshire*, cxix (1967), 67; Dyer, *City of Worcester*, p. 82; Phythian-Adams, 'Economic and Social Structure', pp. 15-20, 39 f.

TABLE 3
York Trades, 1500–1600

A: Freemen Admissions to Trade Groups

	1500-10	1510-20	1520-30	1530-40	1540-50	1550-60	1560-70	1570-80	1580-90	1590-1600	Totals
Clothing	128	81	86	104	128	145	122	141	161	173	1269
Food & Drink	83	116	100	132	119	125	123	132	134	125	1189
Distributive	87	48	85	80	70	73	82	69	90	138	822
Building	42	36	51	50	53	47	49	57	71	58	514
Textile	56	58	43	57	49	52	34	40	26	49	464
Household	35	34	42	52	50	60	55	47	48	44	467
Miscellaneous	60	60	46	43	58	56	37	35	31	29	455
Leather	29	28	26	39	39	39	49	47	47	47	390
Rural	23	37	12	20	23	25	22	25	22	19	228
Personal services	13	20	19	18	11	10	20	16	11	15	153
Net Total:	556	518	510	595	600	632	593	609	641	697	5951
Plus trades not given	9	12	4	12	3	2	1	2	1		46
Gross Total:	565	530	514	607	603	634	594	611	642	697	5997
Of which women numbered	7	2	5	7	5	5	2	2	3	4	42

B: Freemen Admissions to Trade Groups as percentages of all Admissions to Freedom *

	1500–10	1510–20	1520–30	1530–40	1540–50	1550–60	1560–70	1570–80	1580–90	1590–1600	1500–1600
Clothing	23.0	15.6	16.9	17.5	21.4	23.0	20.6	23.2	25.1	24.8	21.4
Food & Drink	14.9	22.4	19.6	22.2	19.8	19.7	20.7	21.7	20.9	17.9	20.0
Distributive	15.7	9.3	16.7	13.4	11.7	11.5	13.8	11.3	14.1	19.8	13.8
Building	7.6	6.9	10.0	8.4	8.8	7.4	8.3	9.4	11.1	8.3	8.6
Textile	10.1	11.2	8.4	9.6	8.2	8.2	5.7	6.6	4.1	7.0	7.8
Household	6.3	6.6	8.2	8.7	8.3	9.5	9.3	7.7	7.5	5.3	7.8
Miscellaneous	10.8	11.6	9.0	7.2	9.7	8.9	6.2	5.7	4.8	4.2	7.6
Leather	5.2	5.4	5.1	6.6	6.5	6.2	8.3	7.7	7.3	6.7	6.6
Rural	4.1	7.1	2.4	3.4	3.8	4.0	3.7	4.1	3.4	2.7	3.8
Personal services	2.3	3.9	3.7	3.0	1.8	1.6	3.4	3.0	1.7	2.2	2.6

*This table analyses the 5,951 freemen whose trades are listed.

40 per cent, making it the most industrialized town for which figures are available.[1]

The largest individual trades and crafts of York, as measured by freemen admissions, are classified in Table 4. The mercers or merchants proper were the largest of all, though if one adds in the associated lesser trades, the draper–tailor–hosier group was slightly larger, with 627 admissions as against 617 merchants and associates. Each of these guilds accounted for just over 10 per cent of all freemen admissions. Next in importance came the cordwainers, bakers, butchers, and tanners, who appeared among the leading seven trades throughout the century, and the carpenters, for whom there was a steady demand in a city of timber-framed houses. The textile trades' slow decline during the century is confirmed by the disappearance of the tapiters and weavers from the leading twelve after 1575. The millers were among the largest twelve trades in the first half of the century, and the glovers in the second. Table 4 underrates the importance of the tilers, however. These craftsmen also laid bricks, and bricklayers occur by name in the register only from the 1590s onwards. If they are included, the tilers rank among the leading twelve from 1525 to the end of the century.

In none of the other inland towns analysed were the merchants and mercers the largest group, though they did understandably hold this position in early sixteenth-century Bristol, Chester, and Exeter. At some the leather crafts held this position—shoemakers at Northampton, glovers and shoemakers in Elizabethan Chester—and at others the textile crafts—weavers at Worcester and Norwich—while Coventry was dominated by butchers and cappers, and Leicester by butchers. Nevertheless, the common pattern in the towns was more significant than the differences between them: mercers and merchants, tailors, shoemakers, butchers, bakers, and tanners appear almost everywhere among the twelve largest trades.

---

[1] The various statistics are drawn from different sources; in particular, Worcester's (in the absence of a freemen's register) are based on wills. This might raise doubts about comparability, but a sample check at York between freemen's admissions and wills (for a period twenty years apart) shows close agreement between the two sources.

TABLE 4
The Leading Occupations 1500–1600

1500–25		1525–50		1550–75		1575–1600	
Merchants	118	Merchants	144	Tailors	152	Merchants	181
Tailors	87	Tailors	114	Merchants	120	Tailors	157
Cordwainers	61	Cordwainers	68	Bakers	75	Bakers	78
Fishers	47	Tapiters	68	Cordwainers	66	Cordwainers	77
Butchers	43	Tanners	58	Tanners	65	Innholders	69
Bakers	41	Bakers	49	Butchers	64	Butchers	64
Tanners	41	Butchers	42	Glovers	44	Tanners	62
Weavers	39	Victuallers	42	Innholders	40	Glovers	54
Tapiters	37	Millers	35	Carpenters	34	Drapers	52
Haberdashers	37	Carpenters	33	Tapiters	34	Carpenters	49
Millers	35	Labourers	32	Tilers	32	Joiners	40
Carpenters	32	Tilers	29	Weavers	30	Blacksmiths	35

Note: Merchants include corn merchants, mercers, and chapmen; cordwainers include shoemakers; tanners include barkers; weavers include woollen, linen and silk weavers; carpenters include sawyers; innholders include innkeepers; drapers include linen drapers.

4

The merchants, the largest and wealthiest group in the city, had very diverse businesses. Unfortunately, no York merchant's papers seem to survive, but scattered references attest the breadth of their interests. Just before the Reformation, one was selling wine, wax, and oil to Newburgh Priory, and another supplying Durham Priory with sugar, currants, spices, and paper.[1] Some merchants dealt in building materials, and some in foodstuffs: in 1565 one was trading in cargoes of beans, malt, cheese, salt, and wine with Berwick and Newcastle.[2] But perhaps the most profitable trade was in lead, which York men exported to the Low Countries, Gascony, Prussia, and possibly also to Spain and the Mediterranean.[3]

The merchants were equally diverse in importance. At the lower end, it was possible for young men to become freemen and members of the merchants' guild while being only agents for the greater merchants;[4] at the upper end, a York merchant might aspire to become a member of one of the national merchants' societies. Few did so, however, for York men were no longer numbered among the really important overseas traders.[5] This became apparent when the Merchants Adventurers, dominated by the Londoners, tried to exclude all retailers from their ranks; it transpired that all York merchants, even the richest, kept shops, and they resisted to such effect that when the ban was at length imposed in 1564, Hull and York merchants were exempted.[6] Nevertheless, in their own city the York merchants were dominant. Numbering a tenth of all freemen, they provided half the Tudor mayors and aldermen; and for eleven years in the sixteenth century the mayor of the city and the master of the mercers' guild were one and the same.

The terminology of trading in Tudor England was confused.

---

[1] P.R.O., C1/341/57; *The Durham Household Book*, ed. J. Raine, Surtees Soc. xviii (1844), pp. 37 f., 116–8, 158, 216 f.

[2] P.R.O., E190/303/2.

[3] *York Mercers*, ed. Sellers, pp. 135 f., 161 f.; *L.P. Hen. VIII* xxi (1), no. 1334.

[4] e.g. B.I.H.R., prob. reg. xxii, fo. 184; xxiii, fos. 153, 315.

[5] Drake, *Eboracum*, pp. 229, 363; *York Mercers*, ed. Sellers, pp. 162 f., 209 f.; B.I.H.R., prob. reg. xxiii, fo. 326ᵛ.

[6] *York Mercers*, ed. Sellers, pp. lviii f., 164 f.

At York, the terms mercer, merchant, grocer, and chapman seem to have overlapped considerably, if indeed they were not synonymous. The real distinction among York's distributive traders was between the great men and the humble. On the one hand, the mercers' or merchants' guild, with its associated grocers, spicers, apothecaries, and corn-chapmen dominated civic life. Separated from them by a wide gulf were the petty chapmen, hawkers, and pedlars (mostly unfree) who traded on a small scale, and the multitude of poor men who operated transport services. A group of mariners operated a freight service between York and Hull, a vital link for a city which was no longer a sea-going port. Long-distance land transport, including a regular service to London, was performed by carriers. Their service was an essential but routine one, and little is heard of them except when epidemics threatened, when the corporation would promptly forbid them to ply to the capital.[1] The peripatetic life of a carrier can be glimpsed in the will of John Greyn, glover and carrier of York. He bequeathed a horse at Hinderskelfe (now Castle Howard), and asked to be buried 'wher it shall happen me to depart furth of this world', an unusual bequest for a citizen, who nearly always specified his own parish church.[2]

Within the city, goods were distributed by porters and labourers from the riverside to homes and warehouses. Heavier goods were moved by horsedrawn sleds, whose owners were rather more prosperous than the porters; one sledman operated a 'fleet' of five horses.[3] The porters and labourers carried mainly grain, vegetables, salt, and fuel. They formed a trade guild of a special kind, closely protected and supervised by the corporation, who fixed their charges, raising them periodically to allow for inflation.[4] Yet another group of carriers were the 'burnleders' or water carriers. Their trade would be vital, except to the rich few who had wells in their own yards, and though only two became freemen during the whole century, there must have been many others. Historians, with a natural interest in progress, have charted the gradual movement towards a piped water supply during the seventeenth

[1] e.g. *Y.C.R.* vi. 64, 70, 72; vii. 15, 181 f.
[2] Y.M.L., MS L2(5)a, f. 139 (1524).   [3] *Y.C.R.* viii. 98.
[4] *Y.C.R.* ii. 122; vii. 40; viii. 32; Y.C.A., B 31, fo. 399.

century: but as late as the 1680s the normal supply was from leather sacks carried on horseback.[1]

York's peak prosperity in the century 1350–1450 had rested on the twin bases of textiles and long-distance trade. The merchants still traded far afield in the Tudor period, if on a smaller scale, but the textile crafts suffered much more heavily. In 1561 the city council told the government that 'where as in olde tymes past the said Citie hath moche prospered in clothe makyng', there were now only fourteen weavers in the city, all of them poor. Weaving had migrated to the West Riding, where water power was available and the cost of living lower.[2] Weaving was preceding by dyeing, carding, and spinning. Numerous dyers figure in the freemen's register, but no carders and only four spinsters, probably because these tasks were left to women: in 1542 a widow bequeathed a gift to 'old Jenet my spynner' and arrears of wages to 'Elisabeth my work woman or carder' in terms suggesting that such servants were not unusual.[3] There were other ancillary crafts, which all tended to disappear as weaving declined: cardmakers last appeared among the new freemen in the 1550s, fullers in the 1570s, and shearmen in the 1580s.

The 'tapiters', who made coverlets, bed-coverings, and wallhangings, survived the textile slump better than the weavers. Ninety-seven were made free between 1510 and 1550; two sat among the Twenty-Four, and one went on to be elected alderman. One tapiter left a net estate of £220, including £100 in debts owed to him, some from villagers near the city, and one from as far away as Newark. He had a workhouse with three looms and three spinning wheels, and in his storehouse and wool chamber were seventy-two stones of yarn, fifty-two of wool, and sixty of 'Wald' (Wolds wool?).[4]

While textiles declined, the leather crafts were growing. York was typical of those towns, situated in mixed agricultural areas, where 'the leather crafts assumed a large importance in the absence of any other dominant industrial

---

[1] R. Plot, *The Natural History of Staffordshire* (Oxford, 1686), p. 38. 'Watterledders' or 'bowrnledders' regularly contributed to the bakers' guild: B.L. Add 33852, fos. 10, 12, *et passim*.

[2] *Y.C.R.* vi. 13 f., 17.   [3] Y.M.L., MS L2(5)a, fo. 208ʳ.

[4] B.I.H.R., original probate records, R. Hewton 1553.

activity'.[1] Between 1550 and 1600 York's four leather crafts—tanners, skinners, saddlers, and curriers—accounted for 7.2 per cent of freemen admissions, and if cordwainers and glovers are included, the figure becomes 14.8. The skinners prepared skins and furs from many different animals. Anthony Appylbe stocked the skins of foxes, hares, cats, fitchews, and lambs in 1541, and he owed substantial debts to two men of Cockermouth, possibly for supplying him with skins.[2] The skins, after being prepared by the skinners, were treated by curriers or leather dressers, while hides were prepared by tanning, usually with bark. Dressing and tanning formed respectively the light and heavy branches of the industry.

Tanners were more numerous than curriers, five of them becoming free every two years in Elizabeth's reign. They secured supplies of cattle hides from the city butchers, but bark was more difficult to obtain as wood became scarce about York. Fortunately oak bark was plentiful in the West Riding, where a leather industry arose to use it. Early in the sixteenth century a York tanner arranged to buy 300 quarters of bark from a tanner of Leeds, for a price of £15 spread over six years.[3] Occasionally tanners' wills provide other glimpses of their trade. One was owed 13 nobles for leather by a Micklegate shoemaker. Another asked that the leather in his 'barkehouse' should not be valued as it stood, but that his executors should retain his servants until it was dressed and worth more.[4]

The clothing crafts suffered a recession early in the sixteenth century, but more than made up the ground under Elizabeth, and by the 1580s and 1590s they comprised a quarter of all new freemen. Plainly they were serving a much wider area than the city, and to do so they were having to use cloth made elsewhere, often by those West Riding workers who had crippled the city's own industry. The largest clothing craft, and the second largest of all crafts, was the tailors'. The drapers were much fewer in number but far more influential:

[1] L. A. Clarkson, 'The leather crafts in Tudor and Stuart England', *Agric. Hist. Rev.* xiv (1966), pp. 32 f., 38.
[2] B.I.H.R., original probate records, A. Appylbe 1541.
[3] P.R.O., C1/342/52.   [4] B.I.H.R., prob. reg. xi, fo. 452; ix, fo. 479.

in 1523 there were only eight, but seven were present or future city councillors.[1] The tailors' and drapers' guilds co-operated from 1492 or earlier, and united by 1551, while a third guild, that of the hosiers, joined them by 1585.[2] The drapers had extensive businesses. John Litster's shop in 1541 contained 479 yards of 'western' cloth and 247½ yards of other sorts, and in 1585 it was said that Christopher Maltby, alderman and draper, owed over £1,700 to four merchant tailors of London for clothes delivered to him.[3]

The other large clothing trades were the leather-working cordwainers and glovers. The glovers steadily increased in numbers until in Elizabeth's reign they were the twelfth largest craft. Their market must have been expanding, though by 1607 they were facing increasing competition from London glovers. They obtained sheepskins from the city butchers, fashioning them not only into gloves but also into purses and keybands.[4] Cordwainers made leather shoes, and the term was used interchangeably with shoemakers. Their numbers, and the absence of clogmakers, suggest that wooden shoes, common in the fifteenth century, had become obsolete.[5] There was a good choice of shoe sizes: one cordwainer in 1522 bequeathed no less than 120 pairs of lasts. The stock of a woman shoemaker in 1589 included thirteen pairs of shoes and 'pantables' (slippers), two pairs of children's shoes, twenty-two pairs of pumps for men or women, and four pairs of double-soled shoes. She was owed money by neighbouring countryfolk as well as by citizens.[6]

Of the 'household' crafts, the most powerful were the gold-smiths, so called from the most valuable of their products, although the bulk of their work was in silver. Theirs was a luxury craft relying heavily on immigrant talent, judging from the names of masters such as John Colan (d. 1490) and his son Herman; certainly the goldsmith and sheriff Martin Soza (d. 1560), was a Spaniard. Four goldsmiths attained

[1] Y.C.A., B 10, fo. 63ᵛ.

[2] Johnson, *Company of Merchant Taylors*, pp. 36–43; *Y.C.R.* v. 58.

[3] B.I.H.R., original probate records, J. Litster 1541; P.R.O., REQ. 2/244/37.

[4] Y.C.A., B 33, fo. 82; *Y.C.R.* iii. 181–4.

[5] Harrison, *Life in a Medieval College*, p. 72; *York Plays*, ed. L. T. Smith (Oxford, 1885), p. xxii.

[6] B.I.H.R., prob. reg. ix, fo. 240; original probate records, anon. 1589.

the aldermanic bench, a sure sign of wealth for a small craft with only one per cent of all freemen admissions. The source of their wealth is obvious from a glance at the wills and inventories of the richer citizens, who amassed silver and silvergilt plate in large quantities, or from the widespread distribution of Elizabethan church plate made at York.[1]

The pewterers, about as numerous as the goldsmiths, made table-ware of an alloy of tin, widely used by those who could not afford plate but did not need to rely entirely on wooden trenchers. A stationer's buttery contained 87 lb. of pewter, and a tapiter had 65 lb., while further up the social scale a Minster canon owned 360 lb.[2] The pewterers, like the goldsmiths, probably served a wide area. In the early sixteenth century, when their numbers were probably at their maximum, the York pewterers enjoyed almost a monopoly of northern manufacture, and were influential enough to join with their London colleagues in securing an Act of Parliament in their favour.[3]

Smaller metal crafts included the specialized cutlers and bladesmiths, and others who manufactured a very miscellaneous range of goods. The pinners and wiredrawers made bread graters, mousetraps, shoe buckles, and fishhooks; the founders made stirrups, spurs, candlesticks, and 'chawfyndishes', those dishes used for keeping food hot which figure so often in York inventories. Girdlers' work included the making of 'daggar chapes, purse knoppes, bulyons, book claspes, dawkes, dog colers, [and] girdilles'.[4] The locksmiths made locks, keys, 'brandrets' (gridirons), and ploughstrakes, while the turners made bowls, dishes, wheels, chairs, and 'dublers' (large plates). Another small but essential craft made the candles which were the only form of artificial light for the well-to-do.

More essential even than these crafts were the victualling trades, which accounted for one in five of all new freemen,

---

[1] e.g. T. M. Fallow and H. B. McCall, *Yorkshire Church Plate*, 2 vols. (Y.A.S. extra series 1912–15), i. pp. xix f.

[2] B.I.H.R., original probate records, N. Mores 1538, R. Hewton 1553, T. Marser 1547.

[3] Bartlett, 'Economy of York', pp. 42–4; Hatcher and Barker, *Hist. British Pewter*, pp. 72–7, 173.

[4] Y.C.A., E 60, fo. 8; *York Memorandum Book*, i. 187; ii. 297; *Y.C.R.* vii. 96 f.

a proportion that suggests they served a wide rural hinterland. The bakers alone accounted for nearly 5 per cent of freemen admissions under Elizabeth, though their numbers might be explained by a lack of home baking within York. The numerous innholders, however, clearly indicate a service industry for the region, since inns were by definition places of accommodation, and from 1578 all innholders were expected to provide at least six beds for guests. Standards of meals for guests were also laid down; a normal dinner was to include pottage, boiled and roast meat, bread, and ale or beer.[1] Star Chamber cases of the 1530s reveal the varied clientèle patronizing York's inns and lodging-houses: the servants of a county gentleman, a German merchant from Hull taking a holiday, and a London law student visiting northern properties which he owned. Even the county sheriff lodged at an inn when he attended sessions of the Council in the North.[2] Even so, it is startling to find that in 1537, when a royal visit was expected, there were 1,035 beds available for strangers in the city and suburbs, over and above those in the city liberties, and those kept by merchants for their friends, apparently amounting to a further two or three hundred.[3]

Until the accession of Elizabeth the number of innholders enfranchised remained steady at between six and nine per decade, but after that they increased enormously: twenty-one in the 1560s, twenty-three in the 1570s, twenty-seven in the 1580s, and thirty in the 1590s. And they became respectable as well as numerous: in Henry VII's reign, as has been seen, elected aldermen had to give up innkeeping, but from 1540 onwards innholders were elected without restrictions. This growth in numbers and worldly esteem can be attributed partly to the general growth of innkeeping in Tudor and Stuart England to keep pace with greater travel and internal trade, and the rise of a major fair at nearby Howden, for instance, brought custom to the York inns.[4] However, the boom in York innkeeping began suddenly around 1560, and was probably linked with the establishment of a Northern

[1] Y.C.R. vi. 44, 140; vii. 7, 181; Y.C.A., B 31, fo. 101ʳ.
[2] Yorks. Star Chamber Proceedings, iii. 21, 26, 83–5, 128–31.
[3] L.P. Hen. VIII, xii (2), no. 22; Addenda i (1), no. 1192. The version in Y.C.R. iv. 21 misprints some figures.
[4] Y.C.R. viii. 16.

Ecclesiastical Commission in the city, and the permanent establishment there of the Council in the North, in 1561. In 1577, of 239 inns in Yorkshire, no fewer than 86 were located in the city and Ainsty. For York alone a figure exists for 1596, when the corporation licensed sixty-four men and women as innholders.[1]

Those making and selling drinks, unlike the innholders, are not fairly represented in the registers, as these trades were largely run on a part-time basis. When the council licensed the sixty-four innholders in 1596, they allowed also eighty-three brewers and 103 tipplers or alehouse-keepers; the lists show that all the tipplers, and all but five brewers, had other occupations. The ratio of alehouses to population was high, one for every 100 people; yet the number increased further, despite corporation disapproval. There were 122 alehouse-keepers at York in 1597, and 156 in 1609.[2] Malt-making, likewise, was by no means confined to the freemen maltsters. In 1540 Layton told Cromwell that there were 'xl. lx. a hundrethe, I knowe not howe many malte kylnes' in York. He recommended their suppression, because 'every marchant of the towne makethe hym a kylne' and neglected his 'olde trade of marchandise'. No action, however, was taken until 1598, when the city council suppressed at least half of York's 117 kilns.[3] One of the citizens who profited by malt-making was Henry Procter, notary public and registrar to the Ecclesiastical Commission, who gave evidence in 1585 that he 'had a kylne of his owne in his owne house at York and that he used then and long before and eversence to convert barly into malt at his said kylne'.[4]

As in all Tudor towns, the victualling crafts were closely watched by a suspicious corporation for signs of malpractices, like adulteration of food or conspiracy to raise prices. There is no reason to expect that they were more (or less) dishonest than any other group, but their role in the urban economy was literally vital, and the York corporation frequently

[1] P.R.O., S.P. 12/117, no. 37; T. P. Cooper, 'Some old York inns', *Associated Architectural Soc. Reports and Papers*, xxxix (1928-9), 292-301.

[2] Cooper, 'Some old York inns', 292-301; Y.C.A., B 31, fo. 273ʳ; Wilson, 'Corporation of York', p. 14.

[3] *L.P. Hen. VIII* xv, no. 515; Addenda i(2), no. 1453; Y.C.A., F 6, fos. 322-6.

[4] P.R.O., REQ. 2/192/24.

intervened in their affairs. The chief grievance against the bakers was a frequent lack of sufficient loaves at the right prices, and throughout the Tudor and early Stuart periods the council struggled, never entirely effectively, to control output and prices. Intermittently, they resorted to the drastic step of destroying the free bakers' monopoly, sanctioning competition by a rival group of 'bolle bakers', some of whom were townsfolk earning a supplementary wage, and others countryfolk. Swift action was likewise taken against the butchers and the millers whenever they conspired to raise prices, including on one occasion the imprisonment of the searchers of the millers' guild.[1] Matters were rarely pushed to the extreme found in some towns, where the entire membership of a victualling guild might be imprisoned or disfranchized for striking against corporation demands, though in 1495 the butchers were imprisoned for nearly three months for 'diverse' offences.[2]

The butchers, who accounted for four per cent of all new freemen in the second half of the sixteenth century, were rich enough to have their own guildhall and to provide several members of the Twenty-Four. They were a clannish trade, all their freemen members living in the same street, and those who became city councillors marrying among themselves to the exclusion of non-butchers.[3] There was a continual battle between the butchers, keen to secure good grazing lands near York, and the city council, who were anxious to keep the city's hinterland under corn.[4] Five butchers' wills made between 1510 and 1535 indicate their sphere of influence, for these men made charitable bequests to nearly a score of villages in the Vale of York, most of them within five or six miles of the city.[5]

Smaller victualling crafts, but none the less vital, were the millers, fishers, fishmongers, and cooks. The millers were indispensable, for while home baking on a small scale was common, milling required more equipment. However, there was no monopolist miller, as there was in many rural manors

[1] *Y.C.R.* iv. 147; v. 91, 98, 102, 125–8, 166 f.; vi. 1; Cartwright, *Chapters Hist. Yorks.*, pp. 278–81.

[2] *Y.C.R.* ii. 121.   [3] Palliser, 'York', pp. 188 f.

[4] *Y.C.R.* ii. 154, 181; iii. 45–8, 67, 172; v. 35 f., 56, 87.

[5] B.I.H.R., prob. reg. ix, fos. 52, 200, 303, 328; xi. fo. 142; xiii, fo. 30.

and a few towns, and citizens could patronise a variety of windmills, watermills, and horsemills. The fishers and fishmongers respectively caught and sold the fish that bulked so large in Tudor diets, for meat-eating without a dispensation was forbidden in Lent and every Wednesday (from 1563), Friday, and Saturday. Curiously, however, the fishers, after a peak of twenty-seven admissions to freedom in the decade 1510–20, declined to a level of only two admissions during the last twenty years of the century, whereas the fishmongers recruited at a steady level. The difference in their fortunes was perhaps brought about by a change in demand from freshwater fish to seafish, or by non-freemen taking over the fishing of the rivers, for as late as 1697 the Ouse was still 'full of good fish', especially cod and salmon.[1]

The tradesmen grouped here as offering 'personal services' accounted for very few freemen. The only ones with more than a handful of members were the barber-surgeons, who were admitted at the rate of about one a year. There were also specialist surgeons, whose charges put their services out of reach of poor citizens; from time to time the council arranged for a surgeon to heal the poor without payment. The need for such a service can be seen from the complaint of a tailor, whose broken arm was treated 'with great expences' by two surgeons, but to no avail; he apparently had to give up his craft and become an inmate in the merchants' hospital.[2]

There was, however, a substantial group of freemen concerned with stationery and similar trades. During the century forty-six parchment makers, fifteen stationers, and three bookbinders were admitted to the freedom, but these were far from all, because some stationers, as well as printers and booksellers, lived within the Minster Liberty. Ursyn Mylner took up the franchise only when he moved his business from Minster Yard to Blake Street, and in 1603 a stationer was enfranchised for a reduced fee because there were no other *free* stationers in the city. Gordon Duff was able to identify twenty-seven stationers, bookbinders, and printers operating in York in the century before 1557, and only sixteen appear

---

[1] *The Journeys of Celia Fiennes*, ed. C. Morris (London, 1947), p. 76.
[2] *York Mercers*, ed. Sellers, p. 151.

in the freemen's register.[1] As he relied largely on printed extracts from the Minster archives for the unfree book dealers, the total number in the stationery trades was probably at least double those who became freemen. Rather startlingly, even on Duff's figures the twenty-seven York men form a larger number than those for any other provincial town except Oxford's forty-four.

York was an early centre of printing and publishing. A breviary for the York use, printed at Venice in 1493, was probably published at York. Between 1507 and 1535 ten other books printed elsewhere are known to have been published at York, and at least six books were printed in the city, by Hugo Goes and Ursyn Mylner, about the years 1509-16. They were probably of Netherlandish origin, as were all the York publishers of this period, except for the Frenchman John Gachet.[2] The histories of the York press by Davies and Duff record no printing in the city between 1516 and 1639, but the account roll of the Corpus Christi Guild for 1534 recorded 3s. 8d. spent on making an image and 'pro pryyntyng iijᶜ letters'.[3] This could mean they were printed locally, for York guild accounts usually specified when work was carried out elsewhere. If so, it would explain a minor problem about the Pilgrimage of Grace: Darcy suggested having the Pilgrims' oath and articles printed, and the Misses Dodds wondered where this could have been done, as they believed the press at York to have closed down about 1516.[4] Likewise the 'printed notes', which a scrivener set up as advertisements at street corners in 1597, were perhaps printed locally.[5] At the most, however, only jobbing printing is likely to have been carried on after 1516, for had many books been printed there, a few would surely have survived. Yet whatever the state of the York press, the range of books to be bought in York was growing. A Stonegate stationer who died in 1538 left a stock of only some 125 books, almost all of them legal or religious,

---

[1] E. G. Duff, *A Century of the English Book Trade* (London, 1905), *passim*; Y.C.A., B 32, fo. 281ʳ.

[2] R. Davies, *A Memoir of the York Press* (Westminster, 1868), pp. 7-27; E. G. Duff, *The English Provincial Printers, Stationers and Bookbinders to 1557* (Cambridge, 1912), pp. 42-65, 133 f.

[3] Y.C.A., C 102/3. [4] Dodds, *Pilgrimage of Grace*, i. 252.

[5] Y.C.A., B 31, fo. 272ʳ.

though they included Ovid and Aesop. By contrast, the stock of another stationer in 1616 ran to nearly 3,000 volumes, and though much was religious, there were also books on ethics, logic, history, law, medicine, education, poetry, plays, fiction, and music. And his stock was kept up to date: at least thirteen of the works he had for sale had been published that year. He catered for a wide market, and was owed money for books by many of the Yorkshire gentry.[1]

Another group of trades has been somewhat arbitrarily described as 'rural', of which the most numerous were smiths, blacksmiths, and spurriers. Their services will have been in considerable demand, not only from citizens, but from visitors; for the York inns provided even more stabling than they did beds, stabling for 1,711 horses in 1537 as against 1,035 beds.[2] The presumption is that there were a great many day visitors arriving on horseback. However, it may be inaccurate to think of the smiths primarily in this connection. Much of the work of urban smiths was the rough working of iron to form the raw material for the locksmiths, lorimers, and other craftsmen.

The remaining group of crafts is those connected with the building industry. Almost all private buildings were timber-framed with tiled roofs, and most furniture was also wooden. It is therefore not surprising that, of the 514 new freemen of these crafts, 160 were carpenters (wrights) and sawyers, 95 were carvers and joiners, and 127 tilers and tile-makers. Masons and bricklayers were few, and the register includes not a single thatcher or dauber. This does not necessarily mean that no humble Tudor cottages of the mud-and-thatch kind were built, but probably the very poor who had such houses would build their own.

Even before the Reformation brought church-building to an end, the masons were few in number compared to the carpenters and tilers, though the largest group of masons, on the Minster payroll, had no need to take up civic freedom. Such a declining group must have felt very angry at the decision in 1490 to build the Red Tower on the city walls in brick instead

---

[1] Palliser and Selwyn, 'The stock of a York stationer', *passim*; Davies, *Memoir of the York Press*, pp. 342-71.

[2] Above, p. 166, n. 3.

of stone, for not only did they break or steal the tools of the tilers working there, but the Minster master mason and his successor were imprisoned on suspicion of murdering a tiler.[1] No masons took up the freedom of the city after 1536-7, except for two admitted in 1592-3, who may have been working on extensions to the King's Manor, and their guild was defunct by 1561.[2] When, therefore, Ouse Bridge collapsed four years later, the city was in a desperate plight. Not only did the overseer of London Bridge have to advise on the re-building, but an outside mason, Christopher Walmesley, was called in to carry out the work. For more than twenty years he returned to the city from time to time to work on the bridge as well as on the city walls and other places, becoming indeed, despite his non-residence, the last Common Mason to the corporation.[3] In a city with public buildings of stone, masoncraft was still needed, but not on a sufficient scale for full-time craftsmen. William Foster, who served as mason to Lord President Huntingdon, was by craft a tiler.[4]

Another trade hard hit by the Reformation was that of the glaziers, men such as Robert Preston, who in 1503 left to his apprentice 'all my bookes that is fitte for one prentesse of his craffte to lerne by', and John Petty, who died in 1508 during his mayoralty, leaving glass to the Minster and St. Mary's Abbey, besides making a bequest to Furness Abbey for their absolution, 'be cause I have wroght mych wark there'.[5] At the Reformation this employment ceased, and after a steady recruitment of five per decade in the first third of the sixteenth century, only one glazier was made free between 1535-6 and 1552-3. The guild must have been at its lowest ebb in 1551, when the city council agreed to reduce their contribution to the mystery plays, because of 'such povertie and skarsitie as is at this present perceyvid in the glasyars of this citie'.[6] Only the new demand for house windows saved the glaziers from suffering the fate of the masons.

The majority of the building craftsmen were woodworkers, who were gradually absorbed into a single guild. The carpenters

[1] *Y.C.R.* ii. 60 f., 77; Harvey, *English Mediaeval Architects*, pp. 138, 144.
[2] *Y.C.R.* vi. 31.   [3] See p. 76.
[4] Y.C.A., vii. 163; viii. 105; *Register of Freemen*, ii. 13, 21.
[5] *Test. Ebor.* iv. 217, 334.   [6] Y.C.A., B 20, fo. 56ʳ.

were united to the joiners and carvers in 1530 to prevent squabbling among them. The ordinances of the guild, revised in 1563, show that the wheelwrights and sawyers also belonged to it, and that there were at the time forty-three masters in the guild.[1] These crafts together not only controlled the building of houses but also tried to monopolize furniture-making.[2] The carpenters must have had demarcation disputes with the tilers, for in 1586 they secured an order 'that no tyler . . . shall take anie bargaine . . . for anye manner of buyldinge of timber worke'.[3]

The tilers built in brick as well as in tile, but their main work must have been in tiling roofs and also in plastering houses; the tilers and plasterers had united in the fifteenth century, and the freemen's register for the Tudor period does not include a single plasterer. In Elizabeth's reign, brick came more to the fore, and eight freemen admitted in the 1580s and 1590s were described as brickmakers and bricklayers. Nevertheless, a move by the brickmakers to form a separate guild was unsuccessful,[4] and it was only in the seventeenth century that they came into their own with the widespread move from timber to brick building.

5

One of the professions not represented in the register is that of schoolmaster, but it should not be concluded that education was rare, or that only gentry and officials patronized schools and bookshops. The chief evidence for literacy is, admittedly, the ambiguous one of lists of signatures and marks attesting documents; but these sources are numerous enough and consistent enough for the late Tudor period to suggest considerable literacy. For example, of forty-two men who came before the council in the year 1585–6 to have deeds attested or quarrels settled, eighteen (43%) signed rather than made marks. In 1594 twenty-three householders out of fifty-five in St. Denys's parish (42%) signed a document, while the others made marks. Signatures were also

[1] *Y.C.R.* iii. 132; iv. 139, 159; v. 99 f., 163; Y.C.A., E 20A, fo. 226ʳ.
[2] *Y.C.R.* iii. 15.   [3] Y.C.A., B 29, fo. 156ʳ.
[4] Davies, *Walks through York*, p. 138.

made by twenty-nine out of forty-nine churchwardens (59%) in a group of six parishes, and by thirty-seven out of fifty-seven masters of the cordwainers between 1623 and 1631 (65%).[1] These figures suggest a literacy rate among adult males between two-fifths and two-thirds, of the same order as the 58 per cent rate at Chester in 1642, the only urban Protestation Return of that year to provide evidence of literacy.[2] One exceptional document yields firmer evidence for an earlier date. On 22 June 1509 the corporation took an important decision about finance, 'and all the sayd presence in recorde herof they that cowthe write hath subscribed thare names with ther owne hands and the resydew hath setto thare markes'. Nine aldermen, including the mayor, signed and two made marks, but of the Twenty-Four in attendance only one signed and four made marks; this suggests clearly that only the very topmost level of the laity could write.[3] Probably literacy was increasing as the century wore on, and certainly the ability to read, more common than writing in semi-literate societies, must have been widespread, or the number of notices in public places would be inexplicable. Offenders were often pilloried or displayed in public with written notices of their offences, and troubled times produced outbreaks of seditious handbills.[4]

An adult literacy rate of perhaps 50 per cent by the end of the period suggests widely-available education. Some children no doubt learned reading and writing at home, as occasional wills testify.[5] Others acquired a vocational education from scriveners, two of whom were by the end of Elizabeth's reign teaching reading, writing, ciphers, and the casting of accounts.[6] Many children apparently acquired the rudiments of education in petty schools, of which there are sufficient casual mentions to suggest the existence of one in every parish. The best-recorded was that of St. Michael-le-Belfrey, known to have been in existence in 1408 and 1508, and still

---

[1] Y.C.A., E 56; C 6, 1585–6 bk., fos. 79–85; B.I.H.R., C.P. G 2800, and all surviving par. reg. transcripts 1599–1609; Y.M.L., MS Ydii.

[2] L. Stone, 'Literacy and education in England 1640–1900', *Past & Present*, xlii (1969), 100.

[3] Y.C.A., B 9, fo. 47^r.   [4] e.g. *Y.C.R.* iv. 7–13; v. 2 f.; vii. 169.

[5] e.g. B.I.H.R., Dean and Chapter prob. reg. v, fos. 65, 113.

[6] Y.C.A., B 29, fo. 184^r; B 31, fo. 272^r.

in being in 1592-3.[1] A similar institution, held in a chamber in the churchyard of St. Martin's, Coney Street, is mentioned in 1529 and 1552-5, and one in the churchyard of Holy Trinity, King's Court, in 1546, 1591, and by inference in 1600.[2] There are casual mentions of five or six similar parish schools in Elizabeth's reign, as well as of schools in the Merchants' Hall in 1546, on Ouse Bridge in 1555 and in St. Anthony's Hall in 1579 and perhaps earlier.[3] The most interesting of these cryptic references was supplied in evidence given before a government commission in 1593. A tapiter of St. Saviourgate testified that in Mary's reign, when he was aged about twelve, he 'beinge then a scholer, dyd helpe one Sir Richard Murtone, preste of St. Margretes in Walmegate in York, to saye masses of requiem for one Agnes Manners; and this examinate, being then scholer to the sayd Sir Richard Murton, dyd helpe to gather the rentes for the sayd sex cotages' which Agnes had left to the church.[4] Such schools obviously lost their *raison d'être* at the Reformation, but there may in compensation have been an increase in elementary parish schools; certainly most of the York references to such schools are Elizabethan, though that may reflect an increase in records rather than in foundations. The availability of such schools would, however, mean little for the very poor unless their education was free. Alderman Drawswerde's bequest in 1529 was to enable a chantry priest 'to teche vij childer of the parishe, and to take nothyng of them', and much would depend on how many such free places were available in the city.[5]

A number of leading citizens left large amounts, some of £10 a year or more, to 'find' their children at school, presumably

---

[1] Raine, *Mediaeval York*, p. 37; *Test. Ebor.* iv. 334; Y.M.L., Acc. 1966/2, 19, fos. 25-8.

[2] *Test. Ebor.* v. 268-9; B.I.H.R., Y/MCS 16, p. 4; prob. reg. xii, fo. 247[V]; xxv, fo. 1357, *Y.A.J.* xvii. 117.

[3] B.I.H.R., Dr Purvis's 'Tudor Crockford', entries for H. Trinity Micklegate, S. Martin Micklegate, S. M. Bishophill Jr. and S. Sampson; Y.M.L., MS S3(4)a, p. 54; B.I.H.R., R IV Be 1, fo. 45[V]; A. F. Leach, *English Schools at the Reformation, 1546-8* (Westminster, 1896), i. 99, ii. 283; *Y.C.R.* v. 64, 130; viii. 22; *V.C.H. York*, p. 158.

[4] P.R.O., E134/35 and 36 Eliz./Mich. 15.

[5] *Test. Ebor.* v. 269. Similar bequests: ibid., iv. 202; B.I.H.R., prob. reg. ix, fo. 357.

at one of the grammar schools.[1] York was well equipped with
two such schools until 1539, and again after about 1575, but
in the interval between there was at first no school at all, and
later only one, despite pious assumptions about the continuous existence of St. Peter's.[2] It is probably no coincidence
that the only three York boys who can be traced at Eton and
Winchester were all there during that difficult middle third of
the century.[3] The tertiary education of the Universities and
Inns of Court naturally catered for an even smaller minority
than the grammar schools. Not a single councillor is known
to have attended either university before 1600 and no York
layman at all before 1570, though some citizens' sons studying for the church did go to early Tudor Cambridge, as did
the sons of local gentry. York laymen did, however, share
fully in the Elizabethan and early Stuart expansion of the
universities, or at least of Cambridge. Between 1570 and
1610 at least eight sons of aldermen and one of a member of
the Twenty-Four studied at Cambridge; six of them went on
afterwards to the Inns of Court, while Alderman Trew's son
William went to Clement's Inn and the Middle Temple without going to Cambridge. One or two citizens below the level
of the councillors also aspired to higher education for their
children; the sons of a York draper and a York fishmonger
both went to Cambridge in the 1580s.[4]

6

Such, in brief, were the main York trades, crafts, and professions; but it must be repeated that the statistical analysis on
which the survey has been largely based is the freemen's
register, and that tabulated admissions from the register cannot be used as a simple guide to occupational structure without a good many qualifications. In particular, there are not

[1] e.g. B.I.H.R., prob. reg. xi, fos. 534, 761; xvi, fo. 64; Dean and Chapter prob.
reg. v, fo. 14.
[2] See p. 222.
[3] J. F. Kirby, *Winchester Scholars* (London, 1888), pp. 122, 140; W. Sterry,
The Eton College Register 1441–1698 (Eton, 1943), p. 153.
[4] J. and J. A. Venn, *Alumni Cantabrigienses: Part I*, 4 vols. (Cambridge, 1922–
7), *sub* Birkby, Brooke, Dawson, Hall, Herbert, Mosley, Myers, Plommer; *Register
of Admissions to the Honourable Society of the Middle Temple*, ed. H. A. C.
Sturgess, 3 vols. (London, 1949), i. 47.

only an unknown number of involuntary omissions from the register (masters who avoided registration, or who registered but were omitted by mistake), but also deliberate limitations: subordinate craftsmen were of course not eligible, most women did not take up freedom even if they ran a business, while even master craftsmen had no need to register if they dwelt in one of the numerous liberties. It is possible, there-fore, that fluctuations in a craft's numbers may reflect not economic changes but a changing attitude to the freedom by applicants, or a more rigorous pursuit of evaders by the cor-poration. In the late fifteenth century there was a rapid in-crease in lawyers, clerks, physicians, and scriveners admitted, while it was also the only period when any city friars became freemen.[1] Most such groups would dwell outside the city franchise, but it may be that the corporation was mounting a campaign to insist that they could not work within the franchise unless they became freemen. Certainly it was at the same period that the textwriters' guild appealed for protec-tion against part-time competition by the lowly-paid city clergy.[2] There is also frequent evidence from the chamber-lains' accounts that non-freemen could trade within the city by paying a yearly fine rather than taking up the freedom. And just as these men could trade without becoming free, so others might become free without wishing to trade. Sir Thomas Fairfax, who had a town house on Bishophill but usually lived at Nun Appleton in the Ainsty, was one of the earliest gentlemen to seek what would later be called honorary freedom. He told the mayor on 10 August 1599, 'I have longe had a desire to be made fre of this cittie, not for that I have purpose to gaine by the same, but for that I am borne within the liberties, and all my auncestors on both sides have bene either cittizens or Ainstye men.' The corporation promptly granted him the franchise free of charge and with exemption from the usual liability to bear civic office.[3]

Nevertheless, the register remains an invaluable source des-pite all these limitations. It has been shown that recorded admissions in the second quarter of the sixteenth century represent something like half the adult males in the city. This

[1] Dobson, 'Admissions to the freedom', p. 14.
[2] Palliser, 'Trade gilds', p. 106.   [3] Y.C.A., B 32, fo. 41[r].

represents a very substantial proportion of the total work-force, especially if an allowance is also made for freemen missing from the register. The proportion at Norwich, Oxford, Leicester, and Exeter seems to have been much lower in the sixteenth century, though in late seventeenth-century Norwich about half the adult males were free.[1] It would be tempting to speculate on the size of the freemen class and its correlation with factors like the prosperity, population, and spread of popular power in the towns; but many more examples are needed before this can profitably be done. Each town was a law unto itself regarding the regulations for enfranchisement, and it may well be that no valid generalizations would emerge.

---

[1] Pound, 'Social and trade structure of Norwich', pp. 67-9; Clark and Slack, *Crisis and Order in English Towns*, p. 274; *Oxford Council Acts 1583-1626*, ed. H. E. Salter (Oxford Hist. Soc. lxxxvii, 1928), p. xi; Hoskins, *Provincial England*, p. 94; MacCaffrey, *Exeter*, pp. 163 f. The last two figures are expressed only as admissions per decade; I have assumed, as at York, an average twenty-year period between admission and death.

VII

COMMERCE AND TRADE

The citie stondeth the best for trade of marchandise
that ever I se, London excepte: balangers, crayese,
goodly vessells may arrive galantly at the towne syde.
Richard Layton to Thomas Cromwell, 1540[1]

The possession of a business or shop was the mark of a freeman. Freemen sold, and often made, products in their own
shops, and were forbidden to keep market stalls; while
'foreigners' (whether living in York or not) could buy and sell
in the markets but were not allowed to keep shop.[2] The freeman's shop seems usually to have been a front ground-floor
room, often used as a workshop or store. It opened to the
street through a shuttered window, the shutters being let
down to form a counter for sales; hence the complaint of the
cooks' guild that a weaver's wife was baking pies and pasties
'and sells the same uppon her wyndos'.[3] The use of the front
room as a workshop drove many craftsmen into encroaching
on the street for sales, building a 'stall' in front of the house
and roofing it against the weather with a 'penthouse'. The
corporation had constantly to watch out for citizens who
built too far into the street, and in 1606–7 'divers men was
forced by the command of my lord mayor to take up their
shop stalls and to have the same to fall upon turned stoopes
which many men grudge for the loss of those necessary
roomes'.[4]

Surviving inventories show that most shops carried only a
small stock of goods, and many wares were probably made
on demand, a pair of shoes being perhaps ordered on one
market day and collected on the next. The craftsman working

[1] H. Ellis, *Original Letters, Illustrative of English History*, 3rd series, iii (London, 1846), 212–3; dating from *L.P. Hen. VIII*, xv, no. 417.
[2] Palliser, 'Trade gilds of Tudor York', p. 102.
[3] Y.C.A., C 5, 1565–6 book, p. 51.
[4] e.g. *Y.C.R.* vii. 177, viii. 35; Bodley, Gough Yorks. 8, p. 122.

in his 'shop' with shutters lowered was visible to passers-by, and the quality of his workmanship could be seen. The frequent guild rules against night-work by candlelight may have been aimed as much at deceitful workmanship as at unfair competition. It was common even for houses in the main streets to have no front window except that of the shop,[1] and so the corporation's method of disfranchising a man—ordering him to shut his shop window—made work as well as trade virtually impossible.[2] A kind of rough equality was imposed by corporation and guilds in limiting each freeman to a single shop as his trading outlet.[3] The shoemaker Francis Newbie, called before the council in 1594 for a breach of such a regulation, said that

> he having a shoppe in Fossgate which is far frome his howse hath of late maid a shoppe in his house in Walmgate and that his customers do not yet knowe that newe shop; and so craveth that he may be permitted to keepe the said shoppes till his shoppe at home be knowne to his customers.

The corporation granted him a month's grace, after which he was to give up the shop in Fossgate.[4]

The butchers' regulations clearly distinguish between shopkeepers and market traders. Free butchers had to 'sell ther flesh in there owne shoppes or howses wher they doe dwell, and not to come to sell ther flesh in Thursdaie Markett or the Towle Bothe ther', while 'forrein bochers' had the right to trade in the market.[5] Markets were gatherings in a specific place on fixed weekdays at which non-freemen set up stalls. Four main markets were held three times weekly, on Tuesday, Thursday, and Saturday—general ones in the 'two faire marketsteads' of Pavement and Thursday Market, a malt market outside St. Martin's, Coney Street, and a leather market in the Common Hall. There were also fish markets at Foss Bridge and Ouse Bridge and swine markets in Swinegate and Peasholme, while in 1546 a new cloth market was opened in the Common Hall. A weekly beast market was held on Toft Green, at least in the fifteenth century, and in 1590 the queen

---

[1] B.I.H.R., C.P. G. 1036; *Y.C.R.* viii. 14.
[2] e.g. *Y.C.R.* i. 91; ii. 106, 121; vi. 145; viii. 14.
[3] Palliser, 'Trade gilds', p. 102.   [4] Y.C.A., B 31, fo. 83^v.
[5] *Y.C.R.* viii. 17.

authorized a horse and cattle fair fortnightly between Lent and Advent.[1] A mention of 'le markesteid' in the Minster Garth suggests a market of the dean and chapter in addition to all these civic markets, and certainly the canons held a Whit Sunday fair, which the corporation regarded as unfair competition.[2]

It is unfortunate that no Tudor market records survive, but it is known that the markets were much used by local villagers. Men of Heworth and Osbaldwick, for instance, came regularly to them, while the street surface of Bootham was kept in repair chiefly for Clifton men and others coming 'to the market'.[3] The city specialized to some extent as a corn market, and attracted corn for sale from the three surrounding wapentakes.[4] Malt was brought for sale from places as far apart as Pocklington and Barnby Dun, and on one occasion a syndicate of five badgers (corn dealers) came from Skipton to buy malt there.[5] Indeed, the lack of navigable rivers seems to have driven many West Riding men to York for their supplies. The corporation said in 1597 that 'her Majesties subiectes of the west countrye and other places xxx^tie or xl^tie myles distante' had 'yearelye used to make theire provision of corne' at York and to carry it away on horseback.[6]

Fairs tended to attract buyers and sellers from greater distances than markets. The corporation had held two major annual fairs since the thirteenth century, at Whitsun and the Feast of SS. Peter and Paul (29 June). Both were held originally in the Horsefair, but from 1586–7 the former expanded into Thursday Market also, and at the same time it was moved from Sunday to Monday, a sign of the growing Sabbatarianism among the corporation.[7] In 1502, in an attempt to revive the city's flagging trade, the corporation secured a royal grant for two more yearly fairs, but they were not a

---

[1] For city markets see H. Richardson, *The Medieval Fairs and Markets of York*, Borth. P. xx (1961), and *V.C.H. York*, pp. 484–91. The quotation is from Bodley, Rawl. C 886, p. 48.

[2] Bodley, Rawl. B 451, fo. 46^r; *Y.C.R.* viii. 119.

[3] Y.M.L., MS V. xii; Y.C.A. E 31, pt. 1, fo. 4^r.

[4] Thirsk, *Agrarian History*, iv. 589; Y.C.R. v. 46 f.

[5] *Y.C.R.* v. 78–80; P.R.O., C1/591/63; Y.C.A., B 31, fo. 223^v.

[6] Y.C.A., B 31, fo. 246^r.   [7] *V.C.H. York*, pp. 489–90.

success.[1] However, the two older fairs remained popular, and attracted customers from as far as Louth.[2] The city fairs were thrown open to freemen as well as 'foreigners', so that for short spells each year the city saw the unusual spectacle of open trading competition. Unwin has well described urban fairs as 'a kind of inoculation with the dreaded virus of free enterprise'.[3]

Older and more important than the corporation's fairs was the Lammas fair of the archbishop, a two-day gathering which began on the afternoon of 31 July. The most notable feature of the fair—one of the principal fairs in all England[4]— was that during it the archbishop had full jurisdiction throughout the city. The sheriffs surrendered their rods of office to him; he used the city gates as toll points; and he could even hang thieves. In 1521 Wolsey's officials claimed the goods of a freeman who mortally wounded a fellow citizen on Lammas Day, and the city council demurred only because the victim died after the fair was over.[5] The explanation for such an astonishing privilege is that the archbishop had held the fair since at least 1135, long before a corporation existed, and it is best viewed as a brief annual extension of his permanent franchise over the Minster Yard.

At least fifty-three other markets were held in Yorkshire in the Tudor and early Stuart periods,[6] and Yorkers are known to have patronized many of them, just as their inhabitants often came to York. Casual references in the York archives show the men of York patronizing nineteen Yorkshire fairs and markets, as well as places outside the county. Quality goods justified long journeys in search of the right outlets. York goldsmiths and drapers were travelling to Stourbridge Fair, near Cambridge, in the 1560s, while by the end of the century York and London merchants were meeting to do business at Howden Fair.[7]

[1] *Y.C.R.* ii. 172–6; Y.C.A., B 31, fo. 134[V].   [2] *Y.C.R.* v. 124.

[3] G. Unwin, *Industrial Organization in the Sixteenth and Seventeenth Centuries* (Oxford, 1904), p. 305.

[4] Harrison's *Description*, ed. Furnivall, ii. 104.

[5] *V.C.H. York*, p. 490; Richardson, *Fairs and Markets of York*, pp. 11–15; Drake, *Eboracum*, p. 218; *Y.C.R.* iii. 75–7, 79–81.

[6] Thirsk, *Agrarian History*, iv. 468–9.

[7] *Y.C.R.* vi. 63 f.; *Yorks. Philosophical Soc. Annual Report 1965*, p. 22; Palliser, 'York under the Tudors', pp. 47, 52 f.; Y.C.A., B 32, fos. 281–5.

By a charter of Richard I, the citizens of York were exempt from tolls and other charges throughout England. This important privilege was jealously guarded, and much information on the citizens' trading transactions is preserved only because the town authorities involved tried to charge toll and the York corporation fought the case. Ripon was a notable offender, trying to levy tolls from citizens between 1554 and 1582, and distraining goods when payment was refused; the dispute was the more serious because twenty-two of York's crafts regularly patronized the fairs and markets there.[1] Again, in 1564 a York founder set up a stall of pans and kettles in Selby market place during the town's Michaelmas fair. On refusing to pay a penny for stallage, he suffered distraint of a kettle worth 3*s.* 4*d.* The Council in the North upheld his complaint, and ordered the toll-gatherer to return the kettle and to pay him £1 for his costs.[2] It is rather surprising that the Lionheart's handsome charter still survives, for in Elizabeth's reign it was frequently taken up to London to be produced as evidence, or even lent to private citizens to exhibit before the offending town authorities.[3] Other corporations acted similarly, and when York levied tolls in 1536 from the men of three Suffolk ports, Blythburgh produced a copy of its own charter of exemption.[4]

York's markets and fairs were among the most important in Yorkshire, for the city was well situated as a meeting-point for traders and farmers from very different rural economies. Goods and livestock brought for sale in the city included horses, cattle, pigs, sheep, rabbits, cheese, butter, fish, wood, bark, peat, leather, and wool.[5] Seafish were brought from Scarborough, and freshwater fish from Thorne and Crowle in Marshland; turves for fuel also from Marshland; corn from Lincolnshire and Holderness; hemp from Cumberland; and leather from Yorkshire and Lancashire.[6] It was at York that the corporation of Beverley bought wildfowl in 1502-3, and

---

[1] *Y.C.R.* v. 103, 131-4, 144, 151, 159-60; vii. 41, 128; viii. 55; Y.C.A., B 22, fos. 74^r, 91^r.

[2] Y.C.A., E 23, fo. 2.   [3] e.g. *Y.C.R.* vii. 23, 47, 74.
[4] ibid., iv. 4.   [5] ibid., iii. 32 f.
[6] *York Memorandum Book*, i. 199, 222; *York Mercers*, p. 169; *Y.C.R.* ii. 57, 182; iv. 121; Y.C.A., B 31, fos. 302^r, 305^r; *L.P. Hen. VIII*, ix, no. 456; Y.C.A., C 5/2.

at York that Durham Priory purchased fish, corn, spices, raisins, sugar, and paper.[1]

Theoretically, all this buying and selling should have taken place within the rigidly organized system of shops, markets, and fairs, controlled by the corporation, the guilds, and the church. That was the ideal of the medieval corporate town, but it is doubtful whether it was ever fully enforced. There must always have been unofficial markets outside corporation control, especially when large crowds gathered for religious services or public entertainments. In 1580 the cordwainers' guild forbade members to 'goo forth of this citie apon any Sunday with any wares belongyng to their said occupacion to sell or putt to sale at any churche doores or in any churche-yard or other places owte of ffayers or markett'.[2] The corporation waged unceasing battle against other evasions of the 'open market' principle, such as touting for sale in the streets.[3] A more dangerous evasion, because less detectable, was sale in inns. The Skipton malt badgers already mentioned tried to forestall malt coming to the market and to buy it privately at their inn, while in 1603 the merchants' guild banned a recent practice by which members

have gone to the common innes, wher the chapmen, buyers of flax, and other marchandize have lodged, and there have often sollicyted them to ther owne shoppes, wairehouses, or sellars, for the ventinge of ther owne flax, iron, and other merchandize.[4]

This type of 'private marketing' was not new, but it grew considerably in the sixteenth and seventeenth centuries, as regulated markets took an ever-shrinking share of the total volume of transactions. 'The Elizabethan and Stuart inn', Professor Everitt points out, 'has no exact counterpart in the modern world. It was the hotel, the bank, the warehouse, the exchange, the scrivener's office, and the market-place of many a private trader.'[5]

---

[1] G. Poulson, *Beverlac* (London, 1829), p. 264; *Durham Household Book*, ed. Raine, pp. 6, 36–8, 50, 115–18, 136, 216–17, 314.
[2] Y.M.L., MS YIdi.   [3] e.g. *Y.C.R.* ii. 175.
[4] *Y.C.R.* v. 78–80; *York Mercers*, p. 277.
[5] Thirsk, *Agrarian History*, iv. 559.

2

Geographically, one can distinguish five areas in trading relations with York. First was the immediate hinterland, roughly
the three surrounding wapentakes, where its commercial
dominance was overwhelming, and was closely linked with
its shops and markets. Next, the Vale of York, with its hilly
fringes, formed a second catchment area, roughly that within which York men traded at other fairs or attracted men to
their own. The rest of northern England depended much less
on York, but relied on it for certain specialized products,
much as England as a whole came to depend on London for
certain goods. Fourth, the city had more limited economic
relationships with England south of the Humber, apart from
its important trade with London. Finally, despite its decline
from the great age of its merchants adventurers, it still
played a part in Anglo-European trade.

The city's economic dominance went unchallenged in only
the first of these zones. It was fortunate in being sited in a
vale of mixed husbandry, so that dairy produce and meat, as
well as grains, were near at hand. In 1539 three monastic
farms in the Ainsty had a combined acreage of 364 acres of
arable, 368 of pasture and 109 of meadow. The Ainsty had
also (in 1546) an exceptionally large number of taxpayers
assessed on goods of over £10, double the proportion in the
West Riding as a whole. They would be 'mostly farmers of
larger holdings, and were probably producing food for the
markets of York'.[1] In return for supplying the city with
agricultural produce, the villages depended on it for a wide
range of goods and services. Citizens' inventories lists debts
of numerous villagers, incurred either through purchases or
through borrowing money at interest. Alderman Birkeby
(d. 1610) was owed money by men of Acaster Selby, Steeton,
Huntington, and other nearby villages, as well as of Dewsbury, Doncaster, and Middleham.[2] Churchwardens of local
parishes came regularly into town to buy church goods, or
summoned York craftsmen to do work on the spot, especially

[1] Smith, 'Landed income and social structure in the West Riding', pp. 21 f.,
361; *Land and Politics*, pp. 110, 112, 119.
[2] B.I.H.R., C.P. H767.

organ-mending.[1] A catchment area could be worked out from the records of York quarter sessions, showing which countryfolk were accused of offences in the city. On 27 February 1573, for instance, a husbandman of Elvington and a yeoman of Wilberfoss were mutually bound over to keep the peace one to another, and a carpenter of Selby was similarly bound towards an Escrick yeoman.[2]

The city's trade with its hinterland shaded imperceptibly into trade with more distant areas of Yorkshire. The building crafts of the city were notable for the wide area they served, a bricklayer going to Temple Newsam to make a structural survey, and a glazier putting in heraldic glass at Gilling Castle.[3] A century earlier, in 1487, another glazier was pardoned at the intercession of the Earl of Northumberland, 'unto whome he haith done service'—presumably at one of the Earl's seats of Topcliffe, Wressle, and Leconfield.[4] By the 1590s, York's pinners were regularly visiting Richmond to buy stockings, and its 'buttermen' were travelling to Swaledale and Wensleydale.[5] Likewise, goods were bought at York by men coming from some distance; a Scriven smith bought iron there, and a Ripon dealer pepper.[6]

Much of York's local trade moved overland, but road surfaces were generally poor and carriage charges high. For bulky consignments even to nearby places, and for nearly all long-distance trade, York depended on the Ouse. Downstream, it linked York with the growing port of Hull, and so with distant regions of England as well as with the Continent. Upstream, it was navigable as far as Boroughbridge, thus enabling York to get a grip on the profitable lead of Richmondshire, which was carted overland to Boroughbridge and then transferred to boats. Throughout the Tudor and Stuart periods, York men protested vociferously at the silting of the river and the increased difficulties of navigation, but there is no clear evidence that the river was less navigable than it had ever been. It remained tidal to Poppleton, just above York,

---

[1] *The Antiquary*, vi. 189; *Y.A.J.* xix. 455-81, xxvi. 178-89.

[2] Y.C.A., F3 (unfoliated).

[3] *L.P. Hen. VIII* xxi (2), no. 181; *Y.A.J.* xxvi. 307 f.; Palliser, 'York', pp. 390 f.

[4] Y.C.A., B 6, fo. 68^r.   [5] Y.C.A., B 31, fos. 323-4.

[6] *Wills and Administrations from the Knaresborough Court Rolls*, ed. F. Collins, 2 vols., Surtees Soc. 1902-5, i. 145; *The Antiquary*, xxxii. 370.

until the eighteenth century, and the silting was and is a perennial problem, owing to the long ebb.[1]

It is difficult, in the case of river traffic, to draw a sharp line between local and long-distance trade. It was much used for short journeys to, from and through York, but superimposed on this pattern were the longer journeys, especially of lead shipped from Boroughbridge to Hull and beyond, and of a wide variety of goods imported to Hull and sent upriver. Hull still owed much of its prosperity to York merchants—in 1609 the largest trader there was still a York man, Christopher Dickinson[2]—but they were trading at one remove, and were therefore vulnerable to impositions and controls by the men of Hull. Traffic on the Ouse provides a classic case of corporate exclusiveness, each town trying to impose controls and charges on other towns while struggling to remain free of them itself. The York corporation fought hard to enforce the custom of 'foreign bought and sold' over Richmondshire lead passing through the city, insisting that 'foreigners' could not buy direct from the Richmondshire men. They were most indignant when Star Chamber ruled that London and Newcastle merchants could override this custom.[3] When Hull decided to copy York's tactics it was of course a different story. Three times—in 1532, 1541, and 1577—the Hull corporation obtained a royal grant of 'foreign bought and sold', and on each occasion York loudly and indignantly demanded its repeal.[4]

Quite apart from the lead trade, river traffic played a vital part in the economy of the city and of the whole Vale. Goods being shipped to York in 1492 and 1512 included wheat, rye, barley, malt, peas, beans, coal, and salt.[5] In the mid-sixteenth century goods shipped between Hull and York included iron, osmunds (Baltic iron), ashes, pitch, tar, clapboards, wainscot, salt, grain, fish and eels, coal, cloth, and

[1] Duckham, *Yorkshire Ouse*, pp. 17–23.

[2] R. Davis, *The Trade and Shipping of Hull 1500–1700* (East Yorks. Local History Series, xvii, 1964), p. 29.

[3] *Yorks. Star Chamber Proceedings*, i. 151–5; iii. 175–8; *Y.C.R.* iii. 70–2, 75, 104, 136–9.

[4] *Y.C.R.* iii. 146 f., 151; iv. 73, 97, 133; vii. 155, 161; Y.C.A., B 11, fo. 132^r; B 15, fo. 65^r; *Statutes of the Realm*, iii. 434; *L.P. Hen. VIII*, xvi, no. 1232 (4); xvii, no. 174.

[5] *Y.C.R.* ii. 82; iii. 38.

lead, probably mostly going upriver except for the last.[1] Some
of these goods can be followed further upstream from 'free
passage' records at York, recording payments by mariners
taking cargoes under Ouse Bridge during the period 1520–
36. Herrings, oil, linen, tar, silk, and osmunds went upstream
to Bedale, while Ripon received herrings, oil, wine, tar, linen,
grain, beans, sprats, and saltfish.[2]

With the river trade so important, the corporation were
very sensitive to obstructions and silting. Duckham points
out that 'whether York was a genuine victim of the kind of
silting which left several medieval harbours high and dry is
doubtful. What really happened is that the larger vessels . . .
made the always chronic silting of the Ouse appear worse
than it really was'.[3] The corporation, however, were convinced that the state of the river was a major reason for
York's economic decline, and spent much time, money, and
energy on the problem. In 1462 they were made conservators
of the Ouse and other rivers, and they battled against powerful vested interests to remove the numerous fishgarths or
large traps which impeded navigation. By 1532 they were
driven desperate by the fishgarth owners, whom they accused
of 'daily imagynyng thutter distruccion ruyne and decaye' of
York, and obtained more extensive powers against them by
Act of Parliament.[4] The turning point probably came when
in 1535 they appealed to Cromwell;[5] and whether owing to
him or not, complaints about fishgarths became much fewer
from the mid-sixteenth century. Secondly, as this problem
was gradually solved, attention was turned to improving the
flow of the river and deepening the channel, usually by
dredging and by strengthening the banks. The first record of
such work is in 1538, and there was a spate of such schemes
for the next forty years, after which they were largely abandoned as ineffective.[6] Finally, in the early seventeenth century, the more ambitious idea was taken up of cutting a tidal

---

[1] *York Mercers*, ed. Sellers, pp. 154–9, 168 f.

[2] Y.C.A., C2, C3, *passim.*   [3] Duckham, *Yorkshire Ouse*, p. 37.

[4] *Statutes of the Realm*, iii. 381 f.; Lehmberg, *Reformation Parliament*, pp. 22 f., 156.

[5] *L.P. Hen. VIII*, viii, nos. 260, 976.

[6] Duckham, *Yorkshire Ouse*, pp. 38 f. Duckham has omitted the earliest of these attempts: Y.C.A., B 13A, fo. 1^r; B 14, fo. 7^v.

canal from just south of York direct to the Humber. It would have considerably shortened York's route to the sea, but it was probably beyond the capacity of contemporary engineering.[1]

3

In the later Middle Ages, York's most important long-distance trade was in cloth, but by the early sixteenth century, the merchants' guild asserted, and the corporation agreed, that 'lede ys our most principall commoditie'.[2] Of the four lead-fields of the Pennines, the northernmost, between Tynedale and Teesdale, played no part in York's trade. The southernmost, in Derbyshire, was also remote from the city, though its merchants did have a share in the market as middlemen.[3] Between the two lie the Richmondshire and Craven fields, which were crucial for the prosperity of York, for their output had all to be floated downstream through York if it was to reach distant markets. The corporation's policy was to insist that lead could not be shipped through the city non-stop, nor be taken up at any private crane, but only at their Common Crane in Skeldergate. At the Crane, they explained, 'all maner foreyns and estraunge merchaunts, for wyndyng, weyng and strykyng of lede and all other merchaunds payeth a certayn [sum] for every fouder and ton weght': the fother, a variable measure of lead, was reckoned at York to weigh 2,505½ lb.[4] The Crane charges were increased to sixpence a fother in 1490 and to sevenpence in 1498, increases which provoked a conflict with the Richmondshire leadmen, and an uneasy compromise in 1500.[5] The dispute revealed the difficulty of enforcing collective trade action. A city merchant, William Staveley, was imprisoned by the council for buying lead weighed at Boroughbridge, 'and in his goyng furth in a gret hastynes said that ilkan among theym had bought more lede than he ded'. Four months later, Staveley showed them

[1] Y.C.A., B 32, fos. 279–80; Duckham, *Yorkshire Ouse*, pp. 44–8; Wilson, 'Corporation of York', pp. 139–41.
[2] *York Mercers*, ed. Sellers, p. 125; *Y.C.R.* iii. 72.
[3] Y.C.A., E 20A, fos. 219–20.
[4] *Y.C.R.* iii. 17; Raistrick and Jennings, *History of Lead Mining*, p. 43.
[5] Y.C.A., B 6, fo. 170ᵛ; B 8, fos. 74–109; *Y.C.R.* ii. 138, 142–4, 159; *Yorks. Star Chamber Proceedings*, ii. 73 f.

that four of their number, including the mayor himself, had bought lead at Boroughbridge, and proved it from their merchants' marks on the pigs. After another four months' delay to swallow their pride, the councillors agreed to fine the offenders and to reimburse Staveley for his costs in searching the tollbooks at Boroughbridge.[1]

Insufficient records survive to chart the fluctuations of York's lead trade in detail. John Chapman, a York notary and merchant (d. 1530/1), bought sixty-two fothers from Bolton Priory for £248 in a single transaction, but he was an untypical citizen, owner or lessee of mines in no less than three Pennine fields—'mineras meas infra franchesia regalia et domini de Hextildesham, Swaledale, et Craven'.[2] The York merchants seem to have been content to buy lead from religious houses which owned mines, but they were less friendly towards those which engaged in the trade as middlemen and were therefore competitors. The merchants' guild complained to the abbot of Fountains in 1502 of his dealings in lead, in rather anticlerical terms.[3] Incidents like this help to explain the passing of a statute in 1529 curtailing the commercial activities of religious houses. Time has its revenges, and in 1542-3 the lead from the roofs of Fountains was being shipped through York by the abbey's purchaser, Sir Richard Gresham of London, while other London merchants bought large shipments of lead at York itself.[4]

York was a distribution centre not only for lead but for foodstuffs. Its citizens often acted as middlemen, buying corn especially from the rich cornfields to the east, and selling it to the men of the pastoral uplands.[5] In 1535 there were thirty-eight cornbuyers in York, and one of them, William Holme, was reported to have regrated Lincolnshire and Holderness corn to the value of £100, thereby increasing the price at York, so Cromwell was informed by Lawson. Lawson

[1] Y.C.A., B 8, fos. 74, 87, 95, 101, 103.

[2] P.R.O. C1/728/2; Raistrick and Jennings, *Lead Mining*, p. 36, which misprints the price as £246; B.I.H.R., prob. reg. x, fos. 52-5.

[3] *York Mercers*, ed. Sellers, pp. 110 f. Her evidence for dating the letter is not clear, but it must certainly date from 1502-7, when Archbishop Savage headed the Council.

[4] *Yorks. Star Chamber Proceedings*, i. 151-5; iii. 175-8; P.R.O., C1/1254/67, 1276/17.

[5] Palliser, 'York under the Tudors', p. 49.

said he was reporting Holme only out of goodwill to the decaying city, but it sounds more like a case of fellow-councillors falling out; certainly Lawson himself had bought up Holderness wheat and malt in 1527, and was a largescale buyer of malt in 1540.[1] Dearths could make the dealers search further afield for supplies; in 1596-7 they imported grains from Nottinghamshire and Leicestershire, and even from the Continent.[2] In a good year, the position was reversed. The York middlemen might ship Holderness corn to London, and from 1585 a bill of lading reveals a York fishmonger shipping wheat and barley from Hull to King's Lynn, perhaps returning with a cargo of fish.[3]

There was plainly money to be made out of transferring grains from one area to another, since local prices differed considerably. In 1567 a Lincolnshire gentleman bought up 120 quarters of barley from local growers and sold it to two Yorkshiremen who shipped it to York for resale.[4] The more unscrupulous York merchants were willing to maximize profits by creating a scarcity, and one member of the Twenty-Four is said to have deliberately tried to raise corn prices at Selby.[5] With such an example in the council chamber, it is not surprising that the future bishop John King should single out corn-profiteering as a sin next to usury when he preached in the Minster in 1595.[6]

With fish, as with grains, the city acted as a distributive centre for a very wide area. There was a freshwater fish market on the Staith, drawing salmon and other fish from the Ouse and Humber, and a seafish market on Foss Bridge. Seafish was brought from ports the length of the Yorkshire coast, from Redcar to Bridlington, by members of the York fishers' guild, who rode there to buy on the spot.[7] Merchants also imported fish from Scandinavia; a casual reference shows a group of York merchants at Drypool near Hull to meet a boat returning from Norway, and one repaying a debt to a

[1] Y.C.A., B 13, fos. 29-31; P.R.O., C1/651/1; *L.P. Hen. VIII* ix, No. 456; xv, No. 417.
[2] *A.P.C. 1596-7*, pp. 516 f.; *A.P.C. 1597*, p. 3; Y.C.A., B 31, fos. 226-7, 246.
[3] *L.P. Hen. VIII* vi, No. 107; John Rylands Library, MS R.45818.
[4] Campbell, *English Yeoman*, pp. 195 f.   [5] B.L., Lansdowne 54, fo. 141[r].
[6] J. King, *A Sermon Preached . . . the Queenes Day* (London, 1597), pp. 704 f.
[7] Drake, *Eboracum*, p. 219; Y.C.A., E 22, fos. 200-1.

colleague with four barrels of 'Norway salmon'.[1] Two Flamborough fishers found it worthwhile to take up freedom of the city in 1497–8, and more distant imports are suggested by the admission of a London stockfishmonger to the Corpus Christi Guild in 1501.[2] East Anglians were regularly selling fish at Hull in the 1530s, and Suffolk men rented shops at York every Lent to catch the peak demand.[3] The citizens were buying far more seafish than they needed themselves, retailing most of it to areas further inland.[4]

Foodstuffs normally passed through the city unprocessed, but York was also an important centre for processing goods drawn from a wide area. The extensive markets served by York pewter and silver have already been noticed, and until the Reformation the city was also the leading Northern supplier of stained glass, bells, stalls, and rood-screens.[5] The building trades, with nearly 10 per cent of all freemen, are known to have served a wide area, and the numbers occupied in the clothing and victualling crafts also imply the servicing of an extensive hinterland. In spite of the rise of Hull to the east and of Leeds to the west, York remained the largest commercial centre in Yorkshire. When, for instance, the smaller religious houses in the diocese read the writing on the wall in the spring of 1536, it was chiefly at York that they tried to dispose of their goods. Apparently the most active trade was in selling plate to the York Mint to melt down for coin.[6] York was also in the forefront of marketing new and improved products. When steel was first made by the partial decarburization of pig-iron, on the Kent–Sussex border from 1565, Thomas Dawson of York was one of the first provincial merchants to order supplies.[7]

---

[1] P.R.O., C1/720/45.

[2] *Register of Freemen*, ed. Collins, i. 221; Y.C.A., C100/3.

[3] *Statutes of the Realm*, iii. 532; *Y.C.R.* iv. 4; Y.C.A., C 3, 1535–6 book, pp. 99, 105; 1538–9 book, fo. 21ʳ.

[4] Wilson, 'Corporation of York', p. 130; *Y.C.R.* v. 31, 96 f.; Y.C.A., F 2, entry for 7 Aug. 1566; *Durham Household Book*, pp. 36, 115, 314.

[5] Bartlett, 'Expansion and decline of York', p. 19; L. Stone, *Sculpture in Britain: the Middle Ages* (Harmondsworth, 1955), pp. 221 f.

[6] G. Burnet, *The History of the Reformation*, ed. E. Nares, 4 vols. (London, n.d.), iv. 467.

[7] *Sidney Ironworks Accounts 1541–73*, ed. D. W. Crossley, Camden Soc. 4th ser. xv (1975), pp. 34, 216, 227–9.

York's most important trade outside its own region was with London, and several lawsuits testify to the large consignments of goods which passed between the two cities. York carriers travelled regularly to London, while most of the leading merchants seem to have gone there at one time or another on business.[1] In 1576 the corporation resolved, quite illegally, to send only one burgess to the forthcoming session of Parliament, but the second member coolly interjected that he would attend also 'for that he hath certaine other busynesse ther that he must needs goe', a revealing comment on how differently provincial merchants and Privy Councillors could view the purpose of a Parliament.[2] The merchants were naturally trading on a large scale to make the long journeys worth their while. In 1570 two of them were said to owe £135 to a grocer and a fishmonger of London, while Alderman Maltby was alleged before his death in 1585 to have bought clothes worth £1,714 from four London merchant tailors.[3]

With long-distance coastal trade one is at last able to use systematic documentation, since Hull's port books, surviving for many years after 1565, cover coastal as well as overseas trade by York merchants. The coastal books specify the cargoes involved, and name the traders, although not their domiciles, so that York merchants can be distinguished from others only by their names. Nevertheless, the source is a fruitful one, and only selective results can be presented here. The books chosen for analysis are three from the beginning of the series, those for the Easter to Michaelmas period in the years 1565, 1566, and 1568, and three consecutive books from the end of the century, covering the eighteen months from Easter 1599 to Michaelmas 1600.[4]

The 1565-8 period covered two mixed cargoes of goods brought from London to Hull by citizens. Christopher Harbert in 1565 dealt in oil, soap, pots, wool, wood, bedding, haberdashery, and grocery, and John Harrison the following summer shipped a very varied cargo, including iron, soap, oil, wine, copperas, alum, currants, hemp, candles, pewter,

[1] Palliser, 'York under the Tudors', pp. 51 f.; Palliser, 'York', pp. 221 f.
[2] *Y.C.R.* vii. 114.   [3] *C.P.R. 1569-72*, p. 27; P.R.O., REQ. 2/244/37.
[4] P.R.O., E190/303/2; 304/9; 305/4; 310/12; 310/9; 310/16.

haberdashery, prunes, and raisins. Cargoes to and from provincial ports, however, tended to concentrate on a single commodity. Thus barley was imported from King's Lynn, while beans were exported to Berwick, London, and Plymouth. The bulkiest cargoes, if not so valuable as the luxuries from London, came to Hull from Newcastle—146 chalders of coal and 140 or more 'weys' of salt. Wood was becoming scarce as a fuel around York, and Tyneside coals, together with Marshland turves, were filling the gap.[1] By the end of the century, if the 1599–1600 books are representative, this trade with Newcastle had come to dominate the coastal traffic. York merchants shipped 208 chalders of coal from Newcastle in the summer of 1599—more than in the three earlier summers combined—and 271 in the summer of 1600. Other cargoes were much smaller: hops and pulses were shipped from Lynn to Hull (and iron and timber in the reverse direction), and pulses, peas, and beans from Hull to Newcastle.

4

Overseas trade is even better documented, since in addition to port books there is ample material in the state archives and the records of the city's merchants, besides which it has received a disproportionately large share of attention from economic historians. It is easy to exaggerate the importance of overseas trade, just as it is easy to exaggerate the part that cloth played within it. York specialized at least as much in lead as in cloth, shipping it to many overseas markets as well as to London. An exact list of exports survives for 1552, when an embargo imposed by the Crown stayed the freighting of lead from Hull. At the time, the York merchants had 158 fothers ready to ship to Flanders, forty-five for Bordeaux, and twenty-nine for Gdansk, all valued at £9. 10s. a fother.[2] Nor were these the only markets, for Hull lead was regularly exported to Normandy.[3] The Netherlands, however,

---

[1] *The Fabric Rolls of York Minster*, ed. J. Raine (Surtees Soc. xxxv, 1859), p. 103; Y.C.A., E 20A, fos. 219–20.

[2] *York Mercers*, ed. Sellers, pp. 135 f. *V.C.H. York*, p. 131, convincingly dates the list 1552.

[3] M. Mollet, *Le Commerce maritime normand à la fin du moyen âge* (Paris, 1952), pp. 149, 160 n.

remained the largest single market for lead as for cloth.
About 1510, York's merchants were sending lead to Flanders
'in suche abundannce and quantiti' that the market was
flooded.[1]

It is, however, in terms of cloth that trade with the Low
Countries is usually considered, and it was with cloth for
Flanders that the national Merchants Adventurers were primarily concerned. In 1489 one merchant was sending to
Holland a consignment of kerseys as well as lead, while in
1508 and 1525 wool and cloth from York were recorded at
Bergen-op-Zoom.[2] At the end of the century York men were
selling cloth at Amsterdam and Middelburg, and the port
book of 1602-3 confirms the importance of cloth exports,
though by then much of them went to other markets. Apart
from one consignment of lead to Bordeaux, all the exports
by York during the six months were of shortcloths and kerseys. One cargo was sent to Middelburg, the others to Gascony
and the Baltic.[3]

In Henry VII's reign the Burgundian Netherlands seem to
have been easily the most important of the overseas territories
with which York traded. If two of Alderman Gilliot's apprentices, resident at the small town of Campveere, could be
accused of defecting there to the Yorkist exiles, that is an
indication of how many young citizens spent time in the Low
Countries as agents and factors.[4] Later in the Tudor period
York men diversified their overseas markets, but the Low
Countries remained important, chiefly as an outlet for cloth
and lead. What was bought in exchange? In 1495 'merchaun-
dise of oreante' was being purchased there, perhaps spices
from the Indies, and Rhenish wine reached York through
Dutch middlemen.[5] Other imports included fish from Holland, Zeeland and Friesland,[6] and the Flanders chests which

---

[1] *York Mercers*, ed. Sellers, p. 124.

[2] *Y.C.R.* ii. 126-7; H. J. Smit, ed., *Bronnen tot de Geschiedenis van den Handel met Engeland, Schotland en Ierland* (Rijks Geschiedkundige Publicatiën 86 and 91, 1942-50), nos. 220, 446, 451.

[3] *Miscellanea*, v (Y.A.S.R.S. cxvi, 1951), p. 12; H.M.C. *Sackville MSS.* ii. 12, 94; P.R.O., E190/311/11.

[4] Y.C.A., B 7, fo. 99ᵛ; *Y.C.R.* ii. 126-7.

[5] *York Mercers*, ed. Sellers, p. 93; *Handel met Engeland*, ed. Smit, nos. 451, 469.

[6] *Y.C.R.* viii. 92.

figure frequently in wills and inventories. An unusually explicit record of 1571 reveals York and Hull merchants sending
'corn, clothe and other comodetes' to Emden in East Friesland, receiving in exchange 'sope, hoppes, and other merchan-
dizes of the lowe countryes'.[1]

Another traditional market for York was France, especially
Gascony, where the province's ancient link with the English
Crown had established close trading ties. Trade between York
and Bordeaux was the most important, lead being exchanged
for Gascon wines. In 1483 six citizens, headed by Alderman
Richard York, were shipping wine from Bordeaux, and in
1586 a single merchant was alleged to have brought back
almost 200 tuns.[2] Their wares were in great demand among
the wealthy, and the tuns of wine presented by the corporation to distinguished visitors and neighbours were more often
than not Gascon. Yet if the rewards were high, so were the
risks, war and piracy interrupting the trade frequently. In
October 1546 Gregory Paycok of York and other English
merchants were arrested with their cargoes at Bordeaux upon
a letter of marque, and released only after negotiations between the two governments. The following spring a French
ship freighted wine at Bordeaux for Hull, and the York merchants involved refused any liability should the ship be
attacked by the Scots.[3]

Apart from Gascony and the Low Countries, York's most
important overseas trade was with northern Germany and
the Baltic. Trading links through the Hanseatic League were
of long standing. The Leaguers or 'Eysterlyngs' secured valuable trading privileges in England in 1474, but refused in
return to open their areas freely to Englishmen, and their
privileges provoked great bitterness. The York merchants
complained in the late fifteenth century that the Easterlings
were selling luxury goods throughout the north but buying
no goods in exchange, thus draining the region of currency.
Furthermore, they 'wold not sover your marchands of York

[1] Sellers, ed. *York Mercers*, p. 186.
[2] F. Michel, *Histoire du commerce et de la navigation à Bordeaux* (Bordeaux,
1867-70), i. 118; P.R.O. REQ. 2/170/49.
[3] *L.P. Hen. VIII*, xxi (2), No. 490 ii; Michel, *Commerce et navigation à Bordeaux*, i. 119 n., 416 n.

to mayk no sall to no stranger but to the fre men of Danysk' (Gdansk).[1] Their main bases in the north were apparently Hull and Newcastle, though an agent from Gdansk was at York ('Gorigk') in 1552,[2] and Easterlings traded often with York merchants. The main English debtors of a Köln burgher who died about 1490 were almost all York men.[3]

Gradually the York and Hull merchants went on to the offensive. A sign of the times was the arrival at Hull in 1541 of three English ships from Prussia. Their cargoes, in which four York men had a stake, were iron, osmunds, timber, tar, ashes, and lime.[4] Three Hull ships a year, on average, passed through the Sound between 1528 and 1547, by 1580 the figure had reached twenty and in 1601, exceptionally, it rose to forty.[5] Many of the cargoes will have belonged to York merchants, sixty-six of whom were listed as trading through the Sound in 1579.[6] The merchants also invaded the Hanse's Atlantic ports. At least three future aldermen lived in Hamburg as agents, while 'dyvers' York merchants 'made their adventure' there.[7] Gdansk itself, the chief Baltic port, was not so amenable, and the English merchants trading with that region formed the Eastland Company in 1579, with a theoretical monopoly of Baltic trade, and set up a residence at Elblag, a small rival of Gdansk. The newly-opened trade with Russia had already (1555) been granted to another monopoly, the Muscovy Company. Neither of these London-dominated companies was popular with the northern merchants, and although some joined them, others carried on as interlopers. The Muscovy Company was unable to prevent a considerable number of York and Hull men from continuing to trade with Narva and Lapland.[8]

---

[1] *York Mercers*, ed. Sellers, pp. xlvii, 107–9, 197; *Y.C.R.* i. 66.

[2] *Danziger Inventar*, ed. P. Simson (Munich and Leipzig, 1913), No. 2443.

[3] *Hansisches Urkundenbuch* xi, ed. W. Stein (Munich and Leipzig, 1916), no. 417.

[4] Bartlett, 'Aspects of the economy of York', p. 122.

[5] N. A. Bang, ed., *Tabeller over Skibsfart og Varetransport gennem Oresund 1497–1660*, i (Copenhagen and Leipzig, 1906), *passim*.

[6] *York Mercers*, ed. Sellers, pp. 201 f. One, Persyvall, had been trading with Gdansk twelve years earlier: *Danziger Inventar*, ed. Simson, No. 5039.

[7] Palliser, 'York', p. 223; *Y.C.R.* viii. 161.

[8] T. S. Willan, *The Early History of the Russia Company* (Manchester, 1956), pp. 67–77, 85–6, 137–9.

What Englishmen needed from the Baltic were raw materials in short supply at home: iron, pitch, hemp, and especially flax for linen-making, as well as grain in years of dearth. Flax and iron from Gdansk were reaching York by the 1560s, and in 1579 the city's merchants could demand special consideration from the newly formed Eastland Company, as they were regular traders to Gdansk, whence 'we serve the northe parts with flax'.[1] In 1572 a Gdansk merchant told the Court of Requests that he had delivered 'flax, pitch and other merchandize' worth £118 to a single York citizen.[2] Of the manufactures that paid for Baltic foodstuffs and raw materials, Yorkshire cloths were apparently the chief. Exports of English kerseys to the Baltic, mostly from Hull, sextupled between 1565 and 1585, and doubled or trebled again in the next ten years. With such a growth rate, it is not surprising that by the early seventeenth century the Hull and York merchants together enjoyed a third of England's trade with the Baltic, as large a proportion as the Londoners'.[3] The two-way traffic, cloth against primary products, is well indicated in the will of Henry Wympnye, an Eastland merchant from York, who died at the English community in Elblag in 1597:

I have restinge owinge unto me the clothiers beinge paid and all my debts paid . . . the some of two thousand three hundreth gildernes polish more that my proffyt of my rye, and of two and one quarter last and odd weighte of flaxe, and two laste iron I hope that will proffytt me one thousand gylderns.

Wympnye was by no means the only York man among the English community. In 1594 two others had settled in Elblag and acquired civic rights.[4]

Raw materials and foodstuffs came to York from the north as well as from the Baltic. The Icelandic fishing-grounds still supplied the city in the late fifteenth century, though by

[1] Raine, *Mediaeval York*, p. 184; *Minster Fabric Rolls*, ed. Raine, p. 115; *York Mercers;* ed. Sellers, p. 209.

[2] P.R.O. REQ 2/164/17.

[3] Davis, *Trade and Shipping of Hull*, pp. 7-9; G. D. Ramsay, *English Overseas Trade during the Centuries of Emergence* (London, 1957), p. 97.

[4] B.I.H.R., prob. reg. xxvii, fo. 248; H. Zins, *England and the Baltic in the Elizabethan Era* (Manchester, 1972), p. 75.

Elizabeth's time the North Sea was the main source.[1] From Scotland came fish, salt, and Fifeshire coal.[2] Ireland, in contrast, supplied cloth,[3] and there is no evidence at York for the hides which were the island's main export.

Finally, the city had trading contacts with Spain and Italy, and during the short period 1505-7 there are terse mentions of Genoese, Lombards, and Spaniards visiting York. The Genoese were apparently selling wine and other imports, while the Spaniards were returning home with West Riding cloth which they had bought at Boroughbridge.[4] They may have brought iron in exchange; Spanish iron was in demand in the city and the county during the early sixteenth century, and was regularly bought by the Minster chapter.[5] In 1530 the Spanish Company was founded as yet another trading monopoly, and it came into serious conflict with the Merchants Adventurers after 1577, when Elizabeth incorporated it. The York merchants at first attempted to secure 'thare fredom of Spanys companye', but were presumably unable to secure favourable terms. Instead they demanded the right to trade there without joining the company, since 'our doyng in thos parties are smale'.[6] Plainly it formed only a minor part of York's overseas trade, and before long the dispute became irrelevant as war closed the Spanish market.

Exports and imports formed probably a very small part of York's total trade, though of course the relative proportions cannot be established in the absence of internal customs records. It should not be denied, however, that overseas trade, concerned as it necessarily was with costly goods worth exchanging over long distances, was proportionately important to the city's economy, and the decline of York's long-distance trade, it will be seen, was a major cause of its general decay. Even the low levels reached in the mid-sixteenth

[1] *York Mercers*, ed. Sellers, p. 85; *Y.C.R.* viii. 92. The licence to Richard York to send a ship to Iceland, 1484, presumably involved fish: *Y.A.J.* xxxvii, plate opp. p. 225.

[2] *York Mercers*, p. 169; *Y.C.R.* vii. 152; *Y.C.R.* viii. 92; Palliser, 'York under the Tudors', pp. 46 f., 51.

[3] *Test. Ebor.* iii. 303; *Y.C.R.* iii. 32.

[4] *Y.C.R.* iii. 15; Y.C.A. B 9, fos. 29^r, 36-7, 39^v.

[5] B.I.H.R., prob. reg. viii, fo. 102; *Y.C.R.* iii. 77 f.; Bartlett, 'Aspects of the Economy of York', p. 105; *Minster Fabric Rolls*, pp. 100-2, 108.

[6] *York Mercers*, ed. Sellers, pp. 203, 216-21, 224, 230-2.

century were not to be despised. In the year ending at Michaelmas 1526, forty-one men identifiable as York merchants were paying poundage at Hull on exports and imports, the total value of which Dr Bartlett estimates at £2,500. Even in the year ending at Michaelmas 1541, thirty-one York merchants were involved, shipping goods worth £2,350. In the latter year one of the merchants involved was Robert Hall, the Mayor of York and only recently master of the merchants' guild. He was appropriately the leading trader that year, exporting and importing goods worth £426.[1]

Long-distance and overseas trade was, therefore, consistently valuable enough to have been a crucial element in York's prosperity. It is therefore unfortunate that the customs records do not permit a comprehensive picture, while for local and inland trade there are no systematic sources at all. York merchants are known to have kept account books throughout the period, but not a single one is known to have survived. Where occasional inland transactions are recorded, it is usually in the dubious form of a lawsuit for debt in which the judgement, and therefore the veracity of the plea, is not known. Even when such cases can be accepted as credible there is no means of knowing how typical they may have been; and even the very quantities specified are suspect. The local weight of a lead fother is known, but it was far from the only variable measure. There is evidence for the simultaneous existence in York of the standard 12-inch foot alongside a shorter measure of 10 inches, while one bulk purchase of barley in 1585 explicitly involved the old 'long hundred' of six score, so that the 490 quarters sold represented 570 in our reckoning.[2] If the long hundred was in general use, many of the statistics quoted in this book would have to be revised upwards. None of these considerations need make one despair of understanding the general nature of the city's commerce, but they do argue for caution in relying too strongly on the few statistics which survive.

---

[1] Bartlett, 'Apsects of the Economy of York', pp. 379–81.
[2] P. Grierson, *English Linear Measures: an Essay in Origins* (Reading, 1972), p. 23; P.R.O. REQ 2/192/24.

VIII

POVERTY AND DECAY, 1460–1560

> Where as in olde tymes past the Citie hath moche
> prospered in clothe makyng . . . but . . . in processe
> of tyme the said occupieng descreased and at last
> utterly decayed in the said Citie; even so the weavers
> of the same . . . have fled the most part forth of the
> said Citie, inhabityng in the contry to the same nigh
> adjoynyng.
>
> *Petition of the corporation to Elizabeth I,* 1561[1]

York's economy has so far been viewed over the century as a
whole, the 'static' elements taking precedence over the 'dyna-
mic'. The basic political and economic structure of the city
survived very little changed from the fourteenth century to
the nineteenth, and an unfashionable emphasis on the static
elements of York's life is perhaps justified. Nevertheless, the
system was able to survive only because it successfully adapted
to the many changes over that long period, changes which
profoundly affected the demography, wealth, trade, and
commerce as well as politics of the city, and which were
rarely so rapid as under the early Tudors.

Precise and statistical indicators of change are not to be
expected, but one of the movements least in doubt is a
dramatic decline in the city's population, lasting roughly
from the early fifteenth century to the mid-sixteenth. In
1487 the corporation assured Henry VII that York's population had been halved within the recent past.[2] Such assertions
by urban corporations are rightly suspect, linked as they so
often were to requests for financial aid, but there is no reason
to doubt its substantial accuracy on this occasion, for the
city's population at its medieval peak far outstripped the
early Tudor level. J. C. Russell suggests a total population of
some 11,000 in 1377, while J. N. Bartlett, accepting his
total, argues for an expansion to perhaps 12,000 around

---

[1] *Y.C.R.* vi. 13.   [2] *Y.C.R.* ii. 9.

1400.[1] Both figures, high though they are, may be under-estimates. Richard II, on his visit to York in 1396, distributed alms to the enormous number of 12,040 poor, from which J. H. Harvey infers that the real population of the city and its neighbourhood can hardly have been less than 15,000. Further evidence is provided by the will of Alderman Nicholas Blakeburn I, who in 1432 left money to provide a penny dole for 6,400 poor.[2]

Between the 1377-81 poll taxes and the 1524 lay subsidy there is a demographic Dark Age: no source survives from which even a rough estimate of the population can be deduced. Edward Miller suggests 'a population of about 13,000 at the end of the 14th century and one of about 7,000 or rather more at the end of the 15th'. This he calculates from freemen admissions, but R. B. Dobson's work on the freemen's register makes one doubt whether admissions can be used in this way, even as a rough guide.[3] Nevertheless, the early Tudor figures are so low that there must have been a huge decline in the fifteenth century, however large the margins of error to be allowed. The number of taxpayers in 1524 would suggest a population 'fewer than 8,000', on the assumption that those exempt formed the same proportion as at Coventry.[4] Too much weight cannot be placed on any single estimate, but confidence is increased when a very different source only 25 years later yields a similar result, making the population of York in 1548 roughly 8,000.[5] Without doubt, the city had declined dramatically both absolutely and relatively. From being the largest provincial city in 1377, York had sunk by the 1520s to about sixth place, below Norwich, Bristol, Exeter, Salisbury, and perhaps Newcastle.[6] However, a falling population is not in itself an argument for poverty and decay, for under the Malthusian conditions allegedly prevalent before 1348 hunger and land-shortage had

[1] J. C. Russell, *British Medieval Population* (Albuquerque, 1948), p. 142; Bartlett, 'Expansion and decline', pp. 25-8, 33.

[2] J. Harvey, 'Richard II and York', p. 210, and *York*, p. 118; Shaw, *An Old York Church*, p. 90.

[3] *V.C.H. York*, p. 84; Dobson, 'Admissions to the freedom', *passim*.

[4] Hoskins, *Provincial England*, p. 72.   [5] See pp. 111 f.

[6] W. G. Hoskins, *Local History in England*, 2nd edn. (London, 1972), p. 238, and *Provincial England*, pp. 71 f.

been widespread, and a smaller population may have enjoyed a higher income per head. Any corroboration of the corporation's repeated allegations of poverty must be looked for elsewhere.

In 1485, the corporation told Henry VII that 'the two parties of the said citie was within fewe yeres after' the battle of Towton (1461), 'utterly prostratid, decaied and waisted', and that throughout Edward's reign the citizens 'fro day to day so decayed, that in thend of this reigne they wer and yit be gretely indebted and utterly impoverished'. As R. B. Dobson comments, 'they were in a position to know', and numerous cases could be cited of internal civic documents relating to poverty, and not merely documents for external consumption like this.[1]

The evidence is worth investigating in detail, since the extent of urban decay in the late Middle Ages is much disputed. The traditional view, accepting most urban pleas of poverty at face value and painting a gloomy picture of urban life, has been vigorously attacked by A. R. Bridbury, who maintains that population decline brought nothing but good to the towns. Added force was given to his argument when K. P. Wilson showed that Chester's pleas of poverty in 1445, 1484, and 1486, which brought successive reductions of their fee-farm by the Crown, were self-contradictory and grossly exaggerated.[2] However, royal remissions of fee-farm to the towns were numerous, and one cannot assume gullibility on every occasion. Mr. Phythian-Adams believes that 'royal dispensations were shrewdly calculated from the findings of detailed inquisitions made on the spot by theoretically impartial commissioners',[3] and indeed, in the case of York, Henry VII acted as his own investigator. After visiting the city in April 1486 he remitted nearly the whole of its fee-farm, stating explicitly that he was moved to act 'at our last being at our Citie there, seing the great ruyne and extreme decay

[1] *Y.C.R.* i. 136; Dobson, 'Admissions to the freedom', p. 17.

[2] A. R. Bridbury, *Economic Growth* (London, 1962), *passim*; K. P. Wilson, 'The port of Chester in the 15th century', *Trans. Hist. Soc. Lancs. and Cheshire*, cxvii (1965), 1–15.

[3] C. Phythian-Adams, 'Coventry and the problem of urban decay in the later middle ages', Urban History Conference paper, York 1971. I am grateful to Mr. Phythian-Adams for permission to cite his paper.

that the same is fallen in'.[1] An analysis of urban decay in general would here be out of place, but it may be worth emphasizing that a surprisingly large number of provincial towns suffered decay in the late fifteenth and early sixteenth centuries, culminating in a nadir in the period 1520–70, from which there was a gradual recovery. York's economic fortunes, as R. B. Dobson rightly says, 'were much more representative of those of other major English towns than has usually been recognized'.[2]

2

J. N. Bartlett has shown that York's commerce and trade, as well as its population, were at their apogee at the start of the fifteenth century. Over the period from 1301 to 1551, admissions of freemen reached their highest levels between 1391 and 1421, while the value of foreign trade through Hull (largely a measure of York's overseas trade) was never again as high as in the decade 1407-17.[3] In that sense the city's decline began in the early fifteenth century, but a community may remain reasonably prosperous when an exceptional commercial peak has been passed, and it may even be that wealth *per capita* increased as the population fell. Freemen admissions are not a reliable guide to prosperity, while the fluctuations of overseas trade reflect the activities of a small and wealthy minority. Had the city's economy been able to stabilize at the mid-century level it would have continued a moderately prosperous community.

The first signs that the times were really out of joint were the purchases of exemption from civic office, by royal letters patent, by several leading citizens in the mid-fifteenth century. A flight from civic office is always a danger signal for the viability of towns in a pre-industrial society, and the corporation naturally took a very serious view of it. They secured an Act of Parliament in 1450 revoking all such exemptions, and authorizing a £40 fine on any citizens

---

[1] *Y.C.R.* i. 167.
[2] R. B. Dobson, 'Urban decline in late medieval England', *Trans. Roy. Hist. Soc.* 5th ser. xxvii (1977), p. 20.
[3] Bartlett, 'Expansion and decline', pp. 23, 28.

obtaining them in future.[1] Civic office being burdensome and often expensive, there were still wealthy citizens wishing to avoid it, but they had thereafter to compound with the corporation, and the fines in turn helped to alleviate the city's financial problems. In 1501–2 a baker paid £20 for exemption from all civic office for life, and in 1509 the fishmonger John Roger, elected sheriff, was forborne for £18 as he was 'not of sufficiaunt stature'. In 1524, having grown to great wealth, he surrendered his exemption and had the £18 repaid him.[2] Even so, some were driven to leave the city rather than accept the unpalatable alternatives of office or a fine. When John Smith was elected sheriff in 1526, he moved out to the nearby manor-house at Shipton, which he had rented, and simply refused to serve. Drake's story that he was elected for five successive years, and that after his death his executors had to pay his share of five years' fee-farm, is a garbled account, but it does seem that the citizen who married Smith's widow was called to account for the shrievalty.[3]

The later fifteenth century saw a decline in competition for freedom as well as for civic office, and admissions of freemen between 1451 and 1501 were nearly 30 per cent below the level of 1351 to 1401.[4] A consequence of the earlier competition had been restrictive practices by the craft guilds, for around 1400 it had been normal to allow each master only one apprentice at a time; from 1459, however, several guilds modified the policy.[5] Another index of decline was falling income from house-rents, either because lower rents had to be charged, or because more of the gross income was taken up by repair bills and property left vacant. Such, at least, was the case with the properties of the city corporation and of the College of Vicars Choral. Real gross income from the houses, gardens, and mills of the Vicars, for instance (over 200 in number) amounted to £85 in 1401, £50 in 1457, and £35 in 1500.[6] A shrinking population inevitably meant

---

[1] *V.C.H. York*, p. 75; *Statutes of the Realm*, ii. 359.

[2] Y.C.A. C5/1; B 9, fo. 50ʳ; B 10, fo. 95.

[3] *Y.C.R.* iii. 106, 110; *Test. Ebor.* v. 216–8; Drake, *Eboracum*, p. 186, followed by *V.C.H. York*, p. 139.

[4] Bartlett, 'Expansion and decline', p. 30.

[5] *York Memorandum Book*, i. 89, 184; ii. 196, 209, 238; *Y.C.R.* iii. 179.

[6] Bartlett, 'Economy of York', pp. 186–7.

houses standing empty, or being demolished to save the costs of upkeep. The corporation first took note of the latter practice in 1494, when they ordained fines of £5 on any carpenter, mason, or tiler who should dismantle a house in the city.[1] The corporation was itself affected as a landlord by the prevailing fall in rents—its house income from 'bridge rents' fell from £55 in 1486-7 to £24. 10s. in 1506-7—and this was one cause of its frequent insolvency. Upkeep of the walls and civic buildings became a heavier drain on the impoverished corporation, and the collapse of Ouse Bridge was staved off only by a private bequest of £20.[2]

The decline of income from real estate bore especially heavily on the chantries in the city's parish churches, for their endowments consisted almost entirely of urban properties and rent charges. The numbers of parochial chantries founded mirrored the economic fortunes of York very closely, twenty-one being founded between 1351 and 1400, fourteen between 1401 and 1450, seven between 1451 and 1500, and only one after 1500. R. B. Dobson has demonstrated that the decline did not imply disenchantment with endowing prayers for the dead, and suggests that the financial plight of existing chantries was the main deterrent.[3] Falling rents, indeed, made some chantries too poor to support a priest even at the low level which was customary in York; in 1478 the mayor, as patron of one decayed chantry, licensed its fusion with another, a precedent that was to be copied several times over the next fifty years.[4] When a Bristol merchant left £20 to found an obit in St. Martin's, Coney Street, the parishioners invested the entire sum in lands and tenements in the East Riding, presumably because rural property was a much safer investment.[5]

Some of the indications of decay, taken in isolation, would be inconclusive, but a conjunction of so many, together with complaints by the citizens and acknowledgement of their truth by the king, seems difficult to dismiss. It may or may not be true that wealth *per capita* diminished, but the absolute

---

[1] Y.C.A., B 7, fo. 112[r].   [2] Y.C.A., B 7, fo. 15[v]; cf. *Test. Ebor.* iv. 85.
[3] R. B. Dobson, 'The foundation of perpetual chantries by the citizens of medieval York', in *Studies in Church History* iv, ed. G. J. Cuming, 22-38.
[4] *York Memorandum Book*, ii. 269 f.   [5] Y.C.A., E 20A, fo. 168[r].

fall in wealth and in population was inevitably a hardship, for
the inflexible tax system made it difficult for York to pay
less than it had at its peak. This was especially true of the lay
subsidies, where a fixed total and fixed parochial assessments
(imposed in 1334) continued to be demanded. Pleas to Henry
VII to reduce the city's total were unavailing, though slight
relief was obtained in 1492 by redistributing the burden
among the parishes.[1] Still more onerous was the fee-farm
payable annually to the king, fixed at £160 by King John. By
the fifteenth century successive kings had granted most of it
away, so that it benefited them little, while to the citizens it
was an increasing burden. As soon as Gloucester became
Protector in 1483 the corporation asked him for a remission
of £50 of the farm, and he proved even more generous than
that, for while visiting York as king he remitted £98. 11s. 2d.
altogether, and granted a further £18. 5s. to the mayor.[2]
Henry VII went further in reducing the farm to £18. 5s. a
year, but he more than once repented of his generosity and
alarmed the corporation; in any case he could not permanently disinherit the Roos family, who owned £100 of the
original farm, and this was to cause great difficulty in the
next reign.[3]

3

The impact of fixed taxation on a declining city certainly
aggravated that decline, but does not explain why it occurred
in the first place. In 1485 the corporation dated the origin of
their misfortunes to the civil wars, whereas Richard III had
suggested that wars with the Scots had been mainly responsible. Henry VII preferred to blame the corporation for their
manner of government—or so he thought it useful to maintain in berating a civic deputation over recent rioting.[4] It is
doubtful whether any of these reasons could have been more
than contributory, though a more promising line of enquiry
is opened up by a corporation claim in 1493 that an epidemic
was largely responsible for the 'miserable ruyne and decaye'

[1] *Y.C.R.* ii. 36-8, 84.   [2] *Y.C.R.* i. 71, 82.
[3] *Y.C.R.* i. 165-8, 174, 178; ii. 1, 31 f.; *V.C.H. York*, p. 66.
[4] *Y.C.R.* i. 73, 135-7; ii. 115.

of York.[1] It prompts the question whether the city suffered especially severely from epidemics, and whether the halving of the population alleged in 1487 could have been so caused.

Evidence for epidemics is very scanty before the introduction of parish registers in 1538. Terse references occur to outbreaks in 1485, 1493-4, 1501, and 1507, while the large numbers of wills proved suggest that the whole decade 1501-10 was very unhealthy.[2] There is no doubt that bubonic plague, at least, became in the fifteenth and sixteenth centuries a largely urban disease, and that towns with concentrated populations in insanitary conditions were prime targets for disease of all kinds. Furthermore, until the eighteenth century many or most towns had a natural surplus of burials over baptisms because of their unhealthy conditions, and without constant and large-scale immigration from the countryside, their population would inevitably shrink. All of this speculation (for it can be no more) suggests a cause of demographic decline which York would share with all other large towns. It does not explain why the city declined more than others, in wealth no less than in population. For if tax returns can provide a ranking even approximately reliable, York's decline was catastrophic. From being the wealthiest provincial town in 1377, it sank to fourteenth place in 1524, below even the small but thriving clothing town of Lavenham.[3]

Cloth, indeed, is probably the key to the decline of York as to the rise of Lavenham, in so far as any one cause predominated. The cloth industry was footloose in the fifteenth century, and in Yorkshire it was deserting York, Ripon, and Beverley for the newer centres of the West Riding. The mayor of York, looking back on the shift afterwards, spoke of

the lak of cloth makyng in the sayd cite as was in old tyme accustomed, which is nowe encreased and used in the towne of Halyfax, Leeds and Wakefield for that not onely the commodite of the water mylnes is there nigh hand, but alsoo the poor folk as spynners, carders and other necessary work folks for the sayd webbyng may there besyds their hand labour have kyen, fyre and other releif good and cheap whiche is in this citie very deare and wantyng.[4]

---

[1] *Y.C.R.* ii. 102.
[2] Palliser, 'Epidemics in Tudor York', pp. 46 f.; P.R.O., C1/531/3.
[3] Hoskins, *Local History in England*, pp. 238-9.   [4] *Y.C.R.* vi. 17.

The ulnage or aulnage accounts, which with all their notorious deficiencies remain useful in the absence of other statistics, suggest a steep decline in the city's clothmaking during the fifteenth century. The annual output of saleable cloths fell by nearly one half between 1394–5 and 1468–9, and then halved again within the following eight or nine years.[1] The corporation acknowledged the decline in 1464, noting how 'in tyme passed' the city had contained many prosperous fullers, 'and nowe thay be fewer and porer for lack of wark, that gothe at thies dayes into the contree'.[2] The collapse was naturally neither sudden nor total. York was still the leading Yorkshire cloth-town until at least 1475, and in 1476 one leading county family, the Plumptons, still bought York cloth as a matter of course.[3] However, at some time during the 1460s or 1470s the important custom of Durham Priory was transferred to Halifax and Leeds, and by 1485 York tailors were stocking West Riding cloth in large quantities.[4] The weavers, the city's oldest craft guild and once the most powerful, had their fee farm halved in 1478 and totally remitted in 1486 because of their 'poverty and distress'.[5]

The corporation, as usual, sought to stave off disaster by regulation. In 1484 they ordered that for every two fothers of lead a freeman might sell, he should have one coarse cloth 28 yards long manufactured in York.[6] It was of no avail, and, as has been indicated, the city's merchants had largely moved from cloth to lead by the early sixteenth century. The main crafts involved in woollen cloth declined even more than the freemen as a whole, and only the tapiters, who worked worsted cloth into coverlets, were able to avoid the catastrophe by concentrating on a specialized product. The fullers' and cardmakers' guilds disappeared in the early sixteenth century, and the lesser crafts of pinners and wire-drawers were able to survive only by amalgamation.[7]

[1] H. Heaton, *The Yorkshire Woollen and Worsted Industries*, 2nd edn. (Oxford, 1965), p. 60.

[2] *York Memorandum Book*, ii. 207.

[3] Heaton, *Yorks. Woollen and Worsted Industries*, p. 75; T. Stapleton, ed., *Plumpton Correspondence* (Camden Soc. iv. 1839), pp. 36 f.

[4] Fowler, ed., *Account Rolls of the Abbey of Durham*, iii. 633, 636–7, 649, 656; *Test. Ebor.* iii. 301.

[5] Heaton, *Yorks. Woollen and Worsted Industries*, pp. 47 f.

[6] *Y.C.R.* i. 94.   [7] Palliser, 'Trade gilds of Tudor York', p. 92.

The fate of York's clothmaking requires no local explanation, for the same decline was apparent in other old-established clothmaking towns like Beverley and Lincoln, Stamford and Winchester, while rural or at least unincorporated communities prospered in their stead: Lavenham and Long Melford, the Cotswold wool-towns, Halifax and Leeds. The natural advantages of hilly rural areas had always existed, but probably preponderated the more as workers felt less need for the protection of town walls and guild membership: water power, proximity to supplies of wool, and availability of food and fuel at prices lower than in the large cities.

Although the manufacture of woollen cloth deserted York, its merchants continued to deal in it, so that cloth, like lead, became a commodity for which York was an entrepôt rather than a point of origin. The continuance of cloth trading is attested by the prosperity of the small group of drapers in the city, and it is clear that many other merchants dealt in cloth. Furthermore, for a short period, York was enabled to recover its ancient position as a major wool-trading centre. The Calais Staple monopolized most English wool exports, but the Newcastle merchants were licensed to ship coarse northern wool direct to the Netherlands, a valuable privilege which they enjoyed throughout the sixteenth century.[1] On 22 August 1523 the King, 'having a tender zele and love to the encrease avauncement and amendment of our ancient Citee of Yorke', granted its freemen a similar privilege.[2] The Staplers, however, persistently attacked the new grant, and the corporation vainly tried to have it confirmed by statute.[3] An appeal by the mayor and aldermen to Wolsey acknowledges its value, and makes it clear that it was the Cardinal who had obtained it for them; that may suffice to explain its repeal as soon as Wolsey fell from power.[4] Perhaps in compensation, the Parliament of 1543 gave York instead a monopoly of coverlet-making north of the Trent. The York tapiters, the only weaving craft still flourishing, made full

---

[1] P. J. Bowden, *The Wool Trade in Tudor and Stuart England* (London, 1962), p. 108.

[2] Widdrington, *Analecta Eboracensia*, photograph opp. p. 276.

[3] *Y.C.R.* iii. 91-4, 98, 100-1, 104, 106, 108, 110, 117.

[4] B.L. Titus B. I., fo. 285; Heaton, op. cit., p. 48 n.; *Statutes of the Realm*, iii. 301-2; Lehmberg, *Reformation Parliament*, p. 97.

use of the privilege, and seem to have prospered until at least the end of the century.[1]

Linked with the decline of York's wool and cloth trade was a general diminution in its long-distance trading, especially overseas trade. Bartlett has shown that its extensive medieval trading sphere, from Gascony to Prussia and Iceland, contracted during the fifteenth century, although as some compensation its trade with Spain increased.[2] This can be attributed partly to York's decay as a market and a manufacturing centre, partly to its exclusive reliance on Hull as an outlet, for Hull was losing ground to other ports and especially to London, and partly to the growing tonnage of shipping and its increasing difficulty in navigating the Ouse. In 1544, the corporation claimed, the city possessed only two seagoing ships, and relied for its trade on ten 'keylls' or 'lightners' of 30 or 40 tons, which conveyed cargoes between Hull and York.[3] London was in the early sixteenth century absorbing much of the export and import trade formerly enjoyed by the outports, and one can see the effect at York in the numbers engaged in manufacture for exports, such as the pewter industry.[4]

4

The city's fortunes seem to have been at their lowest from about 1510 to 1560. Such figures as exist for population, taxable wealth, admissions to the freedom, industry, long-distance trade, and real property income all point to that time as the worst, and although none of the indicators is conclusive in isolation, their conjunction is impressive.

The estimate of under 8,000 for York's population in 1524 is based on the lay subsidy of that year and on an assumption that the untaxed poor formed a similar proportion of the total at both York and Coventry. However, the proportion of poor in York may have been very large, and it is quite possible that York's population was still well in excess

[1] *Statutes of the Realm*, iii. 908–9; Heaton, op. cit., pp. 55–8.

[2] Bartlett, 'Expansion and decline', pp. 27–31.

[3] *Y.C.R.* iv. 99 f., 119 f.; *L.P. Hen. VIII*, xix (1), No. 109, xix (2), No. 602; B.L. Add. 32656, fos. 37–8.

[4] Hatcher and Barker, *History of British Pewter*, pp. 72–9.

of 8,000,[1] in which case a decline would continue to the rather more secure total of some 8,000 in 1548. Epidemics probably hastened the decline, though the evidence before 1538 is inevitably tenuous. Numbers of wills proved, an index of mortality among the prosperous, were high throughout the first decade of the century, and two mayors died in office, a significant coincidence, since mayors were normally among the youngest aldermen. The second decade was apparently less unhealthy, but in 1520-2 mortality was again heavy, and two more mayors died in office. In July of one year (probably 1521), a season when bubonic plague often struck, 'the sickness' was described as increasing rapidly in the city.[2]

The city may have become less attractive to potential freemen, for although the fluctuations in admissions can be variously interpreted, the long-term pattern was of a continuous decline in admissions to a mere 519 in the decade 1521-30, less than half of the admission rate of 1411-20. The corporation were well aware of the problem, and made concessions designed to increase the numbers of both freemen and apprentices. In 1508-9 the franchise was offered by instalments to apprentices willing to lease corporation housing, an offer eloquent of property decay no less than of a declining franchise.[3] Ten years later, as the decline worsened, the concessions became more generous. All applicants willing to be city tenants, whether ex-apprentices or not, were to be enfranchised on easy terms, and the desperate corporation overrode many guild restrictions. New freemen were entitled to membership of any and every craft guild without payment, and could 'take as many prentysez, servaunts and journeymen as it shall please them'. One week's work by the corporation had abolished the restrictive practices of generations, and the new policies remained in force until the economy began to recover.[4]

In encouraging applications for freedom the corporation were sponsoring select immigration rather than a mass influx,

---

[1] Certainly the 1524 Yorks. assessment was not comprehensive: J. Thirsk, *Sources of Information on Population, 1500-1760* (Canterbury, 1965), p. 4.
[2] Palliser, 'Epidemics in Tudor York', pp. 47 f.   [3] *Y.C.R.* iii. 24, 26.
[4] ibid., 67 f.; Palliser, 'Trade gilds', pp. 98, 112.

for the freemen accounted for only half the adult male population, and no doubt (with a few exceptions) the more prosperous half. Despite their awareness of demographic crisis, the city fathers had no intention of encouraging population growth at any price, and the same period witnessed both concessions to skilled immigrants and deterrents to the homeless and destitute. Action against beggary followed the pattern familiar in other Tudor towns, attention being first paid to the problem in the late fifteenth century, and growing throughout the sixteenth. As early as 1482 public proclamation was made forbidding immigrant vagrants to stay more than one night, and in 1501 all six wards were ordered to provide stocks and fetters for 'begars, vacabunds and other mysdoers'.[1] Experience soon convinced the city fathers that their policy was too indiscriminate, and the practice of licensing the deserving poor to beg, first recorded at Gloucester in 1504, was taken up. An order of 1515 authorized wardens to punish beggars 'myghty of body', but the sick or impotent beggar was to 'have a token upon his sholder of his overmost garment that he may be knowen'.[2] The destitute, whether native or immigrant, were very numerous, as bequests for funeral doles testify. A Minster cantarist 'witt thar be dalt a thowsand pence to a thowsand poor peopill', and a retired alderman left £5 'to be distribute to every olde man and woman jd'.[3] Indiscriminate doles, however, slowly lost popularity through attracting poor from outside the city. The registrar to the Minster Chancellor left twenty marks to be distributed to the city poor 'in domibus suis, et non publice in ecclesia aut alio loco'. The date was 1528, one of several indications that the more discriminating use of charity in Yorkshire, which W. K. Jordan links with the Reformation, had already begun to take hold.[4]

The repeated proclamations against immigrant vagabonds put it beyond doubt that the ranks of the native poor had been swollen by newcomers hoping for shelter, work, or merely alms, including probably villagers evicted by

---

[1] *Y.C.R.* i. 55 f.; ii. 165.
[2] *Y.C.R.* iii. 46.
[3] Y.M.L., MS L2 (5)a, fo. 111ʳ (1511/16); *Test. Ebor.* v. 199 (1525).
[4] *Test. Ebor.* v. 241; Jordan, *Charities of Rural England*, pp. 230 f.

desertions.[1] Certainly a large city like York, even in decline, is likely to have attracted the destitute from its hinterland. There was no lack of decaying housing to rent cheaply or even left empty for squatters, and the presence of lay and ecclesiastical magnates assured a source of wealth and of alms even in the midst of poverty.[2] Men dependent on rural incomes or official salaries were not, after all, affected by the economic decline of the city in which they had their headquarters. It was during York's blackest period, in the 1520s and 1530s, that Dean Higden made a regal progress to his cathedral each Christmas, attended by fifty liveried gentlemen and thirty yeomen.[3]

The vacant housing was available for poor immigrants because the decay of urban property, already observed in the late fifteenth century, continued. Income from the houses of the Vicars Choral stabilized about the turn of the century,[4] but corporation rents continued to diminish, and in 1533 the common council looked back nostalgically to the 'tymes past when this citie was in grete prosperte and the rents of this city dyd amownt to a great somme'.[5] The response of the private landlord to property decay was often to demolish, and in 1524 the corporation found it necessary to order citizens to 'take downe no houses that stands towards the commen strete' without permission of the mayor.[6] There was no question, either for individuals or for the corporation, of much new building. The evidence of buildings surviving until the present, or only recently demolished, suggests that many York houses were built or rebuilt in the fifteenth and seventeenth centuries, but very few in the sixteenth. Documentary evidence concurs, for only forty to fifty new houses seem to be mentioned during the century, and of those only seven were built during the first six decades.[7] Such was the hallmark of a city in decay, and it is noteworthy that other towns

---

[1] At least one Ainsty village was depopulated by its lord c.1500: M. W. Beresford, 'The lost villages of Yorkshire', *Y.A.J.* xxxviii (1952-5), 223-5, 232.

[2] e.g. Dr Rokeby: T. D. Whitaker, *A History of Richmondshire, in the North Riding of the County of York* (London, 1823), i. 172.

[3] Bodley, Dodsworth 125, fo. 104ᵛ.

[4] Bartlett, 'Aspects of the economy of York', p. 187.

[5] *Y.C.R.* iii. 148.   [6] ibid., 90.

[7] Palliser, 'York', pp. 394A-394C.

in economic difficulties, like Norwich, Southampton, Stamford, and Worcester, saw little Tudor building in comparison with earlier and later periods.

In 1532, and again the next year, York's MPs were instructed to seek a private Act of Parliament which would permit the corporation to seize the sites of demolished houses if the owners refused to rebuild.[1] Their plea was not immediately successful, but in 1540 a statute was passed 'for reedifieng of townes' which authorized such measures in thirty-six named towns including York. The preamble asserted that they had included many fine dwellings which had now collapsed or become dangerous.[2] In so far as the corporation were successful, however, they merely encouraged decayed houses to be patched up and thus available for just those paupers whom they wished to exclude. In January 1547 they imposed new and stringent controls on demolitions, yet at the same meeting they had to forbid the building of tenements rented at under 6s. 8d. a year, 'for there is so many tenements within this citie of xx^d and ij^s farme by yere that vacabunds and beggars can not be avoyded'. Those who could not pay even a rent of twenty pence would squat wherever there was vacant property. In November 1551 'dumb John', a deaf-and-dumb beggar, moved into a house where the entire family was 'newly dead . . . of the plague'. When the landlord evicted him three or four days later he 'wandered abrode' until the corporation, fearing he might spread infection, placed him in another house emptied by plague.[3]

5

While the city decayed and trade stagnated, the corporation were caught between falling revenue and rising expenditure. The most pressing problem was the old one of the annual fee-farm, for the remission by Henry VII had not proved lasting. At York, as at Lincoln, £100 of the fee-farm had long been alienated to the Roos family, until Lord Roos was attainted in 1461. The reversal of the attainder after Bosworth

---

[1] *Y.C.R.* iii. 139, 146.
[2] *Statutes of the Realm*, iii. 768 f.; Elton, *Reform and Renewal*, pp. 108 f.
[3] *Y.C.R.* iv. 149; Y.C.A., E 40, No. 76.

was therefore a disaster for both cities, allowing the Roos heir to claim the farms despite the remissions by Edward IV and Richard III. From 1492 to 1524 the guardian of the Roos interests was Sir Thomas Lovell, who recognized the decay of both cities and agreed to accept twenty marks a year from each in lieu of the £100. However, Thomas Manners became Lord Roos in 1524 (and first earl of Rutland in 1525), and he quickly set about claiming the full £100 from both cities and took the claim to the Exchequer.[1] Both corporations resisted vigorously, and Dean Higden in January 1528 interceded for York with Wolsey, arguing that the city could not 'amend' unless the fee-farm was reduced and the wool-shipping grant continued.[2] Rutland claimed not only the full £100, but also arrears since Lovell's death, and the hapless mayor wrote to the recorder in London that 'I and my bredern can perceyve none oder but to come up at Mighelmas terme next commyng for to surrender up our libertiez into the Kings hands'. After another appeal to the Cardinal, the corporation secured acquittances from Rutland limiting their obligations to the traditional twenty marks.[3] After Wolsey's fall, however, Rutland again increased his demands, and the corporation were by now embarrassed even by the lesser fee-farm payment of £35. 14s. 7d. to St. Stephen's, Westminster, and by various charges and obits which they were obliged to pay. From 1529 they suspended payment to St. Stephen's, without authorization, and in 1531 they again threatened to surrender the city's liberties if the King's council could grant them no relief.[4] Tripartite negotiations between council, corporation, and Earl dragged on for three years, until finally a statute of 1536 resolved the dispute. Rutland compounded to receive £40 a year instead of £100, and the citizens were allowed to reduce the Westminster payment by £5. 14s. 7d., to cancel another yearly charge of £9. 2s. 6d. to Lord Darcy, and to keep £42 which they had yearly spent on certain

[1] *Y.C.R.* iii. 44; *V.C.H. York*, p. 123; J. W. F. Hill, *Medieval Lincoln* (Cambridge, 1948), p. 285, and *Tudor and Stuart Lincoln* (Cambridge, 1956), p. 26.
[2] *L.P. Hen. VIII*, iv. No. 3843.
[3] *Y.C.R.* iii. 113, 116 f.
[4] P.R.O., C1/687/26; *Y.C.R.* iii. 135, 137–41.

chantries and obits. They were thus discharged in perpetuity from yearly payments of £117.[1]

The civic chest was undoubtedly seriously depleted from 1524 to 1536, and for some time afterwards. The chamberlains' account showed a record deficit of £483 for the year ending 15 January 1537, and measures were immediately taken to reduce the debt by exacting large gifts from the chamberlains-elect.[2] One may, however, question whether the corporation were ever as near to bankruptcy as they claimed. The mayor continued to receive his traditional fee of £50, despite several attempts by members of the Twenty-Four and others to reduce or abolish it. On the third of these occasions the common council pressed for a reduction in the mayor's fee and expenses, and substantial cuts in 'sumptuous and costly feasts' and other entertainments, asking that the economies should be maintained 'unto suche tyme that the city be better inhabit'.[3] Most significant of all, the corporation steadfastly continued to pay wages to their two MPs in every Parliament, resisting the blandishments of gentlemen like Richard Bunny, who offered, if elected, to serve *gratis*.[4] The sum of 8s. a day could mean a substantial outlay for a Parliament, as the corporation acknowledged when in 1486 they tried to cancel their MPs' wages lest the King should doubt their pleas of poverty. Yet they apparently paid the 8s. regularly throughout the long Reformation Parliament, at a time when some boroughs were driven to default on paying their burgesses.[5]

Despite these expenses, which the corporation may have felt to be all the more essential to their dignity in an age of decline, the city's poverty went unquestioned by Crown, corporation, and citizens. All the evidence suggests that the relief afforded in 1536, though it eased the pressure, was insufficient to ensure a revival of prosperity. The Act, after all, affected only civic finances, and did nothing to restore

---

[1] *Statutes of the Realm*, iii. 582-4; A. G. Dickens, 'A municipal dissolution of chantries', *Y.A.J.* xxxvi (1944-7), 164-73; Lehmberg, *Reformation Parliament*, pp. 23, 234.

[2] Y.C.A., C 6/8; *Y.C.R.* iv. 20.

[3] *Y.C.R.* iii. 120-8, 143, 147-9.   [4] Y.C.A., E 40, No. 28 (1553).

[5] *Y.C.R.* i. 152; McKisack, *Parl. Repres. Boroughs*, p. 87; Lehmberg, *Reformation Parliament*, pp. 31-4.

industrial or commercial prosperity directly. The underlying problem remained the loss of the city's twin sources of late medieval prosperity, cloth industry and long-distance trade, and no adequate substitute was yet to hand. Admissions of freemen recovered slightly from their lowest point in the 1520s, but not sufficiently to indicate a real return of prosperity. The corporation, relieved at last of the fee-farm disputes, seem to have diagnosed the chief remaining problem as the navigability of the Ouse, and spent much time considering how the river could be deepened and cleared of obstructions by fishgarths.[1] More fruitfully, encouragement was given to the cloth industry and cloth trade. The corporation paid half the charges of the Coverlet Act of 1543, on the ground that 'the same acte is as muche for the common well of this Citie as [for] the coverlet wevers of the same', and it did indeed bring about a modest prosperity of the York worsted industry.[2] About the end of 1552 a memorandum presented to the mayor and aldermen argued that the next Parliament would be a suitable occasion to have clothmaking better supervised, 'consederyn of the good willes that the Dukes grace of Northethumberland and the Erle of Shrewsberye doethe bear towardes the restoryng of this town to his ancyent esteytt'. The author proposed that a hall in York should be set aside for search and sale of all country cloth, wool, and leather, corresponding to Blackwell Hall in London, and his proposal was sponsored by the corporation during the last Parliament of Edward VI, though without success.[3]

6

The corporation continued to plead poverty throughout Mary's reign, and their successful advocate was Alderman William Holme, who sat for the city in both of Edward's Parliaments and the last three of Mary's. His five elections were a record among York's MPs, and he seems to have acquired valuable experience which he put to good use. It was he who persuaded the York-born London alderman, Sir Martin Bowes,

---

[1] e.g. Y.C.A., B 13[a], fo. 1; B 14, fo. 7[v]; *Y.C.R.* iv. *passim*.
[2] *Y.C.R.* iv. 92; Heaton, *Yorks. Woollen and Worsted Industries*, pp. 55-7.
[3] Y.C.A., E 40, Nos. 26, 67; *Y.C.R.* v. 87.

and his friends, to support a bill for the union of decayed churches at York, help which may have been decisive in securing its passage.[1] It was he who in 1553 persuaded the Privy Council to sanction a tax rebate of £50, more than a third of the sum due from the city. More help might have been forthcoming, as in June Edward VI appointed a commission to investigate the decay of York, but the appointment lapsed on the King's death.[2] In 1555, when Holme was again one of the members, the mayor wrote to them complaining of the difficulty in raising another fifteenth and tenth, for the fixed tax was bearing very heavily on the poorer parishes. In seven of the poorest parishes it had proved impossible to levy the assessment because parishioners had moved out of them, 'for that the payment of one yere taxe is duble and treble more than theyr wholle yere rent'. Again, Holme was able to secure a remission of £50 out of the £136 owed.[3]

Holme's services to his city culminated in the Parliament of 1558. He reported to a delighted city council that he had obtained from the Queen yet another tax remission, of £40, and that Sir Martin Bowes had granted the city £60 in money and some silver-gilt plate. The council at once granted Holme a lease of some market tolls 'for his great diligens, industrie and paynes', and then

after all whiche matters by the sayd Mr. Holme declared to this presens . . . by advyse of the same he forthwyth issued forth of the sayd Counsell Chambre into the Comon Hall whan and where he lykewise made report of his seyd doynges . . . to dyverse of the honest comoners of this cite ther ready assembled whoo greatly reioysyng and prayeng for the queenes royall estat and for the sayd Sir Martyne did greatly allow and prayse the earnest dilygens of the sayd Mr. Holme in all the cite affayres.[4]

No record survives of any commission of enquiry into the poverty of the city, as had been planned in 1553, but Mary's council must have been firmly convinced of the reality of the depression to allow three tax remissions in five years. Doubtless the major causes remained the same as they had been since the late fifteenth century, but the long-term difficulties were exacerbated in the mid-sixteenth century by two short-

[1] *Y.C.R.* iv. 173.   [2] *Y.C.R.* v. 88–98.
[3] ibid., 133, 135.   [4] Y.C.A., B 22, fos. 121–2.

term but severe crises. One was caused by the material effects of the Reformation, and the other by a series of devastating epidemics; it is ironic that the worst of the epidemics killed William Holme as he was about to return to Parliament to fight once more for the city's interests.

Of the two, the Reformation is the more difficult to establish as an agent of economic decline. It was taken for granted by Keep and Drake, two of York's early historians, that the dissolutions of religious houses, hospitals, guilds, and chantries were a major cause of the city's decay,[1] but it must be admitted that none of the corporation's explanations of their plight invokes the dissolutions as a cause, except for their repeated complaints that chantry tenements in Crown ownership were allowed to decay.[2] An argument *ex silentio* would therefore deny that the dissolutions were an economic catastrophe, but this would be to ignore the realities of contemporary politics. The corporation had burned their fingers in the Pilgrimage of 1536, and were thereafter anxious to prove their loyalty to every successive sovereign regardless of religion. The preamble to the Church Unions Act of 1547 asserted that the poorer livings were acceptable only to ex-monks and chantry priests, 'blynde guydes and pastors' who kept the people in ignorance of their duty to God and the King. This can only mean that an argument was being advanced acceptable to an Edwardian Parliament, for it is most unlikely that the corporation themselves believed in such a Protestant argument.[3]

The fall of the monasteries and friaries in 1536-9 had two important economic consequences. There were ten religious houses in the city and suburbs, but another forty, including most of the larger northern houses, owned property there, often including a 'town house' for the abbot or prior on his visits to York.[4] The suppression of all fifty within a few years may have caused a sharp decline in large-scale buying from the city's merchants and tradesmen, for some of the monasteries are known to have made extensive purchases at

[1] Trinity Coll. Cambridge MS 0.4.33, p. 113; Drake, *Eboracum*, pp. 236-7.

[2] *Y.C.R.* v. 87, 93, 96, 136-7, 139; vi. 118; vii. 46. Cf. A. G. Dickens, *The English Reformation* (London, 1964), p. 154.

[3] *Statutes of the Realm*, iv. 14; Palliser, *Reformation in York*, p. 30.

[4] See p. 5, n. 4.

York, and in particular St. Mary's, the richest house in the north, must have been a major customer for a wide variety of goods, whereas after 1539 its extensive lands were sold to different owners, and there would no longer be a concentration of their profits within the city. Furthermore, a very large part (probably at least one quarter) of the domestic houses in York had been monastically owned, and they were suddenly transferred to the Crown and thence to owners who usually lived outside the city and sometimes outside the north. The largest purchase, of over 400 dwellings, was made by the London alderman Sir Richard Gresham, and although he and his son sold at least some of them to citizens, there must for a short period have been a considerable drain of rent to London.[1] One of Aske's fears in 1536 was that the dissolutions would drain the north of coin, a fear which may have been justified. Furthermore, one of the royal acts against church privileges was the closure of the ecclesiastical mints at York and Durham, which together with that at Canterbury had 'provided later medieval England with the bulk of its small change'.[2] Significantly, in 1544 the York corporation asked the earl of Shrewsbury to help re-establish the city mint, as the area was 'stonding in necessytie of money'; the King complied with the request in 1545, and in 1546 turned the dissolutions to positive use by housing the new mint in St. Leonard's Hospital.[3] Scarcely had it reopened, however, when the suppression of guilds and chantries posed a further threat to supplies of coin: another one-quarter of the city's housing passed to distant landlords when two government officials bought the bulk of the chantry properties in 1549, and once again there must have been a heavy drain of money rents from the city, at least temporarily.[4]

The dissolutions also entailed some closures of hospitals, exacerbating the problem of poor relief. Henry VIII's brutal and greedy seizure of the four great London hospitals is well known, and his treatment of the largest northern hospital,

[1] Palliser, *Reformation in York*, pp. 17 f.
[2] C. E. Challis, 'The ecclesiastical mints of the early Tudor period', *Northern History*, x (1975), 88, 96–8.
[3] *Y.C.R.* iv. 120; *L.P. Hen. VIII*, xx (1), pp. 274, 371; R.C.H.M. *York*, ii. 61.
[4] Palliser, *Reformation in York*, pp. 24 f.

St. Leonard's at York, was no better.[1] It fell with the monasteries in 1539, despite being a home for the aged and bed-
ridden rather than a monastery. Their number had fallen to
sixty in 1535 and to about forty-four at the dissolution, still
a substantial figure.[2] True, they received the same pension
(26s. 8d.) as they had from the hospital, but they now had to
find shelter; nor can pensions (which did not rise with inflation) to a diminishing number of poor be considered an
adequate substitute for an establishment continuing to
receive new inmates. It was presumably the hospital's contribution to the problem of poverty that made the corporation
appeal for its restoration in Mary's reign.[3] The sixteenth century also saw the disappearance or suppression of various
smaller hospitals, although their importance is very obscure,
and there is no means of knowing how many poor they had
sheltered between them. Fourteen hospitals out of the city's
total of twenty-two disappeared during the century, and at
least thirteen were closed between the 1530s and the 1560s.
Collectively, their closure must have considerably exacerbated
the already severe problem of poverty in the city.[4] Furthermore, of the two city grammar schools, that in St. Leonard's
fell with the hospital in 1539, and the cathedral school,
which relied on St. Mary's Abbey to keep fifty poor scholars,
may also have closed. The loss was made good in part by
Archbishop Holgate in 1546, but not until the refoundation
of St. Peter's, which took effect after 1565, were there once
again two grammar schools.[5] It is unfortunate that the corporation's financial records are wanting for just this period,
to establish how far they had taken over responsibility for
education in the meantime. It has not, apparently, been

---

[1] J. J. Scarisbrick, *Henry VIII* (London, 1968), p. 515, with ref. to York as
also 'sorely hit'.

[2] *V.C.H. York*, p. 132.   [3] *Y.C.R.* v. 137.

[4] *Yorks. Chantry Certificates*, p. 42; *The Itinerary of John Leland*, ed. L. T.
Smith (London, 1907-10), i. 55; *L.P. Hen. VIII* xiv (2), No. 623; *V.C.H. Yorks.*
iii, 348; Raine, *Mediaeval York*, pp. 242, 251, 259-60, 283; *Y.C.R.* v. 66; Y.C.A.,
B 31, fo. 205[V]; B.I.H.R., probate registers, for last bequests as follows: vii, fo. 60
(Whitefriar Lane m.d. 1507); xi, fo. 10 (St. Andrewgate m.d. 1532); xiii, fo. 304[V]
(St. Christopher's m.d. 1546); xiii, fo. 543[r] (St. Sampson's m.d. 1547-8). The
evidence is listed here because it is contrary to the argument in *V.C.H. York*,
pp. 132 f.

[5] Palliser, *Reformation in York*, pp. 16 f.

noticed previously that the Crown accepted it as one of
the reasons for their poverty. Mary's tax remission of 1553
spoke of 'great charges and expenses that the sayd citizens is
yerelie at for the good education of a greate numbre of
power chyldren', an explanation repeated in 1563.[1]

Both Mary and Elizabeth also cited epidemics among the
causes of York's poverty, and these short-term disasters, coming close on one another, may have been especially devastating
to an already crippled city. After a relatively healthy period
of fifteen years, York was struck hard in 1538-41, 1549-52,
and 1558-9, apparently in increasing order of severity.[2] The
'pestyllence' of 1538, judging from numbers of wills proved,
was more severe than any attack in the previous thirty years.
After only eight years' relief, there was heavy mortality in
1550 and 1551. The parish of St. Martin, Micklegate, may
have lost half its population in those two years alone; and a
very rough calculation would allow 4,000 deaths in the city
in the period 1550-2, or about half the total population.
Too much weight cannot be placed on one estimate as a proportion of another, especially as it has to be based on the
only two reliable parish registers which cover the whole
period. Nevertheless, the disaster was enough for Queen Mary
in 1553 to accept that 'there is a great number of howses
vacante . . . by reason of the great pestylence that was latlie
there', and two years after that seven parishes were still
almost depopulated.[3]

Before the city could well recover from these disasters, it
was struck again in the summer of 1558 by 'extreame and farvent sekenes', alias 'the newe ague'. It has escaped all mention in York histories, probably because it scarcely figures in
the parish registers or the council minutes, yet it was in all
likelihood the worst epidemic of the century, part of the
nationwide influenza which devastated England at the end of
Mary's reign. The indications are all of a high death-rate, and
the lack of evidence in the parish registers was apparently
owing simply to a cessation of registration in an exceptionally
severe epidemic.[4] The effect of the 'new ague', coming so
soon after bubonic plague and the sweat, must have been

[1] *Y.C.R.* v. 98; vi. 67.   [2] Palliser, 'Epidemics in Tudor York', pp. 48-52.
[3] *Y.C.R.* v. 97 f., 133.   [4] Palliser, 'Epidemics in Tudor York', pp. 51 f.

disastrous, even though admissions of immigrants to the freedom rose sharply after 1560 and may have compensated in
part for the loss of manpower. When the corporation spoke
in 1562 of 'the evydent decaye and dymenishyng both of
people and habitacons, by the third part within this cite',
they may well have spoken the sober truth.[1]

As if the effects of dissolutions and epidemics were not
enough, financial troubles loomed large again with the full
impact of Tudor inflation. Its effects may have been especially
severe in a large and decaying city which lived mainly by
commerce and crafts, and had little of its own food. It is
unfortunate that the chamberlains' rolls are entirely missing
for the 1540s and 1550s, but a panic measure of civic
economy in 1558 was justified by 'thexceedyng dearth of
all maner of vitaylls and other necessaries of howskepyng
wiche in theis our dayes doo cost duble and treble the money
that in tymes past they were wont to do', and certainly the
price of one basic commodity, malt, almost exactly doubled
between 1545–6 and 1563–4.[2] Sustained inflation of agricultural prices, it is now widely agreed, began in the 1520s,
and of industrial prices probably in the 1540s,[3] so that
York's artisans, certainly those without livestock or smallholdings, must have come under severe pressure by mid-
century. Impoverishment was acute by 1552, when the
corporation reiterated the statutory maximum wages for
some craftsmen of 4d. a day with meat and 6d. without, laid
down in 1514, and imprisoned some who refused to work for
those wages. The guilds concerned petitioned the mayor on
12 July that they had hitherto worked at rates of 5d. and 8d.
respectively, and that the revived 1514 rates would beggar
them, since 'all thynges ar so dear and outte of the waye'.
The corporation's brusque response was to imprison the
searchers who had presented the petition, but it was easier to
imprison recalcitrants than to solve the problem of declining
real wages.[4] Surviving corporation wage-rates for 1554 and

---

[1] *Y.C.R.* vi. 33.   [2] *Y.C.R.* v. 177; Y.M.L., MSS Vr 34, 35.
[3] e.g. R. B. Outhwaite, *Inflation in Tudor and early Stuart England* (London,
1969), p. 13; P. H. Ramsey, ed., *The Price Revolution in Sixteenth-Century
England* (London, 1971), p. 4.
[4] *Y.C.R.* v. 76–8; Y.C.A., E 40, No. 73.

1559 suggest that they soon gave up the attempt to keep to the 1514 levels.[1]

York by the end of Mary's reign was undoubtedly a very unfortunate city. General economic difficulties produced by inflation, debasement, war, the collapse of the Antwerp market, and the religious dissolutions at home had coincided with local economic difficulties to impoverish a city already in decay. The heavy death-rate of the late 1550s must have seemed the last straw, and councillors whose fathers or fathers-in-law had staved off corporation bankruptcy in the 1530s must have thought that the situation was repeating itself. It would have seemed very unlikely at that time that under Mary's sister the city was to be more than repeopled and to enjoy once more a modest prosperity.

[1] Information kindly supplied by D. M. Woodward, from a forthcoming study of wage regulation at York.

IX

RELIGION AND THE REFORMATION

It seems they took the change in religion much worse
than in the southern parts of the kingdom, and made
several smart struggles against it.

Francis Drake, 1736[1]

York in Henry VII's reign, like any other large city, was to
outward appearance a devoutly Catholic community where
secular and ecclesiastical life interpenetrated at all levels, and
where the most impressive buildings to greet a traveller,
towering over the city walls, were churches and religious
houses. The city and suburbs housed, besides the cathedral
and its associated institutions, four monasteries, one nunnery,
four friaries, forty parish churches, two civic bridge-chapels,
and many lesser chapels, hospitals and *maisons dieu*. There
were perhaps 200 or more religious, and the same number of
parish clergy, in a city of 8,000 people.[2] The wills of many
layfolk testify to friendship and kinship with priests and
religious, who seem, with few exceptions, to have integrated
well with the rest of the population.

Then, as now, the city was physically dominated by the
Minster, one of the nine secular English cathedrals. Its great
wealth and patronage, the power of its Dean and Chapter,
and its numerous clergy, lawyers, and officials, made it a
power to be reckoned with. It housed the tombs of several
archbishops canonized by due process or by popular consent,
and those of St. William (d. 1154), Sewall de Bovill (d. 1258),
and Richard Scrope (d. 1405) were centres of pilgrimage.[3] It
was the obvious church in which to make public appeals to
the leading citizens and country gentry, like the archbishop's

[1] Drake, *Eboracum*, p. 127.

[2] *c.*300 parish clergy in 1436 and *c.*150 religious at the Dissolution: Dobson,
'Foundation of perpetual chantries', p. 38; Palliser, *Reformation in York*, p. 12.

[3] For Bovill and Scrope, see J. Wilson, *The English Martyrologe* (1608, repr.
Amsterdam and New York, 1970), p. 131; *Test. Ebor.* v. 4.

sermons against the papal supremacy in 1534-5, and the corporation even held business meetings there 'behind St. Christopher'.[1] Yet it remained primarily a mother-church for the diocese, and most citizens regarded it 'with the same mixture of respect and indifference that the seamen of a modern trawling fleet might display towards an ocean liner'. Many citizens bequeathed money for its fabric, but the gift was in most cases a traditional fourpence for the mother church, and is not to be compared with the generous sums frequently offered to the parish churches and friaries. Of some 140 chantries known in York, at least fifty-six were housed in the Minster, but most were founded by its canons, and no York laymen established any there after 1400.[2]

The monasteries and nunnery also benefited little from citizens' bequests.[3] Recorded relations between citizens and religious tend to be prosaic, such as the letting and sub-letting of a monastic corrody like any property rent.[4] One might therefore assume that the monastic houses, though an accepted part of the order of things, failed to arouse devoted attachment; but it is difficult to be sure. The paucity of benefactions may simply reflect an awareness that the religious were adequately endowed, and the hostility of the citizens to the monastic suppressions of 1536 is undoubted. There is less room to question the esteem in which the four city friaries were held. One in three of the citizens making wills between 1501 and 1538 remembered them, and the corporation commissioned sermons from friars to the very eve of the dissolutions.[5] It was normal for the corporation to arrange for annual prayers for their benefactors, and for craft guilds to attend obits and requiem masses, 'within one of the frears'.[6] Too little is known of the activities which earned the mendicants such regard, but they were certainly relied on in a variety of ways. Land-owners entrusted them with the keeping

---

[1] Palliser, op. cit., p. 3; Y.C.R. ii. 14; v. 140, 169; vi. 97; vii. 163.

[2] Dobson, 'Foundation of perpetual chantries', pp. 25-7.

[3] Notable exceptions are Test. Ebor. iv. 28 f. and Y.M.L., MS L2 (5)a, fos. 142-3.

[4] P.R.O., C1/302/62 (c.1510).

[5] Palliser, Reformation in York, pp. 2 f.

[6] Y.C.A., B 7, fo. 15ᵛ; Y.C.R. iii. 186-7, iv. 184; J.S. Purvis, 'A York account roll for A.D. 1537-8', Y.A.J. xlii. 52 f.

of deeds and valuables, bishops found their priories useful for
holding ordinations, and the city corporation, besides endowing prayers in them, occasionally held their meetings in a
friary.[1]

It was their parish churches, however, which had the
primary claim on the loyalties of citizens. Most testators
asked for burial in their parish church or churchyard, and the
commonest charitable bequests were to their own churches.[2]
It was the parochial unit which gave the citizens their strong-
est sense of continuity with the past, through those inter-
cessions linking the living with the dead which were at the
heart of late medieval religion. The richest families endowed
chantries for daily intercession, and the well-to-do founded
obits for annual commemoration. A modest bequest could
secure commemoration in the parish bede-roll, a list which
was regularly read out by the priest, and which in a semi-
literate age must have impressed itself deeply on the minds of
the hearers. Witnesses in 1585 could still remember that
Agnes Maners had been prayed for at St. Margaret's under
Henry VIII and again under Mary I.[3] Parochial loyalties could
retain a hold on families even after they had left the city.
Martin Bowes, heir to a patrician family of St. Cuthbert's,
left York as a youth to seek and find a fortune in London. In
1548, a rich goldsmith and alderman, he was able to help
pilot York's Union of Churches bill through Parliament, and
in return he successfully interceded for the preservation of
St. Cuthbert's. He reminded the corporation that in that
parish 'I was borne and my great graundefathere whiche was
Mayer of Yorke and my graunde father Shyrryf, who were
bothe founders and patrons of the same churche and gave
bothe books, bells and all other ornaments to the same'.[4]

---

[1] e.g. *Y.A.J.* xxxii. 151 f.; A. H. Thompson, *The English Clergy and their
Organization in the later Middle Ages* (Oxford, 1947), p. 299; *Y.C.R.* i. 74; iii.
2, 114.

[2] Of 1,725 citizens with surviving wills 1501–1600, three asked for burial in
monasteries, fourteen in friaries, fifty-one in the Minster and Minster Yard, and
some twenty to twenty-five in a parish church other than their own. All the
others, where they mentioned a burial place, asked for their own parish church or
churchyard.

[3] P.R.O., E178/2661. She had died c.1500, leaving nine tenements to the
church: *Test. Ebor.* iv. 97.

[4] *Y.C.R.* iv. 173.

Patronage of the churches was in many hands, with no patron in a dominant position. The Crown held only one advowson, and other laymen five. Nineteen or more were owned by religious houses, eleven by St. Mary's and Holy Trinity. The largest group, fourteen, was held by the archbishop, chapter and Minster clergy.[1] The patrons' influence was restricted by the low level of stipends, for the average living surveyed in 1535 was worth only £4. 5s. 0d. a year. It is therefore not surprising that the city parishes did not attract the better-educated clergy. Only four out of seventy known parish priests between 1534 and 1553 were certainly graduates.[2] It is true that the vicar of All Saints, North Street, owned Erasmus's *Adages* and two of Cicero's works in 1535, but the absence of humanist books from the stock of the bookseller Mores in 1538 scarcely argues a lively intellectual atmosphere among the city clergy.[3]

The poverty of parish livings was compounded by appropriations, an abuse especially common in Yorkshire. Between fifteen and twenty of them were appropriated by their patrons, the Minster chapter and various religious houses, so that in only half the parishes did the incumbent receive the full tithes and dues. Income from tithes was in any case a difficult problem in the towns, where wealth was more difficult to assess than in the countryside, and the conventional payments for 'tithes neglected' in most wills can have been little compensation. The parsons' plight is graphically portrayed in the 1547 Union of Churches Act, no doubt with a little exaggeration:

in the Citie of Yorke and suburbes of the same there is many parishe churches whiche heretofore . . . was good and honest leving for lernyd incumbents by reason for the prevey tythes of the riche merchaunts and of the offerings of a great multitude, which levings is nowe so muche decayd by the ruyne and decay of the said Citie and of the trade of merchaundyse ther that there revenues and profetts of dyverse of the same benefices or at this present not above the clere yerely value of xxvjs viij[d] sterlings. . . .[4]

---

[1] Based on last presentations before the dissolution, from lists in Y.M.L., MS L1(8). The totals include two livings divided into medieties.

[2] Palliser, *Reformation in York*, p. 3.

[3] B.I.H.R., Archbishop's Reg. xxviii, fo. 168[v]; Palliser and Selwyn, 'Stock of a York stationer', p. 212.

[4] *Statutes of the Realm*, iv. 14.

The poverty of many churches, it seems, reflected that of the city, which could no longer afford to maintain forty of them: it implied no lack of devotion by the parishioners. Gifts of vestments, ornaments and books remained frequent items in their wills, and one citizen in 1508 bequeathed a chained bible to his church, suggesting that a number of his fellow-parishioners had enough Latin to profit from it.[1] The churches were crowded with altars, images, and other furnishings, their windows filled with stained glass and their walls covered with frescoes.[2] Most surviving glass is of the fifteenth century or earlier, but St. Michael-le-Belfrey possesses a series of windows of the 1530s donated as part of the rebuilding, while another series of early sixteenth-century windows depicts the legend of Becket's parents.[3]

As was usual, seating for the laity was added late, and its installation can be traced through the wills of prosperous citizens, as requests for burial 'near the place where I usually stand' are succeeded by 'near my stall'. Such mentions occur earliest for the rich central parishes of Christ Church (1511), All Saints Pavement (1513) and St. Crux (1517), and for many churches not until mid-century or even later.[4] The most primitive feature, by later standards, was the flooring. Christ Church was carpeted with green rushes in summer and straw in winter, presumably to cover a floor of beaten earth, for it was unpaved until a much later date. Probably the reason was the practical one of facilitating burials, for when the neighbouring church of St. Crux installed paving, it quickly became uneven because of the frequent interments.[5]

Churches, as the only substantial stone buildings in most parishes, had a variety of uses. Primarily, of course, they were employed for masses and other services, and for private devotions.[6] Many housed chantries, and the priests might have other occupations besides saying soul-masses: at least one

---

[1] *Test. Ebor.* iv. 269.   [2] *Excerpta Antiqua*, ed. J. Croft, pp. 16 f.

[3] E. Milner-White, *Sixteenth Century Glass in York Minster and in the Church of St. Michael-le-Belfrey* (Borth. P. xvii, 1960).

[4] Borthwick Inst., probate reg. viii, fo. 106; ix, fo. 52; *Test. Ebor.* v. 37; etc.

[5] Drake, *Eboracum*, p. 320; Marchant, *Puritans and the Church Courts*, pp. 59, 61. Cf. Croft, *Excerpta Antiqua*, pp. 13 f. For other examples see J. S. Purvis, *Tudor Parish Documents of the Diocese of York* (Cambridge, 1948), pp. 60 f.

[6] *Fabric Rolls of York Minster*, ed. Raine, p. 262.

kept a school.[1] Some churches, if not all, housed parish guilds, shadowy associations the bare existence of which is attested by wills, and which may be assumed, by analogy with other places, to have acted as socio-religious fraternities and mutual-benefit societies. At least seven guilds are recorded, between 1501 and 1554, in different churches.[2] Parish meetings were also held in church; the mayor would, on occasion, deal with business in his own parish church; and views of the poor, wardmote courts, and schools could all be held in churches.[3]

2

Orthodoxy was the keynote of almost all religious attitudes recorded before the 1530s, though it would be remarkable if it were otherwise in a city of so many clergy and church courts. Sometimes the expression of orthodoxy or piety can be seen to go beyond what was required,[4] and in 1505-6 three York laymen found themselves at Rome on pilgrimage, two of them being identifiable as free craftsmen.[5] Signs of zeal (if such they were) remained nevertheless infrequent, and the impression left from their wills is that most laymen, as in London, were 'conventionally pious, steering a middle course between religious apathy and religious enthusiasm'.[6] In one respect, certainly, they displayed considerable enthusiasm: the endowment of prayers for the dead. It is true that additions to the large number of endowed chantries in the city dwindled: none was established after 1509-10, though the augmentation of existing chantries continued until 1529.[7] Yet bequests for soul-masses continued unabated until the

[1] *Test. Ebor.* v. 269.

[2] Raine, *Mediaeval York*, pp. 36, 78, 106, 108, 184, 239, 295; Y.M.L., MS L2 (5)a, fos. 34, 43; B.I.H.R., prob. reg. vi, fos. 36, 201-2, 229; vii, fos. 52, 62; viii, fo. 117; ix, fo. 16; xiv, fo. 270^V; *Test. Ebor.* v. 5; B.I.H.R., orig. prob. records, T. Lytster 1528.

[3] e.g. B.I.H.R., C.P. G2792; *York Memorandum Book*, ii. 292; *Y.C.R.* ii. 48; iii. 20, 31; vii. 157, 159; Y.C.A., B 23, fo. 142; Y.M.L. Acc. 1966/2, 19, fo. between fos. 25-8.

[4] e.g. *Test. Ebor.* iv. 53, 56, 58; Y.M.L., MS L2(5)a, fos. 62-3, 189; the former is printed in *Test. Ebor.* iv. 257, which however omits the vital word 'poure'.

[5] *Collectanea Topographica et Genealogica*, v (London, 1838), 69-71.

[6] J. A. F. Thomson, 'Piety and charity in late medieval London', *Jour. Eccles. Hist.* xvi (1965), 194.

[7] *Test. Ebor.* v. 12-17, 214-15, 268-70.

1540s, and the decline in chantry foundations reflects the city's poverty rather than any loss of faith in the efficacy of the prayers.[1] A good part of the city bellman's duties continued to be the announcing of departed souls to be prayed for.[2]

It is almost impossible to measure spirituality from the records, but one of the few revealing exceptions is the text of the Corpus Christi cycle of fifty-two miracle plays, which survives almost complete in a unique copy.[3] Naturally such a cycle, the product of a small number of hands in the fourteenth and fifteenth centuries, cannot be assumed to represent fairly the religious world-picture of the whole population. Yet its production nearly every year, and its undimmed popularity until the 1570s, suggest that it struck a responsive chord in many citizens. In essence, it provides a good biblical summary of cosmic history from the Creation to Doomsday, with few apocryphal additions. The final play, performed by the wealthiest guild, the mercers, is a stark commentary on Christ's parable of the sheep and the goats: performance of the Six Corporal Acts of Mercy is the decisive test of salvation, and one can see at once why Protestant clergy with solefidian views should detest the plays. The message of the Doomsday play, hammered home by windows and wallpaintings in the churches, must have had a considerable impact, to say the least. The fear of retribution for evil deeds gave powerful support to the oath-taking system which the corporation, like the church, used extensively. A merchant accused of writing seditious bills first denied the charge but later confessed to perjury, 'and nowe intendyth to declare and showe all the trouthe for his sowle heylth'.[4]

The world of orthodoxy is the only one adequately recorded, and it is seldom that one glimpses that other mental world of superstition and magic which K. V. Thomas has explored so fully.[5] Curses were put on aldermen more than once; a 'witch of York' is cryptically mentioned in 1537, and in 1594 Cuthbert Williamson was accused of the beneficent

---

[1] Dobson, 'Foundation of perpetual chantries', pp. 34–8.
[2] e.g. Y.C.A., B 7, fo. 15ᵛ.   [3] Smith, *York Plays, passim.*
[4] *Y.C.R.* iv. 11.
[5] K. Thomas, *Religion and the Decline of Magic* (Harmondsworth, 1973 edition), *passim.*

practice of white magic as a 'cunning man'.[1] The most startling and detailed example dates from 1509-10. A York merchant, Thomas Jameson, consulted a wizard about the
recovery of a runaway servant. The wizard diverted him with
the lure of a chest of gold hidden near Halifax, and together
they gathered a group of men, including two priests, to con-
jure a spirit to advise them on the treasure-hunt. Eventually
the story came to light and they were sentenced to public
penance by the archbishop's vicar-general. The proceedings
revealed an extraordinary mixture of Catholic and magical
beliefs; but it would not be fair to assume that such practices were widespread in orthodox York. At an early stage
Jameson had expressed hesitation because 'there was grate
rumor upon it as well at Yorke as in the countrey'.[2]

For pre-Reformation heresy, evidence is equally scanty.
J. A. F. Thomson found no clear case of Lollardy in the
whole diocese between 1421 and 1512; but A. G. Dickens, to
whom our knowledge of Yorkshire Lollardy is chiefly due,
points out that 'long experience had made the Lollards adept
in the art of concealment', an art that would be specially
requisite in the cathedral city. Only from 1528 did York folk
find themselves prosecuted for heresy, and between then and
1547 seven local heretics were tried there, two being burned
and the others abjuring. Interpretation of the cases is far
from easy: the natural supposition (given the late dates)
would be an infusion of Protestantism from the Continent,
and three or four of the seven were indeed 'Dutch'. Dr Thomson prefers the more obvious interpretation, while Professor
Dickens would rather see Lollard survivalism, the singling out
of aliens meaning only that native heretics were less likely to
be accused.[3]

Yet if overt heresy was rare, orthodox citizens had a viewpoint which in certain respects can only be called Erastian or

[1] *Y.C.R.* iv. 2; v. 73; *L.P. Hen. VIII* xii (1), No. 479; Purvis, *Tudor Parish Documents*, pp. 199 f. Cf. Thomas, *Religion and the Decline of Magic*, pp. 220, 510, 608.

[2] J. Raine, ed. 'Proceedings connected with a remarkable charge of sorcery', *Arch. Jour.* xvi (1859), 79–81. For similar cases see Thomas, *Religion and the Decline of Magic*, p. 327.

[3] J. A. F. Thomson, *The Later Lollards 1414–1520* (Oxford, 1965), pp. 195–200; Dickens, *Lollards and Protestants*, pp. 10, 17 f., 21–3, 30–5, 50, 247.

anticlerical, and which must have smoothed the path of at
least some of the Reformation changes. In 1513 the priests of
St. William's Chapel were summoned before the archbishop's
vicar general, and the mayor pointedly told them to appear
'bycause it were the Kyngs cause and for non other cause'.[1]
The corporation found it easy to combine doctrinal orthodoxy
with a dislike of ecclesiastical power, especially the power of
separate jurisdictions like the Minster close. When two
sheriffs' sergeants drew blood in an affray at the Minster
gates, and the chapter imposed a penance on them, the corporation forbade them to perform it.[2] They were even
willing to move in the same direction as Thomas Cromwell
when spurred on by poverty. In 1536 they managed to
reconcile their belief in prayers for the dead with securing a
statute that suppressed seven chantries and three obits and
confiscated their endowments.[3]

3

Such attitudes, and the fact that papal power had not been a
reality since 1515 (when their archbishop had become the
pope's *legatus a latere*) ensured an easy passage for the first
stages of Henry VIII's revolution. There is no sign that the
aldermen and leading citizens were strongly attached to the
papacy, and all the men 'inhabityng within the libertes' of
York are said to have sworn the oath in support of Henry's
marriage to Ann Boleyn, though the expression can surely
not have been meant literally.[4] Attacks upon time-honoured
rituals and institutions were quite another matter, and the
city seems to have become restive in the summer of 1536,
when many smaller religious houses in Yorkshire were suppressed by the Crown. The citizens lost only St. Clement's
and Holy Trinity, but doubtless feared that the rest would
soon follow.[5]

When the Pilgrimage of Grace started in the East Riding in
October 1536, the York commons were quick to support it,

---

[1] *Y.C.R.* iii. 40.   [2] ibid., ii. 61.
[3] Dickens, 'Municipal dissolution', *passim.*
[4] Palliser, *Reformation in York*, pp. 4 f.; *Y.C.R.* iii. 170.
[5] Palliser, *Reformation in York*, pp. 6 f.

and the mayor and aldermen, after a show of reluctance, admitted Aske and his followers within the walls. The city was occupied for two months by the rebels, who used it as a capital and held a great council there. Without doubt the Pilgrimage was very popular in the city, and the support came largely from hostility to the Crown's religious policies. In particular, it is clear that the two suppressed houses there, and nearby Healaugh, were restored by the Pilgrims, and that the monks of Holy Trinity, once in possession again, remained together for two more years without active interference by the King.[1] This is not to deny that many other motives may have been mixed with religious reaction to account for such support within the city. Partly, no doubt, men were simply upset by the attacks on traditional rituals, and credulous of the rumours sweeping the country about how much further Henry and Cromwell intended to go. Perhaps, too, the corporation shared with many northerners a dislike of Crown policies in the 1530s, secular as much as ecclesiastical. Hatred of Cromwell was voiced at a meeting of leading Pilgrims in the house of Sir George Lawson, whose role during the rising was equivocal, to say the least. As an alderman, Crown official, and member of the Council in the North, he was extremely influential, and he was lucky to escape afterwards with nothing worse than some coolness towards him by Cromwell and the King.[2]

In 1538-9 Cromwell completed the process of monastic dissolutions. The six priories—St. Andrew's, Holy Trinity, and the four orders of friars—surrendered in November and December 1538, while the two giants followed them a year later, St. Mary's Abbey on 29 November 1539 and St. Leonard's Hospital on 1 December.[3] The surrenders, together with those of the forty other monasteries owning property in York, had a shattering impact on the city, and one should not be deceived by the prudent reticence of the corporation

[1] Palliser, *Reformation in York*, pp. 7-11; P.R.O., C1/881/31; Smith, *Land and Politics*, p. 187. The largely secular explanations for the rising by A. G. Dickens, in Cuming, ed. *Studies in Church History*, iv. 39-64, have been convincingly countered by C. S. L. Davies in *Past & Present*, xli (1968), 54-76.

[2] *L.P. Hen. VIII*, xi, No. 762; xii (1), Nos. 116, 306, 369, 449, 968, 1320.

[3] *L.P. Hen. VIII*, xiii (2), Nos. 917-19, 928-9; xiv (2), Nos. 603, 623; J. Solloway, *The Alien Benedictines of York* (Leeds, 1910), p. 316.

about the entire process.[1] The fabrics of the dissolved monasteries and friaries were demolished for building materials,
two major hospitals ceased to admit poor, both grammar
schools apparently fell with the monasteries, and something
like a quarter of the domestic housing in the city came into
the hands of the King, who in 1545 sold much of it to a London alderman. Ninety monks, nuns, and canons were turned
out into the world with pensions, and over sixty friars without pensions: some, at least, took livings, curacies, and chantries in the York district.[2]

Technically the dissolutions of religious houses represented
a reform within the church by the King's vicegerent, and did
not affect doctrine or worship. Practically, however, they did
precisely that, and men could not be unaffected by the cessation of chantries and obits, and the disrespect shown to
furnishings, images, shrines, and tombs. After all, an alderman
had been buried in the Franciscan Priory as late as 1535, and
there is no record that his or any other tomb was spared amid
the destruction.[3] The chronology of spoliation is not clear,
but it was presumably in the later years of Henry VIII and
the short reign of his son that most of it occurred, spreading
from the dissolved houses to the Minster and the parish
churches. As in other areas, tombs were destroyed and
brasses re-used or melted down. Henry Keep, still able to
view the consequences in Charles II's reign, wrote of

many of those stone coffins and other monuments of the dead made
the receptacles for raine water, mangers for horses, hogg troughs to
feed their swine, and the fiture of many a noted senator or other
deserveing person layd on the copeing of some old wall or in some viler
place which are frequently to be mett with in severall parts of the city.[4]

The effigy of a medieval knight, removed from a coffin and
placed on Hob Moor as a landmark, survives as one example
of the desecrations.[5]

The natural consequence was that a cool and pragmatic
approach to the church developed. The Minster chapter looked
on the belfry of St. Leonard's as a quarry for building stone,

[1] The first reference in the minutes is Y.C.A., B 15, fo. 65ʳ (30 Dec. 1541).
[2] Palliser, *Reformation in York*, pp. 12–18.
[3] John Besby: B.I.H.R. prob. reg. xi, fo. 147.
[4] Trinity Coll. Cambridge MS 0.4.33, p. 114.
[5] Davies, *Walks*, pp. 97–9; R.C.H.M. *York*, iii. 58.

just as twenty years later Archbishop Young regarded the
lead roof of his York palace hall as an asset to be realized.[1]
There was passive resistance to the new emphasis on sermons
rather than ritual in services, most parishioners absenting
themselves whenever sermons were preached in at least one
church.[2] The leading citizens, though Catholic in belief as
their wills indicate, did not hesitate to capitalize on the dissolutions. Alderman Richard Goldthorpe bought St. Clement's
nunnery in 1543, and later added to it the priory of St.
Andrew across the river. Sir Leonard Beckwith, a country
gentleman and Yorkshire receiver of the Court of Augmentations, acquired Holy Trinity Priory and the Greyfriars, but a
family of city councillors, the Harpers, bought the latter from
him in 1546, while the Whitefriars was bought by another
civic dynasty, the Beckwiths, who were related to Sir
Leonard. Most striking of all, Sir George Lawson, who lived
adjacent to the Augustinian Priory and seems to have col-
laborated with its prior in supporting the Pilgrimage, sought
and acquired a lease of it as soon as it was surrendered.[3] His
fellow-alderman George Gayle, also a Catholic, invested in
rural property instead: he bought Wilberfoss Priory and other
lands and tithes from the Crown for £615 in 1553. He may
almost be described as having a family interest in the priory,
for his sister-in-law was the last prioress and had come to live
in or near his house after the dissolution.[4] Very likely Gayle
and Lawson regretted the dissolutions, like their Yorkshire
contemporary Sherbrook, but would have said with him,
'Might I not, as well as others, have some profit of the spoil
of the Abbey? For I did see all would away; and therefore I
did as others did.'[5]

The largest and richest ecclesiastical institution, the Minster,
survived largely intact if not unscathed. It was by no means a
foregone conclusion, for the King drastically reordered and

[1] *Minster Fabric Rolls*, ed. Raine, p. 110; Drake, *Eboracum*, p. 454; Stow,
Annales (1631 edn.), p. 662.

[2] Y.M.L., MS L2(3)c, fo. 225a, a visitation of St. Mary Bishophill Junior,
1542, misdated 1481 in the printed transcript in *Fabric Rolls of York Minster*,
p. 258.

[3] Palliser, *Reformation in York*, p. 15; *L.P. Hen. VIII*, xiii (2), No. 761; xiv (1),
No. 969, (2), No. 293; xv, No. 465 and p. 556.

[4] *C.P.R.* 1553, p. 89; B.I.H.R., prob. reg. ix, fo. 368; *Test. Ebor.* vi. 307-8.

[5] A. G. Dickens, ed., *Tudor Treatises* (Y.A.S.R.S. cxxv, 1959), p. 125.

impoverished the monastic cathedrals and utterly destroyed
that of Coventry. Even secular cathedrals like York were
eyed covetously by Henry and suspiciously by the reformers;
Cranmer in 1539 was attacking the 'sect of prebendaries' as
idle and superfluous drones. Yet though York Minster had to
surrender much of its treasure and successive archbishops had
to make unequal exchanges of properties with the Crown, the
cathedral retained most of its large and costly establishment.
Six prebends were suppressed between 1540 and 1549 to
benefit the Crown and its nominees, but the other thirty
remained until the Victorian reorganization of cathedral
chapters. The number compared very favourably with the
twelve prebends which were all that Henry allowed to Durham, and their wealth remained considerable; the *Valor
Ecclesiasticus* suggests a total income of almost £1,000 a year
for the thirty prebends, as well as nearly £500 for the chapter
collectively.[1]

There was no active opposition to the dissolutions of
1538-9 in York, or for that matter to any of the policies of
Henry VIII's later years. No doubt the severe punishment of
the leading Pilgrims, and later of the 1541 Yorkshire plotters
(eleven of whom were executed at York), acted as dire warnings, and the reception of the King by the corporation in
1541 can only be described as grovelling.[2] St. William's
shrine in the Minster was promptly dismantled at his command, although subsequent archaeological discoveries have
shown that it was broken up and carefully hidden for re-
erection at a later date.[3] The malcontents became emboldened
once Henry's heavy hand was removed, and there is some
evidence for seditious activity in 1547-8, including the threat
of a second Pilgrimage. Nothing came of it, and in general a
passive resistance to change is the most that can be detected.
Few of the clergy married even when it became lawful; the

---

[1] Much of this paragraph is drawn from C. Cross, 'From the Reformation to
the Restoration', in *A History of York Minster*, ed. G. E. Aylmer and R. Cant
(Oxford, 1977), pp. 193-232.

[2] A. G. Dickens, 'Sedition and conspiracy in Yorkshire', *Y.A.J.* xxxiv (1938-9),
379-98; *Y.C.R.* iv. 68-70.

[3] *Proceedings and Orders of the Privy Council*, vii (1837), p. 247; R. Thoresby,
Ducatus Leodiensis, ed. T. D. Whitaker (Wakefield, 1816), appended Catalogue
of Rarities, p. 115; Raine, *Mediaeval York*, p. 31.

Minster vicars continued openly to pray for the dead until 1549-50, though the practice was illegal; citizens continued to bequeath money for soul-masses until 1551, and the Corpus Christi cycle continued to be performed uncensored, except for the tactful omission of the Marian plays. Very little evidence of positive Protestantism can be set against these and other records of traditionalism.[1]

Edward's reign was chiefly memorable at York for a series of dissolutions probably more revolutionary in effect than those of 1536-9. In April 1548 the hundred or so chantries were all suppressed, together with almost all the religious guilds,[2] in 1548-50 thirteen parish churches, in 1548 the Colleges of St. William's and the Bedern (though the latter suppression was countermanded), and in 1550 St. Sepulchre's College, while in 1553 most of the ornaments in the remaining parish churches were confiscated by the Crown. The effect was a climate of uncertainty in which parishioners stripped lead from their own church roofs to forestall the Crown. As with the monastic dissolutions, it is chiefly the material effects that are known. Another 500 or so domestic houses in the city fell to the Crown for resale, of which a large part were bought by a Yorkshire chantry commissioner and his partner. Whether most were resold to citizens is not known, but the corporation did succeed in buying the lands of the Guild of SS. Christopher and George, and in leasing those of Corpus Christi. The movable possessions of the guilds, however, like the gold and silver shrine of Corpus Christi valued at £211, were simply seized by the Crown for their monetary value, as was a large part of the Minster's silver. What is not clear from the records is the effect on religious and intellectual life: how far the suppression of chantries and guilds left a void in religious practice and social life, and how far the care of the old and the education of the young was affected.[3] There can be no doubt, however, that the greed of Edward's courtiers provoked widespread resentment.

---

[1] A. G. Dickens, 'Some popular reactions to the Edwardian Reformation in Yorkshire', *Y.A.J.* xxxiv. 151-3; Palliser, *Reformation in York*, pp. 18, 26-9.

[2] The dating of the dissolution of chantries is made clear by Bodley, Lat. Th.d. 15, fo. 134^V.

[3] Palliser, *Reformation in York*, pp. 21-6.

The Court of Augmentations, busy demolishing parts of St. Mary's Abbey in 1550-1, had to be restrained by the Privy Council from pulling down part of the King's Manor itself. Lord President Shrewsbury himself complained that 'such spoyle and defacing [was] made in divers parts of his highnes said palace, that hit wold greve any man to see it'.[1]

The closure of parish churches stands out among the Edwardian measures as the only one which was not part of a nation-wide suppression, and the only one sought by the corporation. A statute of 1545 authorized ecclesiastical authorities to unite parish churches less than a mile apart, if one was worth less than £6 a year, provided that the corporation (in the case of corporate towns) assented to the measure. This enabling act apparently reflected a growing desire to rationalize the parochial structure, and several towns seem to have taken advantage of it or, more cautiously, promoted private Acts to cover themselves. York was one, and it has been shown that the corporation secured an Act for the union of parishes in 1547 as one of its measures against civic poverty.[2] The results were drastic. Thirteen parish churches were closed in the years 1548-9, while two others were closed at the same time if they had not already fallen with the monastic houses. The formal ratification of the unions was delayed, but at length the unions were confirmed by the archbishop and corporation in 1586, with very little amendment: one condemned church was reprieved under Mary, and instead the church of All Saints, Peasholme, was closed, so that the total of casualties remained at fifteen parish churches out of forty. Effectively, however, the unions with these two exceptions had been completed in Edward's reign. Most of the fifteen were sold, and some demolished, by 1553. The main purpose of the unions was to relieve the poverty of the livings and the burden on the parishioners, but the corporation themselves benefited from it by selling the sites and buildings. At first they attempted sales at realistic prices of £30 or £40, but quickly abandoned that in

---

[1] College of Arms, Talbot Papers, B 216, as cited by R.C.H.M. *York* iv. 31. The full letter (modernized) is printed by E. Lodge, *Illustrations of British History* (2nd edn., London, 1838), i. 168-9.

[2] See pp. 219 f.

favour of cheap sales to their own members, and six churches were sold to councillors for a total of barely £10. Once again the council demonstrated a pragmatism, if not callousness, at variance with their doctrinal views, for there is no evidence that even the tombs of former aldermen were spared.[1]

It is not known how promptly the Edwardian religious changes were obeyed in the surviving churches. Parkyn's chronicle is evidence that the reserved sacrament was taken down in the city churches promptly on 1 November 1548, but that the removal of stone altars under injunctions of 1550 was executed much more tardily. They began to be removed 'in the sowthe partts' after Easter, but 'from Trentt northewardes' not until December.[2] The only extant churchwardens' accounts reveal that at St. Michael's, Spurriergate, the rood light and images were destroyed as early as 1547, but there is no means of knowing how typical it may have been.[3] Elizabethan and early Stuart evidence makes it clear that wall paintings often remained exposed until that time, and the superb collection of stained glass in several churches, more extensive than in any other city, indicates that many windows escaped the iconoclasts.

4

The Catholic reaction under Mary was, not surprisingly, welcomed at York. When her accession was proclaimed there on 21 July 1553, the people are said to have greatly rejoiced, 'makynge grette fyers, drynkinge wyne and aylle, prayssing God', and by early September 'masse was songe or saide in Lattin' in nearly all the Yorkshire churches, even before it was legalized.[4] The corporation sent a fulsome letter of allegiance, giving thanks for 'so noble, *godly* and most rightfull a Quene', a description they did not apply to her sister five years later.[5] In November they ordered the altar in St. Thomas's

[1] Palliser, 'Unions of parishes at York', *passim.*
[2] Bodley, Lat. Th. d. 15, fos. 135-6, printed by Dickens, 'Robert Parkyn's narrative', pp. 68 f., 72.
[3] Y.M.L., MS Add. 220/1, fo. 217ᵛ.
[4] Bodley, Lat. Th. d. 15, fos. 139-40, pr. 'Robert Parkyn's narrative', pp. 78, 80.
[5] *Y.C.R.* v. 91 f.

Hospital (which they now controlled) to be 'furthwyth sett up agayn', and soon afterwards they restored the Marian plays to the Corpus Christi cycle, besides reviving the St. George's Day pageant and various processions.[1] Church furnishings were restored piecemeal, perhaps because of the cost: thus at St. Martin's, Coney Street, the holy water stoup was installed in the spring of 1554, and the rood painted in the autumn and set up in the spring of 1555.[2] As money slowly accumulated, the seizures of Edward's commissioners began to be made good: a parishioner of St. Michael's, Ouse Bridge end, left 6s. 8d. in 1556 'to the byenge of the greate bell'.[3] Mary's first Parliament passed an Act empowering the parishioners of St. Helen, Stonegate, to rebuild their church, which had already been partly demolished, and they saved their church by starting rebuilding at once, and almost completing it by the time of the Queen's death.[4] By 1557 a new stained-glass window was commissioned in at least one church, by Councillor Martin Soza.[5]

The city's support for the Marian reaction seems to have sprung from Catholic survivalism rather than Counter-Reformation piety. As has been rightly said, 'if one thinks of Edwardian and Marian York as primarily occupied by disputes and material problems born of the Reformation, one is thrusting aside an immense mass of evidence in favour of an imaginative abstraction'.[6] When the Council in the North ordered bonfires to celebrate the reconciliation of the realm to Rome, the corporation coolly arranged for the fires 'with rejoysyng and thanksgyvyng to God for his mercyfullnesses nowe and alle tymes'.[7] The restoration of suppressed revenues and hospitals was nearer their hearts than the distant concept of papalism. They petitioned Cardinal Pole, though unsuccessfully, for the restoration of St. Leonard's Hospital, and were doubtless pleased when in 1556 Mary surrendered

---

[1] *Y.C.R.* v. 96, 100, 105.   [2] B.I.H.R., MS Y/MCS 16, pp. 8 f, 18.

[3] B.I.H.R., probate reg. xv (1), fo. 64^r.

[4] Palliser, 'Unions of parishes at York', pp. 91, 98 f.; *Statutes of the Realm*, iv. 216–17.

[5] T. Gent, *The Antient and Modern History of the Famous City of York* (York and London, 1730), pp. 219 f.

[6] Dickens, *Lollards and Protestants*, p. 206.

[7] *Y.C.R.* v. 113; cf. Dickens, *Lollards and Protestants*, p. 213.

various Crown revenues from former colleges and chantries, including £157 a year from the city of York.[1]

Not a single prosecution for heresy was undertaken against any citizen under Mary, but Yorkers were made aware of heresy in other towns when offenders were sent to the Minster to do public penance.[2] Such awareness, coupled with the certainty after 1557 that Mary would be succeeded by a Protestant sister, gave a defensive tone to the expression of orthodoxy. In 1557 the dean and chapter refounded St. Peter's School for the education of clergy able to rebut heresy.[3] In August 1558 a parishioner of St. Michael-le-Belfrey bequeathed a sumptuous vestment to Sawley Chapel, but prudently willed it to his family 'if the uses of vestments do cease in churches'. The previous February Sir Martin Bowes had endowed an obit in St. Cuthbert's church with a proviso for alternative use of the money 'if yt shall chanse hereafter by any lawes of this realme . . . that the premysses . . . shalbe . . . deamed to be superstitious or ungodly (as God defende)'.[4]

The change that they feared came with Elizabeth's accession, and the consequence was immediately emphasized in an after-dinner speech at a public banquet in the city, given by 'W.P.', perhaps the Sir William Pickering who was shortly to be rumoured as a favoured suitor for the Queen's hand, roundly condemning the whole Marian reaction.[5] The audience, who clearly approved of the speech, would probably be Protestant gentry, and the corporation and leading citizens probably felt quite otherwise. The religious settlement of 1559 certainly had a much cooler reception in the city than those of Edward or Mary: Elizabeth's injunctions as Supreme Governor of the church were obeyed slowly and with visible reluctance. Archbishop Heath, one of the firmest opponents of the 1559 settlement, was deprived, and a general visitation of the northern clergy was held to enforce the Acts of Supremacy and Uniformity, including a four-day session at York from

[1] *Y.C.R.* v. 137; C. J. Kitching, 'Studies in the Redistribution of Collegiate and Chantry Property in the Diocese and County of York at the Dissolution' (unpubl. Ph.D. thesis, Univ. of Durham, 1970), ii.A.26.

[2] Dickens, *Lollards and Protestants*, pp. 230–1.

[3] A. F. Leach, *Early Yorkshire Schools*, i (Y.A.S.R.S. xxvii, 1899), 50.

[4] Purvis, ed., *Tudor Parish Documents*, p. 142; Y.C.A., B 22, fo. 115^r.

[5] B.L. Royal 17. C. III.

6 to 9 September.[1] At Holy Trinity, Goodramgate, the images were burned in 1559-60 and the altar taken down in 1560-1. St. Martin's, Coney Street, was more tardy: the altars were removed in 1561, the images burned in 1562, the choir walls plastered and painted with scriptures in 1566, a communion table and cover provided in 1568. Its old vestments and candlesticks were not sold until 1567-70, significantly 'by the comandmente of my lord Archebusshoppe'.[2] In his own cathedral church, a Catholic inscription was placed on the tomb of Councillor Soza in 1560, and many Catholic furnishings remained until 1567. In the same year a search of stationers' shops in York revealed that many forbidden Catholic books, especially primers, were being stocked.[3] In 1568 a former civic priest was still openly defending 'prayenge unto saintes', and in 1569 a tanner could casually (if illegally) leave money to his parish priest to pray for him.[4]

The corporation remained 'Catholic survivalists' during the 1560s, and in 1564 Archbishop Young considered only two aldermen out of thirteen 'favorers of religion', Ralph Hall and William Watson.[5] When Sir Martin Bowes wrote to them about the modification of his obit at York, 'for as moch as it hath pleased God to send me life to see certayne alteracons in the world', the corporation explained how 'syns the late change' they had had to depart from his 'godly entent' by altering the form of service: their distaste for the change almost shrieks through the diplomatic phrases.[6] Doubtless a dislike of innovation was mingled with uncertainty whether the new settlement would last. In 1562 a local gentleman, dining at the house of Alderman William Coupland, said 'he durst lay a wager that the crucifix with Marie and John shuld be sett up ageyne in alle cherches betwix this and Christmas next'. When Coupland himself (one of the eleven 'non-favourers' of religion) made his will in 1568 it was in entirely

[1] H. N. Birt, *The Elizabethan Religious Settlement* (London, 1907), pp. 141-65.

[2] B.I.H.R., R.XII Y/HTG 12, pp. 2, 13; Y/MCS 16, pp. 43-5, 64-5, 68, 74-5.

[3] Drake, *Eboracum*, p. 494; *Fabric Rolls of York Minster*, ed. Raine, p. 113 f.; B.I.H.R., High Commission MSS, proceedings against York stationers.

[4] A. G. Dickens, 'The first stages of Romanist recusancy in Yorkshire', *Y.A.J.*, xxxv (1940-3), 162; B.I.H.R., Dean and Chapter prob. reg. v, fo. 45.

[5] 'Original letters from the bishops', ed. Bateson, p. 72.

[6] *Y.C.R.* vi. 27 f. The service, with 'a sermon instead of an Obijt', was still held c. 1680: Trinity Coll. Cambridge MS 0.4.33, pp. 126 f.

traditional form, with an invocation of the Virgin and the saints, and a dole for 1,600 poor. He asked for wax candles to be burned about his body and torches to be carried at his funeral, 'yf the lawe will permitte the same'.[1] Not all his colleagues were such sturdy traditionalists, however. Robert Hall, also called a 'non-favourer' in 1564, made a Protestant will later that year, and his widow, a generous benefactor to the rebuilt Ouse Bridge in 1566, was commemorated in distinctly Protestant form on a brass plate there:

> By works Lady Jane Hall
> Her Faith doth shewe
> Giveing one hundred pounds
> This Bridg to renewe.[2]

The lukewarm Protestantism of the 1560s may have owed something to dissension and weakness within the church leadership. 1559 was the first church settlement to which any of the Minster chapter had refused to subscribe, and the reluctance of some of the resident administrators broke the continuity of church government for eighteen months.[3] Even after that, firm leadership was lacking. The archbishop from 1561 to 1568 was Thomas Young, who presided over both the Northern Ecclesiastical Commission and (from 1564) the Council in the North. Yet he left a poor reputation among zealous Protestants, and Thomas Wood singled him out as one of the worst non-preachers on the episcopal bench.[4] Young's régime is symbolized by the fact that of two York aldermen who sat on the Ecclesiastical Commission until his death, William Watson was a Protestant and Robert Paycok a 'non-favourer'. Not until Matthew Hutton became dean in 1567 and Edmund Grindal archbishop in 1570 did the church have a fervently Protestant leadership.

Just before Grindal's appointment, the Northern Earls had risen in the last Catholic rebellion in the north. The whole area from Tees to Ripon was 'up', and there was plainly

---

[1] *Y.C.R.* vi. 42; B.I.H.R., prob. reg. xviii, fo. 122.

[2] Trinity Coll. Cambridge MS. 0.4.33, p. 103, a text significantly different from Drake, *Eboracum*, p. 280.

[3] J. C. H. Aveling, *Catholic Recusancy in the City of York 1558-1791*, Cath. Rec. Soc. Monograph ii (1970), 20 f., 305 f.

[4] C. Hill, *Society and Puritanism in Pre-Revolutionary England* (1969 Panther edn.), p. 257.

sympathy for such a cause in the York district.[1] The corporation, however, remained loyal, and no citizens of importance
except the castle gaoler joined the rebels. It proved a decisive
event, urging Grindal and Hutton to attack Catholic survivalism in earnest, and compelling those who disliked sedition to
identify themselves reluctantly with the established church.
The Ecclesiastical Commission made a public example of William Allyn, the most firmly Catholic alderman.[2] In June
1571 the corporation took official notice of the problem of
recusancy for the first time, informing the Council in the
North of the absence from church of John Banyster of St.
Margaret's parish; the Northern Council was joining forces
with the Northern Commission in imposing religious uniformity.[3] The Commission also acted against the many
churches in city and county which had been supervised rather
leniently, and the rood-lofts were only now removed from
the city churches, while parishes like Bishophill Senior that
had removed almost none of their Marian furnishings were
attacked.[4] It would also seem that chalices had remained un-
disturbed in many churches until the Rising, when the
authorities insisted on communion cups instead. Of thirty-
one pieces of sixteenth-century church plate made in York,
twenty-four were produced in the year 1570 alone.[5] The city
clergy seem to have been completely conformist after 1570,
one reason no doubt being that the Crown had acquired
monastic advowsons after the dissolutions, and now had an
extensive patronage. Its advowsons, only one out of forty in
1530, numbered eleven out of twenty-five after the unions of
parishes.[6]

The next clashes came over the Catholic, and sometimes
even pagan, pageants and ceremonies that the conservative
citizens were still performing. First to be attacked was the
Creed Play, a lost work which was abandoned in 1568 after

[1] P. Tyler, *The Ecclesiastical Commission and Catholicism in the North* (n.p.,
1960), pp. 52–4.
[2] ibid., pp. 70, 137; Aveling, *Catholic Recusancy in York*, pp. 169–70.
[3] Y.C.A., B 24, fo. 243^r.
[4] e.g. B.I.H.R., R.XII Y/HTG 12, p. 53; Y/MCS 16, p. 94; Purvis, *Tudor Parish
Documents*, p. 187.
[5] Fallow and McCall, *Yorkshire Church Plate*, i, pp. xix f.
[6] Aveling, *Catholic Recusancy in York*, p. 319.

pressure from Dean Hutton. He found much in it 'disagreeing from the sinceritie of the gospell', and added that

thoghe it was plausible 40 yeares agoe, and would now also of the ignorant sort be well liked, yet now in this happie time of the gospell, I knowe the learned will mislike it, and how the state will beare with it, I knowe not.[1]

'The ignorant' did not, however, surrender to 'the learned' without a struggle. William Allyn was elected mayor in 1572, and at once flung down a gauntlet by reviving the Paternoster play (presumably a morality play based on the Lord's Prayer) and placing the last performance at the door of Christopher Harbert, a Protestant alderman. Harbert and another alderman were imprisoned and disfranchised by their colleagues for avoiding the performance and complaining to the Council in the North, 'beyng a foreyne Courte'. The victory for tradition was balanced by a defeat, for the Ecclesiastical Commission then forbade Allyn and his colleagues to stage the 'Yule rydyng', a bawdy ceremony which ushered in the Christmas season.[2] Grindal and Hutton were now on the offensive, and it was probably about this time that they banned the Corpus Christi plays, as they did at Wakefield in 1576; certainly the Paternoster play text was called in by Grindal in 1572 and never seen again.[3] They were aided by the appointment of Huntingdon as Lord President in 1572, and by changes of personnel at York in 1573. Allyn was succeeded as mayor by his personal and confessional enemy, Harbert, and later in the year William Tankerd, the 'Papist' recorder since 1537, died. Harbert significantly urged that the new recorder should be 'a favorer of the word of God', and if William Byrnand did not quite meet that requirement, he at least proved thoroughly conformist.[4] The bench was becoming steadily more Protestant, though Allyn and John Dyneley clung to Catholicism, aided by the election in 1576 of the still more stubborn Robert Criplyng. Nevertheless, they did not form a party in any real sense, and religion seems to have become an individual matter that did not correlate with wealth, occupation or any other divisions among the aldermen.

[1] *Y.C.R.* vi. 134 n.; Y.C.A., B 24, fo. 106[ar].
[2] *Y.C.R.* vii. 46–50, 55, 62 f.   [3] *Y.C.R.* vii. 46–52.
[4] *Y.C.R.* vii. 77, 79 f.; Aveling, *Catholic Recusancy in York*, pp. 341 f.

Under Huntingdon, Grindal and his successor Sandys, and Hutton, the Protestant pressure became stronger throughout the 1570s. From 1573 the corporation were required to submit regular returns of recusants, and from 1574 mayors and sheriffs were expected to take the Oath of Supremacy. The authorities were understandably worried, because from about 1570 a small but well-instructed group of recusants appeared in York, quite distinct from the dwindling number of Catholic survivalists. By the time Grindal moved from York to Canterbury in December 1575 the recusants' vigorous proselytizing had taken effect, thanks partly to the use of York as the chief prison centre for its county. A census in 1576 revealed ninety recusants in the city, many of them converted wives of conformist husbands, like Margaret Clitherow. Huntingdon took vigorous action to imprison or intimidate them, but the city corporation seem to have been understandably reluctant to persecute their own friends and relatives, for the movement affected the highest families. In 1577–8 several wives and widows of aldermen were presented for recusancy, including the wife of Mayor Dyneley himself. As Mr Aveling has observed, the age of traditionalist conservatism was ending. 'From now onwards the majority of citizens would be unenthusiastic but settled Anglicans . . . while, amidst them, would stand two tough minorities—the larger by far "Puritan", converted and earnest, the smaller Catholic recusant'.[1] Doubtless some conformed through fear or indifference, while others experienced a genuine conversion. Of the second group a good representative was 'devout and godly' Mrs Metcalfe, mother-in-law of Councillor Francis Bayne. She died 'heartely sorie that she was so supersticiously and popishely bent in tymes past . . . and fully reposed her whole confidence and trust in the death and passion of Jesus Christ'.[2]

5

The course of the Reformation at York is not in doubt, yet it remains almost impossible to know how most citizens thought

[1] For this paragraph, see Aveling, op. cit., pp. 38–47, and *Y.C.R.* vii, *passim*.
[2] Y.A.S. Library, Leeds, transcript of St. John Micklegate parish register, *s.a.* 1579.

and felt during this crucial chapter of their history. The corporation's official records are discreet, too discreet; the heretics and recusants are untypical; the wills of most citizens are
rather reticent on matters of belief. It may, therefore, be
worth retracing the religious revolution with the aid of the
one source that promises to shed at least a little light into the
citizens' souls—their bequests of those souls, a feature found
in almost every Tudor will. A. G. Dickens has made valuable
use of soul bequest statistics for Yorkshire and Nottinghamshire, while emphasizing the caution needed in their interpretation, while Margaret Spufford has investigated the religious
phraseology of wills for another area in impressive detail.[1]
One difficulty is that testators formed only a minority of the
population; but it has at least been possible to analyse all the
surviving York wills for the sixteenth century, 1,725 in all,
and it is believed to be the first time that a large Tudor community has been so analysed. A more intractable difficulty lies
in deciding whether the testators' religious phraseology reflected their own beliefs or those of the writers of the wills,
who seem usually to have been clergy. It is not possible to
pronounce definitely on the question: the writers may have
had a considerable influence, but a close study of selected
groups of wills shows that men and women of the same
parish during the same period often used different formulae,
and in a few cases there is sworn evidence that the writer
simply transcribed at the dictation of the dying testator.[2]

The pattern revealed by the York wills, summarized in
Table 5, is certainly striking when compared with other local
statistics available in print. It bears out entirely the picture of
York sketched above, as a city moving only slowly and reluctantly from religious traditionalism to Protestantism.[3] In the
first thirty-seven years of the century the wills remained in
fifteenth-century form, with not a single unorthodox soul

[1] Dickens, *Lollards and Protestants*, pp. 171-2, 215-18; M. Spufford, *Con-
trasting Communities: English Villagers in the Sixteenth and Seventeenth Centuries* (Cambridge, 1974), pp. 320-44. Another important regional study of wills,
published while this book was being completed, is in P. Clark, *English Provincial
Society from the Reformation to the Revolution: Religion, Politics and Society
in Kent, 1500-1640* (Hassocks, 1977), pp. 58, 76, 420.

[2] e.g. B.I.H.R., R.VII.G.1510.

[3] For a more detailed discussion of will formulae before 1553, see Palliser,
Reformation in York, pp. 18-21, 28-9.

TABLE 5
Bequests of Testators' Souls in York Wills 1501–1600

	Traditional				Neutral	Protestant		Total
	GMS	GM & GM(S)	G(MS)	GS		G(CP)	G/S	
1501–37	630	5	2	1	10			648
1538–46	135	2	23	3	7			170
1547–8	9		8		2	1		20
1549	10		3	1	9	1		24
1550	15		5	2	12			34
1551	13		10	3	14	5		45
1552–June 1553	4		5			5		14
July 1553–1556	20	2	9	1	8			40
1557	23	1	3	1				28
1558 (to 17 Nov.)	42		13		6	1		62
17 Nov. 1558–1560	18		9	2	5	1		35
1561–70	9		3	15	51	33		111
1571–80	4			12	74	54	2	146
1581–90	1			4	87	45	3	140
1591–1600					92	74	1	167

| | Percentage of Wills | | | Total |
	Trad.	Neutral	Prot.	
1501–1537	98.5	1.5		100
1538–1546	95.9	4.1		100
Edward VI	64.2	27.0	8.8	100
Mary I	88.5	10.8	0.8	(100)
Elizabeth I	12.8	51.6	35.6	100

Note: The tables include 1,684 wills, out of a total of 1,725 known to survive for York city. Of the others, twelve have mixed formulae difficult to classify, and twenty-nine have no formulae at all. *GMS* = bequest to God, B.V.M. and all Saints; *GM* = to God and BVM.; *GM(S)* = to God and B.V.M. asking all Saints to pray for testator; *G(MS)* = to God, asking B.V.M. and all Saints to pray for testator; *GS* = to God and all Saints; *Neutral* = simple bequests to God; *G(CP)* = to God, trusting to be saved through merits of Christ's Passion; *G/S* = to God, trusting to be saved.

bequest, and 98.5 per cent of the testators employing the traditional dedication to God, the Blessed Virgin Mary, and all the holy Company of Heaven. The last nine years of Henry VIII's reign witnessed a slight shift, with a growth in the number of non-committal bequests to God, and more traditionalists using a modified formula. Even so, with 95.9 per cent of the wills traditional, the York pattern was much more orthodox than that revealed by published wills for Yorkshire, Nottinghamshire, and London, where nearly a quarter of all wills in Henry's last nine years were non-traditional. Even more striking, there were no definitely Protestant wills at York before the death of Henry VIII, whereas the printed Yorkshire wills include examples from 1537-8 onwards, and the London selection from 1539. It is scarcely surprising that London was more radical than York, but the contrast between Yorkshire and its county town is more unexpected. The Yorkshire sample includes two mobile classes, the gentry and the textile workers, who did not figure prominently at York, and who included early converts to Protestantism. It is, however, unwise to press a contrast between a sample of published wills for two counties, and a count of all wills for one city, and satisfactory analysis requires the enumeration of many more ordinary wills to avoid the bias inherent in most published collections.

The conservatism of York's testators was even more marked in Edward's reign. Not only did some citizens continue to request prayers for the dead until 1551, but traditional will formulae remained predominant throughout the reign, whereas the printed Yorkshire wills show an increasing majority of non-traditional wills from 1549 onwards. Furthermore, most 'non-traditional' wills at York were of the non-committal type, and it is known in some cases from their other bequests that the testators were traditionalist; and citizens employing clearly Protestant formulae numbered only twelve (8.8%) in the whole reign. It would be interesting to know how far ordinary testators in the rest of the county were equally conservative; the Edwardian wills published for one Wensleydale manor are all traditional.[1] Caution is certainly needed in

---

[1] H. Thwaite, ed., *Abstracts of Abbotside Wills 1552-1688* (Y.A.S.R.S. cxxx, 1968), pp. 1-3 (but only three wills).

interpreting such statistics, but what cannot be doubted is that the York wills indicate a strong conservatism, either of testators or of writers. Bishop Hooper was quite clear that the bequest of a soul to God, the Virgin, and All Saints indicated Catholic belief;[1] and it is significant that the few who still used it by the middle of Elizabeth's reign can nearly all be identified as recusants.

The 130 Marian wills emphasize the widespread support of the citizens for the restoration of the traditional religion. Nearly all used the traditional formulae, and only a single testator at the very end of the reign adopted a positively Protestant form. Once again the pattern contrasts strongly with the published wills of Yorkshire gentry, but corresponds closely to that of the Wensleydale manor for which all wills are in print.[2] The citizens were set an example by their former pastor, the deprived Archbishop Holgate, whose Protestantism collapsed after Mary's accession. He ended his life a sincere Catholic, and it is therefore noteworthy that Holgate began his will, in April 1555, with the time-honoured formula: 'First I bequeth my soule to almightie God, our Ladye Saynt Marie and all tholie Companye of Heaven'.[3] Even in the first two years of Elizabeth's reign traditional wills were the norm at York, and a considerable minority continued to use the same wording until the repression of the Rising of the Earls brought the period of tolerance to an end.

Thereafter, as survivalism gave way to conformity and recusancy, the wills came mostly to use the noncommittal bequest of the soul to God, but with a growing minority preferring the Protestant testimony of salvation through Christ alone. Even so, the traditional form was astonishingly slow to disappear. Edmund Richardson, in 1576, was the last alderman to leave his soul to God and the saints, but William Watson did so as late as 1586, though he prudently added that he trusted to be saved through the Passion of Christ. Outside the city, a few stubborn recusants employed it even later. The widow of Thomas Lord Wharton, of Healaugh,

[1] Frere and Kennedy, *Visitation Arts. of the Reformation*, ii. 306.
[2] Dickens, *Lollards and Protestants*, pp. 220-1; Thwaite, ed., *Abbotside Wills*, pp. 3-6.
[3] P.R.O., P.C.C. 25 Ketchyn.

used the full traditional wording in 1583, and Richard Byrnand of Knaresborough (a relative of the York recorder) employed the modified form in 1591.[1]

6

The course of events was left in the late 1570s, as survivalism was yielding to conformity and recusancy. Active Protestantism, already in command of the machinery of church and state at York, now captured the civic élite. Mayor John Dyneley (1577–8) was the last chief magistrate to rule in the old, easygoing way without provoking a storm. His colleague Robert Criplyng, also the husband of a recusant, suffered a troubled mayoralty two years later. He made no attempt to enforce the recusancy laws, openly criticized a sermon by the Minster Chancellor, and was said to have uttered 'very unsemely and fowle woords' against the clergy, which had encouraged like-minded people to post street bills with 'filthie and lewde speeches'. The Northern Council took the unprecedented step of imprisoning him before his term expired, and on his release the embarrassed corporation hastened to deprive him of his gown and his freedom of the city, lest the Privy Council should think they had been unconcerned 'in electyng so rashe and heady a man to be there chief governour'.[2] One suspects, from their language, that Criplyng had received much support from lesser citizens, and that religious conflict was sharpened by class antagonisms. The episode serves also to illustrate the growth of the secular power, represented by Huntingdon, at the expense of the church, even in matters religious. Huntingdon, though a good friend of Grindal, had not hesitated to try to lease the episcopal manor of Bishopthorpe when Grindal was promoted to Canterbury in 1575 and the see of York was vacant. Had he succeeded, the archbishops, already deprived of their York palace by Young's destructive activities, would have lost their

---

[1] B.I.H.R., prob. reg. xxi. fo. 65; xxiii, fo. 223; *Knaresborough Wills*, ed. Collins, i. 82; D. M. Palliser, 'Popular reactions to the Reformation . . . 1530–70', in F. Heal and R. O'Day, eds., *Church and Society in England: Henry VIII to James I* (London, 1977), p. 45.

[2] *Y.C.R.* viii. 25, 28–30.

only habitable palace in the York district. The attempt failed, but it left Grindal's successor Sandys bitter towards Huntingdon.[1]

It was during Criplyng's mayoralty that Huntingdon asked York to join the growing band of towns employing a civic preacher, and Criplyng put the request to the craft guilds, no doubt with a shrewd idea of their response. Only the two wealthiest were willing to contribute, the rest arguing that York was already well supplied with clergy. Significantly, the post of preacher was created only under Criplyng's Protestant successor, Robert Askwith, and then on the initiative of the city council.[2] Furthermore, it was the common council which petitioned Askwith for the continuance of the Corpus Christi plays, apparently without success.[3] Altogether, the evidence suggests a Protestant city council initially at odds with a more traditional common council and their electors, a division which gradually disappeared as education by preachers and schoolmasters took effect. By 1598 it was the common council which took the initiative on recusancy, and in 1608 they petitioned the corporation to have four civic preachers, one for each ward.[4]

Gradually the corporation shouldered more of the burden of Protestantizing the city, to the pleasure of Huntingdon and the clergy. Christopher Harbert was the first to take action on Sabbatarianism, in 1573, but it was Askwith in 1580 who imposed on the craft guilds a ban on drinking during service time. Once again, the aldermen were probably more zealous than many of their fellow citizens: in 1575 shopkeepers on the Pavement still opened on Sundays and holy days 'if faires and marketts fall on such daies', and in 1590 the corporation found it necessary to appoint four searchers of Sunday shopkeeping and Sunday drinking, offences which the mayor said were widespread.[5] In 1578 the corporation resolved to destroy 'all pictures of challices and hoastes' in the windows of St. Thomas's Hospital, and

[1] Cross, *Puritan Earl*, p. 250.
[2] *Y.C.R.* viii. 7–9, 31, 35, 46; Cross, *Puritan Earl*, pp. 254–5.
[3] *Y.C.R.* viii. 26. [4] Wilson, 'Corporation of York', p. 258.
[5] Palliser, 'Trade gilds', pp. 102–3; Purvis, *Tudor Parish Documents*, p. 91; Y.C.A., B 30, fos. 162, 163, 169.

in 1579 they banned the bawdy and popular custom of blessing bridal beds.[1]

More serious was the challenge of the recusant minority in the city. In 1576–8 most of the leading recusants were scattered or imprisoned, but there were still some eighty or ninety adult recusants in the latter year. Between 1578 and 1581 the Northern Council and Commission acted vigorously against recusants, but the number of adults involved dropped only to seventy-five or eighty, and remained at about this level until the end of the century. Public opinion seems to have prevented the corporation from levying the heavy recusancy fines (2s. per Sunday and feast-day) on lesser citizens; in any case, had they done so, ordinary tradesmen would have been ruined and become a charge on the poor-rate. The intermittence of persecution, the 'occasional conformity' of many recusants, the activities of seminary priests, and the community spirit of the recusants, ensured their survival under pressure, despite many lapses into conformity.[2]

J. C. H. Aveling, who has recently studied the York recusants in greater detail than anyone before, rightly stresses these unheroic facts, and reveals the martyrs as untypical. Nevertheless, one should not forget them in a reaction against nineteenth-century hagiography. No fewer than twenty people were martyred at York between August 1582 and September 1589, many of them natives of the York district,[3] and the figure contrasts sharply with the Marian persecution, when there was not a single martyr in the whole diocese. The most famous York martyr, Margaret Clitherow, was pressed to death in 1586 for refusing to plead to a charge of harbouring priests. She was the wife of a prosperous butcher who had served the city as chamberlain, and the stepdaughter of Henry May, the then mayor. According to Fr. Mush's biography of her, the execution aroused great horror, and Sheriff Gibson broke down during the proceedings.[4] It is a credible story, for when the corporation first began to take vigorous action against recusants, Gibson had protested that 'they doo

---

[1] *Register of Guild of Corpus Christi*, ed. Skaife, p. 310; *Y.C.R.* vii. 183.
[2] For this paragraph see Aveling, *Catholic Recusancy*, pp. 65–76.
[3] *Troubles of our Catholic Forefathers*, ed. Morris, iii. 40.
[4] The life is printed ibid., pp. 360–440.

sitt here to doo nothyng, but to cutt mens throtes'.[1] Catholic
accounts stress the sympathy displayed by spectators at the
executions of priests and laymen, and though this could be
attributed to simple humanitarian feelings, that may not be
the whole explanation. In 1580 York was still considered
'verie unsound' in religion by the Privy Council, and when
two Catholic women were sentenced to burning in 1596 the
Ecclesiastical Commission hastened to reprieve them, fearing
to make martyrs.[2] In 1600 the entire body of constables and
churchwardens of one parish had to be imprisoned for refusing to certify what education recusants' children were receiving, and in 1604 Mayor Thomas Harbert had the mortification
of presenting for recusancy his own brother Christopher, who
had become a Catholic while studying law at Gray's Inn.[3]

A Catholic account preserves an anecdote plausible enough
given the siege-mentality of Elizabethan Protestantism: when
a priest appeared for questioning at York in his robes, 'Mr.
Meares would have had him stript into his doublet and hose,
saying his very habit was able to persuade folks in the streets
to be of his religion'. It was also alleged that Mayor William
Robinson, in 1594, imprisoned a recusant widow, leaving her
five children succourless; when a relative interceded for them
he grew angry, saying, 'All these men where there is condemned felons and other malefactors . . . hath not committed
so great offence as she doth'.[4]

The religious settlement of 1559 was, of course, challenged
by 'Puritans' as well as by Catholics: but there was no persecution of the left as there was of the right. The extreme
sectaries found no foothold in a city like York, even when it
had become thoroughly Protestant: and more moderate Puritans had little difficulty with the church leadership, which
until Archbishop Neile (1632–40) was sympathetic and low-
church. A. G. Dickens has characterized the religion of late
Elizabethan York as 'Anglo-Puritanism', 'a Puritan emphasis
in the interpretation of the Prayer Book and the Articles of

---

[1] *Y.C.R.* vii. 176.

[2] *A.P.C. 1580–1*, pp. 107–8; Tyler, *Eccles. Commission at York*, p. 252.

[3] Y.C.A., B 32, fo. 85ᵛ; A. G. Dickens, 'The extent and character of recusancy',
Y.A.J. xxxvii (1948–51), p. 26; H.M.C. *Hatfield MSS.*, ix. 209.

[4] *Troubles of our Catholic Forefathers*, ed. Morris, iii. 54, 313 f.

Religion'.[1] Ceremonies that gave offence to Puritans, like lay
baptism by midwives, were stopped, and the prevailing spirit,
willing to correct abuses but hostile to radical changes, was
firmly expressed by Archbishop Sandys in 1588 in his will.[2]

It is difficult to form a clear picture of the reformed York
churches between the presentations for Catholic survivals
around 1570 and the accusations of Puritan practices sixty
years later. Doubtless the interiors were fairly bare, with
whitewashed walls covered with scriptural texts, a prominent
pulpit, and a wooden communion table surrounded by seats.
In 1585 a butcher left 10s. to St. John's 'toward makinge
more seates in the queare to sytt at the communyon'.[3] Neile's
prosecutions in the 1630s revealed practices which had
probably become normal: hats were kept on, seats were
ranged around the communion table, and psalms were sung
instead of canticles.[4] Increased emphasis on the Word is
reflected in the growing number of bibles owned by parishes
or individuals, and by a few devotional and theological works
owned by laymen. Texts replaced pictures on the walls of
churches, and even in private households. Whereas pious
citizens before the Reformation had had their walls hung
with painted cloths depicting saints, Huntingdon decorated
the King's Manor with the framed Ten Commandments and a
table of 'the causes of salvacion and damnacion'.[5] The emphasis on instruction rather than ritual caused the Church to
raise the age of confirmation and first communion until
youths were sufficiently catechized: until the 1540s, according to Robert Parkyn, seven was a normal age, but after the
Reformation it became fourteen or even twenty.[6]

The church ceased to be a centre of worship for the whole
community, if indeed it had ever been so, and Archbishop
Grindal's injunctions of 1571 imply that servants and paupers
may not all have attended. Communion became an infrequent
service attended only by the more prosperous, if the lists of

---

[1] *V.C.H. York*, p. 151.
[2] B.I.H.R., prob. reg. xxxi, fo. 103^r; printed in Drake, *Eboracum*, p. 455.
[3] B.I.H.R., prob. reg. xxxii, fo. 638.
[4] Marchant, *Puritans and the Church Courts*, pp. 61, 66.
[5] H.M.C., *MSS. of R. R. Hastings*, i. 355, 358.
[6] Dickens, 'Parkyn's narrative', p. 76; Purvis, *Tudor Parish Documents*, p. 80.

communicants in one wealthy parish can be taken literally. Social precedence was certainly enforced, in that as in all other matters. The Rector of St. Crux described how on Easter Sunday 1569 'he did minister the same sacramentall breade first unto the Lord Mayor of the Citie of Yorke being his parishoner and so to the more worthie parishoners . . . as they sat in order at the table'.[1] One catches a glimpse for the first time of churchgoing as an activity of the prosperous and the powerful. In 1599 the mayor and aldermen complained that many inhabitants of the city, 'especiallie of the inferior sorte', absented themselves from church, preferring

lyinge in there beddes or idlelye sittinge at there dores or in the stretes or walkinge abrode in the feildes . . . sittinge in the ailehouses or taverns . . . [and] playing in the aile howses at unlawfull games so longe as they either have moneye or creditt.[2]

Aveling suggests that the urban environment in post-Reformation Yorkshire was one where 'the feckless, irreligious and very poor non-churchgoers' existed in large numbers, whether the West Riding cloth towns, 'or an ancient town like York, where a great many medieval churches had been demolished or turned into indifferently-served chapels-of-ease, and parish boundaries and government were often in a state of disarray'.[3] And excommunication was plainly losing its force when a churchwarden, in 1595-6, could 'kepe a servante excommunicate'. Sullen indifference to the religion of the élite could turn to active hostility: in 1615 Thomas Nicholson threw snowballs at a congregation coming from a sermon, saying 'that it was never good world since ther were so many sermons'.[4] To the aldermen, of course, matters appeared quite different. To them a struggle was in progress to cleanse the church of corruption and to Christianize a semi-pagan populace. They triumphed in the 1640s and 1650s, which in their eyes was not a period of disruption but a happy culmination of the religious reforms begun a century earlier.[5]

[1] *Registers of St. Michael le Belfrey*, i. 103-6; B.I.H.R., C.P. G 1430.
[2] Y.C.A., B 32, fo. 2^v.
[3] H. Aveling, 'Some aspects of Yorkshire Catholic recusant history, 1558-1791', in *Studies in Church History*, ed. Cuming, iv. 109.
[4] Purvis, *Tudor Parish Documents*, p. 47; Y.C.A., B 34, fo. 54^r.
[5] C. Cross, 'Achieving the millennium: the Church in York during the Commonwealth', *Studies in Church History*, iv. 122-42.

X

STABILITY AND RECOVERY, 1560-1600

Yorke, Yorke for my monie,
The fairest citie I ever did see
For merry pastime or company
Except for the citie of London.
William Elderton, 1584[1]

The city of York was in sorry plight when Elizabeth I was
proclaimed queen there on 24 November 1558. An already
shrunken population had been further reduced by plague,
sweating sickness and the 'new ague', and almost the first act
of the corporation after proclaiming the Queen was to consider the scarcity of bread 'by reason of the unyversall syke-
ness and decay of people'.[2] The traditional textile trades had
almost entirely vanished, and only coverlet-making held its
own. Inflation was dislocating the city's finances, while house-
rents were at so low a level that many properties became
tumbledown for lack of repairs. Little new building was taking
place, and the monasteries and friaries, together with many
of the parish churches, were being gradually demolished for
their materials. Endowments of new grammar schools had
not yet made up for the losses at the Dissolution, while very
few hospitals for the poor still functioned. Yet relief was at
hand. The economic depression had levelled out, and was
gradually to give way to a renewed, if modest, prosperity.

Naturally the recovery was gradual, and for the first decade
of the new reign the corporation betrayed no sense that the
worst of the depression was passing. In 1561 they successfully pleaded for the remission of the weavers' fee farm, and
in 1562 they asked for a reduction in their military service on
the ground of severe population decline. Later that year they
were exercised over the decay of the house-property which
they owned, repairs to which were not covered by income

[1] Elderton, *Yorke, Yorke for my Monie.*
[2] *Y.C.R.* vi. 1.

from rents.[1] Nor was it only the corporation who viewed the city's situation as desperate. An undated scheme by an Elizabethan projector urged that £900 should be raised by public subscription and given for poor relief to Lincoln, Canterbury, and York, presumably thought to be especially decayed. Sir Thomas Gargrave wrote to Cecil in 1560 urging the claims of York as a permanent headquarters for the Council in the North; without its presence the city would 'in shorte tyme moche decay'.[2]

Gargrave was in a position to know. A Yorkshire gentleman and lawyer, he had been attending meetings of the Northern Council in York since 1544, and from 1555 until his death in 1579 he served continuously as vice-president. R. R. Reid's considered judgement was that he was 'the real ruler of the North' for a quarter of a century, and that 'to him must be given most of the credit for developing the Court at York out of the King's Council in the North'.[3] Though he made his home at Kinsley Hall and later Nostell Priory, he was constantly in York on official business, and was much trusted and respected by the aldermen and councillors. In 1547 they had elected him a Member of Parliament for the city, having first enfranchised him to make him eligible, and he sat for York during the whole Parliament of 1547-52.[4] As Speaker in Elizabeth's first Parliament, he made 'a notable oration, touching partly the decays of this realm, with some remedies for the same'; the text has been lost, but it would not be surprising if he had taken the opportunity to rehearse the economic difficulties of the north in general and of York in particular, so well known to him and so foreign to much of his audience.[5] Certainly he was soon urging on Cecil 'a mynt placyd her at Yorke', and in the 1560s he frequently received gifts from a grateful corporation for being 'evere ready bothe by his good word and dede to helpe and pleasure' their city.[6]

---

[1] *Y.C.R.* vi. 13, 17, 33, 43; *C.P.R. 1560-3*, p. 18.

[2] Bodley, Jones 17, fos. 8ᵛ, 9ʳ; Cartwright, *Chapters in the History of Yorks.*, p. 10.

[3] Reid, *King's Council in the North*, p. 184. For Gargrave see *D.N.B.*; Cartwright, *Chapters in Yorks. History*, pp. 1-87.

[4] *York Freemen* i. 267; *Y.C.R.* iv. 164. He was also nominated in 1562 and 1571, but sat for the shire: *Y.C.R.* vi. 47 f.; vii. 21-3.

[5] *Journals of the House of Commons*, i (1803), 53.

[6] Cartwright, *Chapters in Yorks. History*, p. 12; *Y.C.R.* vi. 80, 108, 121, 130, 143.

Gargrave's greatest service to York was, however, his plea for the permanent establishment there of the Queen's Northern Council. It bore fruit in her instructions of January 1561 to the lord president to keep house at York or some other suitable place, and if he were absent, to leave the councillors and secretary there for the convenience of suitors.[1] During the following eighty years the Council's official headquarters was the King's Manor, and its importance during that period is still manifest in its architecture. Hitherto the Council had used the building only spasmodically, being content with the U-shaped medieval house which they had taken over from the abbots of St. Mary's, but successive lords president from Rutland (1561–4) to Strafford (1628–41) enlarged it into a mansion grouped round two courtyards, a true Renaissance palace more than double the size of the original house.[2] The Council was a powerful agency with extensive secular jurisdiction over five counties; and it had only just been permanently established at the Manor when it acquired ecclesiastical powers over an even wider area. For in June 1561 the Queen established the Ecclesiastical Commission for the Northern Province, of which the Councillors were made *ex officio* members. Thus in the first half of 1561 York was equipped with two powerful and complementary bodies that made it once again a true capital of the north.

Gargrave's conviction that the presence of the Northern Council would save York from economic decay was not, apparently, misplaced. A simple proof of cause and effect is impossible, but there can be no doubt that the Council drew large numbers of suitors to the city.[3] Throughout Elizabeth's reign, for example, very few York suits were heard by either Star Chamber or Chancery, whereas under Henry VIII and his father they had been common. One can reasonably suppose that northerners had no wish to appear in London when a powerful court existed on their own doorstep. Similar indirect evidence is provided by the York freemen's register, indicating a surge in demand for accommodation at almost exactly the time that the Council and Commission were established in the city. By 1596 there were no fewer than sixty-four York

[1] Reid, *King's Council in the North*, pp. 188 f.
[2] R.C.H.M. *York*, iv. 30–43.   [3] Reid, *King's Council in the North*, p. 344.

inns, of which forty-six were situated in the central area between Minster, Manor, and Castle, within easy walking distance of the church and county courts and the Northern Council.[1] The recently-demolished 16-18 Micklegate, unusually large for Elizabethan York, was a survival of this innkeeping boom. Certainly an inn by 1602, it had probably been built as such a few years earlier.[2]

The numbers of bakers and butchers among the victualling crafts, and of tailors, drapers, and glovers among the clothing trades, also rose considerably after the middle of the century, and it is reasonable to connect their growth with rising demand from the many gentry and other visitors to York, who whatever their errands would combine legal or administrative business with shopping and entertainment. Furthermore, the Northern Council employed citizens more directly than through increasing demand for goods and services. It employed a large number of servants, messengers, and minor officials, while the major building works at the Manor were probably entrusted to York tilers.[3] Other York tradesmen benefited from the large orders needed to supply the council and the president's own household. Huntingdon received the traditional £1,000 a year for the Council's diet, a sum which was often greatly exceeded in a time of inflation. The surviving expenditure book for 1584-5 shows only £1,020 spent on provisions, at a time of retrenchment, but usually the earl owed £200 or £400 for provisions at York.[4]

The Northern Council and Commission, together with the five old-established church courts and the shire and city courts, made York a miniature Westminster, providing legal employment for those who in early Tudor times had been more likely to seek a legal career in the capital. Numerous judges, registrars, proctors, advocates, notaries, and apparitors were called for, and an ambitious local boy with talent had a wide field open to him. James Birkeby (c.1540-1610), the son of a sheriff's clerk in York, began his career in the same office but ended it as a prosperous attorney with the

---

[1] Above, p. 167; Cooper, 'Some old York inns', pp. 292-301, transcribing a corporation list now lost.

[2] R.C.H.M. *York*, iii, pp. lxiv, 72.   [3] e.g. *Y.C.R.* viii. 105.

[4] Cross, *The Puritan Earl*, p. 100.

Northern Council, a member of the Northern Commission, and a city alderman. Twice mayor of York and twice a burgess in Parliament, he died owning much property in the West Riding and leaving a large York house and over £2,000 to his son Alverey.[1] An even more impressive success was achieved by Henry Swinburne (c.1551-1624), born in York and educated at Holgate's school, who was a clerk of the archbishop's registrar by the age of sixteen. Having taken civil law at Oxford as a mature student, he returned home to practise as an advocate from 1581 until his death, while for the last twenty years of his life he was also judge in several York church courts and a member of the Ecclesiastical Commission. He was known as 'the northern advocate' for his learning, and famous for his two textbooks of canon law, the *Brief Treatise of Testaments and Last Willes* (1590, 1611, and later editions) and the posthumously published *Treatise of Spousals or Matrimonial Contracts*, though the eclipse of canon law by common law has obscured his reputation. He died less wealthy than Birkeby, perhaps because of his well-known charity, but he was nevertheless able to leave £500 in trust for his son Toby.[2]

2

Although the permanent establishment of the Northern Council and Commission in 1561 was almost wholly beneficial to the city, the effects were slow to manifest themselves. In 1562 the corporation were chiefly conscious of decay, poverty, and heavy taxes, and could not be expected to foresee the economic recovery that was just around the corner. It was only gradually, during the next twenty years, that they ceased to complain so much of poverty and became a little more self-confident. The change in attitude can be sensed from their archives, though unfortunately there are no surviving chamberlains' rolls between 1562 and 1576 from which the economic recovery could be charted. Already in 1561-2

---

[1] History of Parliament Trust, Elizabethan files, *sub* Birkby.
[2] Drake, *Eboracum*, p. 377; J. D. M. Derrett, *Henry Swinburne (? 1551-1624); Civil Lawyer of York* (Borth. P. xliv, 1973); A. G. Dickens, 'The writers of Tudor Yorkshire', *Trans. Roy. Hist. Soc.* 5th ser. 13 (1963), 63.

the corporation were out of debt, with a surplus of £50 or more of income over expenditure. In 1562 they felt able to insist on raising the daily payment to their two MPs from 8s. to 13s. 4d., despite opposition by the Commons, and in 1566 they increased the number of city waits from three to four 'for the worship and decentnesse of this ancient Citie'.[1] The numerous presents of wine to local notables in the 1560s also suggest a return to financial solvency, while in 1567 the corporation ventured £20 in the earliest state lottery, though many citizens grudged contributing to the stake.[2] One recipient of gifts from the corporation was Archbishop Young, who between 1564 and 1568 was also President of the Northern Council, and was apparently able to use his official influence for the city's benefit. In 1565 he was given an exceptionally long lease of a city moat and rampart—useful grazing ground—so that he should 'contynewe good and gracyouse lord to this city', and in 1567 Young asked the mayor to be a godfather to his baby son, the corporation in return giving a gilt cup as a christening present.[3]

One cause of the corporation's economic recovery was probably their sales of unprofitable properties and their purchase or lease of others which were more lucrative. In 1562-3 the corporation sold many of their urban tenements, and improved their financial position almost at once.[4] Sales continued for several years, and their completion was vigorously enforced. In September 1563 a tanner, a draper, and a merchant who had promised to buy city tenements were refusing to pay, 'to the hyndrauns of the said sale', and were promptly disfranchised.[5] The sales were followed up at least until the end of the decade, to ensure that early repairs were carried out on the properties remaining in the hands of the corporation. Meanwhile another economy being practised was to reserve the timbers of ruinous houses being demolished, keeping them in a corporation 'storehous' in Jubbergate to be used in repairs on other houses.[6]

The tenement sales were very successful. By the end of 1565, when a further £100 had been raised, the total received

[1] *Y.C.R.* vi. 49 f., 121.
[2] *Y.C.R.* vi. 130, 136-7.
[3] Y.C.A., B 24, fo. 24^V; *Y.C.R.* vi. 131-2.
[4] See p. 84.
[5] Y.C.A., B 23, fo. 108^V.
[6] ibid., fos. 13^V, 106^r.

was apparently £500, a fund which became available for short-term loans to citizens.[1] There may have been other sums from this source, for from 1564 onwards the corporation had the necessary reserves to engage in the purchase of freehold and leasehold lands and even whole manors, on terms which secured them a handsome profit. Frequently such purchases were made from local gentry in need of ready cash; the first was of the manors of Eastburn and Skerne near Great Driffield in 1563.[2] In 1564 the corporation bought the suburban manor of Bustardhall from one of their own number, Thomas Lawson, for £80, and in 1566 they had the resources to try to buy from the Crown three more valuable manors on the city boundaries, Dringhouses, Fulford, and Clifton, though negotiations were abortive.[3] In 1574 they made a good bargain by paying Sir Marmaduke Constable £200 down and £10 a year for a twenty-one-year lease of lands in Drax said to be worth at least £40 a year. This set a pattern for several similar agreements made with the Babthorpe, Layton, Constable, Cholmeley, and Aske families; it had become common form by January 1580, when Robert Aske of Aughton was lent £100 in return for a twenty-one-year lease of the lordship of Deighton, 'after suche ordre as Sir Richard Cholmeley and Sir William Babthorpe, knights, hath done'.[4] The policy was very profitable, bringing in rents of £72 or £73 a year between 1576 and 1579, rising after further leases to £88. 6s. 8d. in 1580–1 and 1582–3.

By 1565–6 the city's finances had already sufficiently recovered to enable a severe crisis to be weathered. On 6 January 1565 a thaw followed heavy snow, and the swollen river undermined Ouse Bridge.[5] The only land connection between the two halves of the walled city was snapped, and the situation was desperate, even though a temporary ferry service was arranged. Eventually, in 1566, a single span of stone was designed to replace the two spans destroyed, and was completed by the end of the year, when the new shops on the bridge

[1] Y.C.A., B 24, fos. 23^V, 29^V–32^r, 101, 123^V.

[2] Y.C.A., B 23, fos. 117^r, 140^V, 147–8; B 24, fos. 11^V, 15^r, 22^V.

[3] Y.C.A., B 23, fo. 140^r; Y.C.R. vi. 118. A further attempt was made to buy the three manors and others in 1571: Y.C.R. vii. 22, 28.

[4] Y.C.A., B 25, fo. 129^r; B 26, fos. 21^V, 45^r, 53^V, 92–3, 101^r, 147^V, 211^r.

[5] See p. 3.

were ready for letting. The cost must have been considerable, though the accounts do not survive; in 1565 £400 was ordered to be raised by a local tax in four instalments, and the final cost was probably higher, as individual donations had to supplement the funds, like the £100 given by Alderman Hall's widow.[1] It was, however, money well spent, and a far-sighted achievement for a city so poor. Camden said that it had the largest arch of any bridge he had seen, and it was indeed seven feet wider than the Ponte di Rialto in Venice, which was in any case built over twenty years later.[2] It proved strong enough to resist subsequent thaws and floods, doing duty as the only bridge over the Ouse until it was replaced in 1818–20.

York must at this time have seemed poor enough for the government to continue to grant tax remissions, and to include the collapse of the bridge among the reasons for the grants. From 1563 it became standard practice to remit £50 of every £136. 10s. 6½d. levied on the city as its share of every fifteenth and tenth, and the grants of remission were explicit about the city's poverty and its causes. In 1563, 1567, and 1571, they were stated to be depopulation by plagues, the cost of military service, and the education of many orphans undertaken by the corporation. Oddly, however, the 'late fall' of Ouse Bridge and the cleansing of the Ouse were first added to the list in the remission of 1576, and later still, in 1581, the Crown could adduce the fall of the bridge and the obstruction caused by the old foundations as reasons for the poverty of the York merchants justifying their new charter.[3] It is hard to believe that the effects of the disaster continued to be felt so late, and it can only be suggested that, however reliable early Tudor tax remissions may have been in their language, those of Elizabeth became stereotyped. It is difficult to credit that the Queen's ministers would show undue tenderness towards taxpayers' problems, but it may be that they had accepted that York had fallen permanently in its economic standing relative to other towns

---

[1] *Y.C.R.* vi. 100–123; R.C.H.M. *York*, iii. 49; Drake, *Eboracum*, p. 280.

[2] Camden, *Britannia* (1586 edn.), p. 407; Harvey, *York*, p. 81.

[3] *Y.C.R.* vi. 66 f.; Y.C.A., B 24, fos. 92–3, 247ʳ; B 26, fo. 70ʳ; *York Mercers*, ed. Sellers, p. 244.

like Hull and Leeds, and that an automatic tax remission was seen as easier and less controversial than a downward readjustment of the total assessment.

Certainly another of the alleged causes of poverty and depopulation was very dubious indeed. The epidemics of 1550-2 and 1558-9 had indeed been devastating, but the gaps in the population were apparently filled fairly rapidly, for the city was recovering its attraction for immigrants, while the absence of any severe epidemic between 1559 and 1604 allowed the native population to increase at the same time. The increase in both natives and immigrants can be gauged, at least for the more prosperous half of the population, from the freemen's register, which divides admissions into freemen by inheritance and all others. The detailed lists of enfranchisements between 1535 and 1566, already analysed, show that 95.5 per cent of the freemen admitted by methods other than inheritance were born outside the city; it is therefore reasonable to treat the two groups of admissions in the register as being roughly equivalent to natives and immigrants.[1] Total admissions of freemen, after reaching their lowest point of about fifty a year in the 1520s, had recovered to about sixty a year in mid-century and then rose gradually to seventy a year by 1600. The separate figures for the two groups of freemen are, however, of more interest. There were massive rises in the numbers of immigrant freemen after both epidemic periods, 132 being admitted in the two years 1551-3 and 125 in 1561-3. In a city with a freeman class about 1,200 strong, these influxes were enormous. The numbers of freemen admitted by inheritance did not fluctuate quite so much from year to year, for they depended on long-term trends in fertility, but there was a slow and steady upward trend in their numbers from 1562 throughout Elizabeth's reign, an increase which was a clear indication of biological recovery in a period free of epidemics, as well as of an economic recovery which encouraged so many sons of freemen to remain in the city. The same recovery can also be traced in the surviving parish registers, which indicate a regular natural surplus of births from 1560 onwards, after the disastrous decade of the 1550s.

The 1560s, therefore, saw the beginnings of healthier

[1] See p. 128.

corporation finances and of an upward trend in population. The corporation minutes also testify to a gradual recovery in self-confidence, as for instance over the perennial problem of the Ouse navigation. In 1567 and 1568, for example, 'common day works' were regularly appointed when at least forty labourers a day were set to work on scouring the river, and a 'new work in St. Georges Closse' was built up.[1] These efforts may not have significantly improved the navigability of the river, but at least they testified to a new vigour on the part of the corporation; and there are indications that the York merchants' long-distance trading through Hull was beginning to expand again. In 1565 the corporation agreed to ask the government to license Alderman William Watson to trade with Narva in Estonia, and Watson was confident enough of its value to promise in return 'xl^{li} yerely toward reparacon of Ousebrige soo long as it shall chance the sayd licens to contynewe in force'.[2] Narva had been captured by the Russians in 1558, giving them direct access to the Baltic, and the Muscovy Company were trying to monopolize the lucrative trade with it. However, Yorkshiremen continued to import goods thence, including Narva hides, and Gregory Watson of York, probably a relative of the alderman, settled at Narva as 'one of the cheife factores for all the stragling merchauntes of Yorke and Hull'.[3] Yet the York merchants remained very poor compared to the Londoners; when the Merchants Adventurers lent £30,000 to the Queen in 1560, the seven York members were assessed at only £425.[4]

The economic recovery was scarcely under way before restrictions were being strengthened against the immigration of skilled craftsmen into York. After half a century in which masters had been free to take on apprentices without restriction, the minstrels' guild imposed limits in 1561, followed by the plasterers and tilers in 1572.[5] In 1568 the common council, obviously worried about limited employment opportunities in a time of rising population, asked that no 'strangers' should be enfranchised for less than £10. The corporation

[1] Y.C.R. vi. 128, 139; Y.C.A., B 24, fos. 83^r, 112^v.   [2] Y.C.R. vi. 96.
[3] Willan, Early History of the Russia Co., pp. 67–77, 85 f.; B.L. Lansdowne 110, fo. 186^r.
[4] York Mercers, ed. Sellers, pp. 162–3.
[5] Palliser, 'Trade gilds', pp. 98, 115.

rejected this as too restrictive, and fixed the entrance fee at a minimum of £3. 6s. 8d., with provision for lower fees from 'such handy craftys man as shall be thought . . . necessarie and profitable for the common weale and amendment of the sayd Citie'.[1] It would be wrong, however, to picture a narrowly selfish freeman class in conflict with a city council of broader economic vision, for in 1564 the two groups took opposite positions on the level of market tolls. The common council asked for tolls on 'strangers and forreners' to be reduced, as 'thrugh gentill intreteamment of foren vyttelers in marketts or good townes thyther is brought plenty of corne and other vyttalls', and it was the city councillors, concerned not to lose the revenue from tolls, who resisted.[2]

3

The Rising of the Northern Earls in 1569–70 marked a turning-point for the citizens in more ways than one. The events of that winter buried the suspicions of York's loyalty which Henry VII and Henry VIII had harboured. One consequence of the rising was that Elizabeth became determined to impose her rule north of the Humber once and for all. On 22 May 1570 she appointed Edmund Grindal to the vacant see of York in succession to the easy-going Thomas Young, and in August 1572 she made Henry, Earl of Huntingdon, Lord President at York; henceforth she was served with unswerving loyalty by them and their successors in the two chief offices in the North. More immediately, however, the role of York during the rising had demonstrated a military, financial, and organizational capacity that revealed a new self-confidence among the city fathers. They responded quickly and vigorously when they learned of the rebellion, putting York into a state of defence that deterred the earls from besieging it, and apparently coping adequately with an influx of 3,000 soldiers from all over the county, as well as all the suburban townsmen, a huge number for a city of perhaps 8,000 or 9,000 to accommodate. When the royal army moved north to pursue the rebels, the generals asked York for a short-term loan of £1,000 or more for soldiers' wages, and although the

[1] Y.C.R. vi. 133; vii. 5.   [2] Y.C.R. vi. 76–9.

councillors felt 'they were not of habilitie' to raise such a sum, they did at once contribute over £500 among themselves.[1]

The late medieval decline of York had been brought about by the decline of the textile industry and long-distance trade. The economic recovery under Elizabeth I and the early Stuarts was based on the city's role as a governmental and social capital, and on a revival of its long-distance trade. Elizabethan York had no major textile manufacturing sector as did Norwich and Worcester, two other ancient corporate towns which were more successful in adapting to the changing circumstances of supply and demand in the cloth industry. The trading function of York, however, proved more resilient than its industries. There had always been a residual role for York's traders, even in the darkest days of the mid-Tudor depression, and by the middle of Elizabeth's reign this minimal level of local trading was being supplemented at the regional, national, and even international levels. Many more gentry and other visitors were coming to the city on official and unofficial business. The gradual growth of long-distance trading was increasing York's function as an entrepôt for goods and services throughout a large area of the north and the northern midlands, and as a link between the northern shires and London by way of the Humber and the Great North Road. Finally, York shared in the revival of Hull's trade from about the middle of the sixteenth century, one of the signs of a relative recovery by the outports against London's dominance of overseas trade.

Alan Everitt has convincingly demonstrated a considerable growth of English inland trade from about 1570, and stressed that the markets, the fairs, and especially the inns of the provincial towns formed an 'ever-expanding network of inland market trade . . . one of the more striking features in the English economy of the Tudor era'.[2] All these features can be discerned among the York records, if not always as fully as one would wish. York inns were regularly patronized

[1] *Y.C.R.* vi. 163-82.

[2] A. Everitt, ed., *Perspectives in English Urban History* (London, 1973), p. 6. See also Everitt, 'The English urban inn, 1560-1760', op. cit., pp. 91-137; 'The marketing of agricultural produce', *passim*; and 'Urban growth, 1570-1770', *The Local Historian*, viii (1968-9), 118-25.

by 'chapmen, buyers of flax and other marchandize', and some chapmen were plainly retained by individual merchants as their own agents.[1] By the 1560s York drapers and goldsmiths were attending Stourbridge Fair near Cambridge, which was rapidly becoming the greatest fair in England, and nearer home many York merchants attended the well-known fairs at Howden and Beverley, where they made contact with London traders.[2] A regular carriers' trade was beginning between York and the capital, and large consignments of metropolitan goods were reaching York to judge from the pleas of London creditors.[3] Some York freemen even chose to serve apprenticeships in or near the capital before returning home to set up shop.[4]

York also benefited from a 'modest maritime growth at Hull from the middle of the sixteenth century', especially from its trade with the Baltic. York merchants exported cloth and lead through Hull, and received in return a wide variety of imported goods. Sixty-six York merchants were trading through the Sound by 1579, and the York and Hull men together captured more and more of England's Baltic trade, until by the early seventeenth century they accounted for a third of the total.[5] The growing trade led to disputes between Hull and York over tolls and dues in both towns, and to an ineffective trade boycott of each by the other, which was settled in 1578 by the mediation of Huntingdon, and again after a renewed dispute in 1586.[6] It was probably during one of these disputes that the York merchants

[1] *York Mercers*, ed. Sellers, p. 277; *Y.C.R.* viii. 45.

[2] *Y.C.R.* vi. 63 f.; viii. 16, 81, 165; *Yorks. Philosophical Soc. Annual Report* 1965, p. 22; Y.C.A., B 30, fos. 347-9; B 31, fo. 33; B 32, fos. 48^r, 281-5; Poulson, *Beverlac*, p. 332.

[3] e.g. B.I.H.R. prob. reg. ix, fo. 157; H.M.C., *MSS. of Duke of Rutland*, i. 194, 299; *Y.C.R.* vi. 64, 70, 72; vii, 15, 181-2; *C.P.R. 1569-72*, p. 27; P.R.O. Req. 2/244/37; 2/213/47.

[4] e.g. B.I.H.R., C.P. G.1430; *Kingston upon Thames Register of Apprentices 1563-1713*, ed. A. Daly (Surrey Record Soc. xxviii, 1974), p. 4 and pl. 2; *Register of Freemen*, ed. Collins, ii. 15.

[5] *York Mercers*, ed. Sellers, pp. 201-2; Davis, *Trade and Shipping of Hull*, p. 6; Palliser, 'York under the Tudors', pp. 44-7; Ramsay, *English Overseas Trade*, p. 97.

[6] Cross, *The Puritan Earl*, pp. 189-90; Reid, *King's Council in the North*, p. 308; *Y.C.R.* vii. 155-6, 161, 164; viii. 2. The agreement of 28 June 1578 is in Y.C.A., E 23, fo. 109.

complained to Burghley that the corporation of Hull 'be evill affectioned againste us, and wolde cutt us from our trade as some of the aldermen have given it out in plaine speches'. The Baltic concentration of York's imports appears from the list of goods interfered with: flax, hemp, wax, tallow, pitch, tar, Narva hides, and Gdansk wheat and rye.[1] York men, in fact, benefited enormously from Hull's position, and were able to play a leading role in Hull's overseas trade well into the seventeenth century. The renewed importance of the York merchants was demonstrated when in 1581 they purchased a royal charter incorporating them as the Society of Merchants Adventurers of York, and granting them a monopoly of all foreign goods imported into York and the Ainsty except fish and salt.[2]

The Elizabethan age also witnessed a turning-point in the supply of domestic and industrial fuel. The traditional source for both was local timber, but much wood was apparently felled by monastic purchasers to pay for their new estates, and industrial needs were also growing.[3] In the 1520s the council chamber on Ouse Bridge had been heated by wood and charcoal, but by the 1550s turves and coals were used instead. These two fuels completely replaced timber in the second half of the century. In 1572 the corporation, like Worcester, even considered managing their own coal-mine, though the scheme was abortive.[4] By 1584 so many 'cole waynes' were entering Micklegate Bar, presumably from the West Riding coalfield, that a special levy was necessary to keep the causeway there repaired, and by the end of the century the largest item of York's coastal trade was 'sea coal' shipped from Newcastle.[5] Even more numerous, however, are references to turves, used for domestic fuel at all levels of society, and by 1597 described as 'nowe the greatest parte of our fewell'.[6]

[1] B.L., Lansdowne 110, fo. 186[r] (undated).

[2] *York Mercers*, ed. Sellers, pp. 244–54; Gross, *The Gild Merchant*, ii. 280–5.

[3] Smith, *Land and Politics*, pp. 22 f., 235; *L.P. Hen. VIII*, xv, no. 515; Addenda i, no. 1453; Elton, *Reform and Renewal*, p. 78; *Y.C.R.* v. 23–5, 87.

[4] Y.C.A., C 2–C 7; *Y.C.R.* vii. 48, 52; cf. Dyer, *Worcester*, p. 55.

[5] *Y.C.R.* viii. 73 f., 100; see p. 194.

[6] e.g. B.I.H.R., orig. probate records, Canon T. Atkynson, 1571; Y.C.A., B 31, fos. 51[v], 305[r].

Another modest spur to York's recovery was the revival of its educational importance. It has been seen that both grammar schools were lost at the Reformation, and Holgate's foundation of a new school in 1546 cannot have fully compensated for the loss. In 1557 the Dean and Chapter refounded a cathedral grammar school with a distinctly counter-Reformation bias, but it is not at all certain that their aim was not a reorganization of Holgate's Protestant foundation.[1] Whatever the truth, the second school of St. Peter had not actually been started in 1565, though it was certainly open, alongside Holgate's, in 1574.[2] The new school was intended for 'a certayne convenient number of scholars therein to be frelie taught theyre grammer', and also for fee-paying pupils. The county gentry patronized it as they had before the Reformation, thereby adding to the city's prosperity. There is no early register of pupils, but two brothers from Plowland Hall, near Patrington, were educated there, and boys at the school in the early 1620s included the sons of gentlemen of Thoraldby, Warter, Swale Hall, Thirkleby, and Welborne, as well as sons of leading city merchants and of the Dean.[3]

York's renewed prosperity was attracting more immigrants, while its freedom from epidemics allowed a continuing natural increase in population, at least in the richer parishes for which registers survive. Gaol fever in the castle in 1581 took no hold in the city, while 'plagues' at Hull in 1575–6 and 1582 were kept at bay by temporary suspensions of trade with that town.[4] The numbers of freemen's sons surviving to inherit the franchise increased, and in 1588–9 they accounted for over half the total admissions for the first time. The new demographic situation caused the corporation and the guilds to tighten controls of apprenticeship in favour of freemen's sons.[5] The policy was not totally exclusive, for immigrant freemen continued to be welcome, especially if they were of good families, and immigrants with special skills

[1] Leach, *Early Yorkshire Schools*, i, pp. 42–50.

[2] ibid., p. xxvi; A. Raine, *History of St. Peter's School: York* (London, 1926), p. 78.

[3] Raine, *Hist. St. Peter's*, p. 87; *The Life of Marmaduke Rawdon of York*, ed. R. Davies (Camden Soc. lxxxv, 1863), pp. 3 f.

[4] Palliser, 'Epidemics in Tudor York', pp. 52 f.

[5] e.g. *Y.C.R.* viii. 87, 111.

lacking in the city could be enfranchised at reduced rates: two Dutch linenweavers were in 1571 enfranchised for only 20*d.* apiece.[1] The greatest threat was feared not from such men but from poor immigrants, who were apparently being attracted to York in unprecedented numbers, and who were often crammed into overcrowded houses or into extensions at the backs of properties. In 1578 the council complained that 'dyverse poore persons ar setled in the fyerhouses of certeyn tenements', while in 1586 they ordered landlords to expel recently-arrived pauper undertenants.[2]

The poor were a perennial concern in Tudor towns, but at York the problem became serious only when poor immigrants were attracted in large numbers; and the reviving prosperity which attracted them also allowed the corporation to spend more on relieving the problem, both of native and immigrant paupers. By 1561 compulsory poor-rates were being levied weekly by the council to prevent begging, and in 1566, for the first time, they ordered a complete census of all 'impotent, aged and poore folke' and all 'ydle and vagrant persons' with a view to relieving the former and punishing the latter. It cannot have been successful, for the next year, spurred on by the Council in the North, they repeated the attempt.[3] In 1569–70 the machinery was overhauled; a 'view' was taken of the poor and eighty-eight poor licensed to beg, while those who 'can not goe abroade' were to be relieved out of the weekly assessments, which were revised; special officials were created to supervise the system. All of this anticipated the Act of 1572, which made poor rates compulsory for the first time, and which was promptly followed up by the corporation.[4] York was also, in some respects, ahead of the Act of 1576, which enjoined the provision of work for the able-bodied unemployed, and the institution of 'Houses of Correction' for those unwilling to work. Weaving establishments for the unemployed were opened in St. Anthony's Hall in 1567 and St. George's Chapel in 1569, although the scheme to sell the cloth made there proved unworkable.[5] In 1574 a different policy was tried: fifty-one 'aged, impotent poore and

[1] *Y.C.R.* vii. 37.   [2] *Y.C.R.* vii. 169; viii. 115.
[3] *Y.C.R.* vi. 6, 14, 110 f., 124.   [4] *Y.C.R.* vi. 150 f., 159 f.; vii. 2, 52 f.
[5] *Y.C.R.* vi. 129–30, 144–8; vii. 3 f., 12 f., 18, 29 f., 32 f., 66–73.

lame people' were to be settled in St. Thomas's Hospital, the Merchants' Hall and St. Anthony's Hall, and a stock of linen, hemp, and tow was to be provided for them to spin.[1] These schemes all presupposed paupers who were willing to work; but as soon as the 1576 Act was passed, the corporation established a House of Correction in St. George's to provide hard labour for those who were not. St. George's continued to be so used until at least 1598, but it quickly proved inadequate for a city of York's size. Fishergate Bar was converted into a second House of Correction in 1584, though it soon became a prison instead, perhaps because it was too small for forced labour. In 1586 part of St. Anthony's Hall was converted for the purpose instead, and its size apparently made it more suitable; in any event, the lower storey of the hall remained a House of Correction until 1814, earning the criticism of Howard the penal reformer.[2]

The normal policy with immigrant paupers who had no work was, however, to send them back to their last place of residence. A thorough investigation of labourers was undertaken in 1577; sixty-five were licensed to work in the city, but twenty-one immigrant labourers and their families were expelled. Most had come from nearby villages, but three families had travelled from Hull, Richmond, and Norwich, while one vagrant who was whipped and expelled later that year was a Hampshire man.[3] Two families expelled from York in February 1577 had come from Lancashire and County Durham, and another native of the Bishopric, Thomas Wiggon, travelled all over the country before his case was investigated at York in 1597. He spent his childhood in York and was then apprenticed in London, but despite this prosperous beginning he fell into poverty and took to the road. He appeared briefly in York again, was pressed into service on the Calais expedition of 1596, and then turned up again in York as a maimed soldier begging for relief.[4] York natives themselves contributed to this unhappy army of homeless vagrants, men like Henry Burton who was arrested while

[1] *Y.C.R.* vii. 86, 90, 93.
[2] *Y.C.R.* vii. 118-121, 125; viii. 78, 114-15, 118; *V.C.H. York*, p. 494; R.C.H.M. *York*, ii. 152.
[3] Y.C.A., B 27, fos. 2-4, partly printed in *Y.C.R.* vii. 144-5; *Y.C.R.* vii. 165.
[4] *Y.C.R.* vii. 146; Y.C.A., B 31, fos. 281-2.

begging at Exeter.[1] Most of the wanderers moved on readily
enough if rewarded with alms or threatened with whipping;
but a few proved obstinate and posed a challenge to law enforcement. Margaret Sheles, 'a notorious vacabonde', arrived
in York about 1570, 'loytred with in and about the Citie of
Yorke' for ten years, despite being whipped, burned through
the ear, and expelled. A York couple whom she pestered
appealed to the Northern Ecclesiastical Commission, but they
were in a quandary: they wanted to be rid of her, but not to
have her executed as a felon, the penalty she risked for returning to York as 'a roge in the secunde degree'. The city fathers
were ordered to banish her again; if she dared to return, they
were to provide 'suche punyshment . . . as yowe thynke shall
restrayne her accesse thether', though the Commissioners
declined to specify what punishment short of death would
keep her away.[2]

The prominence of poor relief and vagrancy in the minutes
of the Elizabethan corporation might suggest a city in economic distress, but such an impression would be misleading.
What was new was the extent of official aid and machinery,
produced partly by an increased social sensitivity on the part
of Parliament and the urban corporations. The provision of
wool in 1579 for 'settyng the pore of this Citie on worke'
cost the corporation and freemen £400, while in 1588 the
common council could contemplate abolishing begging by
setting all the able poor on work and paying a 'better allowance then heretofore' to all the aged and infirm poor who
had lived in York for at least three years, each to have at
least three halfpence a day, 'under whiche some a poore
creator cannot lyve'.[3] The resources were certainly available,
for the surviving civic accounts for the period 1576-83 indicate a net surplus in every year, and the growing expenditure
on civic ceremonial indicates a healthy financial position as
well as a renewed sense of corporate pride. £27 was spent in
1580 on a new mace and cap of maintenance, and £3. 6s. 8d.
in 1586 on a coat of arms from the College of Heralds.[4] The
dignity of the corporation was emphasized ostentatiously.
When Huntingdon first entered York after being appointed

---

[1] MacCaffrey, *Exeter 1540-1640*, p. 95.   [2] *Y.C.R.* viii. 12 f.
[3] *Y.C.R.* viii. 1, 157-9.   [4] *Y.C.R.* viii. 34, 132.

Lord Lieutenant of the northern counties in 1581, the corporation and 200 citizens met him ceremonially at Bootham Bar, and when his commission was renewed in 1586 they staged an even more elaborate welcome, with a deputation 'in their best apparell' at Walmgate Bar, 'the waites plainge over the gates', whence 'they brought him upe into the Cittye, with greate stoore of torches and lightes, Fosse bridge beinge verye well perfumed with frankensence'.[1] The corporation were also by this period wealthy enough to bid for many of the former church properties which they had failed to secure during the dissolutions, and in 1585 the Queen was glad to grant them some 150 tenements and cottages which had originally belonged to chantries and religious houses on condition that they maintained them.[2] The wills and other records of the aldermen confirm the picture, suggesting increasing private as well as public affluence among the members of the corporation. They were improving their houses with wainscotting and glass windows, and accumulating luxuries like silver plate, and some were beginning to make gifts of plate to the city. Most aldermen owned several houses in York and usually rural land as well, while a small but growing number were lords of rural manors.

The career of William Robinson, owner of eight and a half manors, illustrates the reviving importance and prosperity of the York merchants. Apparently an immigrant to York, born about 1534, he was admitted to the freedom in 1558-9, and resided for several years in Hamburg, Lübeck, and other Hanseatic towns, presumably as a factor or agent of other York merchants. He rose rapidly, joining the Twenty-Four in 1569 and the bench of aldermen in 1578, presumably because of his growing wealth and trade, and was one of the city's Baltic traders by 1579. He was five times governor of the York merchants, twice lord mayor, and twice MP for the city, sitting on several committees in both Parliaments. When he died, he left £40 to the merchants' company to be lent to young merchants interest free, as well as £80 to the corporation for similar purposes, and bequeathed a silver bowl to the

---

[1] *Y.C.R.* viii. 41 f., 123-4; Cross, *The Puritan Earl*, pp. 207-8.
[2] Y.C.A., A 42 (royal letters patent of 15 Mar. 1585).

city plate.[1] In 1580, at the end of a third consecutive term as governor of the merchants, he went to London on one of a series of missions to secure the new royal charter reconstituting the guild as the Society of Merchants Adventurers. It is significant that the York merchants were able to spend over £70 on obtaining the charter, as it is that in 1577 'diverse' of them had been ready to invest in Frobisher's second voyage to the Arctic.[2]

Clearly, by the 1580s the merchants and tradesmen of York were prospering again. In 1587 the Queen granted another of her now traditional tax remissions, referring again to York's ruin and decay, but the hollowness of the reasons was made apparent only four months later, when the Privy Council expressed concern at the declining returns from taxes despite the long peace 'and howe greatlye the welth of her subjects is therebye generallye encreased'; the warning was a general one, but a copy was sent to the corporation by the Northern Council with the clear implication that York's citizens were sharing in the general prosperity and under-assessment of taxes.[3] A glimpse of York's growing wealth as a social capital is afforded by a ballad of 1584 by William Elderton, celebrating the great archery match in the city two years previously:

> And never a man that went abroade,
> But thought his monie well bestowde,
> And monie laide in heap and loade,
>   As if it had been at London.
> And gentlemen there so franke and free,
> As a mint at Yorke again should bee. . . .[4]

Prosperity had returned, but it was a more private and less publicly-demonstrated prosperity than before the slump. As in Coventry, 'ceremony and religion together withdrew indoors from the public gaze' after the Reformation, and the old communal processions and pageants which symbolically

---

[1] History of Parliament, Elizabethan files; *Reg. Corpus Christi Guild*, ed. Skaife, p. 311 n.; Jordan, *Charities of Rural England*, p. 293 n.; *York Mercers*, ed. Sellers, pp. 201-4, 324.

[2] *York Mercers*, ed. Sellers, pp. 203-5, 224; *A.P.C. 1575-7*, pp. 302-3.

[3] *Y.C.R.* viii. 146-8, 156. The latter letter, though copied into the minutes later, was issued by the Queen on 15 May 1587 (Y.C.A., B 19, fo. 245^V).

[4] Elderton, *Yorke, Yorke for my Monie*.

united the citizens were reduced or abolished.[1] The pageant-
plays, notably the great Corpus Christi cycle, came to an end
in the 1570s, and the occasional attempts at Midsummer
plays and interludes in the 1580s cannot have provided adequate substitutes.[2] The city fathers, furthermore, were tend-
ing to regard the communal property—city gates, moats,
pastures, and even public rights of way—as assets to be realized
by leasing or selling them to the highest bidder or to those
whose friendship could be useful. In 1586, for instance, they
sold a public lane to Sir Thomas Fairfax for enlarging his
Bishophill property, for a price of 66s. 8d., from which
26s. 8d. was immediately deducted 'in respecte of his frend-
shippe towardes this cittie'.[3] Admittedly such sales and leases
were subject to the consent of the common council, but the
rights of lesser inhabitants, who would be inconvenienced
and would receive no financial benefit, were disregarded.
Once, however, the city council overstepped the mark. In
1574 they closed Haymonger Lane, between the Shambles
and Peter Lane Little, and leased it out in parcels to the
adjoining property owners, most of whom were aldermen and
councillors, at low rents. There were 'many dissencions'
among the citizens, and disputes involving the recorder's legal
advice rumbled on until 1577. The opposition was finally
overborne, but the council never again tried to close a major
right of way.[4] James Ryther, in an attack on the corporation
in 1589, said that 'it may be holden for a principle among
these private people, that their common commodity occupieth
the least part of their care'.[5]

Another of Ryther's complaints concerned the prevalence
of usury at York, 'of all the able sort practised', which he
alleged involved interest rates of 30, 40, or 50 per cent, far
beyond the maximum 10 per cent allowed by statute after
1571.[6] He probably exaggerated, but there is much independent corroboration that money-lending had become a major
source of income in late-Elizabethan York. Archbishop

[1] Clark and Slack, *Crisis and Order in English Towns*, p. 80.
[2] *Y.C.R.* viii. 77, 101, 103.   [3] Y.C.A., B 29, fo. 110ʳ.
[4] Raine, *Mediaeval York*, pp. 188–9; *Y.C.R.* vii. 84; Y.C.A. B 25, fos. 98–9,
106–10; B 26, fos. 34ʳ, 59ʳ, 114ᵛ; B 27, fos. 8ʳ, 28ʳ, 30ʳ, 68ʳ, 71ᵛ; F 3 (unfoliated), entries for 10 Nov. 1572, 23 Mar. 1576.
[5] B.L., Lansdowne 119, fo. 111.   [6] loc. cit., fo. 111ʳ.

Sandys, 'the hammer of the usurers', attacked the taking of interest at his inaugural sermon at York in 1577. In 1585 he launched a major campaign against the merchants and leading citizens involved, telling Burghley that the practice had become a scandal, and that it was practised in York 'more than anywhere else in the world'. Altogether forty York usurers were charged and forced to forfeit all interest, including Sheriff William Gibson, while the contumacious were imprisoned. Sandys was a traditionalist who opposed the 10 per cent interest permitted by law; his campaign against even legal interest was opposed by his own Dean and by the Northern Council, and it ended altogether after his death in 1588. The important point for York's economy, however, is the admitted prevalence of money-lending, practised, in Sandys's words, 'as well by merchants as by artificers and men of all sorts', and suggesting that many citizens had spare capital to invest in this way.[1] John King, preaching in the Minster in 1595, castigated in the severest terms 'you the infamous usurers of the North of England, you the Jewes and Judases of our land that would sell Christ for mony if he were amongst you'. The violence of the language surely reflects not only a conservative theology but a very active money-market.[2]

4

To the very end of the Queen's reign, and beyond, the corporation continued to plead poverty when it suited them. In 1589, struggling to avoid a levy of £600 towards Hull's ships, they asked Huntingdon to

have some consideracon of the estaite of the cittizins of Yorke, the better sort wherof are greatlie charged with relief of many pore, and the great charges we were at with furnishing as well of private as comon soldyers and training of the comon sort, and the great losse many of the best sort of cittizins had by ventring for powder, besides that . . . our cittizins have within thes fewe yeares, had great losses, and their habilities not as yt is reported, and the levieng of money will go very hard emongest the cittizins.

---

[1] I. P. Ellis, 'The archbishop and the usurers', *Jour. Eccles. Hist.* xxi (1970), 33-42.

[2] King, *A Sermon Preached . . . the Queenes Day*, pp. 704-5.

Yet later that year, in the course of a dispute with the lord of the manor of Naburn, they sent him word that they would harry him till he had no land left to sell, 'for they said the Cittie purse had no bottome'; and in the following January they did not hesitate to increase the allowance of gown cloth to the mayor's officers to make them more 'decent in there apparell', which hardly suggests financial stringency.[1] The chamberlains' accounts are missing between 1583 and 1597, but there is no reason to doubt that the city's budget was satisfactorily balanced, as it was in the last years of the reign. The Privy Council's dealings with York's constant excuses over ship money indicate that they were not deceived; and if the Queen yet again reduced York's tax in 1598 because of its 'great ruin and long decay', that indicates only the conservatism of her system of taxation. It has been well said that the late sixteenth century was a relatively healthy period for the city's economy, and that 'one is tempted to think that "decay" had become not so much an economic fact as a habit of mind'.[2]

In the course of the ship money dispute of 1589 the Privy Council assessed York at £600 out of the total £1,015 needed from Hull, 'perceavinge ... their trade and traffique to be thrise as much at the least in the porte of Hull, and their comodytie farre greater then the merchauntes of the said towne'. Their judgement was amply confirmed in 1590, when ninety-one York citizens were assessed to lend the Queen sums ranging from £20 to £100 each, while only three Hull men were assessed, and all for the minumum £20.[3] Another measure of relative wealth, charitable bequests, concurs; the totals calculated by Professor Jordan allow £26,000 given at York, the fourth highest figure for a provincial town in his ten-county sample, as against £12,000 at Hull, and less than £10,000 at Leeds and Halifax. The figures, unfortunately, are for 1480–1660 as a whole, but inflation must have ensured that the totals largely represent the Elizabethan and early Stuart periods.[4]

---

[1] Y.C.A., B 30, fos. 89, 156^V; B 14, fo. 24 (entry misplaced, datable 1589–90).
[2] *Calendar of State Papers Domestic 1598–1601*, p. 126; Wilson, 'Corporation of York', p. 143.
[3] *A.P.C. 1588–9*, pp. 45 f.; Cartwright, *Chapters in Yorks. History*, pp. 372–4.
[4] Jordan, *Charities of Rural England*, pp. 194, 446–8. For a correction of Jordan's Yorkshire data to allow for inflation, see W. G. Bittle and R. T. Lane, 'Inflation and philanthropy in England', *Econ. Hist. Rev.* 2nd ser. xxix (1976), 209.

Undoubtedly there was a quickening of the charitable impulse at York in the last decade of the sixteenth century, which, whatever the testators' motives, suggests increased prosperity as well as a growing awareness of social needs. From about 1590 citizens and resident gentry began to leave money in the form of regulated revolving loan funds, sums to be lent to those in need and, when repaid, to be lent again to others. Those revolving loans administered by the corporation have already been listed, but others were endowed and entrusted to parish or guild officials.[1] More money was also channelled into education. Alongside the two well-known grammar schools, several unendowed schools were appearing for the first time, such as the parish schools of Holy Trinity, Micklegate, St. John Ousebridge End, St. Martin Micklegate, and St. Sampson, all first mentioned between 1590 and 1592.[2] William Woller, a merchant benefactor to York, illustrates a tendency for some York wealth made by immigrants being channelled to their birthplaces: he gave a large legacy 'to the erection of a free school in Bingley where he was borne'.[3]

The increasing wealth of the leading citizens came partly from inland trade, and from the servicing of an increasingly wide hinterland by York's traders and craftsmen. When, in 1581-2, a new rector at Kirkby Misperton wanted an estimate for repairing his rectory, it was York carpenters and bricklayers he called on.[4] In 1590, after six years of pressure, the city secured a grant of fortnightly cattle fairs between Palm Sunday and Christmas, a frequency suggesting many potential customers.[5] In 1585 the merchants of York, Hull, Newcastle, Lynn, and Boston claimed to be supplying ten counties with seafish; and in 1597 York's corn purveyors were buying up grain as far afield as Norfolk and Cambridgeshire, supplying not only their fellow citizens but also Craven and Richmondshire.[6]

---

[1] B.I.H.R., prob. reg. xxiii, fo. 143; xxvii, fo. 541; xxxiv, fo. 171; Sellers, *York Merchants*, p. 288; Jordan, *Charities of Rural England*, p. 293.

[2] Purvis, 'Tudor Crockford'; Y.M.L., MS S3(4)a, p. 54.

[3] Drake, *Eboracum*, p. 495.

[4] J. S. Purvis, 'Dilapidations in parsonage property', *Y.A.J.* xxxvi (1944-7), 334-6.

[5] *Y.C.R.* viii. 81, 94, 106, 129; Y.C.A., B 30, fos. 188^r, 191^r; Richardson, *Medieval Fairs and Markets*, p. 19.

[6] *Y.C.R.* viii. 92 f.; Y.C.A., B 31, fos. 304-5.

Overseas trade also expanded as York and Hull, together with the other outports, staged a recovery against London's dominance. In 1578-9 York merchants were trading with Scotland, Spain, Rouen, Bordeaux (whence came much Gascon wine), Antwerp, Emden, Hamburg, Copenhagen, Lübeck, and Gdansk; and in 1579 they asserted that their 'greteste trafecke' was to Gdansk and the Baltic, 'for that we serve the northe partes with flax, and other commodities growing in this contree'.[1] The only comprehensive account surviving of York's overseas trade in Elizabeth's reign is the port book for the period Michaelmas 1602 to Easter 1603; it does not indicate any further widening of the merchants' trading area, but it does show a diversified pattern of trade. Rye, flax, and iron were imported from the Baltic, wine from Gascony, and a wide range of goods from Holland and Zeeland, including honey, Seville oil, paper, figs, frying pans, and soap. Exports were not so varied, consisting entirely of the old staples of lead and cloth, lead being exported to Bordeaux in return for wine, and shortcloths and kerseys to Bordeaux, La Rochelle, Middelburg, and Elblag.[2] The York merchants had to trade entirely from the port of Hull, but it did not prevent them from growing rich; in a renewed ship money dispute in 1596, when they tried to reduce their contribution to Hull, the Privy Council replied that 'we do not a little marvail hereat, considering the state of that citty and what benefyt yt taketh by that port'.[3]

The population, as well as wealth, of the city continued to increase, partly because the city was still lucky enough, or careful enough, not to suffer any serious epidemic. A 'sicknesse' in St. Denys's parish in 1591 gained only a slight hold, a widespread northern epidemic in 1593 did not enter the city, and neither did another major northern plague in 1597-8.[4] The parish registers show a continuing natural surplus of baptisms over burials in the 1580s and the 1590s, and although the poorer parishes without surviving registers may not have been in such a favourable position, continuing immigration must have helped to keep the total population

---

[1] P.R.O., E 190/307/12; Sellers, *York Mercers*, p. 209.
[2] P.R.O., E 190/311/11.   [3] *A.P.C. 1595-6*, pp. 210-11.
[4] Palliser, 'Epidemics in Tudor York', p. 52.

increasing. There is no satisfactory basis for an estimate of York's population between 1548 and the 1660s, but a very crude calculation for the decade 1601-10 suggests a total of the order of 11,500, representing a 45 per cent increase on the 1548 total, and—allowing for the catastrophic epidemics of the 1550s—suggesting a doubling of the city's population during Elizabeth's reign.[1]

The massive population increase, which was a general European phenomenon, had contradictory consequences. The larger numbers of consumers were a stimulus to trading activity and craft output. On the other hand they brought severe problems of overcrowding, law and order, and impoverishment. In a city like York, where the population had merely recovered to its fifteenth-century level, it might be thought that such problems would not have been acute, and that there would be plenty of available space on which to erect cheap housing for the extra people. This does not, however, seem to have happened. Few new houses were built in Elizabeth's reign, and the monastic sites did not become available for development. The consequence was the crowding of a swollen population into the already built-up areas, either by greater numbers per house, the subdivision of houses, or by the building of cheap cottages in yards and gardens. The process of subdivision began early—one messuage in Stonegate was before 1570 divided into four tenements—but it is documented more frequently by the turn of the century; an example is a messuage in High Petergate 'sometyme in the occupacon of John Geldard and now [1594] in severall tennants occupacons', six tenants being listed.[2] The overcrowding problem was one common to many large Elizabethan towns; both Norwich and Worcester, for example, accommodated most of their increased population within the existing housing stock.[3]

The number of very poor in the city seems to have increased; and times of grain shortage put a severe strain on the city's poor relief measures and food supplies. There were

[1] Calculations in Palliser, 'Social and economic history', pp. 26-35.

[2] Y.C.A., E 23, fo. 34^r; Y.M.L., Acc. 1966/2, 19, fo. 35^r.

[3] Pound, 'Social and trade structure of Norwich', p. 62; J. Campbell, 'Norwich', *Historic Towns*, ii, ed. M. D. Lobel (London, 1975), pp. 19 f.; Dyer, *Tudor Worcester*, pp. 164 f.

increased mortality rates, and even occasional deaths directly from starvation, during the nationwide harvest crises of 1586-8 and 1596-8; and the corporation had to seek for grain from distant counties.[1] Doubtless relief was never fully adequate, but genuine compassion was shown: in 1601 Widow Atkinson and her 'diverse small children' were homeless and in danger of 'starving this next winter', and the corporation ordered the Micklegate wardens to get her a home if they could.[2] On the other hand, responsibility was clearly limited to York's own poor. Those who received relief, it was ordered in 1591, must not beg in the streets, or they would be dealt with as rogues according to the statutes; while country beggars were all to be treated as rogues.[3] One has the impression that the slightest encouragement would bring swarms of paupers into the city; in 1599, as the assizes approached, many vagabonds and beggars flocked into Bootham, and the corporation suspected that they intended to pester the judges on their way from the King's Manor to Bootham Bar. The street was to be patrolled and cleared of beggars.[4]

Undoubtedly begging in the streets long remained a serious problem. When Henry Swinburne died in 1624 he provided that £500 should, if his son died under age, be distributed to the poor of the city 'for setting them on worke that they bee not so clamorous in the streets'.[5] The corporation need not be harshly judged for their repeated failure to prevent beggary, for no other town corporation was able to do so, and even the more elaborate schemes of Norwich in the 1570s and Salisbury in the 1620s had only short-term results.[6] More reprehensible, perhaps, was York's failure to tap its own growing wealth for civic improvements in Elizabeth's reign. Perhaps, as Ryther said, 'their common commodity' occupied the least part of the councillors' care. Even a scheme for piping water into the city, first mooted in 1552-3, did not come to fruition until 1616-28, had lapsed by 1634,

---

[1] See above, pp. 124, 191.   [2] Y.C.A., B 32, fo. 160[V].
[3] Y.C.A., B 30, fo. 237[r].   [4] Y.C.A., B 32, fo. 42[V].
[5] Derrett, *Henry Swinburne*, p. 10.
[6] J. F. Pound, *The Norwich Census of the Poor* (Norfolk Rec. Soc. xl, 1971), *passim*; Clark and Slack, *Crisis and Order in English Towns*, pp. 164-203; *Poverty in Early-Stuart Salisbury*, ed. P. Slack (Wilts. Rec. Soc. xxxi, 1975), pp. 1-15.

and was only renewed and completed after 1677.[1] Yet the
city fathers had much to be pleased with by the end of the
Queen's long reign. The city was prospering again after a long
depression, and the prosperity was beginning to be translated
into new, lofty and lavish merchants' houses, and into many
improvements and additional comforts in existing properties.
Even the 'common commodity' was not entirely neglected:
street-cleansing and street-lighting were both being placed on
a more regular basis than ever before.[2] If Camden and Speed
could judge the city as favourably as they did, there must
have been a sound basis of beauty and prosperity to justify
their praise.

[1] *Y.C.R.* v. 80; Y.C.A., E 40, No. 27; Wilson, 'Corporation of York', p. 169.
[2] Dickens, 'Tudor York', p. 119.

CONCLUSION

The shoes of our predecessors are too big for our
feet. . . . The inhabitants [of York] have many of
them forsaken it, and those who have not, she cannot
maintain. . . . Trade is decayed, the river become
unnavigable by reason of shelves. Leeds is nearer the
manufactures, and Hull more commodious for the
vending of them; so York is, in each respect, furthest
from the profit.

*Mayor and corporation of York, c.*1660[1]

Much recent work on local and provincial history has concerned the identification and study of 'communities', areas
within the realm and smaller than the realm which had a
coherent identity. It is clear that York, large though it was by
contemporary standards, was as much a single community as
any of the villages which have been studied with this concept
in mind. The freemen, those who held political and economic
power in York, had a coherent sense of identity, and they be-
haved with regard to their legal and fiscal rights, and the
boundaries within which their jurisdiction ran, much as any
village community did. There were, of course, close links
between county gentry and city aldermen, who were often
drawn from the ranks of the gentry; but York remained in
terms of its chartered rights and its property tenure an island
clearly separated from the countryside, and with a distinct
sense of identity. Within it, property could be freely transferred by sale or bequest, and power was related directly to
wealth and not to land-ownership, long pedigrees, or social
prestige.

It was a community which would strike a modern observer
as organized on an extremely inequitable and unstable basis,
with a paternal and autocratic corporation, the exclusion of

[1] Widdrington, *Analecta Eboracensia*, p. x, repr. in Thirsk and Cooper, *Seventeenth-Century Economic Documents*, p. 374.

non-freemen from any decision-making, and gross disparities of wealth. It is important, however, not to make anachronistic judgements on a system which plainly worked. The city's local governmental machinery remained essentially unchanged from 1396 to 1835, proving able to adapt within that framework to changing circumstances; and it was a fundamentally stable system in the sense that, during the Tudor century at least, it was not seriously challenged either from below or from outside. To say this is by no means to deny the existence of injustice, corruption, or extreme poverty, but to assert that contemporaries saw no fundamental flaws in the system, given their expectations of what government could and should achieve, and their acquiescence in the inevitability of poverty and inequality as part of the scheme of things.

One of the keys to stability in Tudor York was, paradoxically, the vast extent of population mobility. Life was always uncertain, and 'the authoritarianism of traditional social life and education practice becomes a little easier to understand when the youthfulness of so much of the community is borne in mind'.[1] The aldermen were literally as well as etymologically the older men, normally elected in their late forties at an age beyond the average expectation of life, and living to nearly seventy; they had the advantages of age and experience as well as chartered authority in governing the city. Much of the population was immigrant as well as youthful, for mortality was so heavy that, as in London, massive immigration was essential to keep the population from shrinking, and even more to allow it to grow. York was fortunate in having, in Cumbria and the Pennines, a mountainous region of high human and low agricultural fertility, which acted as a reservoir of immigrants. This made the stability provided by a self-elected corporation all the more necessary.

Furthermore, the oligarchy was an open one. At the broadest level it consisted of a freeman class taking in about half the adult male population, a higher proportion than in many other towns. The higher levels of government were also open, because of biological or financial failure on the part of many councillors. Many had no male heirs to follow them, or perhaps suffered the opposite fate of having too many children

[1] Laslett, *World we Have Lost*, p. 111.

to hand over a substantial legacy to any one son; or they
might suffer business failure, and in an age when 'ability' or
financial wealth was needed to enter the city council, it was
equally necessary to keep one there: several aldermen resigned because of poverty and were granted pensions. All of
these failures created openings for young men of ambition to
rise, by business acumen, luck, bequests from masters, or
marriages of rich widows, and to take up the vacant places.
Such openness must have eased some of the inevitable resent-
ments caused by the distribution of power and wealth, just as
—in a way that can no longer be measured—the teachings of
the church must have done. There are also indications that
the line between masters and servants was blurred, perhaps
because girls of all backgrounds went into service. Certainly
some councillors' daughters became servants, and the wife of
Councillor Martin Straker had herself been a servant in her
youth.[1]

The governing body were punctilious in exacting deference
and obedience in an almost schoolmasterly way, as perhaps
they had to when surrounded by the envious, the paupers,
and the adolescents. There were well-understood if unwritten
rules that citizens must doff their caps to the mayor and
aldermen and address them as 'Master', on no account using
their Christian name or the familiar pronoun 'thou'.[2] Any in-
subordination was liable to be visited by imprisonment at the
mayor's pleasure, whether the offender was a humble servant
or a wealthy master. In 1600 an ostler was thus punished for
abusing Laurence Edwards ('It is pitty that any such cater-
piller as he shold be a sheriff'), but a fortnight earlier a draper
was imprisoned for a similar offence. At a meeting of
parishioners to assess tax, he had said loudly and scornfully
that Alderman Birkeby 'doth no good nor will do no good in
the citty but to rase pore men in sessements'.[3] The corporation were equally zealous in enforcing subordination to other
officials of like status with themselves. When the Lord Lieutenant's secretary complained that a parish constable had

---

[1] Skaife, 'Civic officials', *sub* Mapples, Francis; B.I.H.R., prob. reg. xxviii,
fo. 172; *Y.C.R.* vi. 71.
[2] e.g. *Y.C.R.* iii. 9, 14, 20, 36; iv. 70; v. 55; Y.C.A., B 31, fo. 194[v].
[3] Y.C.A., B 32, fos. 118[v], 120[v].

insulted him, 'comparing him self with the same Mr. Thornborough and thowing him, and saying "I have money to pay
for my aile withall aswell as thow hast" ', the hapless constable was imprisoned at the mayor's pleasure.[1] Respect to
rank and office was exacted even after death: aldermen and
their wives expected to be buried according to their 'place',
'calling', or 'degree'. This apparently meant, as Robert
Hekkylton explained in his will, 'at the day of my buriall to
have my lord mayor and his brethren with the whole parish-
inge beinge householders accordinge to the auncient custome
of this cittie'. The concept of degree was, however, no monopoly of the élite. A saddler requested his executors to bring
up his 'poore children' 'according to their simple degrees'.[2]
York's was a deference society, in which social inequality was
accepted and was emphasized constantly, most of all in the
endless bowing and removal of hats.

The social cement was, in fact, strong. For a large city with
a mobile population, widespread ownership of weapons and
little policing, there was remarkably little serious disorder.
Provided, in fact, that the city fathers did their best to keep
the city governed and supplied they faced little opposition;
and this they generally managed to do. In the severe subsistence crisis of 1596–8 they ensured with difficulty supplies
of distant corn to feed the hungry populace, and during the
major epidemics sufficient councillors stayed at their posts to
prevent disorder.[3] The bonds of law and order strained but
did not snap. The larger English urban communities were
generally successful in preserving the social order in times of
crisis, as a recent survey of subsistence crises has emphasized.
'Given the very limited coercive power at their disposal, the
position of the ruling classes was upheld by a . . . complex of
relationships and expectations . . . it was of crucial importance for the maintenance of the social order that dearth was
not only met, but was *seen* to be met. . . . What is significant
is less that dearth in England provoked occasional outbreaks

---

[1] Loc. cit., fo. 165ʳ.
[2] B.I.H.R., prob. reg. xi, fo. 105; xxiv, fo. 236; xxxii, fo. 72; Dean and Chapter
probate reg. v, fos. 14, 101, 104.
[3] e.g. *Y.C.R.* v. 41–4; Y.C.A., B 32, fo. 340ʳ.

of disorder than that it led to so few.'[1] The 'complex of relationships and expectations' involved assumptions of right and
wrong attitudes and policies shared by rich and poor, attitudes
based on Christian teaching and on a sense of natural justice,
which cut across economic divisions and helped to unite
Yorkers.

The bonds linking the different strata of York's society
had to be strong, or there would have been much more disorder in a city which endured severe disruption of its traditional prosperity and way of life. Under the reigns of the
first four Tudors York suffered an economic depression
which gradually worsened, and which was compounded after
1536 by the negative effects of the Reformation. York shared
with Coventry, Lincoln, Winchester, and other cities an experience of the early Reformation which spelled economic
catastrophe. At the same time the city shared with its region
a sense of provincial grievance against a distant government
in Westminster, which was exacerbated by the ecclesiastical
policies of the Crown after 1534. The Pilgrimage of Grace
was a provincial as well as a religious protest, and it is significant that the citizens appear to have supported it almost
unanimously, from the poor commons to Lawson and most
of his fellow-aldermen, even though commons and corporation had been at odds over enclosures a few months before.
A major issue had overridden local divisions.

The potential for disorder was reduced in Elizabeth's
reign by economic recovery, stimulated by the permanent
presence of the Northern Council and Ecclesiastical Commission in the city from 1561. The Northern Council in particular was of inestimable value in drawing suitors to York; the
corporation bitterly regretted its loss in 1641, even though
they felt obliged to pay lip-service to the general dislike of
prerogative courts. The existence of the reconstituted Council, after 1537, was both a symptom and a cause of a decline
in the isolation and disaffection of the north as it gradually
became more integrated with England south of the Humber.
In 1536 the north was the region the most openly disaffected
to Crown policies; in 1569 the Rising of the Northern Earls

[1] J. Walter and K. Wrightson, 'Dearth and the social order in early modern
England', *Past and Present*, lxxi (1976), 22, 41 f.

showed how much that spirit had changed; and by 1603 the north as a whole was quiet and peaceful, apart from surviving lawlessness on the borders.

It would be, however, misleading to emphasize too much the elements of change in Tudor York at the expense of continuity. Change is naturally better recorded, since the absence of it is so rarely remarked upon; but it can distort the portrait of a city which in many ways, despite a religious revolution, remained much the same in 1603 as in 1485. One is reminded of W. T. MacCaffrey's wise words about the disadvantages of treating a single century and arbitrarily breaking 'into the mid-course of a stream of civic history', of being 'faced with the presence of those glacierlike elements in the city's history which change so slowly . . . that they cannot be measured in the brief span of a century'.[1]

At its most basic the continuity is best seen in a continuance of traditional ethics which were, if anything, re-emphasized after the Reformation, concepts of justice, charity and good governance. They were rarely spelled out baldly in the records, but can be glimpsed indirectly in complaints about abuses. Early Tudor citizens petitioning the equity courts, for example, frequently argued that a particular sheriff or mayor was preventing them from receiving justice in a city court. A century later, the epitaph on Alderman Thomas Harbert (1614) is even more striking, since if the family of an alderman could commission verses like these they could scarcely be accused of an outsider's prejudiced judgement:

> God takes the best whilst worse supply their room.

The writer goes on to describe Harbert as

> He whose white hand would touch no filthy bribe
>   Nor make good laws the sword of private ire. . . .
> Three things which in one man we seldom see
> Were joined in him, wit, wealth and honesty.[2]

These, however, are the commonplaces of the elderly of all periods; what are still more difficult to capture are the attitudes of the Tudor citizens to their city and region, to one another and to the structure of their society. How, specifically, did they see themselves within the overall framework of

[1] MacCaffrey, *Exeter 1540–1640*, p. 5.   [2] Drake, *Eboracum*, p. 299.

Christian ethics and the commonplace concepts of order, degree and so on which they shared with their fellow Englishmen?

In some respects, the citizens were plainly very 'insular'. They expected the corporation to defend their chartered liberties vigorously and even pedantically. The city fathers were judged by how vigorously they had maintained York's rights, privileges, and possessions unimpaired. George Kirk was mayor when, in 1495, the city finally lost the long-drawn-out dispute with the Vicars Choral over grazing rights, and sixteen years later it was still held against him when his turn for a second mayoralty came round.[1] The tenacity of privileges was, however, common to all Tudor officials and landowners, and did not reflect the insularity of the native against the outsider. Of York's freemen 70 per cent were immigrants, including 10 per cent from distant Cumbria. The bench of aldermen included Kirk himself from Lincolnshire, Sir Richard York from Berwick-upon-Tweed, and the brothers John and Robert Petty from Furness; and if they adopted a parochial attitude towards their territory that was what was expected of them.

Within the city there were many bonds to unite as well as to divide men of different backgrounds and levels of wealth, and to give cohesion to the civic community and, within it, to the smaller communities of neighbourhood and parish. Rich and poor lived in close proximity, and the almost universal attendance at church gave each parish a focus for a sense of community, supplemented before the dissolutions by the parish guilds. It is true that civic hospitality tended to be exercised only 'to the riche', as the corporation admitted in 1558, but difficult times could call forth generosity towards those in need, like the £100 remitted taxes which the corporation spent on corn and coals for the poor in 1555.[2] It would also be wrong to stress too much the inequality of the social structure as leading to exploitation; the more fair-minded councillors, subscribing to a paternalist view of society, accepted that those with fewer rights deserved special protection in return for their subordination. The labourers' guild received support from the corporation in

[1] *Y.C.R.* iii. 36; above, p. 65.　　　　[2] *Y.C.R.* v. 136 f., 177.

1593, who were concerned that such an organization had little protection from unfair competition; boat-owners were forbidden to employ labourers who had been 'blacked' by the guild's searchers.[1] A citizen who had slandered his female servant was made to do public penance in church and to ask her forgiveness, while another poor girl, wrongfully imprisoned on suspicion of infanticide, was granted financial compensation.[2] Such acts of simple justice must have eased the tensions produced by inequality. There was also a ready acceptance by the oligarchy of any man, however lowly in origin, who became prosperous and joined their ranks. When a local gentleman in 1500 wrote contemptuously to Mayor Neleson about Alderman Metcalf as 'a carle . . . comen lightly up and of smale substance', Neleson retorted that 'I and my Brether and all this Citie knaweth that he worshipfully hath been and born the charge as the Kyng's lieutenant within this Citie'; the mayoralty obliterated all baseness.[3]

The leading citizens and merchants were members of two worlds. On one plane, they were keen to claim equality with the local gentry, with whom indeed they were often related by ties of blood or marriage, and were eager to be considered gentlemen if not to attain to knighthood. On the other hand they shared with the poorer citizens and non-freemen a civic community which in some ways was a very different world from the agrarian society outside the city boundaries. In some respects it was a world of more opportunity; money could more easily be made in commerce than in agriculture, and could buy a man's way into civic government; property could more easily be bought, sold, and bequeathed outside the constraints of feudal tenure and primogeniture, since all messuages in the city were held directly of the king in free burgage, as near to freehold as might be. On the other hand, the city was in some ways a society with less freedom than the countryside. To practise a craft or trade brought a man under the control of corporation by-laws and usually of a craft guild as well. The corporation also legislated freely on all aspects of daily life, from good hygiene, refuse disposal, and prostitution, to gambling, prices of goods, and styles of

[1] Palliser, 'Trade gilds', p. 95.   [2] *Y.C.R.* vii. 164; viii. 31 f.
[3] *Y.C.R.* ii. 156; above, p. 94.

clothing permitted. It was one of the unspoken assumptions
of civic life that the corporation could and should intervene
in any and every aspect of life, and that legislation, if correctly worded and properly enforced, could solve most problems. It was in some ways a very optimistic view of the limits
of government, despite the pessimism about human nature
which the city fathers constantly voiced.

How, finally, did the corporation see themselves in time?
It has been shown that in the early Tudor period they complained, with some justice, of poverty and decay, looking
back to the vanished golden age of 1350–1450. The complaints continued, however, throughout the reigns of Elizabeth and James, when the city was manifestly recovering in
size, population, and wealth, and one suspects that 'decay'
had become an ingrained habit of mind. York was never again
to be quite so important in national and international commerce as it had been around 1400, but Elizabethan and
Stuart York was undoubtedly modestly prosperous, and the
short-term difficulties of the 1620s and 1640s, which York
shared with other English communities, were too readily
seized upon by the corporation as symptoms of irretrievable
decay. The despairing letter from the corporation to one of
their MPs about 1660, quoted at the head of this chapter,
came just before the hearth taxes showed that York had
recovered its old place as the second wealthiest provincial
town.[1] Nearly all the visitors to seventeenth-century York,
apart from the very critical Celia Fiennes, were impressed
by its beauty and air of prosperity; and the importance
attached by both sides in the civil war to the siege of 1644
testified to its importance as a northern capital as well as a
military stronghold. 'If York be lost', wrote Charles I to
Rupert on the eve of Marston Moor, 'I shall esteem my crown
little less', and so it proved. After the Restoration came the
residence of the second duke of Buckingham, prelude to the
city's role as a social capital in the eighteenth century; and
by the time that Defoe visited York it was well 'furnished
with provisions of every kind . . . the river being so navigable,
and so near the sea, the merchants here trade directly to what

---

[1] Hoskins, *Local History in England*, p. 239.

part of the world they will . . . they import their own wines from France and Portugal, and likewise their own deals and timber from Norway . . .'. York was once again an important centre of trade and commerce, as well as a burgeoning centre for county society.

BIBLIOGRAPHY

All the main manuscript classes which were found useful are listed, together with those printed sources consulted which have a direct bearing on York between 1485 and 1603. Comparative studies of other periods and communities, mentioned in the text, have not been listed. Page references after classes of records in the York Borthwick and City Archives relate to the guides by D. M. Smith and W. Giles respectively.

A. MANUSCRIPT SOURCES

i. British Library, London
    Add. 33595 (civic annals)
    Cotton Titus B. I
    Lansdowne 54, 110, 119 (Burghley Papers)
    Royal 17 C. III (Pickering's speech, 1558)

ii. Public Record Office, London
    C.1 (Early Chancery Proceedings)
    C.142 (Inquisitions Post Mortem)
    E.134 (Exchequer Depositions)
    E.178 (Exchequer Special Commissions)
    E.179 (Lay Subsidies)
    E.190 (Port Books)
    K.B.9 (King's Bench, Ancient Indictments)
    REQ.2 (Court of Requests Proceedings)
    S.P.12/117, no. 37 (census of inns, 1577)

iii. History of Parliament Trust, London
    Files of material for the forthcoming history of the period 1558–1603

iv. Trinity College, Cambridge
    0.4.33 (Henry Keep, 'Monumenta Eboracensia', c.1680)

v. Library of the Yorkshire Archaeological Society, Leeds
    Transcripts of registers and accounts for the York parishes of St. Denys, St. John, and St. Michael Spurriergate

vi. John Rylands Library, Manchester
    R 45818 (bill of lading, 1585)

vii. Bodleian Library, Oxford
 Dodsworth MSS (considerable Yorkshire material)
 Gough Yorks. 8 (civic annals)
 Jones 17 (project to aid decayed towns)
 Lat. Th. d. 15 (Parkyn's chronicle)
 Rawl. B 451 (wardmote court book)
 Rawl. C 886 (civic annals)

viii. Borthwick Institute of Historical Research, York
 High Commission Court Books (HC.AB.) (Smith 52)
 High Commission Cause Papers (HC.CP) (Smith 52)
 Cause Papers, Archiepiscopal Courts (CP) (Smith 57)
 Archbishop's Jurisdiction: Probate Records (Smith 155-7)
 Dean and Chapter Jurisdiction: Probate Records (Smith 158-61)
 Parish Records (registers and churchwardens' accounts) (Smith 187-8)

ix. York City Archives, York City Library
 Class B: House or Minute Books (Giles 21-2)
 Class C: Chamberlains' and Bridgemasters' Accounts (Giles 27-46)
 Class D: Freemen's and Apprentices' Records (Giles 53)
 Class E: Register Books (Giles 63-79)
 Class F: Minutes of Sessions of the Peace (Giles 85)
 York History Room: R. H. Skaife, 'Civic officials of York and parliamentary representatives', 3 MSS volumes

x. York Merchants Adventurers' Archives
 D 55-62, 82 sixteenth-century accounts
 D 74, 75 sixteenth-century correspondence

xi. York Merchant Taylors' Archives
 Box no. 1572 Apprentice book, 1606-1751

xii. York Minster Library
 Class F: Liberty of St. Peter
 Class L: Torre's MS notes on the city, 1691-4 (L1(8)); probate records
 Class M: probate records
 Class V: records of the Vicars Choral
 Class Y.1: city guild records
 Acc. 1966/2: churchwardens' accounts, St. Michael-le-Belfrey

B. PRIMARY PRINTED SOURCES

Acts of the Privy Council of England, ed. J. R. Dasent, 32 vols. (H.M.S.O., 1890-1907).
Bronnen tot de Geschiedenis van den Handel met Engeland, Schotland en Ierland, ed. H. J. Smit, 2 vols. (Rijks Geschiedkundige Publicatiën, 's-Gravenhage, 1942-50).
Calendar of Close Rolls

Calendar of Patent Rolls

Calendar of State Papers relating to Scotland and Mary Queen of Scots, 1547-1603, ed. J. Bain *et al.*, 12 vols. (Edinburgh and Glasgow, 1898-1952).

Calendar of State Papers Venetian

Camden, W., *Britannia* (London, 1586).

Britannia, ed. E. Gibson (London, 1695).

Certificates of the Commissioners appointed to Survey the Chantries, Guilds, Hospitals, etc., in the County of York, ed. W. Page, 2 vols. (Surtees Society, 1894-5).

Collectanea Topographica et Genealogica, ed. J. G. Nichols, 8 vols. (London, 1834-43).

'Collection of original letters from the Bishops to the Privy Council', ed. M. Bateson, *Camden Miscellany*, ix (Camden Society, 1895).

Court Rolls of the Manor of Acomb, ed. H. Richardson, i (Y.A.S.R.S., 1969).

Danziger Inventar, ed. P. Simon (Munich and Leipzig, 1913).

Diary of Lady Margaret Hoby 1599-1605, ed. D. M. Meads (London, 1930, no index).

Durham Household Book, ed. J. Raine (Surtees Society, 1844).

Early Yorkshire Schools, ed. A. F. Leach, i (Y.A.S.R.S., 1899).

Elderton, W., *Yorke, Yorke for my Monie* (London, 1584).

Excerpta Antiqua; or, a Collection of Original Manuscripts, ed. J. Croft (York, 1797).

Extracts from the Account Rolls of the Abbey of Durham, ed. J. T. Fowler, 3 vols. (Surtees Society, 1898-1901).

Extracts from the Municipal Records of the City of York, during the Reigns of Edward IV, Edward V, and Richard III, ed. R. Davies (London, 1843).

Fabric Rolls of York Minster, ed. J. Raine (Surtees Society, 1859).

Feet of Fines of the Tudor Period, ed. F. Collins, 4 vols. (Y.A.S.R.S., 1887-90).

Hansisches Urkundenbuch xi, ed. W. Stein (Munich and Leipzig, 1916).

Harrison, William, *Description of England in Shakespere's Youth*, ed. F. J. Furnivall, 2 vols. (New Shakespere Society, 1908).

Historical Manuscripts Commission:

   Calendar of the MSS of the Most Hon. the Marquis of Salisbury, 24 vols. (1883-1976).

   The MSS of his Grace the Duke of Rutland, 3 vols. (1888-94).

   Report on the MSS of the late R. R. Hastings, ed. J. Harley *et al.*, 2 vols. (1928-30).

   Calendar of the MSS of Major-General Lord Sackville . . . preserved at Knole, ed. A. P. Newton and F. J. Fisher, 2 vols. (1940-66).

Illustrations of British History, Biography and Manners, in the Reigns of Henry VIII, Edward VI, Mary, Elizabeth, and James I, ed. E. Lodge, 3 vols. (London, 1838 edn.).

Itinerary of John Leland, ed. L. T. Smith, 5 vols. (London, 1907-10).

Journals of all the Parliaments during the Reign of Queen Elizabeth, ed. S. d'Ewes (London, 1682).

King, John, *A Sermon Preached . . . the Queenes Day* (London, 1597).

Kingston upon Thames Register of Apprentices 1563-1713, ed. A. Daly (Surrey Record Society, 1974).

Letters and Papers, Foreign and Domestic, of the Reign of Henry VIII, ed. J. Gairdner *et al.*, 22 vols. (H.M.S.O., 1864-1932).

Life of Marmaduke Rawdon of York, ed. R. Davies (Camden Society, 1863).

Major, John, *A History of Greater Britain*, ed. A. Constable (Scottish Historical Society, 1892).

Miscellanea, vol. v, ed. F. W. Brooks (Y.A.S.R.S., 1951).

North Country Wills, ed. J. W. Clay, 2 vols. (Surtees Society, 1908-12).

Original Letters, illustrative of English History, ed. H. Ellis, 11 vols. (London, 1824-46).

Parish Register of All Saints' Church, Pavement, in the City of York, i, ed. T. M. Fisher (Y.P.R.S. 1935).

Parish Registers of Holy Trinity Church, Goodramgate, York, 1573-1812, ed. R. B. Cook (Y.P.R.S. 1911).

Parish Register of St. Crux, York, i, ed. R. B. Cook and Mrs F. Harrison (Y.P.R.S. 1922).

Parish Registers of St. Martin, Coney Street, York, 1557-1812, ed. R. B. Cook (Y.P.R.S. 1909).

Parish Registers of St. Martin-cum-Gregory, in the City of York, i, ed. E. Bulmer (York, 1893-5).

Parish Register of St. Mary, Bishophill Junior, York, 1602 to 1812, ed. F. Collins (Y.P.R.S. 1915).

Parish Register of St. Olave, York, i, ed. Mrs F. Harrison and W. J. Kaye (Y.P.R.S. 1923).

Plumpton Correspondence, ed. T. Stapleton (Camden Society, 1839).

Proceedings and Ordinances of the Privy Council of England, ed. N. H. Nicolas, vii (London, 1847).

'Proceedings connected with a remarkable charge of sorcery', ed. J. Raine, *Archaeological Journal* xvi (1859).

Register of Admissions to the Honourable Society of the Middle Temple, ed. H. A. C. Sturgess, 3 vols. (London, 1949).

Register of the Freemen of the City of York from the City Records, ed. F. Collins, 2 vols. (Surtees Society, 1897, 1900).

Register of the Guild of Corpus Christi in the City of York, ed. R. H. Skaife (Surtees Society, 1872).

Registers of St. Michael le Belfrey, York, i, ed. F. Collins (Y.P.R.S., 1899).

Regulations and Establishment of the Household of Henry Algernon Percy, the Fifth Earl of Northumberland, ed. T. Percy (London, 1827).

Relation, or rather a True Account, of the Island of England, ed. C. A. Sneyd (Camden Society, 1847).

Relazioni degli Ambasciatori Veneti al Senato, ed. E. Alberi, Serie i, vol. ii (Florence, 1840).

Report of the Royal Commission of 1552, ed. W. C. Richardson (Archives of British History and Culture, iii & iv, Morgantown, 1974).

Rymer, Thomas, *Foedera*, 20 vols. (London, 1704-35).

Sanctuarium Dunelmense et Sanctuarium Beverlacense, ed. J. Raine (Surtees Society, 1837).

Select XVI Century Causes in Tithe, ed. J. S. Purvis (Y.A.S.R.S., 1949).

Sidney Ironworks Accounts 1541-1573, ed. D. W. Crossley (Camden Society, 1975).

Speed, John, *The Theatre of the Empire of Great Britaine* (London, 1611).

Statutes of the Realm, 11 vols. (London, 1810-24).

Stow, John, *The Annales of England* (London, 1631 edn.).

'Subsidy roll for York and Ainsty', ed. E. Peacock (unsigned), *Y.A.J.* iv (1875-6).

Swinburn(e), Henry, *A Briefe Treatise of Testaments and Last Willes*, 1st edn. (London, 1590).

Tabeller over Skibsfart og Varetransport gennem Oresund 1497-1660, ed. N. A. Bang, i (Copenhagen and Leipzig, 1906).

Testamenta Eboracensia, ed. J. Raine *et al.*, 6 vols. (Surtees Society, 1836-1902).

Troubles of our Catholic Forefathers, related by Themselves, ed. J. Morris, 3 vols. (London, 1872-7).

Tudor Royal Proclamations, ed. P. L. Hughes and J. F. Larkin, 3 vols. (New Haven and London, 1964-9).

Valor Ecclesiasticus, ed. J. Caley, v (London, 1825).

Visitation Articles and Injunctions of the Period of the Reformation, ed. W. H. Frere and W. P. M. Kennedy, 3 vols. (Alcuin Club, 1910).

Wills and Administrations from the Knaresborough Court Rolls, ed. F. Collins, 2 vols. (Surtees Society, 1902-5).

York Civic Records, ed. A. Raine, 8 vols. (Y.A.S.R.S., 1939-53).

York Memorandum Book, ed. M. Sellers and J. Percy, 3 vols. (Surtees Society, 1912-73).

York Mercers and Merchant Adventurers, 1356-1917, ed. M. Sellers (Surtees Society, 1918).

York Plays: the Plays Performed by the Crafts or Mysteries of York on the Day of Corpus Christi, ed. L. T. Smith (Oxford, 1885).

Yorkshire Deeds, ed. W. Brown *et al.*, 10 vols. (Y.A.S.R.S., 1909-55).

Yorkshire Star Chamber Proceedings, ed. W. Brown *et al.*, 4 vols. (Y.A.S.R.S. 1909-27).

C. SECONDARY PRINTED SOURCES

Anglo, S., *Spectacle, Pageantry, and early Tudor Policy* (Oxford, 1969).

Aveling, J. C. H., 'Some aspects of Yorkshire Catholic recusant history, 1558-1791', in G. J. Cuming (1967) (q.v.).

— *Catholic Recusancy in the City of York 1558-1791* (Catholic Record Society, 1970).

Aylmer, G. E. and Cant, R., eds., *A History of York Minster* (Oxford, 1977).

Baddily, R., *The Life of Dr. Thomas Morton, late Bishop of Duresme*, completed by John Naylor (York, 1669).

Bean, J. M. W., *The Estates of the Percy Family 1416-1537* (Oxford, 1958).

Beckingsale, B. W., 'The characteristics of the Tudor North', *Northern History*, iv (1969).

Beresford, M. W., 'The lost villages of Yorkshire', *Y.A.J.* xxxvii (1948-51), xxxviii (1952-5).

Birt, H. N., *The Elizabethan Religious Settlement* (London, 1907).

Brooke, G. C., *English Coins* (London, 1942).

Burnet, Gilbert, *The History of the Reformation of the Church of England*, ed. E. Nares, 4 vols. (London, n.d.).

Campbell, Mildred, *The English Yeoman under Elizabeth and the Early Stuarts* (New Haven, 1942).

Cartwright, J. J., *Chapters in the History of Yorkshire* (Wakefield, 1872).

Challis, C. E., 'The ecclesiastical mints of the early Tudor period', *Northern History*, x (1975).

Claridge, M., *Margaret Clitherow* (London, 1966).

Clark, Peter, ed., *The Early Modern Town: a Reader* (London, 1976).

Clark, Peter and Slack, Paul, eds., *Crisis and Order in English Towns 1500-1700* (London, 1972).

Clarkson, L. A., 'The leather crafts in Tudor and Stuart England', *Agricultural History Review*, xiv (1966).

Clay, J. W., ed., *Familiae Minorum Gentium*, iii (Harleian Society, 1895).

Cliffe, J. T., *The Yorkshire Gentry from the Reformation to the Civil War* (London, 1969).

Cooper, T. P., *York: the Titles 'Lord Mayor' and 'Right Honourable'* (York, n.d.).

—— 'Some old York inns with special references to the "Star", Stonegate', *Associated Architectural Societies' Reports and Papers*, xxxix (1928-9).

Cowgill, U. M., 'Historical study of the season of birth in the city of York, England', *Nature*, ccix (1966).

—— 'Life and death in the sixteenth century in the city of York', *Population Studies*, xxi (1967).

—— 'The people of York: 1538-1812', *Scientific American*, ccxxii (1970).

Cross, Claire, *The Puritan Earl: the Life of Henry Hastings third Earl of Huntingdon 1536-1595* (London, 1966).

—— 'The economic problems of the see of York', in J. Thirsk, ed., *Land, Church, and People: Essays presented to Professor H. P. R. Finberg* (Reading, 1970).

Cuming, G. J., ed., *Studies in Church History: Volume IV: the Province of York* (Leiden, 1967).

Davies, C. S. L., 'The Pilgrimage of Grace reconsidered', *Past & Present*, xli (1968).

Davies, Robert, *A Memoir of the York Press* (Westminster, 1868).

— 'A memoir of Sir Thomas Herbert of Tinterne', *Y.A.J.* i (1870).

— *Walks through the City of York* (London, 1880).

Davis, Ralph, *The Trade and Shipping of Hull 1500-1700* (East Yorkshire Local History Society, 1964).

Derrett, J. D. M., *Henry Swinburne (? 1551-1624): Civil Lawyer of York* (Borth. P. xliv, 1973).

Dickens, A. G., 'Some popular reactions to the Edwardian Reformation in Yorkshire' and 'Sedition and conspiracy in Yorkshire during the later years of Henry VIII', *Y.A.J.* xxxiv (1938-9).

— 'The first stages of Romanist recusancy in Yorkshire, 1560-90', *Y.A.J.* xxxv (1940-3).

— 'A municipal dissolution of chantries at York, 1536', *Y.A.J.* xxxvi (1944-7).

— 'Robert Parkyn's narrative of the Reformation', *English Historical Review*, lxii (1947).

— 'The extent and character of recusancy in Yorkshire, 1604', *Y.A.J.* xxxvii (1948-51).

— *Robert Holgate: Archbishop of York and President of the King's Council in the North* (Borth. P. viii, 1955).

— *The Marian Reaction in the Diocese of York* (Borth. P. xi, xii, 1957).

— *Lollards and Protestants in the Diocese of York 1509-1558* (Oxford, 1959).

— 'Tudor York', in P. M. Tillott, *Victoria County History* (1961) (q.v.).

— 'The writers of Tudor Yorkshire', *Transactions of the Royal Historical Society*, 5th ser. xiii (1963).

— *The English Reformation* (London, 1964).

— 'Secular and religious motivation in the Pilgrimage of Grace', in G. J. Cuming (1967) (q.v.).

Dobson, R. B., 'The foundation of perpetual chantries by the citizens of medieval York', in G. J. Cuming (1967) (q.v.).

— 'Admissions to the freedom of the city of York in the later middle ages', *Econ. H.R.* 2nd ser. xxvi (1973).

— 'Urban decline in late medieval England', *Transactions of the Royal Historical Society*, 5th ser. xxvii (1977).

Dodds, M. H. and R., *The Pilgrimage of Grace 1536-1537 and the Exeter Conspiracy 1538*, 2 vols. (Cambridge, 1915).

Donaldson, G., *The First Trial of Mary, Queen of Scots* (London, 1969).

Drake, Francis, *Eboracum: or the History and Antiquities of the City of York* (London, 1736).

Duckham, B. F., *The Yorkshire Ouse: the History of a River Navigation* (Newton Abbot, 1967).

Duff, E. Gordon, *A Century of the English Book Trade: Short Notices of all Printers, Stationers, Book-binders . . . from 1457 to . . . 1557* (London, 1905).

Duff, E. Gordon, *The English Provincial Printers, Stationers and Book-binders to 1557* (Cambridge, 1912).

Ellis, I. P., 'The archbishop and the usurers', *Journal of Ecclesiastical History*, xxi (1970).

Elton, G. R., *Reform and Renewal: Thomas Cromwell and the Common Weal* (Cambridge, 1973).

English, B. A. and Barr, C. B. L., 'The records formerly in St. Mary's Tower, York', *Y.A.J.* xlii (1967-70).

Fallow, T. M. and McCall, H. B., *Yorkshire Church Plate*, 2 vols. (Y.A.S.R.S. extra series, 1912-15).

Fonblanque, E. B. de, *Annals of the House of Percy*, 2 vols. (London, 1887).

Gent, Thomas, *The Antient and Modern History of the Famous City of York* (York and London, 1730).

Giles, William, *Catalogue of the Charters . . . and other Books, Deeds and old Documents belonging to the Corporation of York* (York, 1909).

Hanham, A., *Richard III and his Early Historians 1483-1535* (Oxford, 1975).

Harrison, Frederick, *Life in a Medieval College* (London, 1952).

Harvey, John, *English Mediaeval Architects: a Biographical Dictionary down to 1550* (London, 1954).

— *York* (London, 1975).

Hatcher, J. and Barker, T. C., *A History of British Pewter* (London, 1974).

Heaton, H., *The Yorkshire Woollen and Worsted Industries from the Earliest Times up to the Industrial Revolution*, 2nd edn. (Oxford, 1965).

Henry, Louis, 'Some comments on Ursula M. Cowgill's article . . .', *Population Studies*, xxii (1968).

Hoskins, W. G., *Provincial England: Essays in Social and Economic History* (London, 1963).

— *Local History in England*, 2nd edn. (London, 1972).

Hutton, Barbara, 'Timber-framed houses in the Vale of York', *Medieval Archaeology* xvii (1973).

Ingledew, C. J. D., *The Ballads and Songs of Yorkshire* (London, 1860).

Johnson, Bernard P., *The Acts and Ordinances of the Company of Merchant Taylors in the City of York* (York, 1949).

Jordan, W. K., *The Charities of Rural England 1480-1660: the Aspirations and Achievements of the Rural Society* (London, 1961).

Kaye, W. J., 'Yorkshiremen who declined to take up their knighthood', *Y.A.J.* xxxi (1932-4).

Kendall, P. M., *Richard the Third* (London, 1955).

Kirby, J. F., *Winchester Scholars* (London, 1888).

Leach, A. F., *English Schools at the Reformation, 1546-8* (Westminster, 1896).

Lehmberg, S. E., *The Reformation Parliament 1529-1536* (Cambridge, 1970).

Marchant, R. A., *The Puritans and the Church Courts in the Diocese of York 1560–1642* (London, 1960).
— *The Church under the Law: Justice, Administration and Discipline in the Diocese of York 1560–1640* (Cambridge, 1969).
Metcalf, D. M., *Sylloge of Coins of the British Isles: 23: Ashmolean Museum, Oxford: Part III: Coins of Henry VII* (London, 1976).
Michel, F., *Histoire du Commerce et de la Navigation à Bordeaux*, 2 vols. (Bordeaux, 1867–70).
Mill, Anna J., 'The stations of the York Corpus Christi play', *Y.A.J.* xxxvii (1948–51).
Milner-White, E., *Sixteenth Century Glass in York Minster and in the Church of St. Michael-le-Belfrey* (Borth. P. xvii, 1960).
Mollett, M., *Le Commerce Maritime Normand à la Fin du Moyen Age* (Paris, 1952).
Neale, J. E., *The Elizabethan House of Commons* (London, 1949).
Nuttgens, P., *York: the Continuing City* (London, 1976).
Palliser, D. M., *The Reformation in York 1534–1553* (Borth. P. xl, 1971).
— 'The trade gilds of Tudor York', in P. Clark and P. Slack (1972) (q.v.).
— 'Epidemics in Tudor York', *Northern History*, viii (1973).
— 'York under the Tudors: the trading life of the Northern Capital', in A. Everitt, ed., *Perspectives in English Urban History* (London, 1973).
— 'The unions of parishes at York, 1547–86', *Y.A.J.* xlvi (1974).
— 'A hostile view of Elizabethan York', *York Historian* i (1976).
Palliser, D. M. and Selwyn, D. G., 'The stock of a York stationer, 1538', *The Library*, 5th ser. xxvii (1972).
Peck, Francis, *Desiderata Curiosa*, i (London, 1732).
Pevsner, N., *The Buildings of England: Yorkshire: York and the East Riding* (Harmondsworth, 1972).
Phythian-Adams, C., 'The economic and social structure', in *The Fabric of the Traditional Community* (Open University, Milton Keynes, 1977).
Poulson, G., *Beverlac; or, the Antiquities and History of the Town of Beverley* (London, 1829).
Purvis, J. S., *A Mediaeval Act Book, with some Account of Ecclesiastical Jurisdiction at York* (York, n.d.).
— 'Dilapidations in parsonage property', *Y.A.J.* xxxvi (1944–7).
— *Tudor Parish Documents of the Diocese of York* (Cambridge, 1948).
— *The Records of the Admiralty Court of York* (Borth. P. xxii, 1962).
— 'A York account roll for A.D. 1537–8', *Y.A.J.* xlii (1967–70).
Raine, Angelo, *History of St. Peter's School: York* (London, 1926).
— *Mediaeval York: a Topographical Survey based on Original Sources* (London, 1955).
Raine, James, *Historic Towns: York* (London, 1893).
Raistrick, A. and Jennings, B., *A History of Lead Mining in the Pennines* (London, 1965).

Ramsay, G. D., *English Overseas Trade during the Centuries of Emergence* (London, 1957).

Reid, Rachel, R., *The King's Council in the North* (London, 1921).

Richardson, H., *The Medieval Fairs and Markets of York* (Borth. P. xx, 1961).

Ritchie, C. I. A., *The Ecclesiastical Courts of York* (Arbroath, 1956).

Rowse, A. L., *The England of Elizabeth: the Structure of Society* (London, 1950).

R.C.H.M., *An Inventory of the Historical Monuments in the City of York*, 4 vols. (H.M.S.O. 1962-75).

Russell, Josiah C., *British Medieval Population* (Albuquerque, 1948).

Shaw, Patrick J., *An Old York Church: All Hallows in North Street* (York, 1908).

Shaw, William A., *The Knights of England*, 2 vols. (London, 1906).

Smith, David M., *A Guide to the Archive Collections in the Borthwick Institute of Historical Research*, Borthwick Texts and Calendars i (York, 1973).

Smith, Ralph B., *Land and Politics in the England of Henry VIII: The West Riding of Yorkshire: 1530-46* (Oxford, 1970).

Solloway, J., *The Alien Benedictines of York: being a Complete History of Holy Trinity Priory, York* (Leeds, 1910).

Sterry, W., *The Eton College Register 1441-1698* (Eton, 1943).

Stone, Lawrence, *Sculpture in Britain: the Middle Ages* (Harmondsworth, 1955).

— *Family and Fortune: Studies in Aristocratic Finance in the Sixteenth and Seventeenth Centuries* (Oxford, 1973).

Strype, J., *Ecclesiastical Memorials, relating chiefly to Religion, and the Reformation of it . . .* , 3 vols. (London, 1721).

Tenison, Eva M., *Elizabethan England: being the History of this Country 'in Relation to all Foreign Princes'*, 14 vols., privately pr. (Leamington, 1933-61).

Thomson, John A. F., *The Later Lollards 1414-1520* (Oxford, 1965).

Thoresby, Ralph, *Ducatus Leodiensis*, ed. T. D. Whitaker (Wakefield, 1816).

Tyler, P., *The Ecclesiastical Commission and Catholicism in the North, 1562-1577* (n.p., 1960).

— 'The significance of the Ecclesiastical Commission at York', *Northern History*, ii (1967).

Tytler, P. F., *England under the Reigns of Edward VI and Mary*, 2 vols. (London, 1839).

Venn, J. and J. A., *Alumni Cantabrigienses: Part I: from the Earliest Times to 1751*, 4 vols. (Cambridge, 1922-7).

Victoria History of the County of York, The, ed. W. Page, 3 vols. (London, 1907-13).

Victoria History of the County of York, The: East Riding, ed. K. J. Allison, 3 vols. (Oxford, 1969-76).

Victoria History of the County of York, The: North Riding, ed. W. Page, 2 vols. (London, 1914-23).

Victoria History of the County of York, The: The City of York, ed. P. M. Tillott, 1 vol. (Oxford, 1961).

Widdrington, T., *Analecta Eboracensia: or, Some Remaynes of the Ancient City of York*, ed. C. Caine (London, 1897).

Willan, T. S., *The Early History of the Russia Company, 1553-1603* (Manchester, 1956).

Williams, Neville, *Henry VIII and his Court* (London, 1973).

Willson, D. H., *King James VI and I* (London, 1956).

Wilson, J., *The English Martyrologe* (1608, repr. Amsterdam and New York, 1970).

Zins, H., *England and the Baltic in the Elizabethan Era* (Manchester, 1972).

D. UNPUBLISHED THESES

Bartlett, J. N., 'Some aspects of the economy of York in the later middle ages, 1300-1500', University of London Ph.D. thesis (1958).

Ives, E. W., 'Some aspects of the legal profession in the late fifteenth and early sixteenth centuries', University of London Ph.D. thesis (1955).

Kitching, C. J., 'Studies in the redistribution of collegiate and chantry property in the diocese and county of York at the dissolution', University of Durham Ph.D. thesis (1970).

Palliser, D. M., 'Some aspects of the social and economic history of York in the sixteenth century', University of Oxford D.Phil. thesis (1968).

Smith, R. B., 'A study of landed income and social structure in the West Riding of Yorkshire in the period 1535-46', University of Leeds Ph.D. thesis (1962).

Tyler, P., 'The administrative character of the Ecclesiastical Commission for the Province of York, 1561-1585', University of Oxford B.Litt. thesis (1960).

—— 'The Ecclesiastical Commission for the Province of York, 1561-1641', University of Oxford D.Phil. thesis (1965).

Wilson, B. M., 'The corporation of York, 1580-1660', University of York M.Phil. thesis (1967).

INDEX

To facilitate reference, key dates are included in some biographical entries, those of the holding of the offices of alderman (a.), archbishop (abp.), and lord president of the Northern Council (l.p.). Places within Yorkshire are, for convenience, located by Riding: East (E.R.), North (N.R.), and West (W.R.).

Acaster Selby (W.R.), 185
Acomb (W.R.), 99
Admiralty, Court of 4, 109, 147
advocates, 146, 263f.
advowsons, 229, 246
age, proof of, 123
agriculture, 7-10, 29, 185
Agrig, Robert, 33, 37, 143
Ainsty wapentake (W.R.), 7, 9, 15, 17, 30, 78f., 90, 129, 138, 167, 177, 185, 214n., 273
Aire, river, 9
ale, 166
alehouses and taverns, 16, 93, 167, 255, 259
aliens, 94, 130f., 147, 164, 170
Allyn, William (a. 1567-81), 63, 104, 246f.;
    William (councillor), 108
Amsterdam, 195
annals, civic, 64
Antwerp, 225, 284
apothecaries, 154, 161
Appleyarde, John, 123;
    Thomas I (a. 1548-80), 36n., 105;
    Thomas II (a. 1580-1600), 64, 78, 104f.
apprentices, apprenticeship, 128-31, 134, 147, 149f., 153f., 172, 195, 205, 212, 269, 272, 274, 276
appropriations, 229
Appylbe, Anthony, 163
archery, 20, 279
aristocracy, 12-18, 21, 120
armour, 77, 139
armourers, 155
artillery, 50
Aske family, 266;
    Robert, the 'Grand Captain', 50, 221, 235;
    Robert II, 266

Askwith, Robert I (a. 1577-97), 86, 95, 255;
    Robert II (a. 1602-23), 71n.;
    Thomas, 95
Atkinson, Widow, 286
attorneys, 109, 142, 263
Aughton (E.R.), 266
Augmentations, Court of, 237, 240
aulnage, 209
Aveling, J.C.H., 248, 256, 259

Babington plot, 56
Babthorpe family, 266;
    Sir William, 266
Bacon, Sir Francis, 44
bakers, 106, 150, 154, 158f., 166, 168, 205, 263
Baltic Sea, 187, 195-8, 272f., 278, 284
Bankhows, Thomas (a. 1511-21), 107, 141
Banyster, John, 246
baptism, 112f., 115-17, 119f., 258, 265
barbers and barber-surgeons, 130, 150, 154, 169
Barnard Castle, 134
Barnby-upon-Don (Barnby Dun) (W.R.), 181
Barrow-on-Humber, 132
Bartlett, J. Neville, 200f., 204, 211
Barton, John, 16n.;
    Thomas, 33n.
Bayne, Anne, 80;
    Francis, 80, 248
Beane, John (a. 1540-80), 18, 94, 96, 107, 132;
    Mary, 96
Becket, St. Thomas, 230
Beckingsale, B.W., 6
Beckwith family, 237;

Beckwith family (*cont.*)
   Sir Leonard, 18, 237;
   William (a. 1553–86), 36n., 63
Bedale (N.R.), 2, 188
bede-rolls, 228
beer, 166
Beeseley, Christopher, 102
beggars, 25, 76, 81, 144, 213–15, 275,
   286
bells, church, 228, 242
Belt family, 99;
   Leonard, 99;
   Sir Robert, 99;
   Sir William, 99
Bennett, Dr. John, 73
Bergen-op-Zoom, 195
Berwick-upon-Tweed, 47, 51, 109,
   140f., 160, 194, 294
Besby, John (a. 1510–11, 1533–5),
   132, 236n.
Beskwood Lodge (Notts), 42
Beverley (E.R.), 5n., 79, 183, 208,
   210, 272
Beysley, Reginald, 73, 109
Bingley (W.R.), 283
Birkeby, Alverey, 142, 264;
   James (a. 1585–1610), 38, 96f.,
   109f., 141f., 176n., 185, 263f., 290
Bishopthorpe (W.R.), 32, 254f.
Blackamore Hills, 10
blacksmiths, 155, 159
bladesmiths, 165, 171
Blads, James, 71n.
Blakeburn, Nicholas, 202
Blythburgh (Suffolk), 183
Boleyn, Queen Ann, 234
Bolton Priory (W.R.), 5n., 190
bonfires, 241f.
bookbinders, 169
books, 38, 169–71, 173, 228–30, 244,
   258, 264
booksellers, 169, 229
Bordeaux, 194–6, 284
Boroughbridge (W.R.), 2, 74, 186f.,
   189f., 199
Bossall (N.R.), 99
Boston (Lincs.), 2, 283
Bosworth, battle of, 42f., 215
Bovill, Sewall de (abp. 1256–8), 226
Bowes, Sir Martin, 58, 218f., 228,
   243f.
bowling alleys, 105

Bowrow, Henry, 33
bowyers, 102, 155
bread, 166, 168, 260
brewers, 167
brick, building in, 32f., 35, 171–3;
   bricklayers, 158, 171, 186;
   brickmakers, 173
Bridlington (E.R.), 5n., 191
Bristol, 1, 22, 60, 73, 82, 93, 106,
   128, 155, 158, 202, 206
Brooke, Christopher, 98;
   Robert (a. 1579–99), 36n., 86,
   176n.;
   Samuel, 98
Buckingham, duke of, *see* Villiers
building crafts, 154–8, 171–3, 186,
   192
Bulmer wapentake (N.R.), 9
Bunny, Richard, 217
Burghley House, 56;
   Burghley, Lords, *see* Cecil
burial places, 161, 228, 230, 236, 244
Burley, John, 86
Burton, Henry, 276f.
Bustardhall (W.R.), 266
butchers, 63, 86, 106f., 149, 154,
   158f., 164, 168, 180, 256, 258,
   263
butter trade, 186
Byland Abbey (N.R.), 5n., 18
Byrnand, Richard, 254;
   William, 74, 247

Calais, 210, 276
Cambridge, city of, 182, 272;
   University, 176
Cambridgeshire, 249, 283
Camden, William, 1, 7f., 22, 26f., 267,
   287
Campbell, Mildred, 130
Campveere, 195
candles, 154, 165, 180, 193, 245
Canterbury, 45, 128, 221, 248, 261
cappers, 94, 98, 151, 158
caps and hats, doffing of, 134, 291
carders, cardmakers, 162, 209
Carlisle, city of, 15;
   diocese of, 5, 13
carpenters, 32f., 130, 158f., 171–3,
   186, 206
carpet weaving, 131;
   see also coverlet making

carriers, 161, 193, 272
carvers, 171, 173
Castle Howard (N.R.), 161
Catholic reaction, 241-3, 274
Catholic survivalism, 242-8, 254, 258
Catholicism, Roman, 226-35
Catterton (W.R.), 18
cattle, 8, 29, 163, 181, 183, 208, 283
Cawthorne (N.R.), 132
Caxton, William, 144
Cecil, David, 109;
    Robert, 1st Earl of Salisbury, 76;
    Thomas, 2nd Baron Burghley (l.p.
        1599-1603), 20;
    William, 1st Baron Burghley, 13,
        20, 39, 54f., 261, 273, 281
chamber pots, 27, 37
Chancery, Court of, vii, 41, 49, 66
chantries and cantarists, 33, 51, 175,
        206, 213, 217, 220f., 227f.,
        230-2, 234, 236, 239, 243, 278;
    chantry commissioners, 111, 239
Chapman, John, 141, 190
chapmen, 159, 161, 184, 272
charcoal-burning, 9
charitable bequests, 132, 141f., 144,
        282f.
Charles I, 98, 296;
    Charles II, 56
Chester, city of, 15, 93, 151, 155, 158,
        174, 203;
    diocese of, 4f., 99
children, 97, 115-22, 175f., 289f.,
        291
chimneys, 33, 35
Cholmeley family, 266;
    Sir Richard, 266
Christmas festivities, 117, 247
churches, bequests to, 132, 228, 230
churches, parish, see York
churching, 120
churchyards, trading in, 184
Clark, Peter A., 131
clergy, 5, 13, 31, 33, 37, 66, 98f.,
        140, 142f., 146, 155, 175, 177,
        226-59
Cleveland (N.R.), 10
Cleves (Kleve), 51
Cliffe, J.T., 15, 18
Clifford family, earls of Cumberland,
        14;
    Henry de, 14th baron, 60;

George, 3rd earl, 20, 102
Clifton (N.R.), 30, 181, 266
Clitherow, Margaret, 248, 256
cloth industry, 8, 51, 129, 154, 162f.,
        201, 208-11, 218, 252, 260,
        271, 275f.
clothing, 37
cloth trade, 63, 180, 187, 194-6,
        198f., 209-11, 272, 284
coal-mining, 8, 273;
    coal trade, 187, 194, 199, 273,
        294
cobblers, 100
Cockermouth (Cumb.), 2, 163
Cockersand Abbey (Lancs.), 5
cock-fighting, 20
Cocklodge (N.R.), 44
Cok, Thomas, 33
Colan, John and Herman, 164
Cologne, see Köln
Colyns, Martin, 142
Colynson, Robert, 149
Common Pleas, court of, 17, 41, 74
communicants, 111f., 258f.
Concett, Christopher (a. 1597-1615),
        104
Conisbrough (W.R.), 12
Constable family, 15f., 20, 266;
    Sir Marmaduke, 266;
    Sir Robert, 16
Cook(e), Francis, 142;
    Miles, 69f.
cooks, 168, 179
Copenhagen, 284
Copmanthorpe (W.R.), 30
cordwainers, 88, 143, 154, 158f.,
        163f., 174, 180, 184
corn merchants, 159, 161, 190f.
corn supplies, 8, 80, 124, 135, 141,
        161, 168, 181, 183-5, 187f.,
        190f., 194, 196, 198, 270, 273,
        283, 286, 291, 294
Cornwall, 3
corrodies, 227
Cotam, Sir Roger, 43
Cotswold, 10, 210
Cottrell, James, 86
Council in the Northern Parts, King's,
        vii, 4, 6f., 17-20, 28, 42, 45,
        48-51, 53-6, 61, 73f., 81, 89,
        92, 105, 108f., 139f., 146f.,
        166f., 235, 245, 247, 254-7,

Council in the Northern Parts (*cont.*)
    261-5, 275, 279, 281, 292;
    lords president of, *see* Cecil,
    Hastings, Holgate, Hutton,
    Manners, Radcliffe, Sheffield,
    Talbot, Wentworth, Young
Coupland, William (a. 1549-69), 36n.,
    71, 142, 144, 244
Coventry, 56, 98, 111, 137f., 155,
    158, 202, 211, 239, 279, 292
Coverham Abbey (N.R.), 5n.
coverlet making, 209-11, 218, 260
Cowgill, Ursula M., 115-17, 120f.
Cox. J.C., 112
Cranmer, Archbishop Thomas, 238
Craven (W.R.), 14, 189f., 283
Craven, William, 36
crime, 44, 79f., 143f., 148, 182, 295
Criplyng, Robert (a. 1576-80), 102,
    104, 247, 254f.
Cromwell, Thomas, 9, 47f., 55, 112,
    135, 167, 179, 188, 190, 234f.
Crowle (Lincs.), 183
crown lands, 12-14
Cumberland, Cumbria, 3f., 42, 129f.,
    183, 289, 294
Cundall (N.R.), 104
Cure, William (a. 1517, 1521-3), 46,
    67
currency, 196, 221;
    see also York, city of: mints
curriers, 154, 163
cutlers, 143, 165

Danzig, *see* Gdansk
Darcy, Thomas Lord, 13, 170, 216
Davies, Robert, 170
Dawson, Thomas, 192
dearths, 122-5, 191, 198, 285f., 291
Defoe, Daniel, 296f.
Deighton (E.R.), 266
demography, *see* population
Derbyshire, 189
Derwent, river, 9
deserted villages, 11, 213f.
Devereux, Robert, 2nd earl of Essex,
    102
Devon, 3
Dewsbury (W.R.), 185
Dickens, A.G., 6, 61, 69, 127, 233,
    249, 257
Dickinson, Christopher, 187

Dishforth (N.R.), 21
Dobson, R. Barrie, ix, 202-4, 206
Dodds, M.H. and R., 170
Don, river, 9, 12
Doncaster (W.R.), 12, 17, 95, 185
Donne, John, 98
Dorchester (Dorset), 1
Dorset, 3
Drake, Francis, 100, 205, 220, 226
drapers, 33, 106f., 142f., 152, 158f.,
    164, 176, 182, 210, 263, 265,
    272, 290
Drawswerde, Thomas (a. 1508-29), 46,
    140, 175
Drax (W.R.), 5n., 266
Driffield (E.R.), 266
Dringhouses (W.R.), 30, 266
Drypool (E.R.), 191
Duckham, Baron F., 188
Dudley, John, duke of
    Northumberland, 218
Duff, E. Gordon, 169f.
Durham Cathedral, 238;
    city, 45, 221;
    county, 276;
    diocese, 5, 99;
    Priory, 5, 79, 160, 184, 209
'Dutch' immigrants, 130f., 170, 233,
    275
Dyconson, Michael, 148
Dyer, Alan D., vii f., 16
dyers, 149, 162
Dyneley, John (a. 1570-79), 102,
    247f., 254

earl marshal, court of, 61
Easby Abbey (N.R.), 5n.
Eastburn (E.R.), 266
East Indies, 195
Eastland Company, 197f.
Eastrington (E.R.), 100
Ecclesiastical Commission, *see* York,
    province of
Edinburgh, 1, 53
education, 174-6, 222f., 239, 255,
    274
Edward I, 40, 59;
    Edward IV, 41;
    Edward VI, 52, 218f., 238-41
Edwards, Laurence, 290
Edwin, King, 22
Elblag (Elbing), 197f., 284

Elderton, William, 260, 279
elections, municipal, 45f., 64–72, 80;
    parliamentary, 3f., 15, 20, 47, 90
'Elisabeth', a carder, 162
Elizabeth I, 17, 53–6, 59, 72, 81, 201,
    223, 241, 243, 260–2, 267, 270,
    278f., 282
Ellerker, Sir John, 15
Ellerton Priory (E.R.), 5n.
Elvington (E.R.), 186
Elwald, Robert (a. 1533–4, 1535–49),
    63
Emden, 195, 284
Emperor, Holy Roman, ambassador to,
    52
enclosures, of lands, 29, 35, 45, 49,
    80, 84, 293;
    of rights of way, 280
epidemics and plagues, 21, 25, 53, 55,
    81f., 117f., 122–5, 127, 133,
    144, 161, 207f., 212, 215, 220,
    223–5, 260, 267f., 274, 284,
    291
epitaphs, funerary, 25, 293
escheator, 63, 79
Escrick (E.R.), 186
Essex, earl of, see Devereux
Eton College, 176
Eure family, 20;
    Lord William, 102
Everitt, Alan, 184, 271
Evers, George, 121
Exchequer, royal, 41, 74, 216
excommunication, 259
executions, 50, 55, 182, 233, 238,
    257f., 277
Exelby, Edward, 21
Exeter, vii, 29, 69, 82, 93, 106, 137f.,
    151, 155, 158, 178, 202, 277
Eynns, Sir Thomas, 28, 32

Fairfax family, 15, 20, 88;
    Sir Guy, 17;
    Thomas, 17;
    Sir Thomas, 28, 177, 280;
    William, 17, 74
fairs, 51, 166, 181–5, 255, 271f., 283
family reconstitution, 114
Fawcett, Edward (a. 1596–1602), 108
Fawkes, Edward, 140;
    Guy, 140;
    William, 102, 140

Fearne, John, 141
fee-farms, urban, 12, 48, 58, 85, 203,
    205, 207, 209, 215f., 218, 260
feltmakers, 151
fenland, 9
Fiennes, Celia, 169n., 296
Fifeshire, 199
firehouses, 133
fires, 23
Fisher, Isabel, 33
fishermen, 154, 159, 168f., 191f.
fishgarths, 188, 218
fishmongers, 140, 168f., 176, 192f.,
    205
fish trade, 151, 169, 180, 183f., 187f.,
    191f., 195, 198f., 273, 283
Fitzroy, Henry, duke of Richmond,
    109
Flamborough (E.R.), 16, 192
Flanders, 194f.
flax, 184, 198, 222f., 284
fletchers, 155
floods, 2f., 9, 266f.
foodstuffs, 154–7, 166–9, 179–81,
    183–8, 190–6
'foreigners', 147, 179f., 182, 187,
    189, 270
Forster, Gordon C.F., 19
Fortescue, Sir John, 39, 76
Foss, river, 2, 23–6, 139, 151
Foster, William, 172
founders, 143, 183
Fountains Abbey (W.R.), 5n., 8, 18,
    190
France, Frenchmen, 57, 114, 130,
    141, 170, 196, 297
freemen, passim
friaries, see religious houses; York
Friesland, 195f.
Frobisher, Sir Martin, 279
fuel, 161, 183, 187, 194, 208, 210,
    273
Fulford (E.R.), 30, 266
fullers, 149, 162, 209
funerals, 230, 291;
    funeral doles, 144, 202, 213
Furness (Lancs.), 294;
    Abbey, 5, 172
furnishings, church, 186, 192, 230,
    232, 236, 238f., 241–4, 246,
    258
furniture, domestic, 36–8, 144, 173,
    195f., 278

Gachet, John, 141
gallows, 26, 88
Galtres Forest (N.R.), 9, 88
gaol fever, 274;
   gaols, *see* prisons
Gargrave, Sir Thomas, 13, 54f., 73,
   261f.
Gascoigne family, 15, 121;
   William, 121;
   Sir William, 74
Gascony, 160, 195f., 211, 284
Gateforth (W.R.), 104
Gawthorpe (W.R.), 74
Gayle, Francis, 99;
   George (a. 1529-56), 49, 52, 62,
   92, 99, 108, 141, 237
Gdansk (Danzig), 194, 197f., 273, 284
Geldard, John, 285
Genoa, 199
gentlemen, gentry, 15-21, 27f., 41,
   73f., 95-7, 99-103, 105-7, 110,
   120f., 132, 148, 171, 173, 214,
   217, 226, 244, 252f., 261, 263,
   266, 271, 274, 279, 283, 288,
   295
Germany, Germans, 40, 51, 164, 166,
   195f.
Gibson, William, 256f., 281
Gilling Castle (N.R.), 186
Gilliot, Sir John (a. 1487-1510), 101,
   105, 141, 195
girdlers, 165
Girdlyngton, Nicholas, 86
glass windows, 35f., 230, 232, 241f.,
   255, 278
glaziers, 172, 186
Gloucester, city of, 99, 213;
   duke of, *see* Richard III
glovers, 98, 158f., 161, 163f., 263
Godfray, Anne, 132, 144
Goes, Hugo, 170
goldsmiths, 37, 106, 108, 141, 164f.,
   182, 228, 272
Goldthorpe, Richard (a. 1555-60),
   142, 237
Gray, Thomas (a. 1492-1514), 107
Great North Road, 2, 17, 54, 271
Gresham, Sir Richard, 190, 221, 236
Grey, Lady Jane, 52
Greyn, John, 161
Grindal, Edmund (abp. 1570-6),
   245-8, 255, 258, 270

grocers, 161, 193
Grosmont Priory (N.R.), 5n.
guilds, craft and trade, viii, 23, 32, 44,
   62, 68-70, 85, 88, 111, 130f.,
   135, 149-73, 180, 184, 189,
   205, 209, 212, 224, 255, 274,
   295; *see also individual crafts*
guilds, parish, 150, 231, 239, 294
guilds, socio-religious, 23, 150, 220f.,
   239;
   Corpus Christi Guild, 135, 170,
   239;
   Guild of SS. Christopher and
   George, 49, 135, 239
Guisborough Priory (N.R.), 5n.
gunpowder, 281

haberdashers, 106, 142, 151, 159
Hackness (N.R.), 19
Hair, P.E.H., 118
Halifax (W.R.), 208-10, 233, 282
Hall family, 21, 95;
   George, 95;
   Henry (a. 1598-1620), 95;
   Jane, 245, 267;
   Michael, 95;
   Ralph (a. 1556-77), 95, 244;
   Robert, of Leventhorpe, 95;
   Robert (a. 1538-65), 36, 50,
   52, 95, 142, 200, 245;
   William (two), 95
Hallamshire (W.R.), 14
Hamburg, 197, 278, 284
Hampshire, 276
Hanham, Alison, 42f.
Hanseatic League, 38, 196f., 278
Harbert, Christopher I (a. 1568-90),
   36n., 63, 94, 99, 193, 247, 255;
   Christopher II, 257;
   Christopher III, 99;
   Thomas (a. 1599-1614), 99, 257,
   293
Harper family, 237;
   Thomas (a. 1565-7), 105
Har(r)ington, Harryngton, John, 100;
   William (a. 1531-40), 62, 102, 107f.
Harrison, John, 193;
   William, 31
harvests, 118, 122-5, 286
Harvey, John H., 202
Hastings, Henry, 3rd earl of Huntingdon
   (l.p. 1572-95), 17, 54-6, 139,

Hastings, Henry (*cont.*)
    142, 172, 247f., 254f., 258,
    263, 270, 272, 277f., 281
Hatfield, H. Chase, 9, 12
hatters, 142
Healaugh (W.R.), 5n., 18, 50, 235,
    253
Heath, Nicholas (abp. 1555-9), 243
Hekkylton, Robert (a. 1537/8-68),
    291
Helleiner, K.F., 125
Helmsley (N.R.), 12, 14, 48
hemp, 183, 193, 198, 273, 276
Henry VII, 6, 13, 42-5, 59f., 80, 83,
    87, 101, 111, 201, 203, 206f.,
    215;
    Henry VIII, 6, 12f., 45-50, 59,
    68f., 80, 109, 210, 221, 234-7
Henry, Prince of Wales, 98
Heslington (E.R.), 28, 30, 32, 104,
    123
Heworth (N.R.), 30f., 181
Hewton, Richard, 143n., 162, 165
Hexham, 190
Hexter, J.H., 6
Higden, Brian, 214, 216
Hildyard, William, 74
Hinderskelfe (N.R.), 161
Hoby, Lady Margaret, 19f.;
    Sir Thomas, 20
Hogeson, John (a. 1528-48), 62
Holderness (E.R.), 10, 12, 135, 183,
    190f.
Holgate (W.R.), 30
Holgate, Barbara, 121;
    Robert (l.p. 1538-49, abp. 1545-
    54), 13, 50f., 54, 61, 92n., 121,
    222, 253, 274
Holland, 129, 195, 284
Holme, William (a. 1540-58), 36, 53,
    58, 109, 190, 218-20
honours, lordship of, 12
Hooper, Bishop John, 253
hops, 196
horses, 29, 161, 171, 181, 183;
    horse-racing, 15, 20
hosiers, 106, 151, 158, 164
Hoskins, W.G., ix, 154
households, 113f.
house rents, 205f., 211f., 214f., 219,
    221, 260f.
Houses of Correction, 275f.

housing, 1, 11, 19, 22, 25-9, 31-8,
    104f., 133, 171-3, 205f., 212-
    15, 221, 236, 239, 260, 265,
    278, 285, 287;
    decay of, 51, 63, 214f., 220, 260;
    subdivision of, 133, 275, 285
Howard, John, 276
Howards, earls of Surrey and dukes of
    Norfolk:
    John, 1st duke, 43;
    Thomas I, earl of Surrey and 2nd
    duke, 45, 135;
    Thomas II, earl of Surrey and 3rd
    duke, 50, 75
Howden (E.R.), 100, 166, 182, 272
Hull, Kingston-upon-, 2, 7, 19, 38, 52,
    56, 76, 95, 101, 129, 148, 155,
    160f., 166, 186f., 191-8, 200,
    204, 211, 268f., 271-4, 276,
    281-4, 288
Humber, river, 2f., 6, 9f., 185, 189,
    191, 271, 292
Huntingdon, earl of, *see* Hastings
Huntingdon (N.R.), 185
husbandmen, 95, 186
Hutton, Barbara, 11;
    Matthew (abp. 1595-1606, l.p.
    1596-9), 102, 245-8
Hydwyn, John, 71n.

Iceland, 198f., 211
illegitimacy, 119, 147
immigration, *see* population
infant mortality, 115, 119f.
inflation, 13, 73, 84, 143, 161, 224f.,
    263, 282
inheritance customs, 8, 142
innholders, 94, 107, 154, 166f.
inns, 4, 166f., 171, 184, 262f., 271
inventories, probate, 33-8, 141-3, 165
Ireland, 57, 199
iron mining, 15;
    trade in, 15, 184, 186-8, 192f.,
    197-9, 284
ironmongers, 150
Italy, 19, 40, 199

Jackson, Thomas (a. 1586-1611), 104
Jakson, Peter (a. 1522-31), 141
James I, 21, 32, 56f., 98, 101
Jameson, Thomas, 233
'Jenet, old', 162

jerseyman, 132
'John, dumb', 215
John, King, 207
joiners, 159, 171, 173
Jordan, W.K., 86, 141, 213, 282
journeymen, 134, 149f., 212
justices of the peace, 16, 59f., 62, 79,
    81, 109

Keep, Henry, 220, 236
Kendal, 129
Kendall, P.M., 42
Kent, 40, 132, 192, 249n.
Kente, Thomas, 123
King, John, 191, 281
King's Bench, court of, 17, 41
King's Lynn, 2, 155, 191, 194, 283
Kingston-upon-Hull, see Hull
Kingston-upon-Thames (Surrey), 272n.
Kinsley Hall (W.R.), 261
Kirk, George (a. 1491-1514), 65, 294
Kirkby Misperton (N.R.), 283
Kirkham Priory (E.R.), 5n.
Kirkstall Abbey (W.R.), 5n.
Knapton (W.R.), 30
Knaresborough (W.R.), 2, 5n., 12, 74,
    254
knighthood, knights, 44, 57, 101, 295
Köln (Cologne), 197

labourers, 118, 144, 159, 161, 269,
    276, 284f.
Lambeth, 5
Lancashire, 2, 4, 129, 133f., 183, 276
Lancaster, duchy of, 12, 17
Lancaster, Nicholas (a. 1484-1501),
    62
Lapland, 197
La Rochelle, 284
Lavenham (Suffolk), 208, 210
law enforcement, 15f., 79-81, 285,
    291f.
Lawson, Sir George (a. 1527-43), 47-9,
    51f., 62, 99, 101, 109f., 135,
    140-2, 190f., 235, 237;
    Thomas (a. 1560-68), 99, 104,
    266
lawyers, 16f., 20, 98, 101, 106, 146f.,
    177, 226, 261, 263f.
Layton family, 266;
    Richard, 167, 179
lead mining, 8, 189f.;

trade in, 2, 129, 160, 186-90,
    194-6, 200, 209f., 239, 272,
    284
leather trade and industry, 8, 154-8,
    162f., 180, 183, 199, 218, 269,
    273
Leconfield (E.R.), 14, 186
Lee, Edward (abp. 1531-44), 13,
    226f.;
    Dr. Roger, 141
Leeds (W.R.), 9f., 95, 163, 192, 208-
    10, 268, 282, 288
Leicester, 29, 68, 137f., 154f., 158,
    178
Leicestershire, 191
Leventhorpe (W.R.), 21, 95
Lewes, John (a. 1548-53), 36, 64
liberties, 5, 26, 88-90, 146, 153, 166,
    177
Lichfield, diocese of, 99
Lincoln, 48, 82, 215f., 261, 292
Lincolnshire, 9f., 135, 183, 190f., 294
literacy, 173f., 230
Litster, Lytster, John, 33, 37, 142;
    Thomas, 143n.
livery and maintenance, 15-17
loan funds, revolving, 86, 150, 283
locksmiths, 165, 171
Lollardy, 232
Lombardy, 199
London, 2, 4, 22, 24, 27, 45f., 50, 53,
    56, 58, 65, 72, 75, 81, 87, 97f.,
    100, 112, 114, 127, 147, 151,
    160f., 164-6, 172, 176, 179,
    183, 185, 187, 190-4, 211, 218,
    221, 228, 231, 236, 252, 257,
    260, 269, 272, 276, 279, 284,
    289
Long Marston (W.R.), 99; see also
    Marston Moor
Long Melford (Suffolk), 210
Lorimers, 171
lottery, 265
Louth (Lincs.), 182
Lovell, Sir Thomas, 216
Lübeck, 278, 284

MacCaffrey, Wallace T., viif., 293
magic, 232f.
Maitland, F.W., 66
Major (Mair), John, 22
malnutrition, 117f.

malt trade and industry, 9, 160, 167, 180f., 184, 191, 224
Maltby, Christopher (a. 1580-5), 164, 193
Malton (N.R.), 5n.
Mankyn, Thomas, 148
Man(n)ers, Agnes, 175, 228
Manners family, lords Roos and earls of Rutland, 14f., 207;
    Henry, 2nd earl (l.p. 1561-4), 262;
    Thomas, 1st earl, 12, 15, 48, 216
manors, lordship of, 11-14, 94, 103, 205, 266, 278, 282
mariners (sailors), 56, 106, 143, 155, 161, 188
markets, viii, 51, 63, 179-85, 211, 255, 271;
    tolls, 25, 75, 85, 183, 219, 270
marriage, 96f., 101f., 121f., 150, 238, 256, 264
Marser, Thomas, 165n.
Marshall, Thomas, 21
Marshland, 9, 183, 194
Marston Moor, battle of, 296
Marton Priory (N.R.), 5n.
Mary I, 40, 52f., 218f., 223, 241-3
Mary Queen of Scots, 54
Masham (N.R.), 95
masons, 76, 107, 171f., 206
Maunsell, William, 142
May, Henry (a. 1581-96), 36n., 80, 256
Meares (Meres), Lawrence, 257
measurement, units of, 200
Meaux Abbey (E.R.), 5n.
medicine, 20
Mediterranean Sea, 160
mercers, 21, 149, 158f., 161, 232
merchants, *passim*;
    Merchants Adventurers, of England, 160, 195, 199, 269;
    of York, 151, 185, 273, 279
Metcalf(e), John (a. 1496-1502), 94, 295;
    Mrs., 248
Micklethwaite, Ralph, 132
Middelburg, 195, 284
Middleham (N.R.), 185
Middlethorpe (W.R.), 30
Middleton (N.R.), 21
midwives, 64, 120
migration, *see* population

Miller, Edward, 61, 202
millers, 69, 154, 158f., 168
minstrels (waits), 75, 155, 265, 269, 278
monasteries, *see under individual names and* York city
money-lending, 19, 142, 280f.
Monmouthshire, 94, 99
Moore, Thomas, 144
Moors, North York, 10
Mores, Neville, 33, 143n., 165n., 170, 229
Morton, Richard, 98;
    Bishop Thomas, 98f.
Moseley, Thomas (a. 1589-1624), 77, 132
Mountgrace Priory (N.R.), 5n.
Mowbray, Vale of (N.R.), 9f.
Moxby (Molsby) Priory (N.R.), 5n.
murders, 44, 79, 148, 182
Murton(e), Richard, 175
Muscovy Company, 197, 269
Mush, John, 256
musters, military, 23, 26
Mylner, Ursyn, 169f.

Naburn (E.R.), 17, 30, 282
Narva, 197, 269, 273
Neale, Sir John E., 58
Neile, Richard (abp. 1632-40), 257
Neleson, Katherine, 121;
    Thomas (a. ?-1484), 103;
    William (a. 1499-1517), 46, 63, 101, 103, 121, 144, 295
Netherlands, 130f., 160, 194-6, 210
Neville family, 42;
    Charles, 6th earl of Westmorland, 17
Newark (Notts), 162
Newbie, Francis, 180
Newburgh Priory (N.R.), 5n., 160
Newcastle-upon-Tyne, 1f., 10, 52, 141, 147, 160, 187, 194, 202, 210, 273, 283
Newton, Miles, 74f.
Nicholson, Thomas, 259
Nidd, river, 7
Norfolk, 283
Norman, Anthony, 121;
    John (a. 1517, 1521-5), 46, 67, 121
Normandy, 194

North, John (a. 1534-58), 67, 105
Northallerton (N.R.), 2, 9
Northampton, 68, 155, 158
Northamptonshire, 134
Northumberland, county of, 4n., 14;
    duke of, see Dudley;
    earls of, see Percy
Northumbria, 22f.
Norway, 191f., 297
Norwich, 24, 93, 106, 112, 128,
    137f., 155, 158, 178, 202, 215,
    276, 285f.
Nostell Priory (W.R.), 5n., 261
notaries, 101f., 108, 121, 146, 167,
    190, 263
Nottingham, 42, 137, 191
Nottinghamshire, 4, 249, 252
Nun Appleton (W.R.), 5n., 177
Nun Monkton (W.R.), 5n.
Nuttgens, Patrick, 22

oaths, 232, 234, 248
obits, 51, 206, 216f., 227, 234, 236,
    243f.
occupational structure, 144-78
organs, church, 186
orphans, viii, 79, 97f., 267
Osbaldwick (N.R.), 181
ostlers, 290
Otterington, North (N.R.), 99
Ouse and Derwent wapentake, 9
Ouse river, 2, 7-9, 23-7, 57, 75f., 139,
    169, 186-9, 191, 211, 218,
    266f., 298
Overton (N.R.), 99
Oxford, city of, 35, 81, 148, 170,
    178;
    University, 176, 264
Oxfordshire, 35

Page, Sir Richard, 47, 109
pageants, 43, 242; see also plays
Palmes family, 17;
    Brian, 74;
    Guy, 74
panniermen, 155
Papacy, 49, 227, 234
paper, 160, 284
parchment makers, 155, 169
parish churches, see York city under
    individual churches;

unions of, 51, 143, 228, 240f., 242
parish officials, 76-8, 174, 257, 259
parish records, vii, 111-27, 223, 241,
    268, 274, 284
Parkyn, Robert, 241, 258
parliament, 49, 57f., 81, 89, 193, 217-
    20, 261, 277f.;
    acts of, 48, 51, 58, 81, 149, 165,
    188, 190, 204, 210, 215, 218-
    20, 228f., 240, 242f., 275;
    members of, 10, 41, 47, 49, 53,
    57f., 69, 72f., 87, 109, 193,
    215, 217, 261, 264f., 278
Patrington (E.R.), 274
Paycok(e), Gregory (a. 1567-77), 196;
    Robert I (a. 1543-70), 102, 245;
    Robert II (a. 1599-1619), 96
pedlars, 161
Pennine hills, 2f., 8-10, 130, 189, 289
Penrith (Cumb.), 2
pensions, 44, 63, 101
pepper, 186
Percy family, earls of Northumberland,
    11-14, 16, 18;
    Henry, 3rd earl, 14;
    Henry, 4th earl, 44, 186;
    Henry, 5th earl, 14;
    Henry, 6th earl, 14, 18;
    Henry, 8th earl, 14;
    Thomas, 7th earl, 17, 55;
    Sir Thomas, 14;
    Sir William, 16
Persyvall, Sampson, 197n.
Petty, John (a. 1504-8), 107, 172,
    294;
    Robert (a. 1526/7-28), 140, 294
pewter, pewterers, 37, 106, 154, 165,
    192f., 211
physicians, 141, 146, 177
Phythian-Adams, Charles, 154n., 203
Pickering (N.R.), 9, 12, 21
Pickering, Sir William, 243
pigs, 27, 77, 180, 183
pilgrimage, 5, 226, 231
Pilgrimage of Grace, 6, 12, 14, 49f.,
    109, 136, 170, 220, 234f.,
    237f., 292
pillories, 26, 174
pinners, 165, 186, 209
piracy, 196
plague, see epidemics

plasterers, 173, 269
plays, Corpus Christi, 105, 152, 172, 232, 239, 242, 247, 255, 280; Creed, 246f.; Midsummer, 80, 280; Paternoster, 63, 247
Plomer, Richard, 143n.
Plowland Hall (E.R.), 274
Plumpton family, 209
Plymouth, 194
Pocklington (E.R.), 21, 181
Poland, 198
Pole, John de la, earl of Lincoln, 44; Cardinal Reginald, 242
Pontefract (W.R.), 5f., 9, 12-14
poor relief, 76f., 81, 111, 132, 139, 202, 213, 222, 231, 236, 256, 260f., 275-7, 281, 285f., 294
Poppleton, Upper and Lower (W.R.), 30, 186
population, 5, 10, 22, 26, 28-31, 38, 59, 111-34, 144f., 178, 201-5, 207f., 211-14, 217, 223-5, 260, 268f., 274, 284f.; migration and mobility of, 94f., 111, 114, 127-31, 170, 208, 212-15, 228, 233, 268-70, 274-8, 283f., 289, 291, 294
port books, 193-5, 284
porters, 100, 155, 161
Portugal, 297
Preston, Robert, 172
printers, 146, 169f.
prisons, 3, 25f., 46, 65, 88, 276
Privy Council, 56, 76, 139, 240, 254, 257, 279, 284
Procter, Henry, 167
Protestantism, 233, 239, 243-59, 274
Prussia, 160, 197, 211
publishers, 141, 146, 170
Pulleyn, John, 74; Ralph (a. 1528-33, 1534-41), 141
Puritanism, 248, 257-9
Purvis, J.S., 31

quarter sessions, 62, 79, 186

Rabye, Nicholas, 144
Radcliffe, Thomas, 3rd earl of Sussex (l.p. 1568-72), 17
Raine, Angelo, viii, 134
Rasyng, John (a. 1522-7), 71n., 141

Rawcliffe (N.R.), 30
rebellions, 40, 44, 52, 226, 238; see also Pilgrimage; Rising of the Northern Earls
rectones, 99, 103
recusants, Catholic, 81, 132, 248f., 253-7
Redcar (N.R.), 191
Reid, Rachel R., 261
religious houses, 5, 23f., 226-9, 234-7; see also individual houses
religious houses, dissolutions of, 19, 22, 28, 49f., 57, 80, 109, 192, 220-2, 225, 227, 234-40, 246, 260, 278, 285
Requests, Court of, vii, 4
Ribble, river, 130
Riccall (E.R.), 103f.
Richard I, 183; Richard II, 41, 60, 202; Richard III, 6, 41-5, 48, 53, 207
Richardson, Edmund (a. 1569-76), 253
Richmond (N.R.), 186, 276; archdeacon of, 108
Richmondshire, 12, 129, 186f., 189, 283
Rievaulx Abbey (N.R.), 5n., 15
riots, 35, 45f., 48f., 68f., 80, 207
Ripon (W.R.), 2, 9f., 132, 148, 183, 186, 188, 208, 245
Rising of the Northern Earls, 17, 55, 245f., 253, 270f., 292
River, Thomas de la, 16n.
Robinson, Laurence (a. 1588-9), 36n.; William (a. 1578-1616), 103, 257, 278f.
Roche Abbey (W.R.), 5n.
Roger, John, 140, 205; Nicholas, 93
Rogerson, Thomas, 25
Rome, 49, 231
Roos family, 48, 207, 215f.; see also Manners
Rotherham, Thomas (abp. 1480-1500), 32
Rothwell (Northants), 134
Roucliffe, Brian, 74; Guy, 74
Rouen, 284

Rupert, Prince, 296
Russell, Josiah C., 201
Russia, 197, 269
Rutland, earl of, *see* Manners
Ruyskaert, Anthony, 131
Ryther, James, 2, 280, 286

Sabbatarianism, 181, 255
saddlers, 106, 154, 163, 291
sailors, *see* mariners
Salisbury, 202, 286
Salmon, Robert, 132
salt, 151, 160f., 187, 194, 199, 273
Salveyn family, 20
sanctuaries, 79f.
Sandys, Edwin (abp. 1577-88), 248, 255, 258, 281
Savage, Thomas (abp. 1501-7), 13, 61
Savile family, 15, 20
Sawley (Salley), 5n., 133, 243
sawyers, 159, 171, 173
Scandinavia, 191
Scarborough (N.R.), 19, 52, 183
schoolmasters, 146, 173, 255
schools, 174-6, 222f., 231, 236, 243, 260, 264, 274, 283
Scotland, Scots, 2, 7, 21f., 24, 40, 51, 53f., 57, 62, 101, 196, 199, 207, 284
Scriven (W.R.), 186
scriveners, 154, 170, 174, 177
Scrope family, 20;
    Richard (abp. 1398-1405), 226
Scudamore, Thomas, 140
Selby (W.R.), 5n., 13, 18, 38, 183, 186, 191
sermons, 237, 245, 254f., 259, 281
servants, 37f., 107, 111, 118, 132, 134, 144, 149f., 212, 258, 263, 290
Sever, William, abbot of St. Mary's and bishop of Carlisle, 13, 45, 135
sexual offences, 80, 295
Seymour, Edward, 1st earl of Hertford and duke of Somerset, 51f., 92
shearmen, 162
sheep, 8, 10, 29, 31, 183
Sheffield, Edmund, 3rd baron (later 1st earl of Mulgrave) (l.p. 1603-19), 61
Sheffield (W.R.), 10, 14, 128
Sheles, Margaret, 277

Sherbrook, ——, 237
Sheriff Hutton (N.R.), 42, 109, 142
ship money, 56, 281f., 284
shipping, 55f., 179, 186, 188-200, 211
Shipton-in-Galtres (N.R.), 205
shoemakers, *see* cordwainers
shops, 4, 15, 20, 25, 33f., 138, 150, 160, 179f., 184, 255, 263, 266, 272;
    shop-stalls, 26, 179
Shrewsbury, earls of, *see* Talbot
silver, 37f., 50, 154, 164f., 192, 239, 278
Simnel, Lambert, 44
Skaif, John, 141
Skelton (N.R.), 103
Skerne (E.R.), 266
skinners, 154, 163
Skipton (W.R.), 14, 181, 184
slander, 295
sledmen, 155, 161
Smith, John, 205;
    Ralph B., 8, 138
soap, 193, 196, 284
soldiers, 42, 51, 55, 87, 260, 267, 270f., 276, 281
Somerset, duke of, *see* Seymour
Sothabie, Marmaduke, 21, 142
soul bequests, 244f., 249-54
Sound, the (Oresund), 197, 272
Southampton, 137, 215
Sowerby (W.R.), 12
Soza, Martin, 94, 164, 242, 244
Spain, Spaniards, 56, 94, 131, 164, 199, 211, 284
Spanish company, 199
Speed, John, 22, 287
spicers, 161
spices, 160, 195
spinners, spinsters, 162, 208
Sponer, John, 42f.
Spufford, H. Margaret, 249
spurriers, 155, 171
stabling, 171
Stamford (Lincs.), 56, 109, 215
Standeven, John, 108;
    Thomas (a. 1558-67), 108
Stapleton, Sir Brian, 97;
    Sir Robert, 19
Star Chamber, Court of, vii, 4, 16, 49
stationers, 34, 155, 165, 169-71, 244
Staveley, Alan (a. 1502-22), 93;

Staveley, (*cont.*)
   William, 189f.
Steeton (W.R.), 17, 185
Stillingfleet (E.R.), 18
stocking-knitting, 129, 186
stocks, 26, 77, 213
Stourbridge Fair (Cambs.), 182, 272
Strafford, earl of, *see* Wentworth
Straker, Martin, 290
'strangers', 147f., 189, 269f.
street-cleansing, 27, 76, 287
street-lighting, 24, 278, 287
street-paving, 20, 27, 75, 77, 88, 133, 181
streets, *see* York city
subsidies, *see* taxation
Suffolk, 183, 192
suicide, 143f.
surgeons, 101, 154, 169; *see also* barbers
Sussex, 192;
   earl of, *see* Radcliffe
Swaledale, 186, 190;
   Swale Hall, 274
sweating sickness, 122f., 260
Swinburne, Henry, 92n., 264, 286;
   Toby, 264
swine, *see* pigs
Swine Priory (E.R.), 5n.
Synningthwaite Priory (W.R.), 5n., 18

tailors, viii, 33, 106f., 130, 141-3, 148, 151f., 169, 193, 209, 263
Talbot family, earls of Shrewsbury, 14;
   Francis, 5th earl (l.p. 1549-60), 54f., 218, 221, 240
Tankerd, Richard, 74;
   William, 74, 109, 247
tanners, 135, 154, 158f., 163, 265
tapiters, 37, 140, 143, 150, 158f., 162-5, 175, 209-11
taxation, vii, 7f., 48, 53, 57-9, 64, 77, 79, 111, 134-41, 143, 185, 202, 207f., 211, 219, 223, 264, 267f., 279, 282, 290, 294, 296
Teesdale, 189, 245
Tempest family, 15;
   Sir Thomas, 18
Temple Newsam (W.R.), 186
Tennand, John, 143n.
Tessimonde, James, 143n.

testamentary records, *see* inventories; wills
textwriters, 177
thatchers, 32, 171
Thicket Priory (E.R.), 5n.
Thirkleby (E.R.), 274
Thirsk (N.R.), 44
Thomas, Keith V., 232
Thomson, J.A.F., 233
Thoraldby (N.R.), 274
Thornborough, Mr., 291
Thorne (W.R.), 183
Thrupp, Sylvia L., 97f.
Thwaites family, 88
Tickhill (W.R.), 12
tilers, 32, 132, 158f., 171-3, 206, 263, 269
timber, trade in, 197
tipplers, 167
tithes, 31, 103, 229, 237
Todd, Sir William (a. 1481-6, 1487-1503), 44, 101
Topcliffe (N.R.), 2, 14, 186
tourists, 38
Towton, battle of, 203
trade, internal, 179-94, 271f., 283, 296;
   overseas, 47, 151, 194-200, 204, 210f., 269, 271-3, 284, 296f.
transport, coastal, 193-4;
   maritime, 194-200;
   river, 2, 23, 82, 179, 181, 186-92, 269, 289, 296;
   road, 2, 27, 161, 186
Trent, river and Vale of, 2, 9, 51, 210, 241
Trew, Andrew (a. 1581-1604), 176;
   William, 176
Turner, Christopher, 86
Tynedale, Tyneside, 189, 194

Unwin, George, 182
usury, 280f.
Uvedale, Sir John, 9

vagabonds, vagrants, 113, 132-4, 213-15, 275-7, 286
Valor Ecclesiasticus, 109
Venice, 22, 65, 170, 267
Vermuyden, Sir Cornelius, 9
victuallers, 154, 159, 165-9, 192, 270

Villiers, George, 2nd duke of Buckingham, 296
Vycars, Simon (a. 1517-34), 67

wages, 86f., 135-7, 143, 224f.
waits, *see* minstrels
Wakefield (W.R.), 9, 12, 140, 208, 247
Walmesley, Christopher, 76, 172
Walsingham, Sir Francis, 56
Walton (W.R.), 17
wapentakes, 4, 7, 138, 181, 185
warehouses, 184, 265
Warter (E.R.), 5n., 15, 274
water supplies, 161f., 286f.
Watson, Gregory, 269;
    John, 33n., 143n.;
    William (a. 1543-68), 244f., 269;
    William, 253
Watter, Sir Robert (a. 1590-1612), 57, 101, 103f., 142
Watton Priory (E.R.), 5n.
waxchandlers, 37
wealth, distribution of, 134-45, 290
weavers, 131, 149, 152f., 158f., 162, 179, 201, 208f., 260, 275
Welburn, 274
Wells, William (a. ?-1487), 44
Wensleydale, 186, 252f.
Wentworth, Thomas, 1st earl of Strafford (l.p. 1628-41), 262
Wessex, Kingdom of, 23
Westminster, 5f., 41, 48, 58, 216, 263, 292
Westmorland, 18, 96, 129;
    see also Cumbria;
    earl of, *see* Neville
Whalley (Lancs.), 2
Wharfe, river, 7
Wharram Percy (E.R.), 10f.
Wharton, Lady Anne, 253;
    Anthony, 18, 96;
    Thomas, 1st lord Wharton, 18, 96
wheelwrights, 173
Whitby Abbey (N.R.), 5n.
White, Sir Thomas, 86;
    William (a. 1486-1504/5), 141
Widdrington, Sir Thomas, 28
Wiggon, Thomas, 276
Wighill (W.R.), 19, 97
Wigston, William, 138
Wilberfoss (E.R.), 5n., 186, 237

William I, 23
William Fitzherbert, St. (abp. 1141-7, 1153-4), 226
wills, vii, 36, 78, 96f., 122f., 141-3, 165, 208, 212, 223, 226, 244, 249-54, 258, 264, 278
Wilson, K.P., 203
Wilstrop, Oswald, 15
Wiltshire, 3
Winchester, 29, 82, 93, 99, 176, 292
Winestead (E.R.), 74
wine trade, 160, 188, 193, 195f., 199, 284
wiredrawers, 165, 209
witchcraft, 232f.
Wolds, Yorkshire, 10, 162
Wolsey, Cardinal Thomas (abp. 1514-30), 46f., 49, 55, 67, 107, 182, 210, 216
women, occupations of, 132, 150, 164, 177;
    office-holding by, 78;
    status of, 65, 134

Wood, Thomas, 245;
    William, 71n.
woodland, 8-10, 163, 273
wool trade, 47, 87, 183, 195, 210f., 216, 218, 277
Worcester, vii, 15, 114, 155, 158, 215, 273, 285
Wressle (E.R.), 14, 186
Wright, William (a. 1514-43), 107
Wyatt, Sir Thomas, 40, 52
Wympnye, Henry, 198

Yedingham Priory (E.R.), 5n.
yeomen, 95, 100, 155, 186, 214
York, city of:
    almshouses, *see* hospitals
    bounds of, 29f., 288
    bridge chapels, 24, 76, 234
    bridges, 3, 25-7, 29, 70, 75f., 82, 139, 172, 175, 180, 188, 191, 206, 245, 266f., 269, 273, 278
    castle, 3f., 23, 26, 30, 39, 41, 43, 73, 90, 142, 146f., 246
    cathedral, *see* Minster
    churches and parishes:
        All SS. North Street, 126, 229;
        All SS. Pavement, 126, 230;
        All SS. Peasholme, 240;

York, city of: (*cont.*)
    Christ Church (Holy Trinity
        King's Court), 175, 230;
    Holy Trinity Goodramgate,
        126, 244;
    Holy Trinity Micklegate, 117,
        126, 283;
    St. Crux, 113, 119, 126, 230,
        259;
    St. Cuthbert, 125, 228, 243;
    St. Denys, 14, 37, 117, 119,
        126f., 173, 284;
    St. George, 30;
    St. Helen-on-the-Walls, 33, 37,
        143;
    St. Helen Stonegate, 27, 39,
        126, 131, 242;
    St. John Ousebridge, 126, 283;
    St. Lawrence, 33, 90, 144, 153;
    St. Margaret, 175, 228, 246;
    St. Martin Coney Street, 35,
        78, 116, 126, 175, 180, 206,
        242, 244;
    St. Martin Micklegate (-cum-
        Gregory), 126, 223, 283;
    St. Mary Bishophill Senior,
        246;
    St. Mary Castlegate, 114, 143;
    St. Michael-le-Belfrey, 27, 33,
        89, 119f., 126, 131, 174,
        230, 243;
    St. Michael Ousebridge
        (Spurriergate), 113, 241f.;
    St. Olave, 30f., 104, 112, 126;
    St. Sampson, 24, 222n., 283;
    St. Saviour, 33.
Common Crane, 26, 129, 189
Common Hall, ix, 25, 35, 49, 76,
    133, 147, 180, 219
Davy Hall, 88
ferries, 75
fields, commons and strays:
    Bishop's Fields, 29;
    Hob Moor, 29, 236;
    Knavesmire, 29, 48, 88;
    St. George's Close, 269;
    Tang Hall Fields, 84;
    Vicars' Leas, 45, 294
Guildhall, *see* Common Hall
guildhalls, 23, 25;
    merchants' hall, 151, 175,
        276;

St. Anthony's Hall, 25, 175,
    275f.;
    tailors' hall, 152
hospitals, almshouses, and *maisons
    dieu,* 24, 88f., 152, 169, 221f.,
    235f., 241f., 255, 260, 276
King's Manor, 28, 146, 172, 240,
    258, 262f., 286
maisons dieu, see hospitals
mills, 29, 83, 169, 205
Minster (cathedral), ix, 22-4, 26,
    30, 33, 36, 39, 54, 79, 88-90,
    107, 139, 171f., 191, 214,
    227f., 236-9, 244, 281
Minster Yard (Cathedral close),
    88-90, 101, 108, 146, 153, 169,
    181f., 234;
    St. Sepulchre's College, 239;
    St. William's College, 239;
    Treasurer's House, 28
mints, archiepiscopal and royal, 4,
    45, 52, 89, 107f., 147, 192,
    221, 261
moats, city, 24, 76
Old Baile, 23
Peasholme College, 24
religious houses, 23f., 220-2, 226-
    9;
    Augustinian Priory, 14, 235,
        237;
    Carmelite Priory (Whitefriars),
        80, 235, 237;
    Dominican Priory (Blackfriars),
        235;
    Franciscan Priory (Greyfriars),
        105, 235-7;
    Holy Trinity Priory, 18, 24,
        49f., 229, 234f., 237;
    St. Andrew's Priory, 24, 79,
        235, 237;
    St. Clement's Priory, 24, 49f.,
        234f., 237;
    St. George's Chapel, 275f.;
    St. Leonard's Hospital, 24,
        88f., 221f., 235f., 242;
    St. Mary's Abbey, 13, 23f., 32,
        51, 88f., 92n., 109, 172,
        221f., 229, 235, 240
Staith, city, 26, 191
streets and districts:
    Aldwark, 16;
    Bedern, 89f., 239;

(cont.)

　　Bishophill,　23, 28, 177, 280;
　　Blake Street,　139, 169;
　　Bootham,　24, 181, 286;
　　Castlegate,　25;
　　Coney Street,　105, 139;
　　Davygate,　88;
　　Fossgate,　16, 180;
　　Goodramgate,　144;
　　Haymonger Lane,　280;
　　Horsefair,　181;
　　Jubbergate,　265;
　　Lady Peckitt's Yard,　26;
　　Layerthorpe,　104;
　　Lendal,　20;
　　Marygate,　153;
　　Micklegate,　23, 26f., 32, 36,
　　　　105, 139, 149, 163, 263,
　　　　286;
　　North Street, 34f.;
　　Ousegate,　23, 26, 36, 105,
　　　　139;
　　Pavement,　23, 55, 105, 139,
　　　　180, 255;
　　Peasholme Green,　180;
　　Petergate,　24, 33, 89f., 105,
　　　　139, 285;
　　Peter Lane Little,　280;
　　St. Andrewgate,　222n.;
　　St. Saviourgate,　175;
　　Shambles,　23, 26, 149, 169,
　　　　280;
　　Skeldergate,　31f., 189;
　　Spurriergate,　139;
　　Stonegate,　20f., 34, 89f., 105,
　　　　139, 170, 285;
　　Swinegate,　180;
　　Thursday Market,　180f.;
　　Toft Green,　180;
　　Walmgate,　23, 26f., 113, 139,
　　　　175, 180;
　　Whitefriar Lane,　222n.
　suburbs,　28-31, 104, 138, 166
　walls, bars and posterns,　23-9, 32,
　　44, 88, 139, 171, 182, 273, 278,
　　286
　wards,　70, 76-8, 149, 286
York, corporation of:
　aldermen, *passim*
　bellman,　232
　bridgemasters,　70f., 82, 85
　chamberlains,　70f., 79, 82-8, 93,

　　100, 140, 142f., 146, 217, 224,
　　256, 282
　chaplains,　75f.
　charters,　41, 46, 70, 87, 148, 181,
　　183, 279, 288, 294
　common clerks,　ix, 25, 58, 61,
　　74f., 99f., 146
　common council,　46, 61, 67-70,
　　90, 217, 219, 270, 277
　coroners,　75, 79, 89
　courts,　65f., 72, 78f.
　finances,　viii, 82-8
　freemen, *passim*;
　　freemen's registers,　viii, 111,
　　　148f., 153-78, 202, 204f.,
　　　211-13, 218, 224, 262, 268
　high stewards,　76
　macebearers,　42, 64, 75
　mayors, lord, *passim*
　muremasters,　70f., 82, 85
　plate,　85
　preachers,　76, 255
　properties,　69, 83-5, 206, 212,
　　215, 239, 265f
　recorders,　21, 43, 58, 61, 72-4, 87,
　　108, 216, 247, 254, 280
　sheriffs,　60-2, 65f., 78f., 85, 92f.,
　　107, 135, 140, 152, 182, 205,
　　228, 234, 248, 290, 293
　swordbearers,　44, 47, 64, 75
　Twenty Four,　40, 61f., 66, 71, 92-
　　110, 162, 168, 174, 176, 217,
　　278
York, county of, *passim*
　assizes,　3, 16
　courts,　3, 263
　sheriffs,　3, 40f., 60, 88, 166
York, diocese and province of,　4f. *et
　passim*
　archbishops, *see* Bovill, Grindal,
　　Heath, Holgate, Hutton, Lee,
　　Neile, Rotherham, Sandys,
　　Savage, Scrope, William, Wolsey,
　　Young
　cathedral chapter and canons,　66,
　　79, 84, 146, 165, 181, 226f.,
　　229, 234, 238, 245;
　chancellors,　33, 73, 213, 254;
　deans,　108, 214, 216, 281;
　treasurers,　33, 36, 142;
　Vicars Choral,　45, 69, 89, 205,
　　214, 294

York, diocese and province of (*cont.*)
   Convocation, 49
   courts, viii, 5, 73, 108, 140, 146,
      231, 233f., 263f.
   Ecclesiastical Commission, viii, 5,
      53-5, 108f., 167, 245-7, 256f.,
      262-4, 277, 292
   St. Peter's Liberty, 79, 88-90, 108,
      169, 182
York, Sir Richard (a. *c* 1468-98), 44,
   101, 196, 294

York, Vale of, 1-3, 8-11, 14, 16, 99,
   124, 129, 168, 185, 187
Young, Sir George, 28, 140;
   Jane, 140;
   Thomas (abp. 1561-8, l.p. 1564-
     8), 55, 102, 237, 244f., 265,
     270
Yule riding, 247

Zafra (Spain), 94
Zeeland, 195, 284